The Essential Mediterranean
Diet Cookbook

2000 Days of Flavorful and Low-Carb Recipes for Every Occasion. Incl. a 30 Days Personalized Meal Plan to Kickstart Your Health Journey

Anthony K. Herd

Table of Contents

INTRODUCTION

What is a Diet?

When most people hear the word "diet," they immediately think of weight loss. However, it's important to understand that the term refers to the way we eat and the types of food we consume. Your diet is the combination of all the foods and drinks you consume regularly. This includes the nutritious foods that promote well-being, as well as the processed, high-fat, and sugary options that are readily available in our modern food environment.

It's important to note that there is no one-size-fits-all approach to a healthy diet. Everyone's nutritional needs are different, depending on factors such as age, gender, activity level, and underlying health conditions. However, some general guidelines can help to promote good health for most people. For example, it's recommended to consume a variety of fruits and vegetables each day, to choose whole grains over refined grains, and to limit the intake of saturated and trans fats.

The bottom line is that your diet is a critical component of your overall health and well-being. Whether you're trying to lose weight, manage a chronic condition, or simply feel better, making small changes to your diet can have a big impact. By choosing nutritious foods that promote well-being and limiting processed, high-fat, and sugary options, you can help to reduce the risk of chronic diseases and promote optimal health.

Welcome to the World of Mediterranean Diet

Have you ever tasted a dish that transports you to a different place, time, and culture? A dish that captures the essence of a region and its people? This is the magic of the Mediterranean diet. It refers to the traditional diet of the Mediterranean coastal countries. It has several characteristics: it emphasizes a plant-based diet, such as fruits, vegetables, whole grains, legumes, and nuts; it emphasizes the intake of healthy fats, especially monounsaturated fats from olive oil and fish; it emphasizes moderate consumption of dairy products and limits the intake of red meat and sweets. The Mediterranean diet is not only a recipe, but also a lifestyle that includes physical activity, socializing, and enjoying food with family and friends.

Imagine yourself sitting at a cozy and quaint family-owned restaurant in Greece, perched on a cliff overlooking the shimmering Aegean Sea, with the sun slowly setting on the horizon, casting a warm golden glow over everything around you. As you gaze out at the stunning view, the waiter arrives at your table, carrying a sizzling hot plate of grilled octopus, lightly drizzled with a tangy blend of fresh lemon juice and rich olive oil. Alongside it, a colorful bowl of vine-ripe tomatoes and crisp cucumbers, adorned with crumbled feta cheese and an aromatic medley of fresh herbs, awaits you.

As you take the first bite of the succulent octopus, the explosion of flavors and textures on your palate instantly transports you to a different time and place, offering you a glimpse into the authentic Mediterranean way of life. It's not just about the food; it's a cultural experience, a celebration of the region's rich history and traditions, and a reflection of the vibrant, lively spirit of the Mediterranean people.

If you are feeling eager to experience Mediterranean cuisine, don't worry! In this book, I will teach you how to enjoy Mediterranean food with simple and nutrient-rich ingredients and feel the Mediterranean lifestyle without leaving your home!

Chapter 1 Mediterranean Diet Essentials

The Pyramid of Mediterranean Diet

The Mediterranean Diet Food Pyramid is a visual representation of the recommended foods and proportions for a healthy Mediterranean-style diet. At the base of the pyramid are foods that should be consumed in the largest quantities, such as fruits, vegetables, whole grains, legumes, nuts, seeds, bread, pasta, rice, cheese & yogurt, and olive oil. Above the base are foods that should be consumed in moderate amounts, such as fish, seafood, poultry, and eggs. At the top of the pyramid are foods that should be consumed sparingly, such as red meat, sweets, and processed foods.

Common Ingredients in Mediterranean Diet

The Mediterranean diet is renowned for its incorporation of distinct and wholesome ingredients that provide an abundance of health advantages. In this section, I will introduce some of the frequently utilized elements in Mediterranean cooking. By doing so, I hope to provide you with a greater understanding of the unique components that make up this renowned diet and their potential benefits to one's overall health and well-being.

1.Olives & Olive Oil

Olives, particularly the dark kalamata variety from Greece, are staples in Mediterranean cuisine and can be found in many dishes such as salads and dips. While the flavor of kalamata olives is strong, the amount needed in recipes will depend on personal taste preferences. Other types of olives, including dark- and light-green varieties, are commonly found in Italy and Spain. When shopping for olives, it's important to consider whether to choose pitted or non-pitted varieties. Pitted olives are more convenient to use in recipes that require chopped or sliced olives, while non-pitted olives are better suited for serving as a small-plate appetizer or tapas to be eaten one at a time.

Aside from their delicious taste, olives are also a great source of heart-healthy fats due to their high content of monounsaturated fatty acids. Olive oil, in particular, is the cornerstone of Mediterranean cooking and is a healthier alternative to other types of oil. It's best to choose extra-virgin olive oil, which is unrefined, free of additives, and not treated with heat to maximize the health benefits. It's also important to pay attention to the origin of the oil, with products from Italy and Greece being preferred due to their reputation for high-quality olive oil.

When shopping for olive oil, it's essential to read the fine print to ensure that the product is authentic and not just marketed as such. While the front packaging may advertise the product as being from Italy or Greece, it's crucial to verify this information on the label to ensure that you're getting the real deal. By paying attention to the quality and origin of olives and olive oil, you can incorporate these healthy and flavorful ingredients into your cooking to enjoy the many benefits of the Mediterranean diet.

2.Vinegar

Vinegar is a flavorful ingredient that adds a tangy punch to many dishes, without adding any calories or salt. It is commonly used in cooking and as a condiment, and its acidic nature makes it a versatile ingredient in many recipes. However, when purchasing vinegar for dishes where it plays a prominent role, it's important to look for authentic products made in Italy or Spain, using traditional brewing methods. This ensures that you're getting high-quality vinegar with the full range of flavors and aromas that make it so special.

On the other hand, when vinegar is used in small amounts, such as a splash on a salad or a marinade, a generic brand is often sufficient. However, it's still a good idea to check the label to make sure that the vinegar is made from high-quality ingredients and is free from any additives or preservatives. By choosing the right vinegar for your recipes, you can elevate the flavors of your dishes and create a truly authentic Mediterranean dining experience.

3.Seasonal fruits & Vegetables

Incorporating fruits and vegetables into your daily diet is a crucial aspect of the Mediterranean lifestyle. It's recommended that you consume at least one serving of fruit per day to provide your body with essential nutrients. To ensure that you're getting the best flavor and nutritional value, it's important to choose fruits that are in season. During the winter months, when fewer varieties are available, it's a good idea to keep some frozen and dried fruits on hand for use in recipes.

In addition to fruits, it's also recommended that you consume three or more servings of vegetables per day. Most local grocery stores carry a variety of vegetables that are commonly used in Mediterranean cuisine, so you shouldn't have trouble finding the ingredients you need. If you're unable to find a specific vegetable, don't be afraid to substitute it with a similar one. When selecting vegetables, it's important to choose the freshest and best quality ingredients available and to select vegetables that are in season when possible. By incorporating a variety of fruits and vegetables into your diet, you'll not only promote better health and well-being, but you'll also enjoy the rich and diverse flavors of the Mediterranean.

4.Grains

Whole grains are a crucial component of the Mediterranean diet, providing essential nutrients such as fiber, protein, and B vitamins. They are a significant source of complex carbohydrates that provide sustained energy and help maintain a healthy weight. The traditional Mediterranean diet emphasizes whole grains such as bulgur, oats, barley, and quinoa. These grains are highly nutritious and can be used in many dishes, including salads, soups, stews, and baked goods.

In addition to their nutritional value, whole grains are versatile and can be prepared in many ways. For example, brown rice can be used as a base for stir-fries or served alongside grilled vegetables and protein for a filling meal. Bulgur can be used as a substitute for rice or pasta in dishes like tabbouleh or as a stuffing for vegetables.

One of the benefits of incorporating whole grains into your diet is that they are relatively affordable and widely available. You can find them in most grocery stores, and they are often sold in bulk, making them a budget-friendly choice. It is recommended to keep a variety of whole grains on hand to ensure that you have options when meal planning. Try experimenting with different grains and flavor combinations to discover your favorite Mediterranean-inspired dishes.

5.Nuts

Nuts are a vital part of the Mediterranean diet, and they can be enjoyed in a variety of ways. In addition to being rich in heart-healthy fats and protein, nuts are also loaded with vitamins, minerals, and antioxidants. They are an excellent source of energy and make a perfect snack for those who are looking for something quick and healthy.

When it comes to incorporating nuts into your diet, there are numerous ways to do it. You can add them as toppings on your salads, roasted vegetables, fish, and chicken to add an extra crunch and flavor. They can also be used in sauces and dips, like pesto or hummus, to enhance their taste and nutrition.

The top varieties of nuts to keep on hand include roasted unsalted almonds, pistachios, and walnuts. Almonds are a good source of vitamin E, magnesium, and fiber, while pistachios are rich in antioxidants and fiber. Walnuts, on the other hand, are loaded with omega-3 fatty acids, which are essential for brain health and may help reduce inflammation in the body.

When buying nuts, opt for unsalted, raw, or dry-roasted varieties to avoid added salt and unhealthy fats. It's also important to store them properly to keep them fresh for longer. Nuts can be stored in an airtight container in a cool, dry place or the refrigerator or freezer for maximum freshness.

6.Legumes & Beans

Legumes, such as lentils, chickpeas, and fava beans, are highly nutritious foods and an essential part of the Mediterranean diet. They are rich in fiber, plant-based protein, iron, and other vitamins and minerals, making them an excellent choice for a healthy and balanced diet.

Lentils are versatile legumes and come in a variety of colors, including brown, green, and red. Dried lentils are the preferred choice for many Mediterranean recipes, as they hold their shape well when cooked and absorb flavors beautifully. Chickpeas, also known as garbanzo beans, are another popular legume in Mediterranean cuisine. They are commonly used in dishes like hummus, falafel, and salads.

Fava beans are a staple in many Mediterranean countries and are often used in dishes like ful medames, a traditional Egyptian breakfast dish. When purchasing canned legumes, look for "no salt added" options to reduce your sodium intake. However, cooking dried legumes from scratch is easy and budget-friendly, and can be a great way to control the amount of sodium and other additives in your food.

Incorporating legumes into your meals is a great way to boost your intake of essential nutrients while adding variety and flavor to your diet. Experiment with different legumes and try new recipes to discover your favorites.

7.Fish

Fish is an essential component of the Mediterranean diet and is consumed a couple of times a week. The diet recommends consuming different types of fish, which are rich in omega-3 fatty acids, a vital nutrient for maintaining heart health. Depending on your location and proximity to the sea, it can be appropriate to purchase fresh, frozen, or canned seafood. While fresh seafood is an ideal option, frozen and canned seafood can be just as healthy and convenient, especially when fresh seafood is not available.

Canned anchovies and sardines are commonly used in Mediterranean cuisine due to their versatility and flavor. They can be used as a topping on pizzas, and salads, or as an ingredient in dips and spreads. Additionally, readily available and frequently celebrated types of seafood in this diet include salmon, swordfish, tilapia, cod, and shrimp. These types of seafood are packed with essential nutrients and can be prepared in a variety of ways, such as grilling, baking, or sautéing.

When selecting canned seafood, opt for those packed in water rather than oil. Also, check the labels for any added preservatives or excess sodium. Fresh seafood, on the other hand, should have a bright and shiny appearance, and a fresh smell. Make sure to consume seafood within a day or two of purchase to ensure optimal freshness and taste.

8.Yogurt

Yogurt is a staple in the Mediterranean diet, and it's no wonder why. This creamy, tangy, and versatile ingredient is not only delicious but also incredibly nutritious. While sweetened and flavored yogurt varieties are common in the dairy section, plain yogurt is the traditional choice in the Mediterranean. It contains fewer added sugars and provides a neutral base that can be used in both savory and sweet dishes.

One of the main benefits of yogurt is its high protein content. It is an excellent source of complete protein, meaning it contains all the essential amino acids that the body needs to build and repair tissues. Yogurt is also rich in calcium, which is essential for strong bones and teeth. Additionally, it contains vitamin D, which helps the body absorb calcium and maintain healthy bones.

Another significant benefit of yogurt is its probiotic content. These beneficial gut bacteria naturally occur in yogurt and promote healthy digestion and immunity. They help to keep the gut micro-biome balanced, which is essential for overall health.

Overall, incorporating plain yogurt into your diet is a great way to add protein, calcium, and probiotics to your meals while avoiding added sugars and artificial flavors.

However, the Mediterranean diet is more than just a list of ingredients. It's also a way of lifestyle about involving in physical activity, enjoying meals with family and friends, savoring every bite of the meal, and taking pleasure in the simple things in life.

A Healthy Mediterranean Lifestyle

The Mediterranean communities have a comprehensive approach to well-being, prioritizing not only a healthy diet but also social connections, physical activity, and stress management techniques. Numerous studies indicate that strong social connections are essential for physical and mental health, with regular interaction with friends and family associated with an increased lifespan, lower rates of depression and anxiety, and a strengthened immune system. Mediterranean culture values quality time spent with loved ones, often centered around a leisurely meal accompanied by a glass of red wine, which nourishes both the body and soul, promoting a sense of overall well-being. In addition to social connections, daily physical activity is crucial in Mediterranean life, with people frequently walking or cycling to work and buying fresh ingredients for their meals, fostering a sense of community along the way. Taking time off for rest is also a core component of Mediterranean culture, with people prioritizing vacations and midday breaks to enjoy meals with family, which helps manage stress and promote a healthy work-life balance. Ultimately, the Mediterranean approach to life is a celebration of life, family, and community, and an opportunity to nourish both the body and soul with healthy, delicious foods that promote longevity and overall well-being. This cookbook hopes to inspire readers to embrace the Mediterranean way of life and all the benefits that come with it.

Core tenets of the Mediterranean Diet

Various regions of the Mediterranean have their distinct ways of eating and food choices due to the diversity of fresh ingredients available in different areas. Nevertheless, they all adhere to the fundamental tenets of the Mediterranean Diet. Adhering to these tenets guarantees that we enjoy our food, feel satiated, and nourish our bodies in the best possible way.

♦ Incorporate More Plant-based Foods into Your Diet.

Incorporate a colorful variety of fresh fruits and vegetables and locally grown whole grains into your diet to benefit from their numerous vitamins and minerals. Don't forget to include beans and legumes like lentils and chickpeas, which are excellent sources of protein and fiber. The diverse colors in fruits and vegetables represent different phytochemicals, which play a vital role in supporting the body's immune system and regulating various bodily functions. Additionally, the natural fiber present in plant-based foods not only makes you feel fuller for longer but also aids in regulating digestion. It is recommended to aim for at least five servings of fruits and vegetables per day, ensuring that you are getting a wide range of essential nutrients. By adding more plant-based foods to your diet, you can support your overall health and well-being while enjoying a delicious and satisfying range of meals.

♦ Reduce Your Meat Intake.

The Mediterranean diet is well-known for its focus on plant-based protein sources instead of meat. Although meat is consumed in the Mediterranean, it is typically seen as an occasional indulgence rather than a daily staple. Instead, the Mediterranean diet emphasizes the consumption of whole grains, legumes, nuts, and seeds as the primary sources of protein. This approach not only supports optimal health, but it also helps to reduce the risk of chronic diseases such as heart disease and diabetes.

One of the key protein sources in the Mediterranean diet is fish, which is consumed regularly in many countries throughout the region. The proximity of many Mediterranean countries to the sea makes it easier for locals to access a variety of fresh seafood, including salmon, sardines, tuna, and more. Fish is an excellent source of lean protein and contains important nutrients such as omega-3 fatty acids, which are essential for maintaining heart health and reducing inflammation in the body.

♦ Savor Nourishing Fats.

The Mediterranean diet incorporates a significant amount of heart-healthy fats, which can be obtained from olives, nuts, and extra-virgin olive oil. Olive trees are a common sight throughout the region, and their fruit is used in many dishes. Locally pressed extra-virgin olive oil is a staple in Mediterranean cooking, used for everything from sautéing vegetables to dressing salads. Nuts, such as almonds, pistachios, and walnuts, are also an important source of healthy fats in the diet.

In addition to healthy fats, the Mediterranean diet includes fresh fish, which is a rich source of omega-3 fatty acids. Consuming fish 8 to 10 ounces a week is a recommended part of the diet. Omega-3 fatty acids support brain function and have been linked to a reduced risk of degenerative diseases. Incorporating healthy fats into the diet is important for maintaining overall health and well-being.

♦ Enjoy Your Meals at a Leisurely Pace.

The Mediterranean way of eating emphasizes not only the quality of the food but also the importance of taking time to enjoy meals. The tradition of sharing meals with family and friends encourages a slower, more mindful approach to eating. Savoring each bite, chewing slowly, and putting down utensils between bites are all practices that promote mindfulness and prevent overeating. This approach allows the body to properly digest and absorb nutrients, leading to greater satisfaction and a more enjoyable dining experience.

Additionally, taking time to enjoy meals can have psychological benefits as well. It creates a sense of community and social connection, which can reduce stress and promote overall well-being. In contrast, rushed or distracted eating can lead to mindless overeating, indigestion, and feelings of guilt or discomfort.

♦ Enjoy a Glass of Red Wine.

In the Mediterranean, red wine is not only considered as a beverage but also as a part of a healthy diet. Moderate consumption of red wine is believed to offer numerous health benefits, including reduced risk of heart disease and stroke. Red wine contains antioxidants, including resveratrol, which helps to protect the body against inflammation and oxidative stress.

In addition to the health benefits, red wine is also a social lubricant that brings people together, fosters community and strengthens relationships. In the Mediterranean culture, wine is often enjoyed with meals, particularly during festive occasions and family gatherings. This tradition creates a relaxed atmosphere where people can unwind, connect, and share stories with each other.

However, it is important to consume red wine in moderation, as excessive alcohol consumption can have harmful effects on health. A standard serving size of red wine is typically between 3-4 ounces, and it is recommended to limit consumption to one or two times a week.

♦ Stay Active Through Natural Means.

The Mediterranean way of life emphasizes natural movement, which allows the body to function optimally. This entails moving all parts of the body regularly throughout the day by engaging in activities such as walking, household chores, yard work, and gardening. The use of basic tools that require the use of the body's mechanics, rather than technology, is also promoted. The environment is set up to encourage daily movement, and the goal is to avoid a sedentary lifestyle. While structured exercise has its place, it is not the primary source of movement in the Mediterranean lifestyle. Instead, natural movement is prioritized to promote health and wellness. Taking frequent breaks and stretching, and avoiding sitting for prolonged periods, are also encouraged to promote movement throughout the day. By adopting natural movement habits, we can enhance our overall physical and mental well-being.

♦ Find Meaning and Connection.

Having a sense of purpose and belonging are key components of the Mediterranean lifestyle. People in the Mediterranean find fulfillment in their daily activities, whether it's through work, family, or community involvement. They take pride in their roles and feel a sense of satisfaction in contributing to something greater than themselves. This purpose provides motivation and a reason to get out of bed each morning.

Belonging is also important in the Mediterranean culture. People maintain strong ties with their families and often live in close proximity to each other. Friendships are built over time and cherished. The community is a central part of daily life, and people come together for festivals, celebrations, and meals. Being part of a group provides a sense of identity and support that contributes to overall well-being.

DAYS	BREAKFAST	LUNCH	DINNER	SNACK/DESSERT
1	Turkish Egg Bowl	Potatoes with Cumin	Spicy Grilled Veggie Pita	Mexican Potato Skins
2	Crostini with Smoked Trout	Toasted Grain and Almond Pilaf	Ratatouille	Goat'S Cheese & Hazelnut Dip
3	Kagianas	Braised Fennel	Caramelized Root Vegetables	Red Grapefruit Granita
4	Peach Sunrise Smoothie	Mediterranean Lentil Sloppy Joes	Tingly Chili-Roasted Broccoli	Spiced Roasted Cashews
5	Nuts and Fruit Oatmeal	Mashed Sweet Potato Tots	Mushroom-Stuffed Zucchini	Blueberry Panna Cotta
6	Mediterranean-Inspired White Smoothie	Sheet Pan Cauliflower with Parmesan and Garlic	Quinoa Salad in Endive Boats	Citrus-Kissed Melon
7	Mashed Chickpea, Feta, and Avocado Toast	Root Vegetable Hash	Black Beans with Corn and Tomato Relish	Almond Pistachio Biscotti
8	Portobello Eggs Benedict	Crispy Green Beans	Cod with Warm Beet and Arugula Salad	Ultimate Nut Butter
9	Warm Fava Beans with Whole-Wheat Pita	Superflax Tortillas	Crunchy Pea and Barley Salad	
10	Quick Low-Carb Avocado Toasts	Baba Ghanoush	Sweet Potato Black Bean Burgers	Pesto Cucumber Boats
11	Creamy Cinnamon Porridge	Roasted Garlic	Lemon Farro Bowl with Avocado	Greek Island Almond Cocoa Bites
12	Amaranth Breakfast Bowl with Chocolate and Almonds	Herb Vinaigrette Potato Salad	White Beans with Kale	Garlic-Parmesan Croutons
13	Quinoa and Yogurt Breakfast Bowls	Warm Beets with Hazelnuts and Spiced Yogurt	Creamy Yellow Lentil Soup	Banana Cream Pie Parfaits
14	Egg and Pepper Pita	Braised Radishes with Sugar Snap Peas and Dukkah	Lemony Salmon	Honey-Rosemary Almonds
15	Crunchy Vanilla Protein Bars	Garlic Cauliflower with Tahini	Hearty Minestrone Soup	Mini Lettuce Wraps
16	Greek Breakfast Power Bowl	Blackened Zucchini with Kimchi-Herb Sauce	Easy Greek Briami (Ratatouille)	Cocoa and Coconut Banana Slices
17	Peachy Green Smoothie	Cucumbers with Feta, Mint, and Sumac	Green Beans with Pine Nuts and Garlic	Date and Nut Balls
18	Feta and Herb Frittata	Rustic Cauliflower and Carrot Hash	Vegetable Tagine	Baklava and Honey

DAYS	BREAKFAST	LUNCH	DINNER	SNACK/DESSERT
19	Power Peach Smoothie Bowl	Coriander-Cumin Roasted Carrots	Sweet and Crispy Roasted Pearl Onions	Creamy Spiced Almond Milk
20	Egg Salad with Red Pepper and Dill	Root Vegetable Tagine	Citrus-Roasted Broccoli Florets	Fruit Compote
21	Almond Butter Banana Chocolate Smoothie	Zesty Cabbage Soup	Maple-Roasted Tomatoes	Cretan Cheese Pancakes
22	Hearty Berry Breakfast Oats	Vibrant Green Beans	Nordic Stone Age Bread	Red-Wine Poached Pears
23	Mediterranean Breakfast Pita Sandwiches	Glazed Sweet Potato Bites	Fried Fresh Sardines	Cherry-Stuffed Apples
24	Spinach and Feta Egg Bake	Tahini-Lemon Kale	Powerhouse Arugula Salad	Lightened-Up Baklava Rolls
25	Berry Breakfast Smoothie	Zucchini Casserole	Greek Potato Salad	Apricot and Mint No-Bake Parfait
26	Greek Yogurt Parfait with Granola	Roasted Salsa	Greek Black-Eyed Pea Salad	Tahini Baklava Cups
27	Smoked Salmon Egg Scramble with Dill and Chives	Chermoula-Roasted Beets	Lentil and Zucchini Boats	Mascarpone and Fig Crostini
28	Berry Baked Oatmeal	Herbed Shiitake Mushrooms	Brown Rice with Dried Fruit	Lemon Coconut Cake
29	Sunshine Overnight Oats	Potato Vegetable Hash	Riviera Tuna Salad	Toasted Almonds with Honey
30	Savory Sweet Potato Hash	Sweet-and-Sour Brussels Sprouts	Moroccan Fish	Strawberry-Pomegranate Molasses Sauce

A Cookbook For Everyone

This cookbook is designed for everyone who wants to eat well and feel great. Whether you are a seasoned home cook or a beginner in the kitchen, the recipes in this book are easy to follow and will help you to create delicious and nutritious meals. The Mediterranean diet is not just a diet, it is a lifestyle that has been proven to improve health and well-being. By following the principles of the Mediterranean diet, you will be nourishing your body with wholesome and fresh ingredients that are full of vitamins, minerals, and antioxidants.

This cookbook is not about deprivation, but rather about enjoying the wonderful flavors and textures of Mediterranean cuisine. You will find a wide range of recipes in this book, from classic dishes such as Citrus Fennel Salad and Creamy Thyme Polenta to more contemporary creations like Avocado and Asparagus Wraps and Croatian Double-Crust Pizza with Greens and Garlic. With this cookbook, you will be able to satiate all your eating needs, whether you are a vegetarian, vegan, or meat-lover. So, let's get cooking and start on the path to a healthier you!

Chapter 2 Breakfasts

Turkish Egg Bowl

Prep time: 10 minutes | Cook time: 15 minutes | Serves 2

2 tablespoons ghee
½–1 teaspoon red chile flakes
2 tablespoons extra-virgin olive oil
1 cup full-fat goat's or sheep's milk yogurt
1 clove garlic, minced
1 tablespoon fresh lemon juice
Salt and black pepper, to taste
Dash of vinegar
4 large eggs
Optional: pinch of sumac
2 tablespoons chopped fresh cilantro or parsley

1. In a skillet, melt the ghee over low heat. Add the chile flakes and let it infuse while you prepare the eggs. Remove from the heat and mix with the extra-virgin olive oil. Set aside. Combine the yogurt, garlic, lemon juice, salt, and pepper. 2. Poach the eggs. Fill a medium saucepan with water and a dash of vinegar. Bring to a boil over high heat. Crack each egg individually into a ramekin or a cup. Using a spoon, create a gentle whirlpool in the water; this will help the egg white wrap around the egg yolk. Slowly lower the egg into the water in the center of the whirlpool. Turn off the heat and cook for 3 to 4 minutes. Use a slotted spoon to remove the egg from the water and place it on a plate. Repeat for all remaining eggs. 3. To assemble, place the yogurt mixture in a bowl and add the poached eggs. Drizzle with the infused oil, and garnish with cilantro. Add a pinch of sumac, if using. Eat warm.

Per Serving:
calories: 576 | fat: 46g | protein: 27g | carbs: 17g | fiber: 4g | sodium: 150mg

Crunchy Vanilla Protein Bars

Prep time: 10 minutes | Cook time: 5 minutes | Serves 8

Topping:
½ cup flaked coconut
2 tablespoons raw cacao nibs
Bars:
1½ cups almond flour
1 cup collagen powder
2 tablespoons ground or whole chia seeds
1 teaspoon vanilla powder or 1
tablespoon unsweetened vanilla extract
¼ cup virgin coconut oil
½ cup coconut milk
1½ teaspoons fresh lemon zest
⅓ cup macadamia nuts, halved
Optional: low-carb sweetener, to taste

1. Preheat the oven to 350°F (180°C) fan assisted or 380°F (193°C) conventional. 2. To make the topping: Place the coconut flakes on a baking tray and bake for 2 to 3 minutes, until lightly golden. Set aside to cool. 3. To make the bars: In a bowl, combine all of the ingredients for the bars. Line a small baking tray with parchment paper or use a silicone baking tray. A square 8 × 8–inch (20 × 20 cm) or a rectangular tray of similar size will work best. 4. Press the dough into the pan and sprinkle with the cacao nibs, pressing them into the bars with your fingers. Add the toasted coconut and lightly press the flakes into the dough. Refrigerate until set, for about 1 hour. Slice to serve. Store in the refrigerator for up to 1 week.

Per Serving:
calories: 285 | fat: 27g | protein: 5g | carbs: 10g | fiber: 4g | sodium: 19mg

Garlic Scrambled Eggs with Basil

Prep time: 5 minutes | Cook time: 5 minutes | Serves 2

4 large eggs
2 tablespoons finely chopped fresh basil
2 tablespoons grated Gruyère cheese
1 tablespoon cream
1 tablespoon olive oil
2 cloves garlic, minced
Sea salt and freshly ground pepper, to taste

1. In a large bowl, beat together the eggs, basil, cheese, and cream with a whisk until just combined. 2. Heat the oil in a large, heavy nonstick skillet over medium-low heat. Add the garlic and cook until golden, about 1 minute. 3. Pour the egg mixture into the skillet over the garlic. Work the eggs continuously and cook until fluffy and soft. 4. Season with sea salt and freshly ground pepper to taste. Divide between 2 plates and serve immediately.

Per Serving:
calories: 267 | fat: 21g | protein: 16g | carbs: 3g | fiber: 0g | sodium: 394mg

Butternut Squash and Ricotta Frittata

Prep time: 10 minutes | Cook time: 33 minutes | Serves 2 to 3

1 cup cubed (½-inch) butternut squash (5½ ounces / 156 g)
2 tablespoons olive oil
Kosher salt and freshly ground black pepper, to taste
4 fresh sage leaves, thinly sliced
6 large eggs, lightly beaten
½ cup ricotta cheese
Cayenne pepper

1. In a bowl, toss the squash with the olive oil and season with salt and black pepper until evenly coated. Sprinkle the sage on the bottom of a cake pan and place the squash on top. Place the pan in the air fryer and bake at 400°F (204°C) for 10 minutes. Stir to incorporate the sage, then cook until the squash is tender and lightly caramelized at the edges, about 3 minutes more. 2. Pour the eggs over the squash, dollop the ricotta all over, and sprinkle with cayenne. Bake at 300°F (149°C) until the eggs are set and the frittata is golden brown on top, about 20 minutes. Remove the pan from the air fryer and cut the frittata into wedges to serve.

Per Serving:
calories: 289 | fat: 22g | protein: 18g | carbs: 5g | fiber: 1g | sodium: 184mg

Crostini with Smoked Trout

Prep time: 10 minutes | Cook time: 5 minutes | Serves 4

½ French baguette, cut into 1-inch-thick slices
1 tablespoon olive oil
¼ teaspoon onion powder
1 (4-ounce / 113-g) can smoked

trout
¼ cup crème fraîche
¼ teaspoon chopped fresh dill, for garnish

1. Drizzle the bread on both sides with the olive oil and sprinkle with the onion powder. 2. Place the bread in a single layer in a large skillet and toast over medium heat until lightly browned on both sides, 3 to 4 minutes total. 3. Transfer the toasted bread to a serving platter and place 1 or 2 pieces of the trout on each slice. Top with the crème fraîche, garnish with the dill, and serve immediately.

Per Serving:
calories: 206 | fat: 10g | protein: 13g | carbs: 15g | fiber: 1g | sodium: 350mg

Kagianas

Prep time: 5 minutes | Cook time: 10 minutes | Serves 2

2 teaspoons extra virgin olive oil
2 tablespoons finely chopped onion (any variety)
¼ teaspoon fine sea salt, divided
1 medium tomato (any variety), chopped

2 eggs
1 ounce (28 g) crumbled feta
½ teaspoon dried oregano
1 teaspoon chopped fresh mint
Pinch of freshly ground black pepper for serving

1. Heat the olive oil in a small pan placed over medium heat. When the oil begins to shimmer, add the onions along with ⅛ teaspoon sea salt. Sauté for about 3 minutes or until the onions are soft. 2. Add the tomatoes, stir, then reduce the heat to low and simmer for 8 minutes or until the mixture thickens. 3. While the tomatoes are cooking, beat the eggs in a small bowl. 4. When the tomatoes have thickened, pour the eggs into the pan and increase the heat to medium. Continue cooking, using a spatula to stir the eggs and tomatoes continuously, for 2–3 minutes or until the eggs are set. Remove the pan from the heat. 5. Add the feta, oregano, and mint, and stir to combine. 6. Transfer to a plate. Top with a pinch of black pepper and the remaining ⅛ teaspoon sea salt. Serve promptly.

Per Serving:
calories: 156 | fat: 12g | protein: 8g | carbs: 4g | fiber: 1g | sodium: 487mg

Peach Sunrise Smoothie

Prep time: 10 minutes | Cook time: 0 minutes | Serves 1

1 large unpeeled peach, pitted and sliced (about ½ cup)
6 ounces (170 g) vanilla or

peach low-fat Greek yogurt
2 tablespoons low-fat milk
6 to 8 ice cubes

1. Combine all ingredients in a blender and blend until thick and creamy. Serve immediately.

Per Serving:
calories: 228 | fat: 3g | protein: 11g | carbs: 42g | fiber: 3g | sodium: 127mg

Nuts and Fruit Oatmeal

Prep time: 10 minutes | Cook time: 7 minutes | Serves 2

1 cup rolled oats
1¼ cups water
¼ cup orange juice
1 medium pear, peeled, cored, and cubed
¼ cup dried cherries

¼ cup chopped walnuts
1 tablespoon honey
¼ teaspoon ground ginger
¼ teaspoon ground cinnamon
⅛ teaspoon salt

1. Place oats, water, orange juice, pear, cherries, walnuts, honey, ginger, cinnamon, and salt in the Instant Pot®. Stir to combine. 2. Close lid, set steam release to Sealing, press the Manual button, and set time to 7 minutes. When the timer beeps, let pressure release naturally, about 20 minutes. Press the Cancel button, open lid, and stir well. Serve warm.

Per Serving:
calories: 362 | fat: 8g | protein: 7g | carbs: 69g | fiber: 8g | sodium: 164mg

Mediterranean-Inspired White Smoothie

Prep time: 5 minutes | Cook time: 0 minutes | Serves

½ medium apple (any variety), peeled, halved, and seeded
5 roasted almonds
½ medium frozen banana, sliced (be sure to peel the

banana before freezing)
¼ cup full-fat Greek yogurt
½ cup low-fat 1% milk
¼ teaspoon ground cinnamon
½ teaspoon honey

1. Combine all the ingredients in a blender. Process until smooth. 2. Pour into a glass and serve promptly. (This recipe is best consumed fresh.)

Per Serving:
calories: 236 | fat: 7g | protein: 8g | carbs: 40g | fiber: 5g | sodium: 84mg

Mashed Chickpea, Feta, and Avocado Toast

Prep time: 10 minutes |Cook time: 0 minutes| Serves: 4

1 (15-ounce / 425-g) can chickpeas, drained and rinsed
1 avocado, pitted
½ cup diced feta cheese (about 2 ounces / 57 g)
2 teaspoons freshly squeezed

lemon juice or 1 tablespoon orange juice
½ teaspoon freshly ground black pepper
4 pieces multigrain toast
2 teaspoons honey

1. Put the chickpeas in a large bowl. Scoop the avocado flesh into the bowl. 2. With a potato masher or large fork, mash the ingredients together until the mix has a spreadable consistency. It doesn't need to be totally smooth. 3. Add the feta, lemon juice, and pepper, and mix well. 4. Evenly divide the mash onto the four pieces of toast and spread with a knife. Drizzle with honey and serve.

Per Serving:
calories: 301 | fat: 14g | protein: 12g | carbs: 35g | fiber: 11g | sodium: 450mg

Power Peach Smoothie Bowl

Prep time: 15 minutes | Cook time: 0 minutes | Serves 2

2 cups packed partially thawed frozen peaches
½ cup plain or vanilla Greek yogurt
½ ripe avocado
2 tablespoons flax meal
1 teaspoon vanilla extract
1 teaspoon orange extract
1 tablespoon honey (optional)

1. Combine all of the ingredients in a blender and blend until smooth. 2. Pour the mixture into two bowls, and, if desired, sprinkle with additional toppings.

Per Serving:
calories: 213 | fat: 13g | protein: 6g | carbs: 23g | fiber: 7g | sodium: 41mg

Egg Salad with Red Pepper and Dill

Prep time: 5 minutes | Cook time: 10 minutes | Serves 6

6 large eggs
1 cup water
1 tablespoon olive oil
1 medium red bell pepper, seeded and chopped
¼ teaspoon salt
¼ teaspoon ground black pepper
½ cup low-fat plain Greek yogurt
2 tablespoons chopped fresh dill

1. Have ready a large bowl of ice water. Place rack or egg holder into bottom of the Instant Pot®. 2. Arrange eggs on rack or holder and add water to the Instant Pot®. Close lid, set steam release to Sealing, press the Manual button, and set time to 5 minutes. 3. When the timer beeps, let pressure release naturally for 5 minutes, then quick-release the remaining pressure until the float valve drops. Press the Cancel button and open lid. Carefully transfer eggs to the bowl of ice water. Let stand in ice water for 10 minutes, then peel, chop, and add eggs to a medium bowl. 4. Clean out pot, dry well, and return to machine. Press the Sauté button and heat oil. Add bell pepper, salt, and black pepper. Cook, stirring often, until bell pepper is tender, about 5 minutes. Transfer to bowl with eggs. 5. Add yogurt and dill to bowl, and fold to combine. Cover and chill for 1 hour before serving.

Per Serving:
calories: 111 | fat: 8g | protein: 8g | carbs: 3g | fiber: 0g | sodium: 178mg

Almond Butter Banana Chocolate Smoothie

Prep time: 5 minutes | Cook time: 0 minutes | Serves 1

¾ cup almond milk
½ medium banana, preferably frozen
¼ cup frozen blueberries
1 tablespoon almond butter
1 tablespoon unsweetened cocoa powder
1 tablespoon chia seeds

1. In a blender or Vitamix, add all the ingredients. Blend to combine.

Per Serving:
calories: 300 | fat: 16g | protein: 8g | carbs: 37g | fiber: 10g | sodium: 125mg

Berry Baked Oatmeal

Prep time: 10 minutes | Cook time: 45 to 50 minutes | Serves 8

2 cups gluten-free rolled oats
2 cups (10-ounce / 283-g bag) frozen mixed berries (blueberries and raspberries work best)
2 cups plain, unsweetened almond milk
1 cup plain Greek yogurt
¼ cup maple syrup
2 tablespoons extra-virgin olive oil
2 teaspoons ground cinnamon
1 teaspoon baking powder
1 teaspoon vanilla extract
½ teaspoon kosher salt
¼ teaspoon ground nutmeg
⅛ teaspoon ground cloves

1. Preheat the oven to 375ºF (190ºC). 2. Mix all the ingredients together in a large bowl. Pour into a 9-by-13-inch baking dish. Bake for 45 to 50 minutes, or until golden brown.

Per Serving:
calories: 180 | fat: 6g | protein: 6g | carbs: 28g | fiber: 4g | sodium: 180mg

Sunshine Overnight Oats

Prep time: 5 minutes | Cook time: 0 minutes | Serves 2

⅔ cup vanilla, unsweetened almond milk (not Silk brand)
⅓ cup rolled oats
¼ cup raspberries
1 teaspoon honey
¼ teaspoon turmeric
⅛ teaspoon ground cinnamon
Pinch ground cloves

1. In a mason jar, combine the almond milk, oats, raspberries, honey, turmeric, cinnamon, and cloves and shake well. Store in the refrigerator for 8 to 24 hours, then serve cold or heated.

Per Serving:
calories: 82 | fat: 2g | protein: 2g | carbs: 14g | fiber: 3g | sodium: 98mg

Savory Sweet Potato Hash

Prep time: 15 minutes | Cook time: 18 minutes | Serves 6

2 medium sweet potatoes, peeled and cut into 1-inch cubes
½ green bell pepper, diced
½ red onion, diced
4 ounces (113 g) baby bella mushrooms, diced
2 tablespoons olive oil
1 garlic clove, minced
½ teaspoon salt
½ teaspoon black pepper
½ tablespoon chopped fresh rosemary

1. Preheat the air fryer to 380°F(193ºC). 2. In a large bowl, toss all ingredients together until the vegetables are well coated and seasonings distributed. 3. Pour the vegetables into the air fryer basket, making sure they are in a single even layer. (If using a smaller air fryer, you may need to do this in two batches.) 4. Roast for 9 minutes, then toss or flip the vegetables. Roast for 9 minutes more. 5. Transfer to a serving bowl or individual plates and enjoy.

Per Serving:
calories: 91 | fat: 5g | protein: 2g | carbs: 12g | fiber: 1g | sodium: 219mg

Breakfast Pita

Prep time: 5 minutes | Cook time: 6 minutes | Serves 2

1 whole wheat pita
2 teaspoons olive oil
½ shallot, diced
¼ teaspoon garlic, minced
1 large egg

¼ teaspoon dried oregano
¼ teaspoon dried thyme
⅛ teaspoon salt
2 tablespoons shredded
Parmesan cheese

1. Preheat the air fryer to 380°F(193°C). 2. Brush the top of the pita with olive oil, then spread the diced shallot and minced garlic over the pita. 3. Crack the egg into a small bowl or ramekin, and season it with oregano, thyme, and salt. 4. Place the pita into the air fryer basket, and gently pour the egg onto the top of the pita. Sprinkle with cheese over the top. 5. Bake for 6 minutes. 6. Allow to cool for 5 minutes before cutting into pieces for serving.

Per Serving:
calories: 191 | fat: 10g | protein: 8g | carbs: 19g | fiber: 3g | sodium: 312mg

Oat and Fruit Parfait

Prep time: 5 minutes | Cook time: 12 minutes | Serves 2

½ cup whole-grain rolled or
quickcooking oats (not instant)
½ cup walnut pieces
1 teaspoon honey

1 cup sliced fresh strawberries
1½ cups vanilla low-fat Greek
yogurt
Fresh mint leaves for garnish

1. Preheat the oven to 300°F(150°C). 2. Spread the oats and walnuts in a single layer on a baking sheet. 3. Toast the oats and nuts just until you begin to smell the nuts, 10 to 12 minutes. Remove the pan from the oven and set aside. 4. In a small microwave-safe bowl, heat the honey just until warm, about 30 seconds. Add the strawberries and stir to coat. 5. Place 1 tablespoon of the strawberries in the bottom of each of 2 dessert dishes or 8-ounce glasses. Add a portion of yogurt and then a portion of oats and repeat the layers until the containers are full, ending with the berries. Serve immediately or chill until ready to eat.

Per Serving:
calories: 541 | fat: 25g | protein: 21g | carbs: 66g | fiber: 8g | sodium: 124mg

Quinoa Porridge with Apricots

Prep time: 10 minutes | Cook time: 12 minutes | Serves 4

1½ cups quinoa, rinsed and
drained
1 cup chopped dried apricots
2½ cups water

1 cup almond milk
1 tablespoon rose water
½ teaspoon cardamom
¼ teaspoon salt

1. Place all ingredients in the Instant Pot®. Stir to combine. Close lid, set steam release to Sealing, press the Rice button, and set time to 12 minutes. When the timer beeps, let pressure release naturally, about 20 minutes. 2. Press the Cancel button, open lid, and fluff quinoa with a fork. Serve warm.

Per Serving:
calories: 197 | fat: 2g | protein: 3g | carbs: 44g | fiber: 4g | sodium: 293mg

Polenta with Sautéed Chard and Fried Eggs

Prep time: 5 minutes | Cook time: 20 minutes | Serves 4

For the Polenta:
2½ cups water
½ teaspoon kosher salt
¾ cups whole-grain cornmeal
¼ teaspoon freshly ground
black pepper
2 tablespoons grated Parmesan
cheese
For the Chard:
1 tablespoon extra-virgin olive
oil
1 bunch (about 6 ounces / 170

g) Swiss chard, leaves and
stems chopped and separated
2 garlic cloves, sliced
¼ teaspoon kosher salt
⅛ teaspoon freshly ground
black pepper
Lemon juice (optional)
For the Eggs:
1 tablespoon extra-virgin olive
oil
4 large eggs

Make the Polenta: 1. Bring the water and salt to a boil in a medium saucepan over high heat. Slowly add the cornmeal, whisking constantly. 2. Decrease the heat to low, cover, and cook for 10 to 15 minutes, stirring often to avoid lumps. Stir in the pepper and Parmesan, and divide among 4 bowls. Make the Chard: 3. Heat the oil in a large skillet over medium heat. Add the chard stems, garlic, salt, and pepper; sauté for 2 minutes. Add the chard leaves and cook until wilted, about 3 to 5 minutes. 4. Add a spritz of lemon juice (if desired), toss together, and divide evenly on top of the polenta. Make the Eggs: 5. Heat the oil in the same large skillet over medium-high heat. Crack each egg into the skillet, taking care not to crowd the skillet and leaving space between the eggs. Cook until the whites are set and golden around the edges, about 2 to 3 minutes. 6. Serve sunny-side up or flip the eggs over carefully and cook 1 minute longer for over easy. Place one egg on top of the polenta and chard in each bowl.

Per Serving:
calories: 310 | fat: 18g | protein: 17g | carbs: 21g | fiber: 1g | sodium: 500mg

Spinach and Swiss Frittata with Mushrooms

Prep time: 10 minutes | Cook time: 20 minutes | Serves 4

Olive oil cooking spray
8 large eggs
½ teaspoon salt
½ teaspoon black pepper
1 garlic clove, minced
2 cups fresh baby spinach

4 ounces (113 g) baby bella
mushrooms, sliced
1 shallot, diced
½ cup shredded Swiss cheese,
divided
Hot sauce, for serving (optional)

1. Preheat the air fryer to 360°F(182°C). Lightly coat the inside of a 6-inch round cake pan with olive oil cooking spray. 2. In a large bowl, beat the eggs, salt, pepper, and garlic for 1 to 2 minutes, or until well combined. 3. Fold in the spinach, mushrooms, shallot, and ¼ cup of the Swiss cheese. 4. Pour the egg mixture into the prepared cake pan, and sprinkle the remaining ¼ cup of Swiss over the top. 5. Place into the air fryer and bake for 18 to 20 minutes, or until the eggs are set in the center. 6. Remove from the air fryer and allow to cool for 5 minutes. Drizzle with hot sauce (if using) before serving.

Per Serving:
calories: 207 | fat: 13g | protein: 18g | carbs: 4g | fiber: 1g | sodium: 456mg

Spinach and Feta Egg Bake

Prep time: 7 minutes | Cook time: 23 to 25 minutes | Serves 2

Avocado oil spray
⅓ cup diced red onion
1 cup frozen chopped spinach, thawed and drained
4 large eggs
¼ cup heavy (whipping) cream

Sea salt and freshly ground black pepper, to taste
¼ teaspoon cayenne pepper
½ cup crumbled feta cheese
¼ cup shredded Parmesan cheese

1. Spray a deep pan with oil. Put the onion in the pan, and place the pan in the air fryer basket. Set the air fryer to 350ºF (177ºC) and bake for 7 minutes. 2. Sprinkle the spinach over the onion. 3. In a medium bowl, beat the eggs, heavy cream, salt, black pepper, and cayenne. Pour this mixture over the vegetables. 4. Top with the feta and Parmesan cheese. Bake for 16 to 18 minutes, until the eggs are set and lightly brown.

Per Serving:
calories: 366 | fat: 26g | protein: 25g | carbs: 8g | fiber: 3g | sodium: 520mg

Smoked Salmon Egg Scramble with Dill and Chives

Prep time: 5 minutes | Cook time: 5 minutes | Serves 2

4 large eggs
1 tablespoon milk
1 tablespoon fresh chives, minced
1 tablespoon fresh dill, minced
¼ teaspoon kosher salt

⅛ teaspoon freshly ground black pepper
2 teaspoons extra-virgin olive oil
2 ounces (57 g) smoked salmon, thinly sliced

1. In a large bowl, whisk together the eggs, milk, chives, dill, salt, and pepper. 2. Heat the olive oil in a medium skillet or sauté pan over medium heat. Add the egg mixture and cook for about 3 minutes, stirring occasionally. 3. Add the salmon and cook until the eggs are set but moist, about 1 minute.

Per Serving:
calories: 325 | fat: 26g | protein: 23g | carbs: 1g | fiber: 0g | sodium: 455mg

Blender Cinnamon Pancakes with Cacao Cream Topping

Prep time: 10 minutes | Cook time: 10 minutes | Serves 4

Cinnamon Pancakes:
2 cups pecans
4 large eggs
1 tablespoon cinnamon
½ teaspoon baking soda
1 teaspoon fresh lemon juice or apple cider vinegar
1 tablespoon virgin coconut oil or ghee
Cacao Cream Topping:

1 cup coconut cream
1½ tablespoons raw cacao powder
Optional: low-carb sweetener, to taste
To Serve:
9 medium strawberries, sliced
1 tablespoon unsweetened shredded coconut

1. To make the pancakes: Place the pecans in a blender and process until powdered. Add all of the remaining ingredients apart from the ghee. Blend again until smooth. 2. Place a nonstick pan greased with 1 teaspoon of the coconut oil over low heat. Using a ¼-cup (60 ml) measure per pancake, cook in batches of 2 to 3 small pancakes over low heat until bubbles begin to form on the pancakes. Use a spatula to flip over, then cook for 30 to 40 seconds and place on a plate. Grease the pan with more coconut oil between batches. Transfer the pancakes to a plate. 3. To make the cacao cream topping: Place the coconut cream in a bowl. Add the cacao powder and sweetener, if using. Whisk until well combined and creamy. 4. Serve the pancakes with the cacao cream, sliced strawberries and a sprinkle of shredded coconut. You can enhance the flavor of the shredded coconut by toasting it in a dry pan for about 1 minute.

Per Serving:
calories: 665 | fat: 65g | protein: 14g | carbs: 17g | fiber: 9g | sodium: 232mg

Berry Breakfast Smoothie

Prep time: 5 minutes | Cook time: 0 minutes | Serves 1

½ cup vanilla low-fat Greek yogurt
¼ cup low-fat milk
½ cup fresh or frozen

blueberries or strawberries (or a combination)
6 to 8 ice cubes

1. Place the Greek yogurt, milk, and berries in a blender and blend until the berries are liquefied. Add the ice cubes and blend on high until thick and smooth. Serve immediately.

Per Serving:
calories: 158 | fat: 3g | protein: 9g | carbs: 25g | fiber: 1g | sodium: 110mg

Warm Fava Beans with Whole-Wheat Pita

Prep time: 5 minutes | Cook time: 10 minutes | Serves 4

1½ tablespoons olive oil
1 large onion, diced
1 large tomato, diced
1 clove garlic, crushed
1 (15-ounce / 425-g) can fava beans, not drained
1 teaspoon ground cumin

¼ cup chopped fresh parsley
¼ cup lemon juice
Salt
Freshly ground black pepper
Crushed red pepper flakes
4 whole-grain pita bread pockets

1. Heat the olive oil in a large skillet set over medium-high heat. Add the onion, tomato, and garlic and cook, stirring, for about 3 minutes, until the vegetables soften. 2. Add the fava beans, along with the liquid from the can, and bring to a boil. 3. Lower the heat to medium and stir in the cumin, parsley, and lemon juice. Season with salt, pepper, and crushed red pepper. Simmer over medium heat, stirring occasionally, for 5 minutes. 4. While the beans are simmering, heat the pitas in a toaster oven or in a cast-iron skillet over medium heat. To serve, cut the pitas into triangles for dipping into and scooping the bean mixture, or halve the pitas and fill the pockets up with beans.

Per Serving:
calories: 524 | fat: 8g | protein: 32g | carbs: 86g | fiber: 31g | sodium: 394mg

Mediterranean Breakfast Pita Sandwiches

Prep time: 5 minutes | Cook time: 7 minutes | Serves 2

2 eggs
1 small avocado, peeled, halved, and pitted
¼ teaspoon fresh lemon juice
Pinch of salt
¼ teaspoon freshly ground black pepper
1 (8-inch) whole-wheat pocket pita bread, halved

12 (¼-inch) thick cucumber slices
6 oil-packed sun-dried tomatoes, rinsed, patted dry, and cut in half
2 tablespoons crumbled feta
½ teaspoon extra virgin olive oil

1. Fill a small saucepan with water and place it over medium heat. When the water is boiling, use a slotted spoon to carefully lower the eggs into the water. Gently boil for 7 minutes, then remove the pan from the heat and transfer the eggs to a bowl of cold water. Set aside. 2. In a small bowl, mash the avocado with a fork and then add the lemon juice and salt. Mash to combine. 3. Peel and slice the eggs, then sprinkle the black pepper over the egg slices. 4. Spread half of the avocado mixture over one side of the pita half. Top the pita half with 1 sliced egg, 6 cucumber slices, and 6 sun-dried tomato pieces. 5. Sprinkle 1 tablespoon crumbled feta over the top and drizzle ¼ teaspoon olive oil over the feta. Repeat with the other pita half. Serve promptly.

Per Serving:
calories: 427 | fat: 28g | protein: 14g | carbs: 36g | fiber: 12g | sodium: 398mg

Greek Eggs and Potatoes

Prep time: 5 minutes | Cook time: 30 minutes | Serves 4

3 medium tomatoes, seeded and coarsely chopped
2 tablespoons fresh chopped basil
1 garlic clove, minced
2 tablespoons plus ½ cup olive oil, divided

Sea salt and freshly ground pepper, to taste
3 large russet potatoes
4 large eggs
1 teaspoon fresh oregano, chopped

1. Put tomatoes in a food processor and purée them, skins and all. 2. Add the basil, garlic, 2 tablespoons olive oil, sea salt, and freshly ground pepper, and pulse to combine. 3. Put the mixture in a large skillet over low heat and cook, covered, for 20–25 minutes, or until the sauce has thickened and is bubbly. 4. Meanwhile, dice the potatoes into small cubes. Put ½ cup olive oil in a nonstick skillet over medium-low heat. 5. Fry the potatoes for 5 minutes until crisp and browned on the outside, then cover and reduce heat to low. Steam potatoes until done. 6. Carefully crack the eggs into the tomato sauce. Cook over low heat until the eggs are set in the sauce, about 6 minutes. 7. Remove the potatoes from the pan and drain them on paper towels, then place them in a bowl. 8. Sprinkle with sea salt and freshly ground pepper to taste and top with the oregano. 9. Carefully remove the eggs with a slotted spoon and place them on a plate with the potatoes. Spoon sauce over the top and serve.

Per Serving:
calories: 548 | fat: 32g | protein: 13g | carbs: 54g | fiber: 5g | sodium: 90mg

Harissa Shakshuka with Bell Peppers and Tomatoes

Prep time: 10 minutes | Cook time: 20 minutes | Serves 4

1½ tablespoons extra-virgin olive oil
2 tablespoons harissa
1 tablespoon tomato paste
½ onion, diced
1 bell pepper, seeded and diced
3 garlic cloves, minced

1 (28-ounce / 794-g) can no-salt-added diced tomatoes
½ teaspoon kosher salt
4 large eggs
2 to 3 tablespoons fresh basil, chopped or cut into ribbons

1. Preheat the oven to 375ºF (190ºC). 2. Heat the olive oil in a 12-inch cast-iron pan or ovenproof skillet over medium heat. Add the harissa, tomato paste, onion, and bell pepper; sauté for 3 to 4 minutes. Add the garlic and cook until fragrant, about 30 seconds. Add the diced tomatoes and salt and simmer for about 10 minutes. 3. Make 4 wells in the sauce and gently break 1 egg into each. Transfer to the oven and bake until the whites are cooked and the yolks are set, 10 to 12 minutes. 4. Allow to cool for 3 to 5 minutes, garnish with the basil, and carefully spoon onto plates.

Per Serving:
calories: 190 | fat: 10g | protein: 9g | carbs: 15g | fiber: 4g | sodium: 255mg

Spinach and Feta Frittata

Prep time: 10 minutes | Cook time: 26 minutes | Serves 4

1 tablespoon olive oil
½ medium onion, peeled and chopped
½ medium red bell pepper, seeded and chopped
2 cups chopped fresh baby spinach
1 cup water

1 cup crumbled feta cheese
6 large eggs, beaten
¼ cup low-fat plain Greek yogurt
½ teaspoon salt
½ teaspoon ground black pepper

1. Press the Sauté button on the Instant Pot® and heat oil. Add onion and bell pepper, and cook until tender, about 8 minutes. Add spinach and cook until wilted, about 3 minutes. Press the Cancel button and transfer vegetables to a medium bowl to cool. Wipe out inner pot. 2. Place the rack in the Instant Pot® and add water. Spray a 1.5-liter baking dish with nonstick cooking spray. Drain excess liquid from spinach mixture, then add to dish with cheese. 3. In a separate medium bowl, mix eggs, yogurt, salt, and black pepper until well combined. Pour over vegetable and cheese mixture. Cover dish tightly with foil, then gently lower into machine. 4. Close lid, set steam release to Sealing, press the Manual button, and set time to 15 minutes. When the timer beeps, let pressure release naturally for 10 minutes, then quick-release any remaining pressure until the float valve drops. Press the Cancel button and open lid. Let stand for 10–15 minutes before carefully removing dish from pot. 5. Run a thin knife around the edge of the frittata and turn it out onto a serving platter. Serve warm.

Per Serving:
calories: 259 | fat: 19g | protein: 16g | carbs: 6g | fiber: 1g | sodium: 766mg

Portobello Eggs Benedict

Prep time: 10 minutes | Cook time: 10 to 14 minutes | Serves 2

1 tablespoon olive oil
2 cloves garlic, minced
¼ teaspoon dried thyme
2 portobello mushrooms, stems removed and gills scraped out
2 Roma tomatoes, halved lengthwise
Salt and freshly ground black

pepper, to taste
2 large eggs
2 tablespoons grated Pecorino Romano cheese
1 tablespoon chopped fresh parsley, for garnish
1 teaspoon truffle oil (optional)

1. Preheat the air fryer to 400ºF (204ºC). 2. In a small bowl, combine the olive oil, garlic, and thyme. Brush the mixture over the mushrooms and tomatoes until thoroughly coated. Season to taste with salt and freshly ground black pepper. 3. Arrange the vegetables, cut side up, in the air fryer basket. Crack an egg into the center of each mushroom and sprinkle with cheese. Air fry for 10 to 14 minutes until the vegetables are tender and the whites are firm. When cool enough to handle, coarsely chop the tomatoes and place on top of the eggs. Scatter parsley on top and drizzle with truffle oil, if desired, just before serving.

Per Serving:
calories: 189 | fat: 13g | protein: 11g | carbs: 7g | fiber: 2g | sodium: 87mg

Quick Low-Carb Avocado Toasts

Prep time: 10 minutes | Cook time: 10 minutes | Makes 4 toasts

Quick Bread Base:
¼ cup (28 g/1 oz) flax meal
2 tablespoons (16 g/0.6 oz) coconut flour
2 teaspoons (2 g) psyllium powder
⅛ teaspoon baking soda
Optional: ½ teaspoon dried herbs, ¼ teaspoon paprika or ground turmeric
Salt and black pepper, to taste
¼ teaspoon apple cider vinegar
1 teaspoon extra-virgin olive oil or ghee, plus more for greasing
1 large egg

2 tablespoons water
Avocado Topping:
1 large ripe avocado
¼ small red onion or 1 spring onion, minced
1 tablespoon extra-virgin olive oil
1 tablespoon fresh lemon juice
Salt, black pepper, and/or chile flakes, to taste
2 teaspoons chopped fresh herbs, such as parsley or chives
Optional: 2 ounces (57 g) smoked salmon and/or poached egg

Make the bread base: Combine all the dry ingredients in a bowl. Add the wet ingredients. Combine and set aside for 5 minutes. Divide the mixture between two wide ramekins lightly greased with the olive oil and microwave on high for about 2 minutes, checking every 30 to 60 seconds to avoid overcooking. (If the bread ends up too dry, you can "rehydrate" it: Pour 1 tablespoon [15 ml] of water evenly over it, then return it to the microwave for 30 seconds.) Let it cool slightly, then cut widthwise. Place on a dry nonstick pan and toast for 1 to 2 minutes per side. Set aside. Make the topping: In a bowl, mash the avocado with the onion, oil, lemon juice, salt, pepper, and chile flakes. To serve, spread the avocado mixture on top of the sliced bread and add fresh herbs. Optionally, top with smoked salmon. Store the bread separately from the topping at room temperature in a sealed container for 1 day, in the fridge for up to 5 days, or freeze for up to 3 months. Refrigerate the topping in a sealed jar for up to 3 days.

Per Serving:
calories: 112 | fat: 10g | protein: 3g | carbs: 4g | fiber: 3g | sodium: 71mg

Creamy Cinnamon Porridge

Prep time: 10 minutes | Cook time: 10 minutes | Serves 2

¼ cup coconut milk
¾ cup unsweetened almond milk or water
¼ cup almond butter or hazelnut butter
1 tablespoon virgin coconut oil
2 tablespoons chia seeds
1 tablespoon flax meal
1 teaspoon cinnamon

¼ cup macadamia nuts
¼ cup hazelnuts
4 Brazil nuts
Optional: low-carb sweetener, to taste
¼ cup unsweetened large coconut flakes
1 tablespoon cacao nibs

1. In a small saucepan, mix the coconut milk and almond milk and heat over medium heat. Once hot (not boiling), take off the heat. Add the almond butter and coconut oil. Stir until well combined. If needed, use an immersion blender and process until smooth. 2. Add the chia seeds, flax meal, and cinnamon, and leave to rest for 5 or 10 minutes. Roughly chop the macadamias, hazelnuts, and Brazil nuts and stir in. Add sweetener, if using, and stir. Transfer to serving bowls. In a small skillet, dry-roast the coconut flakes over medium-high heat for 1 to 2 minutes, until lightly toasted and fragrant. Top the porridge with the toasted coconut flakes and cacao nibs (or you can use chopped 100% chocolate). Serve immediately or store in the fridge for up to 3 days.

Per Serving:
calories: 646 | fat: 61g | protein: 13g | carbs: 23g | fiber: 10g | sodium: 40mg

Amaranth Breakfast Bowl with Chocolate and Almonds

Prep time: 10 minutes | Cook time: 6 minutes | Serves 6

2 cups amaranth, rinsed and drained
2 cups almond milk
2 cups water
¼ cup maple syrup
3 tablespoons cocoa powder

1 teaspoon vanilla extract
¼ teaspoon salt
½ cup toasted sliced almonds
⅓ cup miniature semisweet chocolate chips

1. Place amaranth, almond milk, water, maple syrup, cocoa powder, vanilla, and salt in the Instant Pot®. Stir to combine. Close lid, set steam release to Sealing, press the Rice button, and set time to 6 minutes. When the timer beeps, quick-release the pressure until the float valve drops, press the Cancel button, open lid, and stir well. 2. Serve hot, topped with almonds and chocolate chips.

Per Serving:
calories: 263 | fat: 12g | protein: 5g | carbs: 35g | fiber: 5g | sodium: 212mg

Greek Breakfast Power Bowl

Prep time: 15 minutes | Cook time: 20 minutes | Serves 2

3 tablespoons extra-virgin avocado oil or ghee, divided
1 clove garlic, minced
2 teaspoons chopped fresh rosemary
1 small eggplant, roughly chopped
1 medium zucchini, roughly chopped
1 tablespoon fresh lemon juice
2 tablespoons chopped mint
1 tablespoon chopped fresh oregano
Salt and black pepper, to taste
6 ounces (170 g) Halloumi cheese, cubed or sliced
¼ cup pitted Kalamata olives
4 large eggs, soft-boiled (or hard-boiled or poached)
1 tablespoon extra-virgin olive oil, to drizzle

1. Heat a skillet (with a lid) greased with 2 tablespoons (30 ml) of the avocado oil over medium heat. Add the garlic and rosemary and cook for 1 minute. Add the eggplant, zucchini, and lemon juice. Stir and cover with a lid, then reduce the heat to medium-low. Cook for 10 to 15 minutes, stirring once or twice, until tender. 2. Stir in the mint and oregano. Optionally, reserve some herbs for topping. Season with salt and pepper to taste. Remove from the heat and transfer to a plate. Cover with the skillet lid to keep the veggies warm. 3. Grease the same pan with the remaining 1 tablespoon (15 ml) avocado oil and cook the Halloumi over medium-high heat for 2 to 3 minutes per side until lightly browned. Place the slices of cooked Halloumi on top of the cooked veggies. Top with the olives and cooked eggs and drizzle with the olive oil. 4. Always serve warm, as Halloumi hardens once it cools. Reheat before serving if necessary.

Per Serving:
calories: 748 | fat: 56g | protein: 40g | carbs: 25g | fiber: 10g | sodium: 275mg

Peachy Green Smoothie

Prep time: 10 minutes | Cook time: 0 minutes | Serves 2

1 cup almond milk
3 cups kale or spinach
1 banana, peeled
1 orange, peeled
1 small green apple
1 cup frozen peaches
¼ cup vanilla Greek yogurt

1. Put the ingredients in a blender in the order listed and blend on high until smooth. 2. Serve and enjoy.

Per Serving:
calories: 257 | fat: 5g | protein: 9g | carbs: 50g | fiber: 7g | sodium: 87mg

Mediterranean Omelet

Prep time: 10 minutes | Cook time: 12 minutes | Serves 2

2 teaspoons extra-virgin olive oil, divided
1 garlic clove, minced
½ red bell pepper, thinly sliced
½ yellow bell pepper, thinly sliced
¼ cup thinly sliced red onion
2 tablespoons chopped fresh basil
2 tablespoons chopped fresh parsley, plus extra for garnish
½ teaspoon salt
½ teaspoon freshly ground black pepper
4 large eggs, beaten

1. In a large, heavy skillet, heat 1 teaspoon of the olive oil over medium heat. Add the garlic, peppers, and onion to the pan and sauté, stirring frequently, for 5 minutes. 2. Add the basil, parsley, salt, and pepper, increase the heat to medium-high, and sauté for 2 minutes. Slide the vegetable mixture onto a plate and return the pan to the heat. 3. Heat the remaining 1 teaspoon olive oil in the same pan and pour in the beaten eggs, tilting the pan to coat evenly. Cook the eggs just until the edges are bubbly and all but the center is dry, 3 to 5 minutes. 4. Either flip the omelet or use a spatula to turn it over. 5. Spoon the vegetable mixture onto one-half of the omelet and use a spatula to fold the empty side over the top. Slide the omelet onto a platter or cutting board. 6. To serve, cut the omelet in half and garnish with fresh parsley.

Per Serving:
calories: 218 | fat: 14g | protein: 14g | carbs: 9g | fiber: 1g | sodium: 728mg

Italian Egg Cups

Prep time: 5 minutes | Cook time: 10 minutes | Serves 4

Olive oil
1 cup marinara sauce
4 eggs
4 tablespoons shredded Mozzarella cheese
4 teaspoons grated Parmesan cheese
Salt and freshly ground black pepper, to taste
Chopped fresh basil, for garnish

1. Lightly spray 4 individual ramekins with olive oil. 2. Pour ¼ cup of marinara sauce into each ramekin. 3. Crack one egg into each ramekin on top of the marinara sauce. 4. Sprinkle 1 tablespoon of Mozzarella and 1 tablespoon of Parmesan on top of each egg. Season with salt and pepper. 5. Cover each ramekin with aluminum foil. Place two of the ramekins in the air fryer basket. 6. Air fry at 350ºF (177ºC) for 5 minutes and remove the aluminum foil. Air fry until the top is lightly browned and the egg white is cooked, another 2 to 4 minutes. If you prefer the yolk to be firmer, cook for 3 to 5 more minutes. 7. Repeat with the remaining two ramekins. Garnish with basil and serve.

Per Serving:
calories: 123 | fat: 7g | protein: 9g | carbs: 6g | fiber: 1g | sodium: 84mg

Hearty Berry Breakfast Oats

Prep time: 5 minutes | Cook time: 0 minutes | Serves 2

1½ cups whole-grain rolled or quickcooking oats (not instant)
¾ cup fresh blueberries, raspberries, or blackberries, or
a combination
2 teaspoons honey
2 tablespoons walnut pieces

1. Prepare the whole-grain oats according to the package directions and divide between 2 deep bowls. 2. In a small microwave-safe bowl, heat the berries and honey for 30 seconds. Top each bowl of oatmeal with the fruit mixture. Sprinkle the walnuts over the fruit and serve hot.

Per Serving:
calories: 556 | fat: 13g | protein: 22g | carbs: 92g | fiber: 14g | sodium: 3mg

Greek Yogurt Parfait with Granola

Prep time: 10 minutes | Cook time: 30 minutes | Serves 4

For the Granola:
¼ cup honey or maple syrup
2 tablespoons vegetable oil
2 teaspoons vanilla extract
½ teaspoon kosher salt
3 cups gluten-free rolled oats
1 cup mixed raw and unsalted nuts, chopped

¼ cup sunflower seeds
1 cup unsweetened dried cherries
For the Parfait:
2 cups plain Greek yogurt
1 cup fresh fruit, chopped (optional)

Make the Granola: 1. Preheat the oven to 325°F (163°C). Line a baking sheet with parchment paper or foil. 2. Heat the honey, oil, vanilla, and salt in a small saucepan over medium heat. Simmer for 2 minutes and stir together well. 3. In a large bowl, combine the oats, nuts, and seeds. Pour the warm oil mixture over the top and toss well. Spread in a single layer on the prepared baking sheet. Bake for 30 minutes, stirring halfway through. 4. Remove from the oven and add in the dried cherries. Cool completely and store in an airtight container at room temperature for up to 3 months. Make the Parfait: 5. For one serving: In a bowl or lowball drinking glass, spoon in ½ cup yogurt, ½ cup granola, and ¼ cup fruit (if desired). Layer in whatever pattern you like.

Per Serving:
calories: 370 | fat: 144g | protein: 19g | carbs: 44g | fiber: 6g | sodium: 100mg

Mediterranean Frittata

Prep time: 10 minutes | Cook time: 15 minutes | Serves 2

4 large eggs
2 tablespoons fresh chopped herbs, such as rosemary, thyme, oregano, basil or 1 teaspoon dried herbs
¼ teaspoon salt
Freshly ground black pepper
4 tablespoons extra-virgin olive oil, divided

1 cup fresh spinach, arugula, kale, or other leafy greens
4 ounces (113 g) quartered artichoke hearts, rinsed, drained, and thoroughly dried
8 cherry tomatoes, halved
½ cup crumbled soft goat cheese

1. Preheat the oven to broil on low. 2. In small bowl, combine the eggs, herbs, salt, and pepper and whisk well with a fork. Set aside. 3. In a 4- to 5-inch oven-safe skillet or omelet pan, heat 2 tablespoons olive oil over medium heat. Add the spinach, artichoke hearts, and cherry tomatoes and sauté until just wilted, 1 to 2 minutes. 4. Pour in the egg mixture and let it cook undisturbed over medium heat for 3 to 4 minutes, until the eggs begin to set on the bottom. 5. Sprinkle the goat cheese across the top of the egg mixture and transfer the skillet to the oven. 6. Broil for 4 to 5 minutes, or until the frittata is firm in the center and golden brown on top. 7. Remove from the oven and run a rubber spatula around the edge to loosen the sides. Invert onto a large plate or cutting board and slice in half. Serve warm and drizzled with the remaining 2 tablespoons olive oil.

Per Serving:
calories: 520 | fat: 44g | protein: 22g | carbs: 10g | fiber: 5g | sodium: 665mg

Egg and Pepper Pita

Prep time: 10 minutes | Cook time: 10 minutes | Serves 4

2 pita breads
2 tablespoons olive oil
1 red or yellow bell pepper, diced
2 zucchini, quartered lengthwise and sliced
4 large eggs, beaten
Sea salt

Freshly ground black pepper
Pinch dried oregano
2 avocados, sliced
½ to ¾ cup crumbled feta cheese
2 tablespoons chopped scallion, green part only, for garnish
Hot sauce, for serving

1. In a large skillet, heat the pitas over medium heat until warmed through and lightly toasted, about 2 minutes. Remove the pitas from the skillet and set aside. 2. In the same skillet, heat the olive oil over medium heat. Add the bell pepper and zucchini and sauté for 4 to 5 minutes. Add the eggs and season with salt, black pepper, and the oregano. Cook, stirring, for 2 to 3 minutes, until the eggs are cooked through. Remove from the heat. 3. Slice the pitas in half crosswise and fill each half with the egg mixture. Divide the avocado and feta among the pita halves. Garnish with the scallion and serve with hot sauce.

Per Serving:
calories: 476 | fat: 31g | protein: 17g | carbs: 36g | fiber: 11g | sodium: 455mg

Lemon–Olive Oil Breakfast Cakes with Berry Syrup

Prep time: 5 minutes | Cook time: 10 minutes | Serves 4

For the Pancakes:
1 cup almond flour
1 teaspoon baking powder
¼ teaspoon salt
6 tablespoon extra-virgin olive oil, divided
2 large eggs
Zest and juice of 1 lemon

½ teaspoon almond or vanilla extract
For the Berry Sauce:
1 cup frozen mixed berries
1 tablespoon water or lemon juice, plus more if needed
½ teaspoon vanilla extract

Make the Pancakes: 1. In a large bowl, combine the almond flour, baking powder, and salt and whisk to break up any clumps. 2. Add the 4 tablespoons olive oil, eggs, lemon zest and juice, and almond extract and whisk to combine well. 3. In a large skillet, heat 1 tablespoon of olive oil and spoon about 2 tablespoons of batter for each of 4 pancakes. Cook until bubbles begin to form, 4 to 5 minutes, and flip. Cook another 2 to 3 minutes on second side. Repeat with remaining 1 tablespoon olive oil and batter. Make the Berry Sauce 1. In a small saucepan, heat the frozen berries, water, and vanilla extract over medium-high for 3 to 4 minutes, until bubbly, adding more water if mixture is too thick. Using the back of a spoon or fork, mash the berries and whisk until smooth.

Per Serving:
calories: 381 | fat: 35g | protein: 8g | carbs: 12g | fiber: 4g | sodium: 183mg

Savory Breakfast Oats

Prep time: 10 minutes | Cook time: 15 minutes | Serves 2

½ cup steel-cut oats
1 cup water
1 large tomato, chopped
1 medium cucumber, chopped
1 tablespoon olive oil
Freshly grated, low-fat

Parmesan cheese
Flat-leaf parsley or mint,
chopped, for garnish
Sea salt and freshly ground
pepper, to taste

1. Put the oats and 1 cup of water in a medium saucepan and bring to a boil on high heat. 2. Stir continuously until water is absorbed, about 15 minutes. 3. To serve, divide the oatmeal between 2 bowls and top with the tomatoes and cucumber. 4. Drizzle with olive oil, then top with the Parmesan cheese and parsley or mint. 5. Season to taste. 6. Serve immediately.

Per Serving:
calories: 240 | fat: 10g | protein: 8g | carbs: 32g | fiber: 6g | sodium: 10mg

Garlicky Beans and Greens with Polenta

Prep time: 5 minutes | Cook time: 20 minutes | Serves 4

2 tablespoons olive oil, divided
1 roll (18 ounces / 510-g)
precooked polenta, cut into
½"-thick slices
4 cloves garlic, minced
4 cups chopped greens, such as
kale, mustard greens, collards,

or chard
2 tomatoes, seeded and diced
1 can (15 ounces / 425-g) small
white beans, drained and rinsed
Kosher salt and ground black
pepper, to taste

1. In a large skillet over medium heat, warm 1 tablespoon of the oil. Cook the polenta slices, flipping once, until golden and crispy, about 5 minutes per side. Remove the polenta and keep warm. 2. Add the remaining 1 tablespoon oil to the skillet. Cook the garlic until softened, 1 minute. Add the greens, tomatoes, and beans and cook until the greens are wilted and bright green and the beans are heated through, 10 minutes. Season to taste with the salt and pepper. To serve, top the polenta with the beans and greens.

Per Serving:
calories: 329 | fat: 8g | protein: 12g | carbs: 54g | fiber: 9g | sodium: 324mg

Veggie Hash with Eggs

Prep time: 20 minutes | Cook time: 6¼ hours | Serves 2

Nonstick cooking spray
1 onion, chopped
2 garlic cloves, minced
1 red bell pepper, chopped
1 yellow summer squash,
chopped
2 carrots, chopped
2 Yukon Gold potatoes, peeled
and chopped
2 large tomatoes, seeded and

chopped
¼ cup vegetable broth
½ teaspoon salt
⅛ teaspoon freshly ground
black pepper
½ teaspoon dried thyme leaves
3 or 4 eggs
½ teaspoon ground sweet
paprika

1. Spray the slow cooker with the nonstick cooking spray. 2. In the slow cooker, combine all the ingredients except the eggs and paprika, and stir. 3. Cover and cook on low for 6 hours. 4. Uncover and make 1 indentation in the vegetable mixture for each egg. Break 1 egg into a small cup and slip the egg into an indentation. Repeat with the remaining eggs. Sprinkle with the paprika. 5. Cover and cook on low for 10 to 15 minutes, or until the eggs are just set, and serve.

Per Serving:
calories: 381 | fat: 8g | protein: 17g | carbs: 64g | net carbs: 52g | sugars: 17g | fiber: 12g | sodium: 747mg | cholesterol: 246mg

Chickpea Hash with Eggs

Prep time: 20 minutes | Cook time: 35 minutes | Serves 4

1 cup dried chickpeas
4 cups water
2 tablespoons extra-virgin olive
oil, divided
1 medium onion, peeled and
chopped
1 medium zucchini, trimmed
and sliced
1 large red bell pepper, seeded

and chopped
1 teaspoon minced garlic
½ teaspoon ground cumin
½ teaspoon ground black
pepper
¼ teaspoon salt
4 large hard-cooked eggs,
peeled and halved
½ teaspoon smoked paprika

1. Place chickpeas, water, and 1 tablespoon oil in the Instant Pot®. Close lid, set steam release to Sealing, press the Manual button, and set time to 30 minutes. 2. When the timer beeps, quick-release the pressure until the float valve drops, press the Cancel button, and open lid. Drain chickpeas well, transfer to a medium bowl, and set aside. 3. Clean and dry pot. Return to machine, press the Sauté button, and heat remaining 1 tablespoon oil. Add onion, zucchini, and bell pepper. Cook until tender, about 5 minutes. Add garlic, cumin, black pepper, and salt and cook for 30 seconds. Add chickpeas and turn to coat. 4. Transfer chickpea mixture to a serving platter. Top with eggs and paprika and serve immediately.

Per Serving:
calories: 274 | fat: 14g | protein: 15g | carbs: 36g | fiber: 16g | sodium: 242mg

Quinoa and Yogurt Breakfast Bowls

Prep time: 10 minutes | Cook time: 12 minutes | Serves 8

2 cups quinoa, rinsed and
drained
4 cups water
1 teaspoon vanilla extract
¼ teaspoon salt

2 cups low-fat plain Greek
yogurt
2 cups blueberries
1 cup toasted almonds
½ cup pure maple syrup

1. Place quinoa, water, vanilla, and salt in the Instant Pot®. Close lid and set steam release to Sealing. Press the Rice button and set time to 12 minutes. 2. When the timer beeps, let pressure release naturally, about 20 minutes. Open lid and fluff quinoa with a fork. 3. Stir in yogurt. Serve warm, topped with berries, almonds, and maple syrup.

Per Serving:
calories: 376 | fat: 13g | protein: 16g | carbs: 52g | fiber: 6g | sodium: 105mg

Garden Scramble

Prep time: 10 minutes | Cook time: 10 minutes | Serves 4

1 teaspoon extra-virgin olive oil	1 tablespoon chopped fresh parsley
½ cup diced yellow squash	½ teaspoon salt
½ cup diced green bell pepper	¼ teaspoon freshly ground black pepper
¼ cup diced sweet white onion	
6 cherry tomatoes, halved	8 large eggs, beaten
1 tablespoon chopped fresh basil	

1. In a large nonstick skillet, heat the olive oil over medium heat. Add the squash, pepper, and onion and sauté until the onion is translucent, 3 to 4 minutes. 2. Add the tomatoes, basil, and parsley and season with salt and pepper. Sauté for 1 minute, then pour the beaten eggs over the vegetables. Cover the pan and reduce the heat to low. 3. Cook until the eggs are cooked through, 5 to 6 minutes, making sure that the center is no longer runny. 4. To serve, slide the frittata onto a platter and cut into wedges.

Per Serving:
calories: 165 | fat: 11g | protein: 13g | carbs: 3g | fiber: 1g | sodium: 435mg

Homemade Pumpkin Parfait

Prep time: 5 minutes | Cook time: 0 minutes | Serves 4

1 (15-ounce / 425-g) can pure pumpkin purée	¼ teaspoon ground cinnamon
4 teaspoons honey, additional to taste	2 cups plain, unsweetened, full-fat Greek yogurt
1 teaspoon pumpkin pie spice	1 cup honey granola

1. In a large bowl, mix the pumpkin purée, honey, pumpkin pie spice, and cinnamon. Cover and refrigerate for at least 2 hours. 2. To make the parfaits, in each cup, pour ¼ cup pumpkin mix, ¼ cup yogurt and ¼ cup granola. Repeat Greek yogurt and pumpkin layers and top with honey granola.

Per Serving:
calories: 264 | fat: 9g | protein: 15g | carbs: 35g | fiber: 6g | sodium: 90mg

Feta and Herb Frittata

Prep time : 10 minutes | Cook time: 30 minutes | Serves 6

¼ cup olive oil, divided	¼ cup chopped flat-leaf parsley, plus additional for garnish
1 medium onion, halved and thinly sliced	1 teaspoon salt
1 clove garlic, minced	½ teaspoon freshly ground black pepper
8 sheets phyllo dough	
8 eggs	4 ounces (113 g) crumbled feta cheese
¼ cup chopped fresh basil, plus additional for garnish	

1. Preheat the oven to 400°F(205°C). 2. Heat 2 tablespoons of the olive oil in a medium skillet over medium-high heat. Add the onions and cook, stirring frequently, until softened, about 5 minutes. Add the garlic and cook, stirring, for 1 minute more. Remove from the heat and set aside to cool. 3. While the onion mixture is cooling, make the crust. Place a damp towel on the counter and cover with a sheet of parchment paper. Lay the phyllo sheets in a stack on top of the parchment and cover with a second sheet of parchment and then a second damp towel. 4. Brush some of the remaining olive oil in a 9-by-9-inch baking dish or a 9-inch pie dish. Layer the softened phyllo sheets in the prepared dish, brushing each with some of the olive oil before adding the next phyllo sheet. 5. Next, make the filling. In a large bowl, whisk the eggs with the onion mixture, basil, parsley, salt, and pepper. Add the feta cheese and mix well. Pour the egg mixture into the prepared crust, folding any excess phyllo inside the baking dish. 6. Bake in the preheated oven for about 25 to 30 minutes, until the crust is golden brown and the egg filling is completely set in the center. Cut into rectangles or wedges and serve garnished with basil and parsley.

Per Serving:
calories: 298 | fat: 20g | protein: 12g | carbs: 17g | fiber: 1g | sodium: 769mg

Egg Baked in Avocado

Prep time: 5 minutes | Cook time: 15 minutes | Serves 2

1 ripe large avocado	serving
2 large eggs	2 tablespoons chopped tomato, for serving
Salt	
Freshly ground black pepper	2 tablespoons crumbled feta, for serving (optional)
4 tablespoons jarred pesto, for	

1. Preheat the oven to 425°F(220°C). 2. Slice the avocado in half and remove the pit. Scoop out about 1 to 2 tablespoons from each half to create a hole large enough to fit an egg. Place the avocado halves on a baking sheet, cut-side up. 3. Crack 1 egg in each avocado half and season with salt and pepper. 4. Bake until the eggs are set and cooked to desired level of doneness, 10 to 15 minutes. 5. Remove from oven and top each avocado with 2 tablespoons pesto, 1 tablespoon chopped tomato, and 1 tablespoon crumbled feta (if using).

Per Serving:
calories: 248 | fat: 23g | protein: 10g | carbs: 2g | fiber: 1g | sodium: 377mg

Summer Day Fruit Salad

Prep time: 5 minutes | Cook time: 0 minutes | Serves 8

2 cups cubed honeydew melon	½ cup unsweetened toasted coconut flakes
2 cups cubed cantaloupe	
2 cups red seedless grapes	¼ cup honey
1 cup sliced fresh strawberries	¼ teaspoon sea salt
1 cup fresh blueberries	½ cup extra-virgin olive oil
Zest and juice of 1 large lime	

1. Combine all of the fruits, the lime zest, and the coconut flakes in a large bowl and stir well to blend. Set aside. 2. In a blender, combine the lime juice, honey, and salt and blend on low. Once the honey is incorporated, slowly add the olive oil and blend until opaque. 3. Pour the dressing over the fruit and mix well. Cover and refrigerate for at least 4 hours before serving, stirring a few times to distribute the dressing.

Per Serving:
calories: 249 | fat: 15g | protein: 1g | carbs: 30g | fiber: 3g | sodium: 104mg

C+C Overnight Oats

Prep time: 5 minutes | Cook time: 0 minutes | Serves 2

½ cup vanilla, unsweetened almond milk (not Silk brand)
½ cup rolled oats
2 tablespoons sliced almonds
2 tablespoons simple sugar

liquid sweetener
1 teaspoon chia seeds
¼ teaspoon ground cardamom
¼ teaspoon ground cinnamon

1. In a mason jar, combine the almond milk, oats, almonds, liquid sweetener, chia seeds, cardamom, and cinnamon and shake well. Store in the refrigerator for 8 to 24 hours, then serve cold or heated.

Per Serving:
calories: 131 | fat: 6g | protein: 5g | carbs: 17g | fiber: 4g | sodium: 45mg

Mexican Breakfast Pepper Rings

Prep time: 5 minutes | Cook time: 10 minutes | Serves 4

Olive oil
1 large red, yellow, or orange bell pepper, cut into four ¾-inch rings

4 eggs
Salt and freshly ground black pepper, to taste
2 teaspoons salsa

1. Preheat the air fryer to 350ºF (177ºC). Lightly spray a baking pan with olive oil. 2. Place 2 bell pepper rings on the pan. Crack one egg into each bell pepper ring. Season with salt and black pepper. 3. Spoon ½ teaspoon of salsa on top of each egg. 4. Place the pan in the air fryer basket. Air fry until the yolk is slightly runny, 5 to 6 minutes or until the yolk is fully cooked, 8 to 10 minutes. 5. Repeat with the remaining 2 pepper rings. Serve hot.

Per Serving:
calories: 76 | fat: 4g | protein: 6g | carbs: 3g | fiber: 1g | sodium: 83mg

Mediterranean Fruit Bulgur Breakfast Bowl

Prep time: 5 minutes |Cook time: 15 minutes| Serves: 6

1½ cups uncooked bulgur
2 cups 2% milk
1 cup water
½ teaspoon ground cinnamon
2 cups frozen (or fresh, pitted) dark sweet cherries

8 dried (or fresh) figs, chopped
½ cup chopped almonds
¼ cup loosely packed fresh mint, chopped
Warm 2% milk, for serving (optional)

1. In a medium saucepan, combine the bulgur, milk, water, and cinnamon. Stir once, then bring just to a boil. Cover, reduce the heat to medium-low, and simmer for 10 minutes or until the liquid is absorbed. 2. Turn off the heat, but keep the pan on the stove, and stir in the frozen cherries (no need to thaw), figs, and almonds. Stir well, cover for 1 minute, and let the hot bulgur thaw the cherries and partially hydrate the figs. Stir in the mint. 3. Scoop into serving bowls. Serve with warm milk, if desired. You can also serve it chilled.

Per Serving:
calories: 273 | fat: 7g | protein: 10g | carbs: 48g | fiber: 8g | sodium: 46mg

Spinach Pie

Prep time: 10 minutes | Cook time: 25 minutes | Serves 8

Nonstick cooking spray
2 tablespoons extra-virgin olive oil
1 onion, chopped
1 pound (454 g) frozen spinach, thawed
¼ teaspoon garlic salt
¼ teaspoon freshly ground black pepper

¼ teaspoon ground nutmeg
4 large eggs, divided
1 cup grated Parmesan cheese, divided
2 puff pastry doughs, (organic, if available), at room temperature
4 hard-boiled eggs, halved

1. Preheat the oven to 350°F(180°C). Spray a baking sheet with nonstick cooking spray and set aside. 2. Heat a large sauté pan or skillet over medium-high heat. Put in the oil and onion and cook for about 5 minutes, until translucent. 3. Squeeze the excess water from the spinach, then add to the pan and cook, uncovered, so that any excess water from the spinach can evaporate. Add the garlic salt, pepper, and nutmeg. Remove from heat and set aside to cool. 4. In a small bowl, crack 3 eggs and mix well. Add the eggs and ½ cup Parmesan cheese to the cooled spinach mix. 5. On the prepared baking sheet, roll out the pastry dough. Layer the spinach mix on top of dough, leaving 2 inches around each edge. 6. Once the spinach is spread onto the pastry dough, place hard-boiled egg halves evenly throughout the pie, then cover with the second pastry dough. Pinch the edges closed. 7. Crack the remaining egg in a small bowl and mix well. Brush the egg wash over the pastry dough. 8. Bake for 15 to 20 minutes, until golden brown and warmed through.

Per Serving:
calories: 417 | fat: 28g | protein: 17g | carbs: 25g | fiber: 3g | sodium: 490mg

Poached Eggs on Whole Grain Avocado Toast

Prep time: 5 minutes | Cook time: 7 minutes | Serves 4

Olive oil cooking spray
4 large eggs
Salt
Black pepper

4 pieces whole grain bread
1 avocado
Red pepper flakes (optional)

1. Preheat the air fryer to 320°F(160°C). Lightly coat the inside of four small oven-safe ramekins with olive oil cooking spray. 2. Crack one egg into each ramekin, and season with salt and black pepper. 3. Place the ramekins into the air fryer basket. Close and set the timer to 7 minutes. 4. While the eggs are cooking, toast the bread in a toaster. 5. Slice the avocado in half lengthwise, remove the pit, and scoop the flesh into a small bowl. Season with salt, black pepper, and red pepper flakes, if desired. Using a fork, smash the avocado lightly. 6. Spread a quarter of the smashed avocado evenly over each slice of toast. 7. Remove the eggs from the air fryer, and gently spoon one onto each slice of avocado toast before serving.

Per Serving:
calories: 232 | fat: 14g | protein: 11g | carbs: 18g | fiber: 6g | sodium: 205mg

Spanish Tuna Tortilla with Roasted Peppers

Prep time: 15 minutes | Cook time: 15 minutes | Serves 4

6 large eggs
¼ cup olive oil
2 small russet potatoes, diced
1 small onion, chopped
1 roasted red bell pepper, sliced

1 (7-ounce / 198-g) can tuna packed in water, drained well and flaked
2 plum tomatoes, seeded and diced
1 teaspoon dried tarragon

1. Preheat the broiler on high. 2. Crack the eggs in a large bowl and whisk them together until just combined. Heat the olive oil in a large, oven-safe, nonstick or cast-iron skillet over medium-low heat. 3. Add the potatoes and cook until slightly soft, about 7 minutes. Add the onion and the peppers and cook until soft, 3–5 minutes. 4. Add the tuna, tomatoes, and tarragon to the skillet and stir to combine, then add the eggs. 5. Cook for 7–10 minutes until the eggs are bubbling from the bottom and the bottom is slightly brown. 6. Place the skillet into the oven on 1 of the first 2 racks, and cook until the middle is set and the top is slightly brown. 7. Slice into wedges and serve warm or at room temperature.

Per Serving:
calories: 247 | fat: 14g | protein: 12g | carbs: 19g | fiber: 2g | sodium: 130mg

Broccoli-Mushroom Frittata

Prep time: 10 minutes | Cook time: 20 minutes | Serves 2

1 tablespoon olive oil
1½ cups broccoli florets, finely chopped
½ cup sliced brown mushrooms
¼ cup finely chopped onion

½ teaspoon salt
¼ teaspoon freshly ground black pepper
6 eggs
¼ cup Parmesan cheese

1. In a nonstick cake pan, combine the olive oil, broccoli, mushrooms, onion, salt, and pepper. Stir until the vegetables are thoroughly coated with oil. Place the cake pan in the air fryer basket and set the air fryer to 400°F (204°C). Air fry for 5 minutes until the vegetables soften. 2. Meanwhile, in a medium bowl, whisk the eggs and Parmesan until thoroughly combined. Pour the egg mixture into the pan and shake gently to distribute the vegetables. Air fry for another 15 minutes until the eggs are set. 3. Remove from the air fryer and let sit for 5 minutes to cool slightly. Use a silicone spatula to gently lift the frittata onto a plate before serving.

Per Serving:
calories: 329 | fat: 23g | protein: 24g | carbs: 6g | fiber: 0g | sodium: 793mg

Chapter 3 Beef, Pork, and Lamb

Saucy Beef Fingers

Prep time: 30 minutes | Cook time: 14 minutes | Serves 4

1½ pounds (680 g) sirloin steak	Coarse sea salt and ground
¼ cup red wine	black pepper, to taste
¼ cup fresh lime juice	1 teaspoon red pepper flakes
1 teaspoon garlic powder	2 eggs, lightly whisked
1 teaspoon shallot powder	1 cup Parmesan cheese
1 teaspoon celery seeds	1 teaspoon paprika
1 teaspoon mustard seeds	

1. Place the steak, red wine, lime juice, garlic powder, shallot powder, celery seeds, mustard seeds, salt, black pepper, and red pepper in a large ceramic bowl; let it marinate for 3 hours. 2. Tenderize the cube steak by pounding with a mallet; cut into 1-inch strips. 3. In a shallow bowl, whisk the eggs. In another bowl, mix the Parmesan cheese and paprika. 4. Dip the beef pieces into the whisked eggs and coat on all sides. Now, dredge the beef pieces in the Parmesan mixture. 5. Cook at 400ºF (204ºC) for 14 minutes, flipping halfway through the cooking time. 6. Meanwhile, make the sauce by heating the reserved marinade in a saucepan over medium heat; let it simmer until thoroughly warmed. Serve the steak fingers with the sauce on the side. Enjoy!

Per Serving:
calories: 483 | fat: 29g | protein: 49g | carbs: 4g | fiber: 1g | sodium: 141mg

Beef Stew with Red Wine

Prep time: 15 minutes | Cook time: 46 minutes | Serves 8

1 pound (454 g) beef stew meat, cut into 1" pieces	minced
	4 sprigs thyme
2 tablespoons all-purpose flour	2 bay leaves
¼ teaspoon salt	8 ounces (227 g) baby carrots
¼ teaspoon ground black pepper	8 ounces (227 g) frozen pearl onions, thawed
2 tablespoons olive oil, divided	1 cup red wine
1 pound (454 g) whole crimini mushrooms	½ cup beef broth
2 cloves garlic, peeled and	¼ cup chopped fresh parsley

1. In a medium bowl, toss beef with flour, salt, and pepper until thoroughly coated. Set aside. 2. Press the Sauté button on the Instant Pot® and heat 1 tablespoon oil. Add half of the beef pieces in a single layer, leaving space between each piece to prevent steaming, and brown well on all sides, about 3 minutes per side. Transfer beef to a medium bowl and repeat with remaining 1 tablespoon oil and beef. Press the Cancel button. 3. Add mushrooms, garlic, thyme, bay leaves, carrots, onions, wine, and broth to the Instant Pot®. Stir well. Close lid, set steam release to Sealing, press the Stew button,

and set time to 40 minutes. When the timer beeps, quick-release the pressure until the float valve drops, open lid, and stir well. Remove and discard thyme and bay leaves. Sprinkle with parsley and serve hot.

Per Serving:
calories: 206 | fat: 13g | protein: 12g | carbs: 6g | fiber: 1g | sodium: 186mg

Savoy Cabbage Rolls

Prep time: 10 minutes | Cook time: 16 minutes | Serves 10

1 medium head savoy cabbage	1 tablespoon olive oil
3 cups water, divided	2 tablespoons minced fresh
½ pound (227 g) ground beef	mint
1 cup long-grain rice	1 teaspoon dried tarragon
1 small red bell pepper, seeded and minced	1 teaspoon salt
1 medium onion, peeled and diced	½ teaspoon ground black pepper
1 cup beef broth	2 tablespoons lemon juice

1. Remove the large outer leaves from cabbage and set aside. Remove remaining cabbage leaves and place them in the Instant Pot®. Pour in 1 cup water. 2. Close lid, set steam release to Sealing, press the Steam button, and set time to 1 minute. Press the Adjust button to change the pressure to Low. When the timer beeps, quick-release the pressure until the float valve drops and then open lid. Press the Cancel button. Drain cabbage leaves in a colander and then move them to a kitchen towel. 3. In a medium mixing bowl, add ground beef, rice, bell pepper, onion, broth, olive oil, mint, tarragon, salt, and black pepper. Stir to combine. 4. Place the large uncooked cabbage leaves on the bottom of the Instant Pot®. 5. Remove the stem running down the center of each steamed cabbage leaf and tear each leaf in half lengthwise. Place 1 tablespoon ground beef mixture in the center of each cabbage piece. Loosely fold the sides of the leaf over the filling and then fold the top and bottom of the leaf over the folded sides. As you complete them, place each stuffed cabbage leaf in the pot. 6. Pour remaining 2 cups water and lemon juice over the stuffed cabbage rolls. Close lid, set steam release to Sealing, press the Manual button, and set time to 15 minutes. When the timer beeps, let pressure release naturally for 10 minutes. Quick-release any remaining pressure until the float valve drops and then open lid. 7. Carefully move stuffed cabbage rolls to a serving platter. Serve warm.

Per Serving:
calories: 117 | fat: 3g | protein: 6g | carbs: 15g | fiber: 0g | sodium: 337mg

Prep time: 30 minutes | Cook time: 8 to 10 minutes | Serves 4

1 pound (454 g) flank steak	½ cup crumbled feta cheese
1 teaspoon garlic powder	½ cup peeled and diced
1 teaspoon ground cumin	cucumber
½ teaspoon sea salt	⅓ cup sliced red onion
½ teaspoon freshly ground	¼ cup seeded and diced tomato
black pepper	2 tablespoons pitted and sliced
5 ounces (142 g) shredded	black olives
romaine lettuce	Tzatziki sauce, for serving

1. Pat the steak dry with paper towels. In a small bowl, combine the garlic powder, cumin, salt, and pepper. Sprinkle this mixture all over the steak, and allow the steak to rest at room temperature for 45 minutes. 2. Preheat the air fryer to 400°F (204°C). Place the steak in the air fryer basket and air fry for 4 minutes. Flip the steak and cook 4 to 6 minutes more, until an instant-read thermometer reads 120°F (49°C) at the thickest point for medium-rare (or as desired). Remove the steak from the air fryer and let it rest for 5 minutes. 3. Divide the romaine among plates. Top with the feta, cucumber, red onion, tomato, and olives.

Per Serving:

calories: 229 | fat: 10g | protein: 28g | carbs: 5g | fiber: 2g | sodium: 559mg

Prep time: 15 minutes | Cook time: 33 minutes | Serves 4

1 head green cabbage	1 teaspoon ground cinnamon
1 pound (454 g) lean ground	2 tablespoons chopped fresh
beef	mint
½ cup long-grain brown rice	Juice of 1 lemon
4 garlic cloves, minced	Olive oil cooking spray
1 teaspoon salt	½ cup beef broth
½ teaspoon black pepper	1 tablespoon olive oil

1. Cut the cabbage in half and remove the core. Remove 12 of the larger leaves to use for the cabbage rolls. 2. Bring a large pot of salted water to a boil, then drop the cabbage leaves into the water, boiling them for 3 minutes. Remove from the water and set aside. 3. In a large bowl, combine the ground beef, rice, garlic, salt, pepper, cinnamon, mint, and lemon juice, and mix together until combined. Divide this mixture into 12 equal portions. 4. Preheat the air fryer to 360°F(182°C). Lightly coat a small casserole dish with olive oil cooking spray. 5. Place a cabbage leaf on a clean work surface. Place a spoonful of the beef mixture on one side of the leaf, leaving space on all other sides. Fold the two perpendicular sides inward and then roll forward, tucking tightly as rolled (similar to a burrito roll). Place the finished rolls into the baking dish, stacking them on top of each other if needed. 6. Pour the beef broth over the top of the cabbage rolls so that it soaks down between them, and then brush the tops with the olive oil. 7. Place the casserole dish into the air fryer basket and bake for 30 minutes.

Per Serving:

calories: 329 | fat: 10g | protein: 29g | carbs: 33g | fiber: 7g | sodium: 700mg

Prep time: 30 minutes | Cook time: 18 minutes | Serves 6

3 cube steaks (6 ounces / 170 g each)	1 teaspoon dried basil
	1 teaspoon dried oregano
1 (16-ounce / 454-g) bottle	1 teaspoon dried parsley
Italian dressing	¼ cup beef broth
1 cup Italian-style bread crumbs	1 to 2 tablespoons oil
½ cup grated Parmesan cheese	

1. In a large resealable bag, combine the steaks and Italian dressing. Seal the bag and refrigerate to marinate for 2 hours. 2. In a medium bowl, whisk the bread crumbs, cheese, basil, oregano, and parsley until blended. Stir in the beef broth. 3. Place the steaks on a cutting board and cut each in half so you have 6 equal pieces. Sprinkle with the bread crumb mixture. Roll up the steaks, jelly roll-style, and secure with toothpicks. 4. Preheat the air fryer to 400°F (204°C). 5. Place 3 roll-ups in the air fryer basket. 6. Cook for 5 minutes. Flip the roll-ups and spritz with oil. Cook for 4 minutes more until the internal temperature reaches 145°F (63°C). Repeat with the remaining roll-ups. Let rest for 5 to 10 minutes before serving.

Per Serving:

calories: 307 | fat: 15g | protein: 24g | carbs: 17g | fiber: 1g | sodium: 236mg

Prep time: 30 minutes | Cook time: 12 to 18 minutes | Serves 4

23 tablespoons red curry paste	3 scallions, minced
¼ cup olive oil	1½ pounds (680 g) flank steak
2 teaspoons grated fresh ginger	Fresh cilantro (or parsley)
2 tablespoons soy sauce	leaves
2 tablespoons rice wine vinegar	

1. Mix the red curry paste, olive oil, ginger, soy sauce, rice vinegar and scallions together in a bowl. Place the flank steak in a shallow glass dish and pour half the marinade over the steak. Pierce the steak several times with a fork or meat tenderizer to let the marinade penetrate the meat. Turn the steak over, pour the remaining marinade over the top and pierce the steak several times again. Cover and marinate the steak in the refrigerator for 6 to 8 hours. 2. When you are ready to cook, remove the steak from the refrigerator and let it sit at room temperature for 30 minutes. 3. Preheat the air fryer to 400°F (204°C). 4. Cut the flank steak in half so that it fits more easily into the air fryer and transfer both pieces to the air fryer basket. Pour the marinade over the steak. Air fry for 12 to 18 minutes, depending on your preferred degree of doneness of the steak (12 minutes = medium rare). Flip the steak over halfway through the cooking time. 5. When your desired degree of doneness has been reached, remove the steak to a cutting board and let it rest for 5 minutes before slicing. Thinly slice the flank steak against the grain of the meat. Transfer the slices to a serving platter, pour any juice from the bottom of the air fryer over the sliced flank steak and sprinkle the fresh cilantro on top.

Per Serving:

calories: 397 | fat: 24g | protein: 38g | carbs: 6g | fiber: 3g | sodium: 216mg

Beesteya (Moroccan-Style Lamb Pie)

2 tablespoons olive oil
1 medium onion, chopped
(about 1¼ cups)
3 carrots, finely chopped (about
1 cup)
1 teaspoon ground turmeric
2 garlic cloves, minced
1 pound (454 g) ground lamb,
turkey, or lean beef
⅓ cup golden raisins

½ cup pistachios, toasted
¼ cup chopped fresh cilantro
1 teaspoon ground cinnamon
6 eggs
1 (5-ounce / 142-g) container
2% Greek yogurt
Olive oil cooking spray or other
nonstick cooking spray
12 sheets frozen phyllo dough,
thawed

1. Preheat the oven to 375°F (190°C). 2. In a large skillet, heat 1 tablespoon of the olive oil over medium heat. Add the onion and carrots and cook, stirring occasionally for 5 to 6 minutes, until the onion is translucent. Stir in the turmeric and garlic; cook for 1 minute. Add the remaining 1 tablespoon olive oil and the ground lamb to the skillet. Cook, breaking up the meat with a wooden spoon as it cooks, for 6 to 8 minutes, until the lamb is browned. 3. Stir in the raisins, pistachios, cilantro, and cinnamon until well combined; set aside. 4. In a medium bowl, whisk the eggs and yogurt together; set aside. 5. Spray a 9-inch springform pan with olive oil cooking spray or other cooking spray. On a clean work surface, stack 4 phyllo sheets, spray both sides with cooking spray, and place in the stack in the prepared pan, extending the edges of the stack up the sides of the pan. Repeat with a second stack of 4 phyllo sheets; place them crosswise over the first stack, extending the edges over the top edge of the pan. 6. Fill the phyllo crust with the lamb mixture, then pour in the egg mixture. Spray the remaining 4 phyllo sheets with cooking spray and cut in half. Place them over the filling to cover it completely. Fold the phyllo toward the center over the filling. Spray with additional cooking spray. 7. Bake for 45 to 50 minutes, until golden brown. Let stand for 15 minutes before serving.

Per Serving:
1 cup: calories: 362 | fat: 19g | protein: 22g | carbs: 28g | fiber: 3g | sodium: 241mg

Smoked Paprika and Lemon Marinated Pork Kabobs

⅓ cup finely chopped flat-leaf
parsley
¼ cup olive oil
2 tablespoons minced red onion
1 tablespoon lemon juice
1 tablespoon smoked paprika
2 teaspoons ground cumin
1 clove garlic, minced

¼ teaspoon cayenne pepper
½ teaspoon salt
2 pork tenderloins, each about
1 pound (454 g), trimmed of
silver skin and any excess fat,
cut into 1¼-inch cubes
1 lemon, cut into wedges, for
serving

1. In a large bowl, whisk together the parsley, olive oil, onion, lemon juice, smoked paprika, cumin, garlic, cayenne, and salt. Add the pork and toss to coat well. Cover and refrigerate, stirring occasionally, for at least 4 hours (or as long as overnight). 2. Soak bamboo skewers in water for 30 minutes. 3. Preheat the grill to high heat. 4. Remove the meat from the marinade, discarding the marinade. Thread the meat onto the soaked skewers and place the skewers on the grill. Cook, with the lid closed, turning occasionally, until the pork is cooked through and browned on all sides, about 8 to 10 minutes total. 5. Transfer the skewers to a serving platter and serve immediately with the lemon wedges.

Per Serving:
calories: 447 | fat: 21g | protein: 60g | carbs: 3g | fiber: 1g | sodium: 426mg

Smoky Herb Lamb Chops and Lemon-Rosemary Dressing

4 large cloves garlic
1 cup lemon juice
⅓ cup fresh rosemary
1 cup extra-virgin olive oil

1½ teaspoons salt
1 teaspoon freshly ground black
pepper
6 (1-inch-thick) lamb chops

1. In a food processor or blender, blend the garlic, lemon juice, rosemary, olive oil, salt, and black pepper for 15 seconds. Set aside. 2. Put the lamb chops in a large plastic zip-top bag or container. Cover the lamb with two-thirds of the rosemary dressing, making sure that all of the lamb chops are coated with the dressing. Let the lamb marinate in the fridge for 1 hour. 3. When you are almost ready to eat, take the lamb chops out of the fridge and let them sit on the counter-top for 20 minutes. Preheat a grill, grill pan, or lightly oiled skillet to high heat. 4. Cook the lamb chops for 3 minutes on each side. To serve, drizzle the lamb with the remaining dressing.

Per Serving:
calories: 484 | fat: 42g | protein: 24g | carbs: 5g | fiber: 1g | sodium: 655mg

Baked Lamb Kofta Meatballs

¼ cup walnuts
½ small onion
1 garlic clove
1 roasted piquillo pepper
2 tablespoons fresh parsley
2 tablespoons fresh mint

¼ teaspoon salt
¼ teaspoon cumin
¼ teaspoon allspice
Pinch cayenne pepper
8 ounces (227 g) lean ground
lamb

1. Preheat the oven to 350°F (180°C) and set the rack to the middle position. Line a baking sheet with foil. 2. In the bowl of a food processor, combine the walnuts, onion, garlic, roasted pepper, parsley, mint, salt, cumin, allspice, and cayenne pepper. Pulse about 10 times to combine everything. 3. Transfer the spice mixture to the bowl and add the lamb. With your hands or a spatula, mix the spices into the lamb. 4. Roll into 1½-inch balls (about the size of golf balls). 5. Place the meatballs on the foil-lined baking sheet and bake for 30 minutes, or until cooked to an internal temperature of 160°F (71°C).

Per Serving:
calories: 408 | fat: 23g | protein: 22g | carbs: 7g | fiber: 3g | sodium: 429mg

Steak with Bell Pepper

Prep time: 30 minutes | Cook time: 20 to 23 minutes | Serves 6

¼ cup avocado oil
¼ cup freshly squeezed lime juice
2 teaspoons minced garlic
1 tablespoon chili powder
½ teaspoon ground cumin
Sea salt and freshly ground black pepper, to taste
1 pound (454 g) top sirloin steak or flank steak, thinly sliced against the grain
1 red bell pepper, cored, seeded, and cut into ½-inch slices
1 green bell pepper, cored, seeded, and cut into ½-inch slices
1 large onion, sliced

1. In a small bowl or blender, combine the avocado oil, lime juice, garlic, chili powder, cumin, and salt and pepper to taste. 2. Place the sliced steak in a zip-top bag or shallow dish. Place the bell peppers and onion in a separate zip-top bag or dish. Pour half the marinade over the steak and the other half over the vegetables. Seal both bags and let the steak and vegetables marinate in the refrigerator for at least 1 hour or up to 4 hours. 3. Line the air fryer basket with an air fryer liner or aluminum foil. Remove the vegetables from their bag or dish and shake off any excess marinade. Set the air fryer to 400ºF (204ºC). Place the vegetables in the air fryer basket and cook for 13 minutes. 4. Remove the steak from its bag or dish and shake off any excess marinade. Place the steak on top of the vegetables in the air fryer, and cook for 7 to 10 minutes or until an instant-read thermometer reads 120ºF (49ºC) for medium-rare (or cook to your desired doneness). 5. Serve with desired fixings, such as keto tortillas, lettuce, sour cream, avocado slices, shredded Cheddar cheese, and cilantro.

Per Serving:
calories: 252 | fat: 18g | protein: 17g | carbs: 6g | fiber: 2g | sodium: 81mg

Beef Ragù

Prep time: 15 minutes | Cook time: 4½ hours | Serves 6

1 medium yellow onion, diced small
3 cloves garlic, minced
6 tablespoons tomato paste
3 tablespoons chopped fresh oregano leaves (or 3 teaspoons dried oregano)
1 (4-pound / 1.8-kg) beef chuck roast, halved
Coarse sea salt
Black pepper
2 cups beef stock
2 tablespoons red wine vinegar

1. Combine the onion, garlic, tomato paste, and oregano in the slow cooker. 2. Season the roast halves with salt and pepper and place on top of the onion mixture in the slow cooker. Add the beef stock. 3. Cover and cook until meat is tender and can easily be pulled apart with a fork, on high for 4½ hours, or on low for 9 hours. Let cool 10 minutes. 4. Shred the meat while it is still in the slow cooker using two forks. Stir the vinegar into the sauce. Serve hot, over pasta.

Per Serving:
calories: 482 | fat: 19g | protein: 67g | carbs: 13g | fiber: 1g | sodium: 292mg

Beef Meatballs in Garlic Cream Sauce

Prep time: 15 minutes | Cook time: 6 to 8 hours | Serves 4

For the Sauce:
1 cup low-sodium vegetable broth or low-sodium chicken broth
1 tablespoon extra-virgin olive oil
2 garlic cloves, minced
1 tablespoon dried onion flakes
1 teaspoon dried rosemary
2 tablespoons freshly squeezed lemon juice
Pinch sea salt
Pinch freshly ground black pepper

For the Meatballs:
1 pound (454 g) raw ground beef
1 large egg
2 tablespoons bread crumbs
1 teaspoon ground cumin
1 teaspoon salt
½ teaspoon freshly ground black pepper
TO FINISH
2 cups plain Greek yogurt
2 tablespoons chopped fresh parsley

Make the Sauce: In a medium bowl, whisk together the vegetable broth, olive oil, garlic, onion flakes, rosemary, lemon juice, salt, and pepper until combined. Make the Meatballs: In a large bowl, mix together the ground beef, egg, bread crumbs, cumin, salt, and pepper until combined. Shape the meat mixture into 10 to 12 (2½-inch) meatballs. 1. Pour the sauce into the slow cooker. 2. Add the meatballs to the slow cooker. 3. Cover the cooker and cook for 6 to 8 hours on Low heat. 4. Stir in the yogurt. Replace the cover on the cooker and cook for 15 to 30 minutes on Low heat, or until the sauce has thickened. 5. Garnish with fresh parsley for serving.

Per Serving:
calories: 345 | fat: 20g | protein: 29g | carbs: 13g | fiber: 1g | sodium: 842mg

Lamb and Bean Stew

Prep time: 15 minutes | Cook time: 35 minutes | Serves 4

4 tablespoons olive oil, divided
1 pound (454 g) lamb shoulder, cut into 2-inch cubes
Sea salt
Freshly ground black pepper
2 garlic cloves, minced (optional)
1 large onion, diced
1 cup chopped celery
1 cup chopped tomatoes
1 cup chopped carrots
⅓ cup tomato paste
1 (28-ounce/ 794-g) can white kidney beans, drained and rinsed
2 cups water

1. In a stockpot, heat 1 tablespoon of olive oil over medium-high heat. Season the lamb pieces with salt and pepper and add to the stockpot with the garlic, if desired. Brown the lamb, turning it frequently, for 3 to 4 minutes. Add the remaining 3 tablespoons of olive oil, the onion, celery, tomatoes, and carrots and cook for 4 to 5 minutes. 2. Add the tomato paste and stir to combine, then add the beans and water. Bring the mixture to a boil, reduce the heat to low, cover, and simmer for 25 minutes, or until the lamb is fully cooked. 3. Taste, adjust the seasoning, and serve.

Per Serving:
calories: 521 | fat: 24g | protein: 36g | carbs: 43g | fiber: 12g | sodium: 140mg

Balsamic Pork Chops with Figs and Pears

Prep time: 15 minutes | Cook time: 13 minutes | Serves 2

2 (8-ounce/ 227-g) bone-in pork chops	2 tablespoons olive oil
½ teaspoon salt	1 medium sweet onion, peeled and sliced
1 teaspoon ground black pepper	3 medium pears, peeled, cored, and chopped
¼ cup balsamic vinegar	5 dried figs, stems removed and halved
¼ cup low-sodium chicken broth	
1 tablespoon dried mint	

1. Pat pork chops dry with a paper towel and season both sides with salt and pepper. Set aside. 2. In a small bowl, whisk together vinegar, broth, and mint. Set aside. 3. Press the Sauté button on the Instant Pot® and heat oil. Brown pork chops for 5 minutes per side. Remove chops and set aside. 4. Add vinegar mixture and scrape any brown bits from sides and bottom of pot. Layer onion slices in the pot, then scatter pears and figs over slices. Place pork chops on top. Press the Cancel button. 5. Close lid, set steam release to Sealing, press the Steam button, and set time to 3 minutes. When the timer beeps, let pressure release naturally for 10 minutes. Quick-release any remaining pressure until the float valve drops and then open lid. 6. Using a slotted spoon, transfer pork, onion, figs, and pears to a serving platter. Serve warm.

Per Serving:
calories: 672 | fat: 32g | protein: 27g | carbs: 68g | fiber: 13g | sodium: 773mg

Ground Lamb with Lentils and Pomegranate Seeds

Prep time: 15 minutes | Cook time: 15 minutes | Serves 4

1 tablespoon extra-virgin olive oil	2 cups cooked, drained lentils
½ pound (227 g) ground lamb	1 hothouse or English cucumber, diced
1 teaspoon red pepper flakes	⅓ cup fresh mint, chopped
½ teaspoon ground cumin	⅓ cup fresh parsley, chopped
½ teaspoon kosher salt	Zest of 1 lemon
¼ teaspoon freshly ground black pepper	1 cup plain Greek yogurt
2 garlic cloves, minced	½ cup pomegranate seeds

1. Heat the olive oil in a large skillet or sauté pan over medium-high heat. Add the lamb and season with the red pepper flakes, cumin, salt, and black pepper. Cook the lamb without stirring until the bottom is brown and crispy, about 5 minutes. Stir and cook for another 5 minutes. Using a spatula, break up the lamb into smaller pieces. Add the garlic and cook, stirring occasionally, for 1 minute. Transfer the lamb mixture to a medium bowl. 2. Add the lentils to the skillet and cook, stirring occasionally, until brown and crisp, about 5 minutes. Return the lamb to the skillet, mix, and warm through, about 3 minutes. Transfer to the large bowl. Add the cucumber, mint, parsley, and lemon zest, mixing together gently. 3. Spoon the yogurt into 4 bowls and top each with some of the lamb mixture. Garnish with the pomegranate seeds.

Per Serving:
calories: 370 | fat: 18g | protein: 24g | carbs: 30g | fiber: 10g | sodium: 197mg

Pork Stew with Leeks

Prep time: 15 minutes | Cook time: 55 minutes | Serves 4

2 tablespoons olive oil	pork loin chops, cut into 2-inch pieces
2 leeks, white parts only, chopped and rinsed well	4 cups beef broth
1 onion, chopped	2 cups water
2 garlic cloves, minced	3 potatoes, peeled and chopped
1 carrot, chopped	1 tablespoon tomato paste
1 celery stalk, chopped	Sea salt
2 pounds (907 g) boneless	Freshly ground black pepper

1. In a large skillet, heat the olive oil over medium-high heat. Add the leeks, onion, and garlic and sauté for 5 minutes, or until softened. Add the carrot and celery and cook for 3 minutes. Add the pork, broth, water, potatoes, and tomato paste and bring to a boil. 2. Reduce the heat to low, cover, and simmer for 45 minutes, or until the pork is cooked through. Season to taste with salt and pepper and serve.

Per Serving:
calories: 623 | fat: 16g | protein: 57g | carbs: 60g | fiber: 8g | sodium: 193mg

Quinoa Pilaf–Stuffed Pork

Prep time: 15 minutes | Cook time: 45 minutes | Serves 6

1 (1½-pound / 680-g) pork tenderloin	parsley
2 tablespoons olive oil, divided	1 tablespoon lemon juice
1 clove garlic, peeled and minced	½ cup quinoa, rinsed and drained
½ medium tomato, diced	2 cups water, divided
¼ cup chopped fresh flat-leaf	¼ cup crumbled goat cheese
	¼ teaspoon salt

1. Butterfly pork tenderloin. Open tenderloin and top with a sheet of plastic wrap. Pound pork out to ½" thick. Wrap and refrigerate until ready to use. 2. Press the Sauté button on the Instant Pot® and heat 1 tablespoon oil. Add garlic and cook 30 seconds, then add tomato, parsley, and lemon juice. Cook an additional minute. Transfer mixture to a small bowl. Press the Cancel button. 3. Add quinoa and 1 cup water to the pot. Close lid, set steam release to Sealing, press the Multigrain button, and set time to 20 minutes. When the timer beeps, let pressure release naturally, about 20 minutes, then open lid. Press the Cancel button. Fluff quinoa with a fork. Transfer quinoa to bowl with tomato mixture and mix well. 4. Spread quinoa mixture over pork. Top with goat cheese. Season with salt. Roll pork over filling. Tie pork every 2" with butcher's twine to secure. 5. Press Sauté on the Instant Pot® and heat remaining 1 tablespoon oil. Brown pork on all sides, about 2 minutes per side. Press the Cancel button. Remove pork and clean out pot. Return to machine, add remaining 1 cup water, place rack in pot, and place pork on rack. 6. Close lid, set steam release to Sealing, Press the Manual button, and set time to 20 minutes. When the timer beeps, quick-release the pressure until the float valve drops. Open lid and transfer pork to cutting board. Let rest for 10 minutes, then remove twine and cut into 1" slices. Serve hot.

Per Serving:
calories: 207 | fat: 9g | protein: 25g | carbs: 11g | fiber: 1g | sodium: 525mg

Pork and Beef Egg Rolls

Prep time: 30 minutes | Cook time: 7 to 8 minutes per batch | Makes 8 egg rolls

¼ pound (113 g) very lean ground beef
¼ pound (113 g) lean ground pork
1 tablespoon soy sauce
1 teaspoon olive oil
½ cup grated carrots
2 green onions, chopped
2 cups grated Napa cabbage
¼ cup chopped water chestnuts
¼ teaspoon salt
¼ teaspoon garlic powder
¼ teaspoon black pepper
1 egg
1 tablespoon water
8 egg roll wraps
Oil for misting or cooking spray

1. In a large skillet, brown beef and pork with soy sauce. Remove cooked meat from skillet, drain, and set aside. 2. Pour off any excess grease from skillet. Add olive oil, carrots, and onions. Sauté until barely tender, about 1 minute. 3. Stir in cabbage, cover, and cook for 1 minute or just until cabbage slightly wilts. Remove from heat. 4. In a large bowl, combine the cooked meats and vegetables, water chestnuts, salt, garlic powder, and pepper. Stir well. If needed, add more salt to taste. 5. Beat together egg and water in a small bowl. 6. Fill egg roll wrappers, using about ¼ cup of filling for each wrap. Roll up and brush all over with egg wash to seal. Spray very lightly with olive oil or cooking spray. 7. Place 4 egg rolls in air fryer basket and air fry at 390°F (199°C) for 4 minutes. Turn over and cook 3 to 4 more minutes, until golden brown and crispy. 8. Repeat to cook remaining egg rolls.

Per Serving:
calories: 176 | fat: 5g | protein: 11g | carbs: 22g | fiber: 2g | sodium: 339mg

Roast Pork Loin with Juniper Berries and Honey

Prep time: 5 minutes | Cook time: 1 hour | Serves 6

2 cloves garlic, chopped
3 or 4 leaves fresh sage, chopped
1 tablespoon chopped fresh rosemary
1 tablespoon juniper berries, crushed
2 tablespoons olive oil, divided
1 bone-in pork loin roast (3–4 pounds/ 1.4 to 1.8 kg), trimmed
1 cup low-sodium chicken broth
2 teaspoons honey
½ teaspoon kosher salt
¼ teaspoon ground black pepper

1. Preheat the oven to 400°F(205°C) . 2. In a small bowl, stir together the garlic, sage, rosemary, juniper berries, and 1 tablespoon of the oil. Rub this mixture all over the pork loin and place in a large baking dish. 3. Roast the pork loin, turning the meat over once, until a thermometer placed in the center reads 150°F(66°C), about 50 minutes. Remove the pork from the baking dish and set aside to rest. 4. Strain the juices from the baking dish into a small saucepan. Add the broth, honey, salt, and pepper and bring to a boil. Reduce the heat to a simmer and cook until thickened, about 8 minutes. 5. To serve, slice the pork and drizzle the sauce over top.

Per Serving:
calories: 366 | fat: 16g | protein: 50g | carbs: 4g | fiber: 0g | sodium: 342mg

Greek Lamb Chops

Prep time: 10 minutes | Cook time: 6 to 8 hours | Serves 6

3 pounds (1.4 kg) lamb chops
½ cup low-sodium beef broth
Juice of 1 lemon
1 tablespoon extra-virgin olive oil
2 garlic cloves, minced
1 teaspoon dried oregano
1 teaspoon sea salt
½ teaspoon freshly ground black pepper

1. Put the lamb chops in a slow cooker. 2. In a small bowl, whisk together the beef broth, lemon juice, olive oil, garlic, oregano, salt, and pepper until blended. Pour the sauce over the lamb chops. 3. Cover the cooker and cook for 6 to 8 hours on Low heat.

Per Serving:
calories: 325 | fat: 13g | protein: 47g | carbs: 1g | fiber: 0g | sodium: 551mg

Balsamic Beef and Vegetable Stew

Prep time: 30 minutes | Cook time: 54 minutes | Serves 8

1 pound (454 g) beef stew meat, cut into 1" pieces
2 tablespoons all-purpose flour
¼ teaspoon salt
¼ teaspoon ground black pepper
2 tablespoons olive oil, divided
2 medium carrots, peeled and sliced
2 stalks celery, sliced
1 medium onion, peeled and chopped
8 ounces (227 g) whole crimini mushrooms, quartered
3 cloves garlic, peeled and
minced
4 sprigs thyme
2 tablespoons chopped fresh oregano
2 bay leaves
¼ cup balsamic vinegar
1½ cups beef broth
1 (14½-ounce / 411-g) can diced tomatoes, drained
1 medium russet potato, cut into 1" pieces
1 (6-ounce / 170-g) can large black olives, drained and quartered
¼ cup chopped fresh parsley

1. In a medium bowl, add beef, flour, salt, and pepper. Toss meat with seasoned flour until thoroughly coated. Set aside. 2. Press the Sauté button on the Instant Pot® and heat 1 tablespoon oil. Place half of the beef pieces in a single layer, leaving space between each piece to prevent steaming, and brown well on all sides, about 3 minutes per side. Transfer beef to a medium bowl and repeat with remaining 1 tablespoon oil and beef. 3. Add carrots, celery, and onion to the pot. Cook until tender, about 8 minutes. Add mushrooms, garlic, thyme, oregano, and bay leaves. Stir well. 4. Slowly add balsamic vinegar and beef broth, scraping bottom of pot well to release any brown bits. Add tomatoes, potato, and browned beef along with any juices. Press the Cancel button. 5. Close lid, set steam release to Sealing, press the Stew button, and set time to 40 minutes. When the timer beeps, quick-release the pressure until the float valve drops, open lid, and stir well. Remove and discard thyme and bay leaves. Stir in olives and parsley. Serve immediately.

Per Serving:
calories: 332| fat: 17g | protein: 16g | carbs: 15g | fiber: 5g | sodium: 404mg

Braised Lamb Shanks

Prep time: 10 minutes | Cook time: 2 hours | Serves 4 to 6

3 tablespoons extra-virgin olive oil	1 (15-ounce/ 425-g) can diced tomatoes
6 lamb shanks	6 cups water
1 large onion, chopped	3 bay leaves
3 carrots, chopped	1 teaspoon salt

1. Place a large pot with a lid or Dutch oven over high heat and add the olive oil and lamb shanks. Brown on each side, about 8 minutes total. 2. Put the shanks onto a plate and add the onion and carrots to the same pot; cook for 5 minutes. 3. Add the tomatoes, water, bay leaves, and salt. Stir to combine. Add the lamb shanks back to the pot and bring to a simmer. 4. Turn the heat down to low and cover the pot. Let the shanks cook for 1 hour and 30 minutes. Remove the cover and let cook for another 20 minutes. 5. Remove the bay leaves from the pot and spoon the lamb shanks and sauce onto a serving dish. Serve warm with rice or couscous.

Per Serving:
calories: 462 | fat: 18g | protein: 69g | carbs: 8g | fiber: 3g | sodium: 670mg

Spiced Oven-Baked Meatballs with Tomato Sauce

Prep time: 25 minutes | Cook time: 1 hour 5 minutes | Serves 4

For the Meatballs:	2 tablespoons dry red wine
1 pound (454 g) ground chuck	1 teaspoon fresh lemon juice
¼ cup unseasoned breadcrumbs	For the sauce
2 garlic cloves, minced	3 medium tomatoes, chopped, or 1 (15-ounce / 425-g) can chopped tomatoes
1 teaspoon salt	
½ teaspoon black pepper	
1 teaspoon ground cumin	1 tablespoon plus 1 teaspoon tomato paste
3 tablespoons chopped fresh parsley	¼ cup extra virgin olive oil
1 egg, lightly beaten	1 teaspoon fine sea salt
3 tablespoons extra virgin olive oil	¼ teaspoon black pepper
	¼ teaspoon granulated sugar
1 teaspoon tomato paste	1¾ cups hot water
1 teaspoon red wine vinegar	

1. Begin making the meatballs by combining all the ingredients in a large bowl. Knead the mixture for 3 minutes or until all the ingredients are well incorporated. Cover the bowl with plastic wrap and transfer the mixture to the refrigerator to rest for at least 20 minutes. 2. While the meatball mixture is resting, preheat the oven to 350°F (180°C) and begin making the sauce by placing all the ingredients except the hot water in a food processor. Process until smooth and then transfer the mixture to a small pan over medium heat. Add the hot water and mix well. Let the mixture come to a boil and then reduce the heat to low and simmer for 10 minutes. 3. Remove the meatball mixture from the refrigerator and shape it into 24 oblong meatballs. 4. Spread 3 tablespoons of the sauce into the bottom of a large baking dish and place the meatballs in a single layer on top of the sauce. Pour the remaining sauce over the top of the meatballs. 5. Bake for 45 minutes or until the meatballs are lightly brown and then turn the meatballs and bake for an additional 10 minutes. (If the sauce appears to be drying out, add another ¼ cup hot water to the baking dish.) 6. Transfer the meatballs to a serving platter. Spoon the sauce over the meatballs before serving. Store covered in the refrigerator for up to 3 days or in an airtight container in the freezer for up to 3 months.

Per Serving:
calories: 221 | fat: 16g | protein: 14g | carbs: 5g | fiber: 1g | sodium: 661mg

Roasted Pork with Apple-Dijon Sauce

Prep time: 15 minutes | Cook time: 40 minutes | Serves 8

1½ tablespoons extra-virgin olive oil	¼ cup apple jelly
	¼ cup apple juice
1 (12-ounce/ 340-g) pork tenderloin	2 to 3 tablespoons Dijon mustard
¼ teaspoon kosher salt	½ tablespoon cornstarch
¼ teaspoon freshly ground black pepper	½ tablespoon cream

1. Preheat the oven to 325°F(165°C). 2. In a large sauté pan or skillet, heat the olive oil over medium heat. 3. Add the pork to the skillet, using tongs to turn and sear the pork on all sides. Once seared, sprinkle pork with salt and pepper, and set it on a small baking sheet. 4. In the same skillet, with the juices from the pork, mix the apple jelly, juice, and mustard into the pan juices. Heat thoroughly over low heat, stirring consistently for 5 minutes. Spoon over the pork. 5. Put the pork in the oven and roast for 15 to 17 minutes, or 20 minutes per pound. Every 10 to 15 minutes, baste the pork with the apple-mustard sauce. 6. Once the pork tenderloin is done, remove it from the oven and let it rest for 15 minutes. Then, cut it into 1-inch slices. 7. In a small pot, blend the cornstarch with cream. Heat over low heat. Add the pan juices into the pot, stirring for 2 minutes, until thickened. Serve the sauce over the pork.

Per Serving:
calories: 146 | fat: 7g | protein: 13g | carbs: 8g | fiber: 0g | sodium: 192mg

Mexican-Style Shredded Beef

Prep time: 5 minutes | Cook time: 35 minutes | Serves 6

1 (2-pound / 907-g) beef chuck roast, cut into 2-inch cubes	pepper
	½ cup no-sugar-added chipotle sauce
1 teaspoon salt	
½ teaspoon ground black	

1. In a large bowl, sprinkle beef cubes with salt and pepper and toss to coat. Place beef into ungreased air fryer basket. Adjust the temperature to 400ºF (204ºC) and air fry for 30 minutes, shaking the basket halfway through cooking. Beef will be done when internal temperature is at least 160ºF (71ºC). 2. Place cooked beef into a large bowl and shred with two forks. Pour in chipotle sauce and toss to coat. 3. Return beef to air fryer basket for an additional 5 minutes at 400ºF (204ºC) to crisp with sauce. Serve warm.

Per Serving:
calories: 204 | fat: 9g | protein: 31g | carbs: 0g | fiber: 0g | sodium: 539mg

Herbed Lamb Steaks

Prep time: 30 minutes | Cook time: 15 minutes | Serves 4

½ medium onion	1 teaspoon cayenne pepper
2 tablespoons minced garlic	1 teaspoon salt
2 teaspoons ground ginger	4 (6-ounce / 170-g) boneless
1 teaspoon ground cinnamon	lamb sirloin steaks
1 teaspoon onion powder	Oil, for spraying

1. In a blender, combine the onion, garlic, ginger, cinnamon, onion powder, cayenne pepper, and salt and pulse until the onion is minced. 2. Place the lamb steaks in a large bowl or zip-top plastic bag and sprinkle the onion mixture over the top. Turn the steaks until they are evenly coated. Cover with plastic wrap or seal the bag and refrigerate for 30 minutes. 3. Preheat the air fryer to 330°F (166°C). Line the air fryer basket with parchment and spray lightly with oil. 4. Place the lamb steaks in a single layer in the prepared basket, making sure they don't overlap. You may need to work in batches, depending on the size of your air fryer. 5. Cook for 8 minutes, flip, and cook for another 7 minutes, or until the internal temperature reaches 155°F (68°C).

Per Serving:
calories: 255 | fat: 10g | protein: 35g | carbs: 5g | fiber: 1g | sodium: 720mg

Lamb and Onion Tagine

Prep time: 10 minutes | Cook time: 2 hours 15 minutes | Serves 4

2 tablespoons finely chopped fresh flat-leaf parsley	3 tablespoons extra-virgin olive oil
2 tablespoons finely chopped fresh cilantro	4 bone-in leg of lamb steaks, ½' thick (about 2½ pounds / 1.1 kg)
2 cloves garlic, minced	1 can (28 ounces / 794-g) whole peeled plum tomatoes, drained
½ teaspoon ground turmeric	
½ teaspoon ground ginger	2 large red onions, 1 finely chopped, the other sliced in ⅛' rounds
1 teaspoon ground cinnamon, divided	
1 teaspoon plus a pinch kosher salt	2 teaspoons honey, divided
½ teaspoon ground black pepper	1 tablespoon toasted sesame seeds
2 tablespoons plus ⅓ cup water	

1. In a large bowl, combine the parsley, cilantro, garlic, turmeric, ginger, ¼ teaspoon of the cinnamon, 1 teaspoon of the salt, and the pepper. Add 2 tablespoons of the water and the oil and mix. Add the lamb steaks and turn to coat each one. Cover and refrigerate, turning the steaks occasionally, for at least 1 hour. 2. Make a small cut into each tomato and squeeze out the seeds and excess juices. 3. In a 12' tagine or a deep heavy-bottom skillet, scatter the chopped onion. Arrange the lamb steaks snugly in a single layer. Drizzle the remaining marinade over the top. Add the tomatoes around the lamb. Drizzle 1 teaspoon of the honey and ¼ teaspoon of the cinnamon over the top. 4. Lay the onion rounds on top of the lamb. Drizzle the remaining 1 teaspoon honey. Sprinkle the remaining ½ teaspoon cinnamon and the pinch of salt. Turn the heat on to medium (medium-low if using a pot) and cook, uncovered, nudging the lamb occasionally, until the chopped onion below is translucent, about 15 minutes. 5. Pour in the ⅓ cup water around the outer edges of the food. Cover with a lid, slightly askew to keep air flowing in and out of the tagine or skillet. Reduce the heat to low and simmer gently, nudging the lamb occasionally to prevent sticking. Cook until the lamb is very tender, adding water as needed to keep the sauce moist, about 2 hours. 6. Sprinkle with the sesame seeds and serve.

Per Serving:
calories: 537 | fat: 25g | protein: 63g | carbs: 19g | fiber: 6g | sodium: 791mg

Hamburger Steak with Mushroom Gravy

Prep time: 20 minutes | Cook time: 29 to 34 minutes | Serves 4

Mushroom Gravy:	½ cup Italian-style bread crumbs
1 (1-ounce / 28-g) envelope dry onion soup mix	
⅓ cup cornstarch	2 teaspoons Worcestershire sauce
1 cup diced mushrooms	1 teaspoon salt
Hamburger Steak:	1 teaspoon freshly ground black pepper
1 pound (454 g) ground beef (85% lean)	
¾ cup minced onion	1 to 2 tablespoons oil

Make the Mushroom Gravy 1. In a metal bowl, whisk the soup mix, cornstarch, mushrooms, and 2 cups water until blended. 2. Preheat the air fryer to 350°F (177°C). 3. Place the bowl in the air fryer basket. 4. Cook for 10 minutes. Stir and cook for 5 to 10 minutes more to your desired thickness. Make the Hamburger Steak 5. In a large bowl, mix the ground beef, onion, bread crumbs, Worcestershire sauce, salt, and pepper until blended. Shape the beef mixture into 4 patties. 6. Decrease the air fryer's temperature to 320°F (160°C). 7. Place the patties in the air fryer basket. 8. Cook for 7 minutes. Flip the patties, spritz them with oil, and cook for 7 minutes more, until the internal temperature reaches 145°F (63°C).

Per Serving:
calories: 383 | fat: 21g | protein: 24g | carbs: 23g | fiber: 1g | sodium: 810mg

Mediterranean Beef Steaks

Prep time: 20 minutes | Cook time: 20 minutes | Serves 4

2 tablespoons coconut aminos	pepper
3 heaping tablespoons fresh chives	½ teaspoon dried basil
2 tablespoons olive oil	½ teaspoon dried rosemary
3 tablespoons dry white wine	1 teaspoon freshly ground black pepper
4 small-sized beef steaks	
2 teaspoons smoked cayenne	1 teaspoon sea salt, or more to taste

1. Firstly, coat the steaks with the cayenne pepper, black pepper, salt, basil, and rosemary. 2. Drizzle the steaks with olive oil, white wine, and coconut aminos. 3. Finally, roast in the air fryer for 20 minutes at 340°F (171°C). Serve garnished with fresh chives. Bon appétit!

Per Serving:
calories: 320 | fat: 17g | protein: 37g | carbs: 5g | fiber: 1g | sodium: 401mg

Garlic-Marinated Flank Steak

Prep time: 30 minutes | Cook time: 8 to 10 minutes | Serves 6

½ cup avocado oil
¼ cup coconut aminos
1 shallot, minced
1 tablespoon minced garlic
2 tablespoons chopped fresh oregano, or 2 teaspoons dried

1½ teaspoons sea salt
1 teaspoon freshly ground black pepper
¼ teaspoon red pepper flakes
2 pounds (907 g) flank steak

1. In a blender, combine the avocado oil, coconut aminos, shallot, garlic, oregano, salt, black pepper, and red pepper flakes. Process until smooth. 2. Place the steak in a zip-top plastic bag or shallow dish with the marinade. Seal the bag or cover the dish and marinate in the refrigerator for at least 2 hours or overnight. 3. Remove the steak from the bag and discard the marinade. 4. Set the air fryer to 400ºF (204ºC). Place the steak in the air fryer basket (if needed, cut into sections and work in batches). Air fry for 4 to 6 minutes, flip the steak, and cook for another 4 minutes or until the internal temperature reaches 120ºF (49ºC) in the thickest part for medium-rare (or as desired).

Per Serving:
calories: 373 | fat: 26g | protein: 33g | carbs: 1g | fiber: 0g | sodium: 672mg

Beef and Mushroom Stroganoff

Prep time: 15 minutes | Cook time: 31 minutes | Serves 6

2 tablespoons olive oil
1 medium onion, peeled and chopped
2 cloves garlic, peeled and minced
1 pound (454 g) beef stew meat, cut into 1" pieces
3 tablespoons all-purpose flour
¼ teaspoon salt

¼ teaspoon ground black pepper
2 cups beef broth
1 pound (454 g) sliced button mushrooms
1 pound (454 g) wide egg noodles
½ cup low-fat plain Greek yogurt

1. Press the Sauté button on the Instant Pot® and heat oil. Add onion and cook until soft, about 5 minutes. Add garlic and cook until fragrant, about 30 seconds. 2. Combine beef, flour, salt, and pepper in a medium bowl and toss to coat beef completely. Add beef to the pot and cook, stirring often, until browned, about 10 minutes. Stir in beef broth and scrape any brown bits from bottom of pot. Stir in mushrooms and press the Cancel button. 3. Close lid, set steam release to Sealing, press the Manual button, and set time to 10 minutes. When the timer beeps, quick-release the pressure until the float valve drops, open lid, and stir well. Press the Cancel button. 4. Add noodles and stir, making sure noodles are submerged in liquid. Close lid, set steam release to Sealing, press the Manual button, and set time to 5 minutes. 5. When the timer beeps, quick-release the pressure until the float valve drops. Open lid and stir well. Press the Cancel button and cool for 5 minutes, then stir in yogurt. Serve hot.

Per Serving:
calories: 446 | fat: 13g | protein: 19g | carbs: 63g | fiber: 4g | sodium: 721mg

Lamb Shanks and Potatoes

Prep time: 10 minutes | Cook time: 8 hours | Serves 6

1(15-ounce/ 425-g) can crushed tomatoes in purée
3 tablespoons tomato paste
2 tablespoons apricot jam
6 cloves garlic, thinly sliced
3 strips orange zest
¾ teaspoon crushed dried rosemary
½ teaspoon ground ginger

½ teaspoon ground cinnamon
Coarse sea salt
Black pepper
3½ pounds (1.6 kg) lamb shanks, trimmed of excess fat and cut into 1½-inch slices
1¼ pounds (567 g) small new potatoes, halved (or quartered, if large)

1. Stir together the tomatoes and purée, tomato paste, jam, garlic, orange zest, rosemary, ginger, and cinnamon in the slow cooker. Season with salt and pepper. 2. Add the lamb and potatoes, and spoon the tomato mixture over the lamb to coat. 3. Cover and cook until the lamb and potatoes are tender, on low for 8 hours or on high for 5 hours. Season again with salt and pepper, if desired. 4. Serve hot.

Per Serving:
calories: 438 | fat: 10g | protein: 62g | carbs: 26g | fiber: 4g | sodium: 248mg

Lamb with Olives and Potatoes

Prep time: 20 minutes | Cook time: 4 hours | Serves 4

1¼ pounds (567 g) small potatoes, halved
4 large shallots, cut into ½-inch wedges
3 cloves garlic, minced
1 tablespoon lemon zest
3 sprigs fresh rosemary
Coarse sea salt
Black pepper
4 tablespoons all-purpose flour

¾ cup chicken stock
3½ pounds (1.6 kg) lamb shanks, cut crosswise into 1½-inch pieces and fat trimmed
2 tablespoons extra-virgin olive oil
½ cup dry white wine
1 cup pitted green olives, halved
2 tablespoons lemon juice

1. Combine the potatoes, shallots, garlic, lemon zest, and rosemary sprigs in the slow cooker. Season with salt and pepper. 2. In a small bowl, whisk together 1 tablespoon of the flour and the stock. Add to the slow cooker. 3. Place the remaining 3 tablespoons flour on a plate. Season the lamb with salt and pepper; then coat in the flour, shaking off any excess. 4. In a large skillet over medium-high, heat the olive oil. In batches, cook the lamb until browned on all sides, about 10 minutes. Transfer to the slow cooker. 5. Add the wine to the skillet and cook, stiring with a wooden spoon and scraping up the flavorful browned bits from the bottom of the pan, until reduced by half, about 2 minutes. Then add to the slow cooker. 6. Cover and cook until the lamb is tender, on high for about 3½ hours, or on low for 7 hours. 7. Stir in olive halves, then cover, and cook 20 additional minutes. 8. To serve, transfer the lamb and vegetables to warm plates. 9. Skim the fat from the cooking liquid, then stir in the lemon juice, and season the sauce with salt and pepper. 10. Serve the sauce with the lamb and vegetables.

Per Serving:
calories: 765 | fat: 26g | protein: 93g | carbs: 38g | fiber: 5g | sodium: 596mg

Beef and Goat Cheese Stuffed Peppers

Prep time: 10 minutes | Cook time: 30 minutes | Serves 4

1 pound (454 g) lean ground beef	1 teaspoon salt
½ cup cooked brown rice	½ teaspoon black pepper
2 Roma tomatoes, diced	¼ teaspoon ground allspice
3 garlic cloves, minced	2 bell peppers, halved and seeded
½ yellow onion, diced	4 ounces (113 g) goat cheese
2 tablespoons fresh oregano, chopped	¼ cup fresh parsley, chopped

1. Preheat the air fryer to 360°F(182°C). 2. In a large bowl, combine the ground beef, rice, tomatoes, garlic, onion, oregano, salt, pepper, and allspice. Mix well. 3. Divide the beef mixture equally into the halved bell peppers and top each with about 1 ounce (28 g a quarter of the total) of the goat cheese. 4. Place the peppers into the air fryer basket in a single layer, making sure that they don't touch each other. Bake for 30 minutes. 5. Remove the peppers from the air fryer and top with fresh parsley before serving.

Per Serving:
calories: 298 | fat: 12g | protein: 32g | carbs: 17g | fiber: 3g | sodium: 695mg

Smoky Pork Tenderloin

Prep time: 5 minutes | Cook time: 19 to 22 minutes | Serves 6

1½ pounds (680 g) pork tenderloin	1 teaspoon garlic powder
1 tablespoon avocado oil	1 teaspoon sea salt
1 teaspoon chili powder	1 teaspoon freshly ground black pepper
1 teaspoon smoked paprika	

1. Pierce the tenderloin all over with a fork and rub the oil all over the meat. 2. In a small dish, stir together the chili powder, smoked paprika, garlic powder, salt, and pepper. 3. Rub the spice mixture all over the tenderloin. 4. Set the air fryer to 400°F (204°C). Place the pork in the air fryer basket and air fry for 10 minutes. Flip the tenderloin and cook for 9 to 12 minutes more, until an instant-read thermometer reads at least 145°F (63°C). 5. Allow the tenderloin to rest for 5 minutes, then slice and serve.

Per Serving:
calories: 149 | fat: 5g | protein: 24g | carbs: 1g | fiber: 0g | sodium: 461mg

Rosemary Roast Beef

Prep time: 30 minutes | Cook time: 30 to 35 minutes | Serves 8

1 (2-pound / 907-g) top round beef roast, tied with kitchen string	2 teaspoons minced garlic
	2 tablespoons finely chopped fresh rosemary
Sea salt and freshly ground black pepper, to taste	¼ cup avocado oil

1. Season the roast generously with salt and pepper. 2. In a small bowl, whisk together the garlic, rosemary, and avocado oil. Rub this all over the roast. Cover loosely with aluminum foil or plastic wrap and refrigerate for at least 12 hours or up to 2 days. 3. Remove the roast from the refrigerator and allow to sit at room temperature for about 1 hour. 4. Set the air fryer to 325°F (163°C). Place the roast in the air fryer basket and roast for 15 minutes. Flip the roast and cook for 15 to 20 minutes more, until the meat is browned and an instant-read thermometer reads 120°F (49°C) at the thickest part (for medium-rare). 5. Transfer the meat to a cutting board, and let it rest for 15 minutes before thinly slicing and serving.

Per Serving:
calories: 208 | fat: 12g | protein: 25g | carbs: 0g | fiber: 0g | sodium: 68mg

Beef Burger

Prep time: 20 minutes | Cook time: 12 minutes | Serves 4

1¼ pounds (567 g) lean ground beef	½ teaspoon cumin powder
1 tablespoon coconut aminos	¼ cup scallions, minced
1 teaspoon Dijon mustard	⅓ teaspoon sea salt flakes
A few dashes of liquid smoke	⅓ teaspoon freshly cracked mixed peppercorns
1 teaspoon shallot powder	1 teaspoon celery seeds
1 clove garlic, minced	1 teaspoon parsley flakes

1. Mix all of the above ingredients in a bowl; knead until everything is well incorporated. 2. Shape the mixture into four patties. Next, make a shallow dip in the center of each patty to prevent them puffing up during air frying. 3. Spritz the patties on all sides using nonstick cooking spray. Cook approximately 12 minutes at 360°F (182°C). 4. Check for doneness, an instant-read thermometer should read 160°F (71°C). Bon appétit!

Per Serving:
calories: 193 | fat: 7g | protein: 31g | carbs: 1g | fiber: 0g | sodium: 304mg

Parmesan-Crusted Pork Chops

Prep time: 5 minutes | Cook time: 12 minutes | Serves 4

1 large egg	½ teaspoon salt
½ cup grated Parmesan cheese	¼ teaspoon ground black pepper
4 (4-ounce / 113-g) boneless pork chops	

1. Whisk egg in a medium bowl and place Parmesan in a separate medium bowl. 2. Sprinkle pork chops on both sides with salt and pepper. Dip each pork chop into egg, then press both sides into Parmesan. 3. Place pork chops into ungreased air fryer basket. Adjust the temperature to 400°F (204°C) and air fry for 12 minutes, turning chops halfway through cooking. Pork chops will be golden and have an internal temperature of at least 145°F (63°C) when done. Serve warm.

Per Serving:
calories: 218 | fat: 9g | protein: 32g | carbs: 1g | fiber: 0g | sodium: 372mg

Greek-Inspired Beef Kebabs

6 ounces (170 g) beef sirloin tip, trimmed of fat and cut into 2-inch pieces
3 cups of any mixture of vegetables: mushrooms, zucchini, summer squash, onions, cherry tomatoes, red peppers
½ cup olive oil
¼ cup freshly squeezed lemon juice
2 tablespoons balsamic vinegar
2 teaspoons dried oregano
1 teaspoon garlic powder
1 teaspoon minced fresh rosemary
1 teaspoon salt

1. Place the meat in a large shallow container or in a plastic freezer bag. 2. Cut the vegetables into similar-size pieces and place them in a second shallow container or freezer bag. 3. For the marinade, combine the olive oil, lemon juice, balsamic vinegar, oregano, garlic powder, rosemary, and salt in a measuring cup. Whisk well to combine. Pour half of the marinade over the meat, and the other half over the vegetables. 4. Place the meat and vegetables in the refrigerator to marinate for 4 hours. 5. When you are ready to cook, preheat the grill to medium-high (350–400°F) and grease the grill grate. 6. Thread the meat onto skewers and the vegetables onto separate skewers. 7. Grill the meat for 3 minutes on each side. They should only take 10 to 12 minutes to cook, but it will depend on how thick the meat is. 8. Grill the vegetables for about 3 minutes on each side or until they have grill marks and are softened.

Per Serving:
calories: 285 | fat: 18g | protein: 21g | carbs: 9g | fiber: 4g | sodium: 123mg

Mediterranean Chimichurri Skirt Steak

Prep time: 10 minutes | Cook time: 15 minutes | Serves 4

¾ cup fresh mint
¾ cup fresh parsley
⅔ cup extra-virgin olive oil
⅓ cup lemon juice
Zest of 1 lemon
2 tablespoons dried oregano
4 garlic cloves, peeled
½ teaspoon red pepper flakes
½ teaspoon kosher salt
1 to 1½ pounds (454 to 680 g) skirt steak, cut in half if longer than grill pan

1. In a food processor or blender, add the mint, parsley, olive oil, lemon juice, lemon zest, oregano, garlic, red pepper flakes, and salt. Process until the mixture reaches your desired consistency—anywhere from a slightly chunky to smooth purée. Remove a half cup of the chimichurri mixture and set aside. 2. Pour the remaining chimichurri mixture into a medium bowl or zip-top bag and add the steak. Mix together well and marinate for at least 30 minutes, and up to 8 hours in the refrigerator. 3. In a grill pan over medium-high heat, add the steak and cook 4 minutes on each side (for medium rare). Cook an additional 1 to 2 minutes per side for medium. 4. Place the steak on a cutting board, tent with foil to keep it warm, and let it rest for 10 minutes. Thinly slice the steak crosswise against the grain and serve with the reserved sauce.

Per Serving:
calories: 460 | fat: 38g | protein: 28g | carbs: 5g | fiber: 2g | sodium: 241mg

Pepper Steak

Prep time: 30 minutes | Cook time: 16 to 20 minutes | Serves 4

1 pound (454 g) cube steak, cut into 1-inch pieces
1 cup Italian dressing
1½ cups beef broth
1 tablespoon soy sauce
½ teaspoon salt
¼ teaspoon freshly ground
black pepper
¼ cup cornstarch
1 cup thinly sliced bell pepper, any color
1 cup chopped celery
1 tablespoon minced garlic
1 to 2 tablespoons oil

1. In a large resealable bag, combine the beef and Italian dressing. Seal the bag and refrigerate to marinate for 8 hours. 2. In a small bowl, whisk the beef broth, soy sauce, salt, and pepper until blended. 3. In another small bowl, whisk ¼ cup water and the cornstarch until dissolved. Stir the cornstarch mixture into the beef broth mixture until blended. 4. Preheat the air fryer to 375°F (191°C). 5. Pour the broth mixture into a baking pan. Cook for 4 minutes. Stir and cook for 4 to 5 minutes more. Remove and set aside. 6. Increase the air fryer temperature to 400°F (204°C). Line the air fryer basket with parchment paper. 7. Remove the steak from the marinade and place it in a medium bowl. Discard the marinade. Stir in the bell pepper, celery, and garlic. 8. Place the steak and pepper mixture on the parchment. Spritz with oil. 9. Cook for 4 minutes. Shake the basket and cook for 4 to 7 minutes more, until the vegetables are tender and the meat reaches an internal temperature of 145°F (63°C). Serve with the gravy.

Per Serving:
calories: 302 | fat: 14g | protein: 27g | carbs: 15g | fiber: 1g | sodium: 635mg

Garlic Butter Steak Bites

Prep time: 5 minutes | Cook time: 16 minutes | Serves 3

Oil, for spraying
1 pound (454 g) boneless steak, cut into 1-inch pieces
2 tablespoons olive oil
1 teaspoon Worcestershire
sauce
½ teaspoon granulated garlic
½ teaspoon salt
¼ teaspoon freshly ground black pepper

1. Preheat the air fryer to 400°F (204°C). Line the air fryer basket with parchment and spray lightly with oil. 2. In a medium bowl, combine the steak, olive oil, Worcestershire sauce, garlic, salt, and black pepper and toss until evenly coated. 3. Place the steak in a single layer in the prepared basket. You may have to work in batches, depending on the size of your air fryer. 4. Cook for 10 to 16 minutes, flipping every 3 to 4 minutes. The total cooking time will depend on the thickness of the meat and your preferred doneness. If you want it well done, it may take up to 5 additional minutes.

Per Serving:
calories: 293| fat: 17g | protein: 32g | carbs: 1g | fiber: 0g | sodium: 494mg

Kheema Meatloaf

Prep time: 10 minutes | Cook time: 15 minutes | Serves 4

1 pound (454 g) 85% lean ground beef	1 tablespoon minced garlic
2 large eggs, lightly beaten	2 teaspoons garam masala
1 cup diced yellow onion	1 teaspoon kosher salt
¼ cup chopped fresh cilantro	1 teaspoon ground turmeric
1 tablespoon minced fresh ginger	1 teaspoon cayenne pepper
	½ teaspoon ground cinnamon
	⅛ teaspoon ground cardamom

1. In a large bowl, gently mix the ground beef, eggs, onion, cilantro, ginger, garlic, garam masala, salt, turmeric, cayenne, cinnamon, and cardamom until thoroughly combined. 2. Place the seasoned meat in a baking pan. Place the pan in the air fryer basket. Set the air fryer to 350ºF (177ºC) for 15 minutes. Use a meat thermometer to ensure the meat loaf has reached an internal temperature of 160ºF / 71ºC (medium). 3. Drain the fat and liquid from the pan and let stand for 5 minutes before slicing. 4. Slice and serve hot.

Per Serving:
calories: 205 | fat: 8g | protein: 28g | carbs: 5g | fiber: 1g | sodium: 696mg

Mediterranean Pork with Olives

Prep time: 10 minutes | Cook time: 6 to 8 hours | Serves 4

1 small onion, sliced	1 teaspoon dried oregano
4 thick-cut, bone-in pork chops	1 teaspoon dried parsley
1 cup low-sodium chicken broth	½ teaspoon freshly ground black pepper
Juice of 1 lemon	2 cups whole green olives, pitted
2 garlic cloves, minced	1 pint cherry tomatoes
1 teaspoon sea salt	

1. Put the onion in a slow cooker and arrange the pork chops on top. 2. In a small bowl, whisk together the chicken broth, lemon juice, garlic, salt, oregano, parsley, and pepper. Pour the sauce over the pork chops. Top with the olives and tomatoes. 3. Cover the cooker and cook for 6 to 8 hours on Low heat.

Per Serving:
calories: 339 | fat: 14g | protein: 42g | carbs: 6g | fiber: 4g | sodium: 708mg

Tenderloin with Crispy Shallots

Prep time: 30 minutes | Cook time: 18 to 20 minutes | Serves 6

1½ pounds (680 g) beef tenderloin steaks	4 medium shallots
Sea salt and freshly ground black pepper, to taste	1 teaspoon olive oil or avocado oil

1. Season both sides of the steaks with salt and pepper, and let them sit at room temperature for 45 minutes. 2. Set the air fryer to 400ºF (204ºC) and let it preheat for 5 minutes. 3. Working in batches if necessary, place the steaks in the air fryer basket in a single layer and air fry for 5 minutes. Flip and cook for 5 minutes longer, until an instant-read thermometer inserted in the center of the steaks registers 120ºF (49ºC) for medium-rare (or as desired). Remove the steaks and tent with aluminum foil to rest. 4. Set the air fryer to 300ºF (149ºC). In a medium bowl, toss the shallots with the oil. Place the shallots in the basket and air fry for 5 minutes, then give them a toss and cook for 3 to 5 minutes more, until crispy and golden brown. 5. Place the steaks on serving plates and arrange the shallots on top.

Per Serving:
calories: 166 | fat: 8g | protein: 24g | carbs: 1g | fiber: 0g | sodium: 72mg

Spice-Rubbed Pork Loin

Prep time: 5 minutes | Cook time: 20 minutes | Serves 6

1 teaspoon paprika	1 (1½-pound / 680-g) boneless pork loin
½ teaspoon ground cumin	½ teaspoon salt
½ teaspoon chili powder	¼ teaspoon ground black pepper
½ teaspoon garlic powder	
2 tablespoons coconut oil	

1. In a small bowl, mix paprika, cumin, chili powder, and garlic powder. 2. Drizzle coconut oil over pork. Sprinkle pork loin with salt and pepper, then rub spice mixture evenly on all sides. 3. Place pork loin into ungreased air fryer basket. Adjust the temperature to 400ºF (204ºC) and air fry for 20 minutes, turning pork halfway through cooking. Pork loin will be browned and have an internal temperature of at least 145ºF (63ºC) when done. Serve warm.

Per Serving:
calories: 192 | fat: 9g | protein: 26g | carbs: 1g | fiber: 0g | sodium: 257mg

Greek-Style Meatloaf

Prep time: 5 minutes | Cook time: 25 minutes | Serves 6

1 pound (454 g) lean ground beef	1 teaspoon dried thyme
2 eggs	1 teaspoon salt
2 Roma tomatoes, diced	1 teaspoon black pepper
½ white onion, diced	2 ounces (57 g) mozzarella cheese, shredded
½ cup whole wheat bread crumbs	1 tablespoon olive oil
1 teaspoon garlic powder	Fresh chopped parsley, for garnish
1 teaspoon dried oregano	

1. Preheat the oven to 380ºF (193ºC). 2. In a large bowl, mix together the ground beef, eggs, tomatoes, onion, bread crumbs, garlic powder, oregano, thyme, salt, pepper, and cheese. 3. Form into a loaf, flattening to 1-inch thick. 4. Brush the top with olive oil, then place the meatloaf into the air fryer basket and cook for 25 minutes. 5. Remove from the air fryer and allow to rest for 5 minutes, before slicing and serving with a sprinkle of parsley.

Per Serving:
calories: 220 | fat: 10g | protein: 22g | carbs: 10g | fiber: 1g | sodium: 547mg

Calabrian Braised Beef with Caramelized Onions and Potatoes

Prep time: 10 minutes | Cook time: 4 hours 30 minutes | Serves 6 to 8

5 tablespoons olive oil, divided
3 medium onions, thinly sliced
4 cloves garlic, very thinly sliced
1½ teaspoons salt, divided
2 pounds (907 g) top sirloin steak
½ teaspoon freshly ground black pepper

2 tablespoons chopped fresh thyme, divided
3 medium potatoes, peeled and thinly sliced
2 sprigs fresh rosemary, leaves picked and finely chopped, divided
¼ cup grated Parmesan cheese, plus 4 tablespoons, divided
1 (28-ounce / 794-g) can crushed tomatoes

1. Preheat the oven to 325°F(165ºC). 2. Heat 2 tablespoons of olive oil in a large skillet over medium heat. Add the onions and garlic along with ½ teaspoon of salt, reduce the heat to medium-low, and cook, stirring frequently, until they become very soft and golden brown, about 20 minutes. Remove from the heat. 3. Add 1 tablespoon of olive oil to a Dutch oven over medium-high heat. Pat the meat dry with paper towels and sprinkle with the remaining 1 teaspoon of salt and the pepper. Brown the meat on both sides in the Dutch oven, about 10 minutes. 4. Place about half of the cooked onions on top of the meat in an even layer. Sprinkle 1 tablespoon of thyme over the onions, then top with half of the potato slices, arranging them in an even layer. Drizzle with 1 tablespoon of olive oil, and top with half of the rosemary, and 2 tablespoons of cheese. Pour half of the tomatoes over the top. Repeat with the remaining onions, thyme, potatoes, the remaining tablespoon of olive oil, rosemary, 2 tablespoons of cheese, and the tomatoes. Place the lid on the Dutch oven and cook in the preheated oven for about 4 hours, until the meat is very tender. Sprinkle the remaining ¼ cup of cheese over the top and cook under the broiler for a few minutes, until the cheese is melted and golden brown. Serve hot.

Per Serving:
calories: 399 | fat: 23g | protein: 29g | carbs: 19g | fiber: 4g | sodium: 516mg

Chapter 4 Fish and Seafood

Chilean Sea Bass with Olive Relish

Prep time: 10 minutes | Cook time: 10 minutes | Serves 2

Olive oil spray	½ teaspoon ground cumin
2 (6-ounce / 170-g) Chilean sea	½ teaspoon kosher salt
bass fillets or other firm-fleshed	½ teaspoon black pepper
white fish	⅓ cup pitted green olives, diced
3 tablespoons extra-virgin olive	¼ cup finely diced onion
oil	1 teaspoon chopped capers

1. Spray the air fryer basket with the olive oil spray. Drizzle the fillets with the olive oil and sprinkle with the cumin, salt, and pepper. Place the fish in the air fryer basket. Set the air fryer to 325°F (163°C) for 10 minutes, or until the fish flakes easily with a fork. 2. Meanwhile, in a small bowl, stir together the olives, onion, and capers. 3. Serve the fish topped with the relish.

Per Serving:
calories: 379 | fat: 26g | protein: 32g | carbs: 3g | fiber: 1g | sodium: 581mg

Cod with Warm Beet and Arugula Salad

Prep time: 15 minutes | Cook time: 8 minutes | Serves 4

¼ cup extra-virgin olive oil,	broth
divided, plus extra for drizzling	1 tablespoon dukkah, plus extra
1 shallot, sliced thin	for sprinkling
2 garlic cloves, minced	¼ teaspoon table salt
1½ pounds (680 g) small beets,	4 (6-ounce / 170-g) skinless cod
scrubbed, trimmed, and cut into	fillets, 1½ inches thick
½-inch wedges	1 tablespoon lemon juice
½ cup chicken or vegetable	2 ounces (57 g) baby arugula

1. Using highest sauté function, heat 1 tablespoon oil in Instant Pot until shimmering. Add shallot and cook until softened, about 2 minutes. Stir in garlic and cook until fragrant, about 30 seconds. Stir in beets and broth. Lock lid in place and close pressure release valve. Select high pressure cook function and cook for 3 minutes. Turn off Instant Pot and quick-release pressure. Carefully remove lid, allowing steam to escape away from you. 2. Fold sheet of aluminum foil into 16 by 6-inch sling. Combine 2 tablespoons oil, dukkah, and salt in bowl, then brush cod with oil mixture. Arrange cod skinned side down in center of sling. Using sling, lower cod into Instant Pot; allow narrow edges of sling to rest along sides of insert. Lock lid in place and close pressure release valve. Select high pressure cook function and cook for 2 minutes. 3. Turn off Instant Pot and quick-release pressure. Carefully remove lid, allowing steam to escape away from you. Using sling, transfer cod to large plate. Tent with foil and let rest while finishing beet salad. 4. Combine lemon juice and remaining 1 tablespoon oil in large bowl. Using slotted spoon, transfer beets to bowl with oil mixture. Add arugula and gently toss to combine. Season with salt and pepper to taste. 5 Serve cod with salad, sprinkling individual portions with extra dukkah and drizzling with extra oil.

Per Serving:
calories: 340 | fat: 16g | protein: 33g | carbs: 14g | fiber: 4g | sodium: 460mg

Escabeche

Prep time: 10 minutes | Cook time: 20 minutes | Serves 4

1 pound (454 g) wild-caught	and cut into 2-inch pieces
Spanish mackerel fillets, cut	1 (13¾-ounce / 390-g) can
into four pieces	artichoke hearts, drained and
1 teaspoon salt	quartered
½ teaspoon freshly ground	4 large garlic cloves, peeled and
black pepper	crushed
8 tablespoons extra-virgin olive	2 bay leaves
oil, divided	¼ cup red wine vinegar
1 bunch asparagus, trimmed	½ teaspoon smoked paprika

1. Sprinkle the fillets with salt and pepper and let sit at room temperature for 5 minutes. 2. In a large skillet, heat 2 tablespoons olive oil over medium-high heat. Add the fish, skin-side up, and cook 5 minutes. Flip and cook 5 minutes on the other side, until browned and cooked through. Transfer to a serving dish, pour the cooking oil over the fish, and cover to keep warm. 3. Heat the remaining 6 tablespoons olive oil in the same skillet over medium heat. Add the asparagus, artichokes, garlic, and bay leaves and sauté until the vegetables are tender, 6 to 8 minutes. 4. Using a slotted spoon, top the fish with the cooked vegetables, reserving the oil in the skillet. Add the vinegar and paprika to the oil and whisk to combine well. Pour the vinaigrette over the fish and vegetables and let sit at room temperature for at least 15 minutes, or marinate in the refrigerator up to 24 hours for a deeper flavor. Remove the bay leaf before serving.

Per Serving:
calories: 459 | fat: 34g | protein: 26g | carbs: 13g | fiber: 6g | sodium: 597mg

Salmon with Provolone Cheese

Prep time: 5 minutes | Cook time: 15 minutes | Serves 4

1 pound (454 g) salmon fillet,	grated
chopped	1 teaspoon avocado oil
2 ounces (57 g) Provolone,	¼ teaspoon ground paprika

1. Sprinkle the salmon fillets with avocado oil and put in the air fryer. 2. Then sprinkle the fish with ground paprika and top with Provolone cheese. 3. Cook the fish at 360°F (182°C) for 15 minutes.

Per Serving:
calories: 204 | fat: 10g | protein: 27g | carbs: 0g | fiber: 0g | sodium: 209mg

Cayenne Flounder Cutlets

Prep time: 15 minutes | Cook time: 10 minutes | Serves 2

1 egg
1 cup Pecorino Romano cheese, grated
Sea salt and white pepper, to taste
½ teaspoon cayenne pepper
1 teaspoon dried parsley flakes
2 flounder fillets

1. To make a breading station, whisk the egg until frothy. 2. In another bowl, mix Pecorino Romano cheese, and spices. 3. Dip the fish in the egg mixture and turn to coat evenly; then, dredge in the cracker crumb mixture, turning a couple of times to coat evenly. 4. Cook in the preheated air fryer at 390ºF (199ºC) for 5 minutes; turn them over and cook another 5 minutes. Enjoy!

Per Serving:
calories: 280 | fat: 13g | protein: 36g | carbs: 3g | fiber: 1g | sodium: 257mg

Cod with Parsley Pistou

Prep time: 15 minutes | Cook time: 10 minutes | Serves 4

1 cup packed roughly chopped fresh flat-leaf Italian parsley
1 to 2 small garlic cloves, minced
Zest and juice of 1 lemon
1 teaspoon salt
½ teaspoon freshly ground black pepper
1 cup extra-virgin olive oil, divided
1 pound (454 g) cod fillets, cut into 4 equal-sized pieces

1. In a food processor, combine the parsley, garlic, lemon zest and juice, salt, and pepper. Pulse to chop well. 2. While the food processor is running, slowly stream in ¾ cup olive oil until well combined. Set aside. 3. In a large skillet, heat the remaining ¼ cup olive oil over medium-high heat. Add the cod fillets, cover, and cook 4 to 5 minutes on each side, or until cooked through. Thicker fillets may require a bit more cooking time. Remove from the heat and keep warm. 4. Add the pistou to the skillet and heat over medium-low heat. Return the cooked fish to the skillet, flipping to coat in the sauce. Serve warm, covered with pistou.

Per Serving:
calories: 580 | fat: 55g | protein: 21g | carbs: 2g | fiber: 1g | sodium: 591mg

Breaded Shrimp Tacos

Prep time: 10 minutes | Cook time: 9 minutes |
Makes 8 tacos

2 large eggs
1 teaspoon prepared yellow mustard
1 pound (454 g) small shrimp, peeled, deveined, and tails removed
½ cup finely shredded Gouda or Parmesan cheese
½ cup pork dust
For Serving:
8 large Boston lettuce leaves
¼ cup pico de gallo
¼ cup shredded purple cabbage
1 lemon, sliced
Guacamole (optional)

1. Preheat the air fryer to 400ºF (204ºC). 2. Crack the eggs into a large bowl, add the mustard, and whisk until well combined. Add the shrimp and stir well to coat. 3. In a medium-sized bowl, mix together the cheese and pork dust until well combined. 4. One at a time, roll the coated shrimp in the pork dust mixture and use your hands to press it onto each shrimp. Spray the coated shrimp with avocado oil and place them in the air fryer basket, leaving space between them. 5. Air fry the shrimp for 9 minutes, or until cooked through and no longer translucent, flipping after 4 minutes. 6. To serve, place a lettuce leaf on a serving plate, place several shrimp on top, and top with 1½ teaspoons each of pico de gallo and purple cabbage. Squeeze some lemon juice on top and serve with guacamole, if desired. 7. Store leftover shrimp in an airtight container in the refrigerator for up to 3 days. Reheat in a preheated 400ºF (204ºC) air fryer for 5 minutes, or until warmed through.

Per Serving:
calories: 115 | fat: 4g | protein: 18g | carbs: 2g | fiber: 1g | sodium: 253mg

Pistachio-Crusted Whitefish

Prep time: 10 minutes | Cook time: 20 minutes | Serves 2

¼ cup shelled pistachios
1 tablespoon fresh parsley
1 tablespoon grated Parmesan cheese
1 tablespoon panko bread crumbs
2 tablespoons olive oil
¼ teaspoon salt
10 ounces (283 g) skinless whitefish (1 large piece or 2 smaller ones)

1. Preheat the oven to 350°F(180°C) and set the rack to the middle position. Line a sheet pan with foil or parchment paper. 2. Combine all of the ingredients except the fish in a mini food processor, and pulse until the nuts are finely ground. Alternatively, you can mince the nuts with a chef's knife and combine the ingredients by hand in a small bowl. 3. Place the fish on the sheet pan. Spread the nut mixture evenly over the fish and pat it down lightly. 4. Bake the fish for 20 to 30 minutes, depending on the thickness, until it flakes easily with a fork.

Per Serving:
calories: 267 | fat: 18g | protein: 28g | carbs: 1g | fiber: 0g | sodium: 85mg

Blackened Red Snapper

Prep time: 13 minutes | Cook time: 8 to 10 minutes |
Serves 4

1½ teaspoons black pepper
¼ teaspoon thyme
¼ teaspoon garlic powder
⅛ teaspoon cayenne pepper
1 teaspoon olive oil
4 (4-ounce / 113-g) red snapper fillet portions, skin on
4 thin slices lemon
Cooking spray

1. Mix the spices and oil together to make a paste. Rub into both sides of the fish. 2. Spray the air fryer basket with nonstick cooking spray and lay snapper steaks in basket, skin-side down. 3. Place a lemon slice on each piece of fish. 4. Roast at 390ºF (199ºC) for 8 to 10 minutes. The fish will not flake when done, but it should be white through the center.

Per Serving:
calories: 128 | fat: 3g | protein: 23g | carbs: 1g | fiber: 1g | sodium: 73mg

Crushed Marcona Almond Swordfish

Prep time: 25 minutes | Cook time: 15 minutes | Serves 4

½ cup almond flour
¼ cup crushed Marcona almonds
½ to 1 teaspoon salt, divided
2 pounds (907 g) Swordfish, preferably 1 inch thick
1 large egg, beaten (optional)
¼ cup pure apple cider
¼ cup extra-virgin olive oil, plus more for frying
3 to 4 sprigs flat-leaf parsley,
chopped
1 lemon, juiced
1 tablespoon Spanish paprika
5 medium baby portobello mushrooms, chopped (optional)
4 or 5 chopped scallions, both green and white parts
3 to 4 garlic cloves, peeled
¼ cup chopped pitted kalamata olives

1. On a dinner plate, spread the flour and crushed Marcona almonds and mix in the salt. Alternately, pour the flour, almonds, and ¼ teaspoon of salt into a large plastic food storage bag. Add the fish and coat it with the flour mixture. If a thicker coat is desired, repeat this step after dipping the fish in the egg (if using). 2. In a measuring cup, combine the apple cider, ¼ cup of olive oil, parsley, lemon juice, paprika, and ¼ teaspoon of salt. Mix well and set aside. 3. In a large, heavy-bottom sauté pan or skillet, pour the olive oil to a depth of ⅛ inch and heat on medium heat. Once the oil is hot, add the fish and brown for 3 to 5 minutes, then turn the fish over and add the mushrooms (If using), scallions, garlic, and olives. Cook for an additional 3 minutes. Once the other side of the fish is brown, remove the fish from the pan and set aside. 4. Pour the cider mixture into the skillet and mix well with the vegetables. Put the fried fish into the skillet on top of the mixture and cook with sauce on medium-low heat for 10 minutes, until the fish flakes easily with a fork. Carefully remove the fish from the pan and plate. Spoon the sauce over the fish. Serve with white rice or home-fried potatoes.

Per Serving:
calories: 620 | fat: 37g | protein: 63g | carbs: 10g | fiber: 5g | sodium: 644mg

Italian Baccalà

Prep time: 2 to 3 hours | Cook time: 4 to 6 hours | Serves 4

1½ pounds (680 g) salt cod
1 (15-ounce / 425-g) can no-salt-added diced tomatoes
½ onion, chopped
2 garlic cloves, minced
½ teaspoon red pepper flakes
¼ cup chopped fresh parsley, plus more for garnish
Juice of ½ lemon

1. Wash the salt cod to remove any visible salt. Completely submerge the cod in a large bowl of water and let it soak for at least 2 to 3 hours. If you are soaking it for longer than 24 hours, change the water after 12 hours. 2. In a slow cooker, combine the tomatoes, onion, garlic, red pepper flakes, parsley, and lemon juice. Stir to mix well. Drain the cod and add it to the slow cooker, breaking it apart as necessary to make it fit. 3. Cover the cooker and cook for 4 to 6 hours on Low heat. 4. Garnish with the remaining fresh parsley for serving.

Per Serving:
calories: 211 | fat: 2g | protein: 39g | carbs: 8g | fiber: 2g | sodium: 179mg

Tuna Cakes

Prep time: 10 minutes | Cook time: 10 minutes | Serves 4

4 (3-ounce / 85-g) pouches tuna, drained
1 large egg, whisked
2 tablespoons peeled and chopped white onion
½ teaspoon Old Bay seasoning

1. In a large bowl, mix all ingredients together and form into four patties. 2. Place patties into ungreased air fryer basket. Adjust the temperature to 400ºF (204ºC) and air fry for 10 minutes. Patties will be browned and crispy when done. Let cool 5 minutes before serving.

Per Serving:
calories: 113 | fat: 2g | protein: 22g | carbs: 1g | fiber: 0g | sodium: 56mg

Mediterranean Grilled Shrimp

Prep time: 20 minutes | Cook time: 5 minutes | Serves 4 to 6

2 tablespoons garlic, minced
½ cup lemon juice
3 tablespoons fresh Italian parsley, finely chopped
¼ cup extra-virgin olive oil
1 teaspoon salt
2 pounds (907 g) jumbo shrimp (21-25), peeled and deveined

1. In a large bowl, mix the garlic, lemon juice, parsley, olive oil, and salt. 2. Add the shrimp to the bowl and toss to make sure all the pieces are coated with the marinade. Let the shrimp sit for 15 minutes. 3. Preheat a grill, grill pan, or lightly oiled skillet to high heat. While heating, thread about 5 to 6 pieces of shrimp onto each skewer. 4. Place the skewers on the grill, grill pan, or skillet and cook for 2 to 3 minutes on each side until cooked through. Serve warm.

Per Serving:
calories: 217 | fat: 10g | protein: 31g | carbs: 2g | fiber: 0g | sodium: 569mg

Baked Swordfish with Herbs

Prep time: 10 minutes | Cook time: 20 minutes | Serves 4

Olive oil spray
1 cup fresh Italian parsley
¼ cup fresh thyme
¼ cup lemon juice
2 cloves garlic
¼ cup extra-virgin olive oil
½ teaspoon salt
4 swordfish steaks (each 5 to 7 ounces / 142 to 198 g)

1. Preheat the oven to 450ºF (235ºC). Coat a large baking dish with olive oil spray. 2. In a food processor, pulse the parsley, thyme, lemon juice, garlic, olive oil, and salt 10 times. 3. Place the swordfish in the prepared baking dish. Spoon the parsley mixture over the steaks. 4. Put the fish in the oven to bake for 17 to 20 minutes.

Per Serving:
calories: 397 | fat: 22g | protein: 44g | carbs: 3g | fiber: 1g | sodium: 495mg

Pesto Shrimp with Wild Rice Pilaf

Prep time: 5 minutes | Cook time: 5 minutes | Serves 4

1 pound (454 g) medium shrimp, peeled and deveined
¼ cup pesto sauce

1 lemon, sliced
2 cups cooked wild rice pilaf

1. Preheat the air fryer to 360°F(182°C). 2. In a medium bowl, toss the shrimp with the pesto sauce until well coated. 3. Place the shrimp in a single layer in the air fryer basket. Put the lemon slices over the shrimp and roast for 5 minutes. 4. Remove the lemons and discard. Serve a quarter of the shrimp over ½ cup wild rice with some favorite steamed vegetables.

Per Serving:
calories: 265 | fat: 9g | protein: 28g | carbs: 19g | fiber: 2g | sodium: 277mg

Halibut Fillets with Vegetables

Prep time: 20 minutes | Cook time: 5 minutes | Serves 2

1 cup chopped broccoli
1 large potato, peeled and diced
1 large carrot, peeled and grated
1 small zucchini, trimmed and grated
4 ounces (113 g) mushrooms, sliced
¼ teaspoon dried thyme
¼ teaspoon grated lemon zest

1 (½-pound / 227-g) halibut fillet
½ cup white wine
½ cup lemon juice
1 teaspoon dried parsley
¼ teaspoon salt
¼ teaspoon ground black pepper
⅛ teaspoon ground nutmeg

1. Place the rack and steamer basket in the Instant Pot®. Place broccoli, potato, carrot, zucchini, and mushrooms in layers in the basket. Sprinkle thyme and lemon zest over vegetables. 2. Place fish over vegetables. Pour wine and lemon juice over fish. Sprinkle parsley, salt, and pepper over the fish and vegetables. 3. Close lid, set steam release to Sealing, press the Manual button, and set time to 5 minutes. When the timer beeps, quick-release the pressure until the float valve drops and open lid. Divide fish and vegetables between two plates. Sprinkle nutmeg over each serving.

Per Serving:
calories: 278 | fat: 3g | protein: 31g | carbs: 23g | fiber: 5g | sodium: 409mg

Shrimp over Black Bean Linguine

Prep time: 10 minutes | Cook time: 15 minutes | Serves 4

1 pound (454 g) black bean linguine or spaghetti
1 pound (454 g) fresh shrimp, peeled and deveined
4 tablespoons extra-virgin olive

oil
1 onion, finely chopped
3 garlic cloves, minced
¼ cup basil, cut into strips

1. Bring a large pot of water to a boil and cook the pasta according to the package instructions. 2. In the last 5 minutes of cooking the pasta, add the shrimp to the hot water and allow them to cook for 3 to 5 minutes. Once they turn pink, take them out of the hot water, and, if you think you may have overcooked them, run them under cool water. Set aside. 3. Reserve 1 cup of the pasta cooking water

and drain the noodles. In the same pan, heat the oil over medium-high heat and cook the onion and garlic for 7 to 10 minutes. Once the onion is translucent, add the pasta back in and toss well. 4. Plate the pasta, then top with shrimp and garnish with basil.

Per Serving:
calories: 668 | fat: 19g | protein: 57g | carbs: 73g | fiber: 31g | sodium: 615mg

Herb-Marinated Flounder

Prep time: 5 minutes | Cook time: 10 minutes | Serves 4

½ cup lightly packed flatleaf parsley
¼ cup olive oil
4 garlic cloves, peeled and halved
2 tablespoons fresh rosemary
2 tablespoons fresh thyme

leaves
2 tablespoons fresh sage
2 tablespoons lemon zest
Sea salt and freshly ground pepper, to taste
4 flounder fillets

1. Preheat the oven to 350°F (180°C). 2. Place all the ingredients except the fish in a food processor. Blend to form a thick paste. 3. Place the fillets on a baking sheet, and brush this paste on them. Refrigerate for at least 1 hour. 4. Bake for 8–10 minutes, or until the flounder is slightly firm and opaque. Season with sea salt and freshly ground pepper.

Per Serving:
calories: 283 | fat: 18g | protein: 27g | carbs: 3g | fiber: 1g | sodium: 322mg

Caramelized Fennel and Sardines with Penne

Prep time: 15 minutes | Cook time: 30 minutes | Serves 4

8 ounces (227 g) whole-wheat penne
2 tablespoons extra-virgin olive oil
1 bulb fennel, cored and thinly sliced, plus ¼ cup fronds
2 celery stalks, thinly sliced, plus ½ cup leaves
4 garlic cloves, sliced

¾ teaspoon kosher salt
¼ teaspoon freshly ground black pepper
Zest of 1 lemon
Juice of 1 lemon
2 (4.4-ounce / 125-g) cans boneless/skinless sardines packed in olive oil, undrained

1. Cook the penne according to the package directions. Drain, reserving 1 cup pasta water. 2. Heat the olive oil in a large skillet or sauté pan over medium heat. Add the fennel and celery and cook, stirring often, until tender and golden, about 10 to 12 minutes. Add the garlic and cook for 1 minute. 3. Add the penne, reserved pasta water, salt, and black pepper. Increase the heat to medium-high and cook for 1 to 2 minutes. 4. Remove the pan from the heat and stir in the lemon zest, lemon juice, fennel fronds, and celery leaves. Break the sardines into bite-size pieces and gently mix in, along with the oil they were packed in.

Per Serving:
calories: 400 | fat: 15g | protein: 22g | carbs: 46g | fiber: 6g | sodium: 530mg

Salmon Burgers with Creamy Broccoli Slaw

Prep time: 15 minutes | Cook time: 10 minutes | Serves 4

For the salmon burgers
1 pound (454 g) salmon fillets, bones and skin removed
1 egg
¼ cup fresh dill, chopped
1 cup whole wheat bread crumbs
½ teaspoon salt
½ teaspoon cayenne pepper
2 garlic cloves, minced
4 whole wheat buns

For the broccoli slaw
3 cups chopped or shredded broccoli
½ cup shredded carrots
¼ cup sunflower seeds
2 garlic cloves, minced
½ teaspoon salt
2 tablespoons apple cider vinegar
1 cup nonfat plain Greek yogurt

Make the salmon burgers 1. Preheat the air fryer to 360°F(182°C). 2. In a food processor, pulse the salmon fillets until they are finely chopped. 3. In a large bowl, combine the chopped salmon, egg, dill, bread crumbs, salt, cayenne, and garlic until it comes together. 4. Form the salmon into 4 patties. Place them into the air fryer basket, making sure that they don't touch each other. 5. Bake for 5 minutes. Flip the salmon patties and bake for 5 minutes more. Make the broccoli slaw 6. In a large bowl, combine all of the ingredients for the broccoli slaw. Mix well. 7. Serve the salmon burgers on toasted whole wheat buns, and top with a generous portion of broccoli slaw.

Per Serving:
calories: 504 | fat: 14g | protein: 40g | carbs: 54g | fiber: 5g | sodium: 631mg

Spanish Fish Stew with Saffron

Prep time: 10 minutes | Cook time: 10 minutes | Serves 4

Pinch of saffron (about 8 threads)
¾ cup olive oil, divided
2 medium onions, diced
1 teaspoon salt, divided
1 tablespoon tomato paste
½ cup dry white wine
3 cups fish broth or bottled

clam juice
2 cloves garlic, peeled and minced
3 slices toasted bread
2½ pounds (1.1 kg) cod or other meaty white fish
1 tablespoon finely chopped flat-leaf parsley

1. In a small bowl, combine the saffron threads with 2 tablespoons of warm water. 2. Heat ½ cup of olive oil in a large Dutch oven over medium-high heat. Add the onions and ½ teaspoon of salt and cook, stirring frequently, until softened, about 5 minutes. Add the tomato paste and cook, stirring, for 1 more minute. Add the wine and bring to a boil. Add the fish broth or clam juice and the soaked saffron and bring back to a boil. Reduce the heat to low and let simmer, uncovered, for 10 minutes. 3. Meanwhile, in a food processor, combine the garlic and bread and process until coarsely ground. Add the remaining ¼ cup of olive oil and ½ teaspoon of salt and pulse just to mix. Add the fish to the pot, cover, and cook for about 6 minutes, or until the fish is just cooked through. Stir in the sauce. Taste and adjust seasoning if needed. Ladle the stew into serving bowls and serve immediately, garnished with parsley.

Per Serving:
calories: 712 | fat: 44g | protein: 56g | carbs: 16g | fiber: 2g | sodium: 813mg

Poached Octopus

Prep time: 10 minutes | Cook time: 16 minutes | Serves 8

2 pounds (907 g) potatoes (about 6 medium)
3 teaspoons salt, divided
1 (2-pound / 907-g) frozen octopus, thawed, cleaned, and rinsed
3 cloves garlic, peeled, divided

1 bay leaf
2 teaspoons whole peppercorns
½ cup olive oil
¼ cup white wine vinegar
½ teaspoon ground black pepper
½ cup chopped fresh parsley

1. Place potatoes in the Instant Pot® with 2 teaspoons salt and enough water to just cover the potatoes halfway. Close lid, set steam release to Sealing, press the Manual button, and set time to 6 minutes. When the timer beeps, quick-release the pressure until the float valve drops and open lid. Press the Cancel button. 2. Remove potatoes with tongs (reserve the cooking water), and peel them as soon as you can handle them. Dice potatoes into bite-sized pieces. Set aside. 3. Add octopus to potato cooking water in the pot and add more water to cover if needed. Add 1 garlic clove, bay leaf, and peppercorns. Close lid, set steam release to Sealing, press the Manual button, and set time to 10 minutes. When the timer beeps, quick-release the pressure until the float valve drops and open lid. Remove and discard bay leaf. 4. Check octopus for tenderness by seeing if a fork will sink easily into the thickest part of the flesh. If not, close the top and bring it to pressure for another minute or two and check again. 5. Remove octopus and drain. Chop head and tentacles into small, bite-sized chunks. 6. Crush remaining 2 garlic cloves and place in a small jar or plastic container. Add olive oil, vinegar, remaining 1 teaspoon salt, and pepper. Close the lid and shake well. 7. In a large serving bowl, mix potatoes with octopus, cover with vinaigrette, and sprinkle with parsley.

Per Serving:
calories: 301 | fat: 15g | protein: 15g | carbs: 30g | fiber: 2g | sodium: 883mg

Lemon-Oregano Grilled Shrimp

Prep time: 10 minutes | Cook time: 6 minutes | Serves 6

½ cup oregano leaves
1 clove garlic, minced
1 teaspoon finely grated lemon zest
3 tablespoons lemon juice
¾ teaspoon salt, plus more for seasoning shrimp

½ teaspoon freshly ground black pepper, plus more for seasoning shrimp
½ cup olive oil, plus 2 tablespoons, divided
2½ pounds (1.1 kg) large shrimp, peeled and deveined

1. In a small bowl, stir together the oregano, garlic, lemon zest, lemon juice, salt, and pepper. Whisk in ½ cup of olive oil until well combined. 2. Preheat the grill to high heat. 3. Place the shrimp in a large bowl and toss with the remaining 2 tablespoons of olive oil and a pinch or two of salt and pepper. Thread the shrimp onto skewers, 3 to 5 at a time depending on the size of the shrimp. Place the skewers on the grill and cook for 2 to 3 minutes per side, just until the shrimp are cooked through and just beginning to char. As the shrimp are cooked, transfer the skewers to a serving platter. Spoon the sauce over the skewers and serve immediately.

Per Serving:
calories: 389 | fat: 26g | protein: 36g | carbs: 8g | fiber: 3g | sodium: 530mg

Paprika Crab Burgers

Prep time: 30 minutes | Cook time: 14 minutes | Serves 3

2 eggs, beaten
1 shallot, chopped
2 garlic cloves, crushed
1 tablespoon olive oil
1 teaspoon yellow mustard
1 teaspoon fresh cilantro, chopped

10 ounces (283 g) crab meat
1 teaspoon smoked paprika
½ teaspoon ground black pepper
Sea salt, to taste
¾ cup Parmesan cheese

1. In a mixing bowl, thoroughly combine the eggs, shallot, garlic, olive oil, mustard, cilantro, crab meat, paprika, black pepper, and salt. Mix until well combined. 2. Shape the mixture into 6 patties. Roll the crab patties over grated Parmesan cheese, coating well on all sides. Place in your refrigerator for 2 hours. 3. Spritz the crab patties with cooking oil on both sides. Cook in the preheated air fryer at 360ºF (182ºC) for 14 minutes. Serve on dinner rolls if desired. Bon appétit!

Per Serving:
calories: 288 | fat: 16g | protein: 32g | carbs: 4g | fiber: 1g | sodium: 355mg

Baked Red Snapper with Potatoes and Tomatoes

Prep time: 10 minutes | Cook time: 45 minutes | Serves 4

5 sprigs fresh thyme, divided
2 sprigs fresh oregano, divided
1½ pounds (680 g) new potatoes, halved (or quartered if large)
4 Roma tomatoes, quartered lengthwise
1 tablespoon plus 1 teaspoon olive oil
4 cloves garlic, halved, divided

1¼ teaspoons kosher salt, divided
¾ teaspoon ground black pepper, divided
1 cleaned whole red snapper (about 2 pounds / 907 g), scaled and fins removed
½–1 lemon, sliced
4 cups (4 ounces) baby spinach

1. Preheat the oven to 350°F(180ºC). 2. Strip the leaves off 2 sprigs thyme and 1 sprig oregano and chop. In a 9' × 13' baking dish, toss the potatoes and tomatoes with 1 tablespoon of the oil, the chopped thyme and oregano leaves, 2 cloves of the garlic, 1 teaspoon of the salt, and ½ teaspoon of the pepper. 3. Cut 3 or 4 diagonal slashes in the skin on both sides of the snapper. Rub the skin with the remaining 1 teaspoon oil. Sprinkle the cavity of the snapper with the remaining ¼ teaspoon salt and pepper. Fill it with the lemon slices, the remaining thyme and oregano sprigs, and the remaining 2 cloves garlic. Sprinkle the outside of the snapper with a pinch of salt and pepper. Set the fish on the vegetables. 4. Cover the baking dish with foil and bake for 20 minutes. Remove the foil and continue baking until the potatoes are tender and the fish flakes easily with a fork, 20 to 25 minutes. 5. Transfer the fish to a serving platter. Toss the spinach with the tomatoes and potatoes in the baking dish, until wilted. 6. Using forks, peel the skin off the fish fillets. Scatter the vegetables around the fish and serve.

Per Serving:
calories: 345 | fat: 6g | protein: 39g | carbs: 33g | fiber: 5g | sodium: 782mg

Tomato-Basil Salmon

Prep time: 10 minutes | Cook time: 4 to 6 hours | Serves 4

1 (15-ounce / 425-g) can no-salt-added crushed tomatoes
½ cup chopped onion
4 teaspoons dried basil
3 garlic cloves, minced
2 pounds (907 g) fresh salmon

fillets, skin on or off as preferred
1 teaspoon sea salt
¼ teaspoon freshly ground black pepper
¼ cup chopped fresh basil

1. In a slow cooker, combine the tomatoes, onion, basil, and garlic. Stir to mix well. 2. Season the salmon all over with salt and pepper. Add the salmon to the slow cooker, cutting it into pieces to fit if needed, and spoon some of the tomato mixture on top. 3. Cover the cooker and cook for 4 to 6 hours on Low heat. 4. Garnish with fresh basil for serving.

Per Serving:
calories: 471 | fat: 24g | protein: 58g | carbs: 9g | fiber: 3g | sodium: 733mg

Fish Tagine

Prep time: 25 minutes | Cook time: 12 minutes | Serves 4

2 tablespoons extra-virgin olive oil, plus extra for drizzling
1 large onion, halved and sliced ¼ inch thick
1 pound (454 g) carrots, peeled, halved lengthwise, and sliced ¼ inch thick
2 (2-inch) strips orange zest, plus 1 teaspoon grated zest
¾ teaspoon table salt, divided
2 tablespoons tomato paste
4 garlic cloves, minced, divided
1¼ teaspoons paprika
1 teaspoon ground cumin

¼ teaspoon red pepper flakes
¼ teaspoon saffron threads, crumbled
1 (8-ounce / 227-g) bottle clam juice
1½ pounds (680 g) skinless halibut fillets, 1½ inches thick, cut into 2-inch pieces
¼ cup pitted oil-cured black olives, quartered
2 tablespoons chopped fresh parsley
1 teaspoon sherry vinegar

1. Using highest sauté function, heat oil in Instant Pot until shimmering. Add onion, carrots, orange zest strips, and ¼ teaspoon salt, and cook until vegetables are softened and lightly browned, 10 to 12 minutes. Stir in tomato paste, three-quarters of garlic, paprika, cumin, pepper flakes, and saffron and cook until fragrant, about 30 seconds. Stir in clam juice, scraping up any browned bits. 2. Sprinkle halibut with remaining ½ teaspoon salt. Nestle halibut into onion mixture and spoon some of cooking liquid on top of pieces. Lock lid in place and close pressure release valve. Select high pressure cook function and set cook time for 0 minutes. Once Instant Pot has reached pressure, immediately turn off pot and quick-release pressure. 3. Discard orange zest. Gently stir in olives, parsley, vinegar, grated orange zest, and remaining garlic. Season with salt and pepper to taste. Drizzle extra oil over individual portions before serving.

Per Serving:
calories: 310 | fat: 15g | protein: 34g | carbs: 18g | fiber: 4g | sodium: 820mg

Garlic Prawns with Tomatoes and Basil

Prep time: 10 minutes | Cook time: 10 minutes | Serves 4

2 tablespoons olive oil
1¼ pounds (567 g) shrimp, peeled and deveined
3 cloves garlic, minced
⅛ teaspoon crushed red pepper flakes
¾ cup dry white wine

1½ cups grape tomatoes
¼ cup finely chopped fresh basil, plus more for garnish
¾ teaspoon salt
½ teaspoon freshly ground black pepper

1. Heat the olive oil in a medium skillet over medium-high heat. Add the shrimp and cook about 1 minute on each side, until just cooked through. Transfer the shrimp to a plate, leaving the oil in the pan. 2. Add the garlic and red pepper flakes to the oil in the pan and cook, stirring, for 30 seconds. Stir in the wine and cook until it is reduced by about half. Add the tomatoes and cook, stirring, for 3 to 4 minutes more, until the tomatoes begin to break down. Stir in the basil, salt, pepper, and the reserved shrimp. Cook 1 to 2 minutes more, until heated through. Serve hot, garnished with the remaining basil.

Per Serving:
calories: 282 | fat: 10g | protein: 33g | carbs: 7g | fiber: 1g | sodium: 299mg

Parmesan Mackerel with Coriander

Prep time: 10 minutes | Cook time: 7 minutes | Serves 2

12 ounces (340 g) mackerel fillet
2 ounces (57 g) Parmesan,

grated
1 teaspoon ground coriander
1 tablespoon olive oil

1. Sprinkle the mackerel fillet with olive oil and put it in the air fryer basket. 2. Top the fish with ground coriander and Parmesan. 3. Cook the fish at 390ºF (199ºC) for 7 minutes.

Per Serving:
calories: 522 | fat: 39g | protein: 42g | carbs: 1g | fiber: 0g | sodium: 544mg

Halibut in Parchment with Zucchini, Shallots, and Herbs

Prep time: 15 minutes | Cook time: 15 minutes | Serves 4

½ cup zucchini, diced small
1 shallot, minced
4 (5-ounce / 142-g) halibut fillets (about 1 inch thick)
4 teaspoons extra-virgin olive oil

¼ teaspoon kosher salt
⅛ teaspoon freshly ground black pepper
1 lemon, sliced into ⅛-inch-thick rounds
8 sprigs of thyme

1. Preheat the oven to 450ºF (235ºC). Combine the zucchini and shallots in a medium bowl. 2. Cut 4 (15-by-24-inch) pieces of parchment paper. Fold each sheet in half horizontally. Draw a large half heart on one side of each folded sheet, with the fold along the center of the heart. Cut out the heart, open the parchment, and lay it flat. 3. Place a fillet near the center of each parchment heart. Drizzle 1 teaspoon olive oil on each fillet. Sprinkle with salt and pepper.

Top each fillet with lemon slices and 2 sprigs of thyme. Sprinkle each fillet with one-quarter of the zucchini and shallot mixture. Fold the parchment over. 4. Starting at the top, fold the edges of the parchment over, and continue all the way around to make a packet. Twist the end tightly to secure. 5. Arrange the 4 packets on a baking sheet. Bake for about 15 minutes. Place on plates; cut open. Serve immediately.

Per Serving:
calories: 190 | fat: 7g | protein: 27g | carbs: 5g | fiber: 1g | sodium: 170mg

Italian Fish

Prep time: 10 minutes | Cook time: 3 minutes | Serves 4

1 (14½-ounce / 411-g) can diced tomatoes
¼ teaspoon dried minced onion
¼ teaspoon onion powder
¼ teaspoon dried minced garlic
¼ teaspoon garlic powder
¼ teaspoon dried basil
¼ teaspoon dried parsley
⅛ teaspoon dried oregano
¼ teaspoon sugar

⅛ teaspoon dried lemon granules, crushed
⅛ teaspoon chili powder
⅛ teaspoon dried red pepper flakes
1 tablespoon grated Parmesan cheese
4 (4-ounce / 113-g) cod fillets, rinsed and patted dry

1. Add tomatoes, minced onion, onion powder, minced garlic, garlic powder, basil, parsley, oregano, sugar, lemon granules, chili powder, red pepper flakes, and cheese to the Instant Pot® and stir to mix. Arrange the fillets over the tomato mixture, folding thin tail ends under to give the fillets even thickness. Spoon some of the tomato mixture over the fillets. 2. Close lid, set steam release to Sealing, press the Manual button, and set time to 3 minutes. When the timer beeps, quick-release the pressure until the float valve drops and open lid. Serve immediately.

Per Serving:
calories: 116 | fat: 3g | protein: 20g | carbs: 5g | fiber: 2g | sodium: 400mg

Fried Fresh Sardines

Prep time: 5 minutes | Cook time: 5 minutes | Serves 4

Avocado oil
1½ pounds (680 g) whole fresh sardines, scales removed
1 teaspoon salt

1 teaspoon freshly ground black pepper
2 cups flour

1. Preheat a deep skillet over medium heat. Pour in enough oil so there is about 1 inch of it in the pan. 2. Season the fish with the salt and pepper. 3. Dredge the fish in the flour so it is completely covered. 4. Slowly drop in 1 fish at a time, making sure not to overcrowd the pan. 5. Cook for about 3 minutes on each side or just until the fish begins to brown on all sides. Serve warm.

Per Serving:
calories: 581 | fat: 20g | protein: 48g | carbs: 48g | fiber: 2g | sodium: 583mg

Blackened Salmon

Prep time: 10 minutes | Cook time: 8 minutes | Serves 2

10 ounces (283 g) salmon fillet
½ teaspoon ground coriander
1 teaspoon ground cumin
1 teaspoon dried basil
1 tablespoon avocado oil

1. In the shallow bowl, mix ground coriander, ground cumin, and dried basil. 2. Then coat the salmon fillet in the spices and sprinkle with avocado oil. 3. Put the fish in the air fryer basket and cook at 395°F (202°C) for 4 minutes per side.

Per Serving:
calories: 249 | fat: 13g | protein: 29g | carbs: 1g | fiber: 1g | sodium: 109mg

Red Snapper with Peppers and Potatoes

Prep time: 15 minutes | Cook time: 4 to 6 hours | Serves 4

1 pound (454 g) red potatoes, chopped
1 green bell pepper, seeded and sliced
1 red bell pepper, seeded and sliced
½ onion, sliced
1 (15-ounce / 425-g) can no-salt-added diced tomatoes
⅓ cup whole Kalamata olives, pitted
5 garlic cloves, minced
1 teaspoon dried thyme
1 teaspoon dried rosemary
Juice of 1 lemon
Sea salt
Freshly ground black pepper
1½ to 2 pounds (680 to 907 g) fresh red snapper fillets
2 lemons, thinly sliced
¼ cup chopped fresh parsley

1. In a slow cooker, combine the potatoes, green and red bell peppers, onion, tomatoes, olives, garlic, thyme, rosemary, and lemon juice. Season with salt and black pepper. Stir to mix well. 2. Nestle the snapper into the vegetable mixture in a single layer, cutting it into pieces to fit if needed. Top it with lemon slices. 3. Cover the cooker and cook for 4 to 6 hours on Low heat, or until the potatoes are tender. 4. Garnish with fresh parsley for serving.

Per Serving:
calories: 350 | fat: 5g | protein: 45g | carbs: 41g | fiber: 8g | sodium: 241mg

Maple Balsamic Glazed Salmon

Prep time: 5 minutes | Cook time: 10 minutes | Serves 4

4 (6-ounce / 170-g) fillets of salmon
Salt and freshly ground black pepper, to taste
Vegetable oil
¼ cup pure maple syrup
3 tablespoons balsamic vinegar
1 teaspoon Dijon mustard

1. Preheat the air fryer to 400°F (204°C). 2. Season the salmon well with salt and freshly ground black pepper. Spray or brush the bottom of the air fryer basket with vegetable oil and place the salmon fillets inside. Air fry the salmon for 5 minutes. 3. While the salmon is air frying, combine the maple syrup, balsamic vinegar and Dijon mustard in a small saucepan over medium heat and stir to blend well. Let the mixture simmer while the fish is cooking. It should start to thicken slightly, but keep your eye on it so it doesn't burn. 4. Brush the glaze on the salmon fillets and air fry for an additional 5 minutes. The salmon should feel firm to the touch when finished and the glaze should be nicely browned on top. Brush a little more glaze on top before removing and serving with rice and vegetables, or a nice green salad.

Per Serving:
calories: 279 | fat: 8g | protein: 35g | carbs: 15g | fiber: 0g | sodium: 146mg

White Wine–Sautéed Mussels

Prep time: 10 minutes | Cook time: 10 minutes | Serves 4

3 pounds (1.4 kg) live mussels, cleaned
4 tablespoons (½ stick) salted butter
2 shallots, finely chopped
2 tablespoons garlic, minced
2 cups dry white wine

1. Scrub the mussel shells to make sure they are clean; trim off any that have a beard (hanging string). Put the mussels in a large bowl of water, discarding any that are not tightly closed. 2. In a large pot over medium heat, cook the butter, shallots, and garlic for 2 minutes. 3. Add the wine to the pot, and cook for 1 minute. 4. Add the mussels to the pot, toss with the sauce, and cover with a lid. Let cook for 7 minutes. Discard any mussels that have not opened. 5. Serve in bowls with the wine broth.

Per Serving:
calories: 468 | fat: 15g | protein: 41g | carbs: 21g | fiber: 0g | sodium: 879mg

Moroccan Fish

Prep time: 10 minutes | Cook time: 2 to 4 hours | Serves 4

Ras Al-Hanout:
¼ teaspoon ground cumin
¼ teaspoon ground ginger
¼ teaspoon ground turmeric
¼ teaspoon paprika
¼ teaspoon garlic powder
¼ teaspoon red pepper flakes
⅛ teaspoon ground cinnamon
⅛ teaspoon ground coriander
⅛ teaspoon ground nutmeg
⅛ teaspoon ground cloves
⅛ teaspoon sea salt
⅛ teaspoon freshly ground black pepper
Fish:
Nonstick cooking spray
2 pounds (907 g) fresh white-fleshed fish fillets of your choice
2 garlic cloves, minced

Make the Ras Al-Hanout: In a small bowl, stir together the cumin, ginger, turmeric, paprika, garlic powder, red pepper flakes, cinnamon, coriander, nutmeg, cloves, salt, and pepper. Make the Fish: 1. Coat a slow-cooker insert with cooking spray, or line the bottom and sides with parchment paper or aluminum foil. 2. Season the fish all over with the ras al-hanout and garlic. Place the fish in the prepared slow cooker in a single layer, cutting it into pieces to fit if needed. 3. Cover the cooker and cook for 2 to 4 hours on Low heat.

Per Serving:
calories: 243 | fat: 2g | protein: 51g | carbs: 1g | fiber: 0g | sodium: 216mg

Catfish in Creole Sauce

Prep time: 10 minutes | Cook time: 5 minutes | Serves 4

1 (1½-pound / 680-g) catfish fillet, rinsed in cold water, patted dry, cut into bite-sized pieces	1 teaspoon hot paprika
	¼ teaspoon dried tarragon
	1 medium green bell pepper, seeded and diced
1 (14½-ounce / 411-g) can diced tomatoes	1 stalk celery, finely diced
2 teaspoons dried minced onion	¼ teaspoon sugar
¼ teaspoon onion powder	½ cup chili sauce
1 teaspoon dried minced garlic	½ teaspoon salt
¼ teaspoon garlic powder	½ teaspoon ground black pepper

1. Add all ingredients to the Instant Pot® and stir to mix. 2. Close lid, set steam release to Sealing, press the Manual button, and set time to 5 minutes. When the timer beeps, quick-release the pressure until the float valve drops and open lid. Gently stir and serve.

Per Serving:
calories: 284 | fat: 9g | protein: 31g | carbs: 7g | fiber: 3g | sodium: 696mg

Chili Tilapia

Prep time: 5 minutes | Cook time: 20 minutes | Serves 4

4 tilapia fillets, boneless	1 tablespoon avocado oil
1 teaspoon chili flakes	1 teaspoon mustard
1 teaspoon dried oregano	

1. Rub the tilapia fillets with chili flakes, dried oregano, avocado oil, and mustard and put in the air fryer. 2. Cook it for 10 minutes per side at 360ºF (182ºC).

Per Serving:
calories: 146 | fat: 6g | protein: 23g | carbs: 1g | fiber: 0g | sodium: 94mg

Mussels with Potatoes

Prep time: 15 minutes | Cook time: 12 minutes | Serves 6

2 pounds (907 g) baby Yukon Gold potatoes, cut in half	¼ teaspoon salt
½ cup water	¼ teaspoon ground black pepper
2 tablespoons olive oil, divided	1 (15-ounce / 425-g) can diced tomatoes
1 medium yellow onion, peeled and diced	1½ cups water
1 tablespoon chopped fresh oregano	2 pounds (907 g) mussels, scrubbed and beards removed
½ teaspoon paprika	½ cup sliced green olives
4 cloves garlic, peeled and minced	2 tablespoons chopped fresh parsley

1. Place potatoes, water, and 1 tablespoon oil in the Instant Pot®. Close lid, set steam release to Sealing, press the Manual button, and set time to 2 minutes. When the timer beeps, quick-release the pressure until the float valve drops. Press the Cancel button. Open lid and drain potatoes. Set aside. Wash and dry pot. 2. Press the Sauté button and heat remaining 1 tablespoon oil. Add onion and cook until tender, about 4 minutes. Add oregano, paprika, garlic, salt, and pepper, and cook until very fragrant, about 30 seconds. Add tomatoes and water, and stir well. Press the Cancel button. 3. Stir in mussels, olives, and potatoes. Close lid, set steam release to Sealing, press the Manual button, and set time to 5 minutes. When the timer beeps, quick-release the pressure until the float valve drops and open lid. Discard any mussels that haven't opened. Garnish with parsley and serve immediately.

Per Serving:
calories: 272 | fat: 8g | protein: 15g | carbs: 35g | fiber: 4g | sodium: 560mg

Lemony Salmon

Prep time: 30 minutes | Cook time: 10 minutes | Serves 4

1½ pounds (680 g) salmon steak	Fresh chopped chives, for garnish
½ teaspoon grated lemon zest	½ cup dry white wine
Freshly cracked mixed peppercorns, to taste	½ teaspoon fresh cilantro, chopped
⅓ cup lemon juice	Fine sea salt, to taste

1. To prepare the marinade, place all ingredients, except for salmon steak and chives, in a deep pan. Bring to a boil over medium-high flame until it has reduced by half. Allow it to cool down. 2. After that, allow salmon steak to marinate in the refrigerator approximately 40 minutes. Discard the marinade and transfer the fish steak to the preheated air fryer. 3. Air fry at 400ºF (204ºC) for 9 to 10 minutes. To finish, brush hot fish steaks with the reserved marinade, garnish with fresh chopped chives, and serve right away!

Per Serving:
calories: 244 | fat: 8g | protein: 35g | carbs: 3g | fiber: 0g | sodium: 128mg

Trout Cooked in Parchment

Prep time: 10 minutes | Cook time: 10 minutes | Serves 4

4 (4 ounces / 113 g each) trout fillets	Zest and juice of 1 lemon
3 cloves garlic, finely chopped	⅓ cup extra-virgin olive oil
8 fresh sage leaves, finely chopped	1 teaspoon unrefined sea salt or salt
½ cup finely chopped fresh parsley	Freshly ground pepper
	Lemon wedges

1. Preheat the oven to 425ºF (220ºC). Combine the garlic, sage, parsley, lemon zest and juice, olive oil, salt, and pepper in a small bowl. Cut four pieces of parchment paper—each more than double the size of the trout. 2. Place 1 trout on top of each piece of parchment and equally distribute ¼ of garlic herb mixture on each fish. Brush any remaining garlic herb mixture over the fish and fold the parchment over the fish. Fold and crimp the edges to seal tightly and place in a baking dish. 3. Bake about 10 minutes, until fish is cooked through. Remove from the oven, and serve with lemon wedges, allowing guests to open their own individual packages at the table.

Per Serving:
calories: 339 | fat: 26g | protein: 24g | carbs: 3g | fiber: 1g | sodium: 646mg

Simple Poached Turbot

Prep time: 10 minutes | Cook time: 50 minutes | Serves 4

1 cup vegetable or chicken stock	1 lemon, sliced
½ cup dry white wine	4 sprigs fresh dill
1 yellow onion, sliced	½ teaspoon sea salt
	4 (6-ounce / 170-g) turbot fillets

1. Combine the stock and wine in the slow cooker. Cover and heat on high for 20 to 30 minutes. 2. Add the onion, lemon, dill, salt, and turbot to the slow cooker. Cover and cook on high for about 20 minutes, until the turbot is opaque and cooked through according to taste. Serve hot.

Per Serving:
calories: 210 | fat: 5g | protein: 29g | carbs: 6g | fiber: 1g | sodium: 565mg

Roasted Sea Bass

Prep time: 5 minutes | Cook time: 15 minutes | Serves 6

¼ cup olive oil	¼ cup dry white wine
Whole sea bass or fillets	3 teaspoons fresh dill
Sea salt and freshly ground pepper, to taste	2 teaspoons fresh thyme
	1 garlic clove, minced

1. Preheat the oven to 425ºF (220ºC). 2. Brush the bottom of a roasting pan with olive oil. Place the fish in the pan and brush the fish with oil. 3. Season fish with sea salt and freshly ground pepper. Combine the remaining ingredients and pour over the fish. Bake for 10–15 minutes, depending on the size of the fish. Sea bass is done when the flesh is firm and opaque.

Per Serving:
calories: 217 | fat: 12g | protein: 24g | carbs: 1g | fiber: 0g | sodium: 88mg

Monkfish with Sautéed Leeks, Fennel, and Tomatoes

Prep time: 20 minutes | Cook time: 35 minutes | Serves 4

1 to 1½ pounds (454 to 680 g) monkfish	½ onion, julienned
3 tablespoons lemon juice, divided	3 garlic cloves, minced
1 teaspoon kosher salt, divided	2 bulbs fennel, cored and thinly sliced, plus ¼ cup fronds for garnish
⅛ teaspoon freshly ground black pepper	1 (14½-ounce / 411-g) can no-salt-added diced tomatoes
2 tablespoons extra-virgin olive oil	2 tablespoons fresh parsley, chopped
1 leek, white and light green parts only, sliced in half lengthwise and thinly sliced	2 tablespoons fresh oregano, chopped
	¼ teaspoon red pepper flakes

1. Place the fish in a medium baking dish and add 2 tablespoons of the lemon juice, ¼ teaspoon of the salt, and the black pepper. Place in the refrigerator. 2. Heat the olive oil in a large skillet or sauté pan over medium heat. Add the leek and onion and sauté until translucent, about 3 minutes. Add the garlic and sauté for 30 seconds. Add the fennel and sauté 4 to 5 minutes. Add the tomatoes and simmer for 2 to 3 minutes. 3. Stir in the parsley, oregano, red pepper flakes, the remaining ¾ teaspoon salt, and the remaining 1 tablespoon lemon juice. Place the fish on top of the leek mixture, cover, and simmer for 20 to 25 minutes, turning over halfway through, until the fish is opaque and pulls apart easily. Garnish with the fennel fronds.

Per Serving:
calories: 220 | fat: 9g | protein: 22g | carbs: 11g | fiber: 3g | sodium: 345mg

Balsamic Tilapia

Prep time: 5 minutes | Cook time: 15 minutes | Serves 4

4 tilapia fillets, boneless	1 teaspoon avocado oil
2 tablespoons balsamic vinegar	1 teaspoon dried basil

1. Sprinkle the tilapia fillets with balsamic vinegar, avocado oil, and dried basil. 2. Then put the fillets in the air fryer basket and cook at 365ºF (185ºC) for 15 minutes.

Per Serving:
calories: 129 | fat: 3g | protein: 23g | carbs: 1g | fiber: 0g | sodium: 92mg

Salmon Fritters with Zucchini

Prep time: 15 minutes | Cook time: 12 minutes | Serves 4

2 tablespoons almond flour	diced
1 zucchini, grated	1 teaspoon avocado oil
1 egg, beaten	½ teaspoon ground black pepper
6 ounces (170 g) salmon fillet,	

1. Mix almond flour with zucchini, egg, salmon, and ground black pepper. 2. Then make the fritters from the salmon mixture. 3. Sprinkle the air fryer basket with avocado oil and put the fritters inside. 4. Cook the fritters at 375ºF (191ºC) for 6 minutes per side.

Per Serving:
calories: 102 | fat: 4g | protein: 11g | carbs: 4g | fiber: 1g | sodium: 52mg

Apple Cider Mussels

Prep time: 10 minutes | Cook time: 2 minutes | Serves 5

2 pounds (907 g) mussels, cleaned, peeled	1 teaspoon ground cumin
1 teaspoon onion powder	1 tablespoon avocado oil
	¼ cup apple cider vinegar

1. Mix mussels with onion powder, ground cumin, avocado oil, and apple cider vinegar. 2. Put the mussels in the air fryer and cook at 395ºF (202ºC) for 2 minutes.

Per Serving:
calories: 187 | fat: 7g | protein: 22g | carbs: 7g | fiber: 0g | sodium: 521mg

Summer Mackerel Niçoise Platter

Prep time: 10 minutes | Cook time: 15 minutes | Serves 2

For the Dressing:
3 tablespoons red wine vinegar
4 tablespoons olive oil
1 teaspoon Dijon mustard
¼ teaspoon salt
Pinch freshly ground black pepper
For the Salad:
2 teaspoons salt

2 small red potatoes
1 cup tender green beans
2 cups baby greens
2 hard-boiled eggs
½ cup cherry tomatoes, halved
⅓ cup Niçoise olives
2 (4-ounce / 113-g) tins of mackerel fillets, drained

Make the Dressing: Combine the vinegar, olive oil, Dijon mustard, salt, and pepper in a lidded jar. Shake or whisk the dressing until thoroughly combined. Taste and add more salt and pepper to taste, if needed. Make the Salad: 1. Fill a large saucepan with about 3 inches of water, add salt, and bring to a boil. Add the potatoes and cook for 10 to 15 minutes, or until you can pierce them with a sharp knife, but they are still firm. 2. Remove the potatoes and add the green beans to the water. Reduce the heat and let the beans simmer for 5 minutes. 3. Place both the potatoes and green beans in a colander and run it under cold water until vegetables are cool. 4. Lay the baby greens on a large platter. 5. Slice the potatoes and arrange them on one section of the platter. Add the green beans to another section of the platter. Slice the hard-boiled eggs and arrange them in another section. 6. Continue with the tomatoes, olives, and mackerel fillets. Pour the dressing over the salad.

Per Serving:
calories: 657 | fat: 47g | protein: 25g | carbs: 38g | fiber: 7g | sodium: 355mg

South Indian Fried Fish

Prep time: 20 minutes | Cook time: 8 minutes | Serves 4

2 tablespoons olive oil
2 tablespoons fresh lime or lemon juice
1 teaspoon minced fresh ginger
1 clove garlic, minced
1 teaspoon ground turmeric

½ teaspoon kosher salt
¼ to ½ teaspoon cayenne pepper
1 pound (454 g) tilapia fillets (2 to 3 fillets)
Olive oil spray
Lime or lemon wedges (optional)

1. In a large bowl, combine the oil, lime juice, ginger, garlic, turmeric, salt, and cayenne. Stir until well combined; set aside. 2. Cut each tilapia fillet into three or four equal-size pieces. Add the fish to the bowl and gently mix until all of the fish is coated in the marinade. Marinate for 10 to 15 minutes at room temperature. (Don't marinate any longer or the acid in the lime juice will "cook" the fish.) 3. Spray the air fryer basket with olive oil spray. Place the fish in the basket and spray the fish. Set the air fryer to 325°F (163°C) for 3 minutes to partially cook the fish. Set the air fryer to 400°F (204°C) for 5 minutes to finish cooking and crisp up the fish. (Thinner pieces of fish will cook faster so you may want to check at the 3-minute mark of the second cooking time and remove those that are cooked through, and then add them back toward the end of the second cooking time to crisp.) 4. Carefully remove the fish from the basket. Serve hot, with lemon wedges if desired.

Per Serving:
calories: 175 | fat: 9g | protein: 23g | carbs: 2g | fiber: 0g | sodium: 350mg

Chapter 5 Poultry

Garlic Chicken (Shish Tawook)

Prep time: 15 minutes | Cook time: 15 minutes |
Serves 4 to 6

2 tablespoons garlic, minced
2 tablespoons tomato paste
1 teaspoon smoked paprika
½ cup lemon juice
½ cup extra-virgin olive oil
1½ teaspoons salt
½ teaspoon freshly ground

black pepper
2 pounds (907 g) boneless and
skinless chicken (breasts or
thighs)
Rice, tzatziki, or hummus, for
serving (optional)

1. In a large bowl, add the garlic, tomato paste, paprika, lemon juice, olive oil, salt, and pepper and whisk to combine. 2. Cut the chicken into ½-inch cubes and put them into the bowl; toss to coat with the marinade. Set aside for at least 10 minutes. 3. To grill, preheat the grill on high. Thread the chicken onto skewers and cook for 3 minutes per side, for a total of 9 minutes. 4. To cook in a pan, preheat the pan on high heat, add the chicken, and cook for 9 minutes, turning over the chicken using tongs. 5. Serve the chicken with rice, tzatziki, or hummus, if desired.

Per Serving:
calories: 350 | fat: 22g | protein: 34g | carbs: 3g | fiber: 0g | sodium: 586mg

Southward Pesto Stuffed Peppers

Prep time: 20 minutes | Cook time: 15 minutes |
Serves 4 to 6

Nonstick cooking spray
3 large bell peppers, halved
2 tablespoons extra-virgin olive
oil, plus more to garnish
¼ cup cooked chickpeas
½ shredded carrot
2 garlic cloves, minced
1 pound (454 g) ground turkey
or chicken
Salt
Freshly ground black pepper

1 cup cooked brown rice
½ cup halved cherry tomatoes
½ zucchini, chopped
1 tablespoon dried Italian herb
medley
2 tablespoons chopped black
olives
6 tablespoons prepared pesto
½ cup shredded Italian cheese
blend

1. Preheat the oven to 350°F(180°C). Lightly spray a medium-size casserole or glass baking dish with cooking spray. 2. Bring a medium pot of water to a boil and reduce to a steady simmer. Using tongs to lower the peppers in the water, simmer each pepper half for about 3 minutes, just to soften. Remove from the water and drain in a colander. 3. In a large sauté pan or skillet, heat the olive oil over medium-high heat and sauté the chickpeas and carrot for about 5 minutes, until tender. Add the garlic and sauté for 1 minute, until fragrant. Then add the turkey, season with salt and pepper, and toss

to cook evenly. 4. Just before the turkey is cooked through, add the rice, cherry tomatoes, zucchini, and herbs, and sauté an additional 5 to 7 minutes, until cooked through. 5. Remove from the heat and stir in the olives. Place the prepared pepper halves in the greased casserole dish. 6. Divide the filling evenly among the peppers. Top each pepper with 1 tablespoon of pesto and a sprinkle of Italian cheese. Bake the peppers for 7 to 10 minutes, until heated through. Allow the peppers to rest for 10 minutes before serving. Drizzle with a dash of your favorite olive oil and enjoy!

Per Serving:
calories: 546 | fat: 38g | protein: 26g | carbs: 28g | fiber: 5g | sodium: 493mg

Skillet Creamy Tarragon Chicken and Mushrooms

Prep time: 10 minutes | Cook time: 20 minutes | Serves 2

2 tablespoons olive oil, divided
½ medium onion, minced
4 ounces (113 g) baby bella
(cremini) mushrooms, sliced
2 small garlic cloves, minced
8 ounces (227 g) chicken cutlets
2 teaspoons tomato paste
2 teaspoons dried tarragon

2 cups low-sodium chicken
stock
6 ounces (170 g) pappardelle
pasta
¼ cup plain full-fat Greek
yogurt
Salt
Freshly ground black pepper

1. Heat 1 tablespoon of the olive oil in a sauté pan over medium-high heat. Add the onion and mushrooms and sauté for 5 minutes. Add the garlic and cook for 1 minute more. 2. Move the vegetables to the edges of the pan and add the remaining 1 tablespoon of olive oil to the center of the pan. Place the cutlets in the center and let them cook for about 3 minutes, or until they lift up easily and are golden brown on the bottom. 3. Flip the chicken and cook for another 3 minutes. 4. Mix in the tomato paste and tarragon. Add the chicken stock and stir well to combine everything. Bring the stock to a boil. 5. Add the pappardelle. Break up the pasta if needed to fit into the pan. Stir the noodles so they don't stick to the bottom of the pan. 6. Cover the sauté pan and reduce the heat to medium-low. Let the chicken and noodles simmer for 15 minutes, stirring occasionally, until the pasta is cooked and the liquid is mostly absorbed. If the liquid absorbs too quickly and the pasta isn't cooked, add more water or chicken stock, about ¼ cup at a time as needed. 7. Remove the pan from the heat. 8. Stir 2 tablespoons of the hot liquid from the pan into the yogurt. Pour the tempered yogurt into the pan and stir well to mix it into the sauce. Season with salt and pepper. 9. The sauce will tighten up as it cools, so if it seems too thick, add a few tablespoons of water.

Per Serving:
calories: 556 | fat: 18g | protein: 42g | carbs: 56g | fiber: 2g | sodium: 190mg

Bell Pepper and Tomato Chicken

Prep time: 15 minutes | Cook time: 5 hours | Serves 6 to 8

1 medium yellow onion, sliced thickly
1 bell pepper, any color, cored, seeded, and sliced thickly
4 cloves garlic, minced
6 ounces (170 g) pitted black olives, drained
1 (28-ounce / 794-g) can stewed tomatoes
1 (15-ounce / 425-g) can stewed tomatoes
1 (6-ounce / 170-g) can tomato paste
1 cup red or white wine
2 tablespoons lemon juice
4 to 6 boneless, skinless chicken breasts, cut in half
¼ cup chopped fresh parsley, or 2 tablespoons dried parsley
1 tablespoon dried basil
½ teaspoon ground nutmeg
Sea salt
Black pepper
1 tablespoon red pepper flakes (optional)

1. Place the onion, bell pepper, garlic, and olives in slow cooker. 2. Add the stewed tomatoes, tomato paste, wine, and lemon juice. Stir to combine. 3. Place the chicken pieces in the slow cooker. Make sure all the pieces are covered with the liquid. 4. Sprinkle with the parsley, basil, and nutmeg. Season with salt and black pepper, and add the red pepper flakes, if using. Cover and cook on high for 5 hours or on low for 8 hours. Make sure the chicken is cooked thoroughly. 5. Serve hot over cooked pasta of your choice or cooked spaghetti squash.

Per Serving:
calories: 280 | fat: 7g | protein: 34g | carbs: 15g | fiber: 5g | sodium: 423mg

Greek Roasted Lemon Chicken with Potatoes

Prep time: 10 minutes | Cook time: 1 hour 20 minutes | Serves 4

2 pounds (907 g) potatoes (russet or white varieties), peeled
1½ pounds (680 g) chicken pieces (breasts, thighs, legs)
1 cup wine (any variety), for rinsing
1½ teaspoons freshly ground black pepper, divided
2 tablespoons dried oregano, divided
1 teaspoon salt, divided
½ cup extra virgin olive oil
2 tablespoons fresh lemon juice
2 to 3 allspice berries
2 to 3 cloves
2 garlic cloves, cut into quarters

1. Preheat the oven to 375°F (190°C). Place the peeled potatoes in a large bowl and cover them with cold water. Set aside. 2. Rinse the chicken pieces with the wine, pat dry with paper towels, and transfer to a large plate. In a small bowl, mix 1 teaspoon of black pepper, 1 tablespoon of oregano, and ½ teaspoon of salt to make a rub. Apply the rub to the chicken pieces and then set aside. 3. Remove the potatoes from the water. Rinse and pat dry the potatoes, then cut them into wedges and then cut again into half wedges. Place them in a large bowl. 4. Add the olive oil, lemon juice, remaining tablespoon of the oregano, remaining ½ teaspoon of the black pepper, and remaining ½ teaspoon of salt to the potatoes. Mix until all the potatoes are coated with the spices and olive oil. 5. Transfer the potatoes to a large baking dish and spread them into a single layer. Place the chicken pieces on top of the potatoes

and then scatter the allspice berries, cloves, and garlic around the chicken. 6. Add hot water to one corner of the dish and then tilt the dish until the water is distributed throughout and fills about ¼ of the depth of the dish. (Do not pour the water directly over the potatoes because it will rinse off the olive oil and spices.) 7. Transfer to the oven and roast for 20 minutes, then reduce the oven temperature to 350°F (180°C) and roast for 1 more hour or until the potatoes and chicken are done. (If the water in the dish evaporates too quickly, add more hot water, ¼ cup at a time.) The potatoes are done when they have a golden color and a knife can be inserted easily. Serve hot. Store in the refrigerator for up to 3 days.

Per Serving:
calories: 629 | fat: 34g | protein: 38g | carbs: 43g | fiber: 3g | sodium: 761mg

Hot Goan-Style Coconut Chicken

Prep time: 20 minutes | Cook time: 4 to 6 hours | Serves 6

Spice Paste:
8 dried Kashmiri chiles, broken into pieces
2 tablespoons coriander seeds
2-inch piece cassia bark, broken into pieces
1 teaspoon black peppercorns
1 teaspoon cumin seeds
1 teaspoon fennel seeds
4 cloves
2 star anise
1 tablespoon poppy seeds
1 cup freshly grated coconut, or desiccated coconut shreds
6 garlic cloves
⅓ cup water
Chicken:
12 chicken thigh and drumstick pieces, on the bone, skinless
1 teaspoon salt (or to taste)
1 teaspoon turmeric
2 tablespoons coconut oil
2 medium onions, finely sliced
⅓ cup water
½ teaspoon ground nutmeg
2 teaspoons tamarind paste
Handful fresh coriander leaves, chopped for garnish
1 or 2 fresh red chiles, for garnish

Make the Spice Paste: 1. In a dry frying pan, roast the Kashmiri chiles, coriander seeds, cassia bark, peppercorns, cumin seeds, fennel seeds, cloves, and star anise until fragrant, about 1 minute. Add the poppy seeds and continue roasting for a few minutes. Then remove from the heat and leave to cool. 2. Once cooled, grind the toasted spices in your spice grinder and set aside. 3. In the same pan, add the dried coconut and toast it for 5 to 7 minutes, until it just starts to turn golden. 4. Transfer to a blender with the garlic, and add the water. Blend to make a thick, wet paste. 5. Add the ground spices and blend again to mix together. Make the Chicken: 6. In a large bowl, toss the chicken with the salt and turmeric. Marinate for 15 to 20 minutes. In the meantime, heat the slow cooker to high. 7. Heat the oil in a frying pan (or in the slow cooker if you have a sear setting). Cook the sliced onions for 10 minutes, and then add the spice and coconut paste. Cook until it becomes fragrant. 8. Transfer everything to the slow cooker. Add the chicken, then the water. Cover and cook on low for 6 hours, or on high for 4 hours. 9. Sprinkle in the nutmeg and stir in the tamarind paste. Cover and cook for another 5 minutes. 10. Garnish with fresh coriander leaves and whole red chiles to serve.

Per Serving:
calories: 583 | fat: 26g | protein: 77g | carbs: 7g | net carbs: 4g | sugars: 2g | fiber: 3g | sodium: 762mg | cholesterol: 363mg

Breaded Turkey Cutlets

Prep time: 5 minutes | Cook time: 8 minutes | Serves 4

½ cup whole wheat bread crumbs	⅛ teaspoon garlic powder
¼ teaspoon paprika	1 egg
¼ teaspoon salt	4 turkey breast cutlets
¼ teaspoon black pepper	Chopped fresh parsley, for serving
⅛ teaspoon dried sage	

1. Preheat the air fryer to 380°F(193°C). 2. In a medium shallow bowl, whisk together the bread crumbs, paprika, salt, black pepper, sage, and garlic powder. 3. In a separate medium shallow bowl, whisk the egg until frothy. 4. Dip each turkey cutlet into the egg mixture, then into the bread crumb mixture, coating the outside with the crumbs. Place the breaded turkey cutlets in a single layer in the bottom of the air fryer basket, making sure that they don't touch each other. 5. Bake for 4 minutes. Turn the cutlets over, then bake for 4 minutes more, or until the internal temperature reaches 165°F(74°C). Sprinkle on the parsley and serve.

Per Serving:
calories: 234 | fat: 5g | protein: 37g | carbs: 10g | fiber: 1g | sodium: 260mg

Hoisin Turkey Burgers

Prep time: 30 minutes | Cook time: 20 minutes | Serves 4

Olive oil	crumbs
1 pound (454 g) lean ground turkey	¼ cup hoisin sauce
¼ cup whole-wheat bread	2 tablespoons soy sauce
	4 whole-wheat buns

1. Spray the air fryer basket lightly with olive oil. 2. In a large bowl, mix together the turkey, bread crumbs, hoisin sauce, and soy sauce. 3. Form the mixture into 4 equal patties. Cover with plastic wrap and refrigerate the patties for 30 minutes. 4. Place the patties in the air fryer basket in a single layer. Spray the patties lightly with olive oil. 5. Air fry at 370ºF (188ºC) for 10 minutes. Flip the patties over, lightly spray with olive oil, and cook until golden brown, an additional 5 to 10 minutes. 6. Place the patties on buns and top with your choice of low-calorie burger toppings like sliced tomatoes, onions, and cabbage slaw.

Per Serving:
calories: 330 | fat: 13g | protein: 26g | carbs: 29g | fiber: 3g | sodium: 631mg

Chicken with Lettuce

Prep time: 15 minutes | Cook time: 14 minutes | Serves 4

1 pound (454 g) chicken breast tenders, chopped into bite-size pieces	thinly sliced
	1 tablespoon olive oil
½ onion, thinly sliced	1 tablespoon fajita seasoning
½ red bell pepper, seeded and thinly sliced	1 teaspoon kosher salt
	Juice of ½ lime
½ green bell pepper, seeded and	8 large lettuce leaves
	1 cup prepared guacamole

1. Preheat the air fryer to 400ºF (204ºC). 2. In a large bowl, combine the chicken, onion, and peppers. Drizzle with the olive oil and toss until thoroughly coated. Add the fajita seasoning and salt and toss again. 3. Working in batches if necessary, arrange the chicken and vegetables in a single layer in the air fryer basket. Pausing halfway through the cooking time to shake the basket, air fry for 14 minutes, or until the vegetables are tender and a thermometer inserted into the thickest piece of chicken registers 165ºF (74ºC). 4. Transfer the mixture to a serving platter and drizzle with the fresh lime juice. Serve with the lettuce leaves and top with the guacamole.

Per Serving:
calories: 273 | fat: 15g | protein: 27g | carbs: 9g | fiber: 5g | sodium: 723mg

Simply Terrific Turkey Meatballs

Prep time: 10 minutes | Cook time: 7 to 10 minutes | Serves 4

1 red bell pepper, seeded and coarsely chopped	ground turkey
	1 egg, lightly beaten
2 cloves garlic, coarsely chopped	½ cup grated Parmesan cheese
	1 teaspoon salt
¼ cup chopped fresh parsley	½ teaspoon freshly ground
1½ pounds (680 g) 85% lean	black pepper

1. Preheat the air fryer to 400ºF (204ºC). 2. In a food processor fitted with a metal blade, combine the bell pepper, garlic, and parsley. Pulse until finely chopped. Transfer the vegetables to a large mixing bowl. 3. Add the turkey, egg, Parmesan, salt, and black pepper. Mix gently until thoroughly combined. Shape the mixture into 1¼-inch meatballs. 4. Working in batches if necessary, arrange the meatballs in a single layer in the air fryer basket; coat lightly with olive oil spray. Pausing halfway through the cooking time to shake the basket, air fry for 7 to 10 minutes, until lightly browned and a thermometer inserted into the center of a meatball registers 165ºF (74ºC).

Per Serving:
calories: 388 | fat: 25g | protein: 34g | carbs: 5g | fiber: 1g | sodium: 527mg

Chicken Nuggets

Prep time: 10 minutes | Cook time: 15 minutes | Serves 4

1 pound (454 g) ground chicken thighs	1 large egg, whisked
	½ teaspoon salt
½ cup shredded Mozzarella cheese	¼ teaspoon dried oregano
	¼ teaspoon garlic powder

1. In a large bowl, combine all ingredients. Form mixture into twenty nugget shapes, about 2 tablespoons each. 2. Place nuggets into ungreased air fryer basket, working in batches if needed. Adjust the temperature to 375ºF (191ºC) and air fry for 15 minutes, turning nuggets halfway through cooking. Let cool 5 minutes before serving.

Per Serving:
calories: 195 | fat: 8g | protein: 28g | carbs: 1g | fiber: 0g | sodium: 419mg

Fried Chicken Breasts

Prep time: 30 minutes | Cook time: 12 to 14 minutes | Serves 4

1 pound (454 g) boneless, skinless chicken breasts
¾ cup dill pickle juice
¾ cup finely ground blanched almond flour
¾ cup finely grated Parmesan

cheese
½ teaspoon sea salt
½ teaspoon freshly ground black pepper
2 large eggs
Avocado oil spray

1. Place the chicken breasts in a zip-top bag or between two pieces of plastic wrap. Using a meat mallet or heavy skillet, pound the chicken to a uniform ½-inch thickness. 2. Place the chicken in a large bowl with the pickle juice. Cover and allow to brine in the refrigerator for up to 2 hours. 3. In a shallow dish, combine the almond flour, Parmesan cheese, salt, and pepper. In a separate, shallow bowl, beat the eggs. 4. Drain the chicken and pat it dry with paper towels. Dip in the eggs and then in the flour mixture, making sure to press the coating into the chicken. Spray both sides of the coated breasts with oil. 5. Spray the air fryer basket with oil and put the chicken inside. Set the temperature to 400ºF (204ºC) and air fry for 6 to 7 minutes. 6. Carefully flip the breasts with a spatula. Spray the breasts again with oil and continue cooking for 6 to 7 minutes more, until golden and crispy.

Per Serving:
calories: 319 | fat: 17g | protein: 37g | carbs: 5g | fiber: 3g | sodium: 399mg

Tahini Chicken Rice Bowls

Prep time: 10 minutes |Cook time: 15 minutes| Serves: 4

1 cup uncooked instant brown rice
¼ cup tahini or peanut butter (tahini for nut-free)
¼ cup 2% plain Greek yogurt
2 tablespoons chopped scallions, green and white parts (2 scallions)
1 tablespoon freshly squeezed lemon juice (from ½ medium lemon)
1 tablespoon water

1 teaspoon ground cumin
¾ teaspoon ground cinnamon
¼ teaspoon kosher or sea salt
2 cups chopped cooked chicken breast (about 1 pound / 454 g)
½ cup chopped dried apricots
2 cups peeled and chopped seedless cucumber (1 large cucumber)
4 teaspoons sesame seeds
Fresh mint leaves, for serving (optional)

1. Cook the brown rice according to the package instructions. 2. While the rice is cooking, in a medium bowl, mix together the tahini, yogurt, scallions, lemon juice, water, cumin, cinnamon, and salt. Transfer half the tahini mixture to another medium bowl. Mix the chicken into the first bowl. 3. When the rice is done, mix it into the second bowl of tahini (the one without the chicken). 4. To assemble, divide the chicken among four bowls. Spoon the rice mixture next to the chicken in each bowl. Next to the chicken, place the dried apricots, and in the remaining empty section, add the cucumbers. Sprinkle with sesame seeds, and top with mint, if desired, and serve.

Per Serving:
calories: 448 | fat: 13g | protein: 30g | carbs: 53g | fiber: 5g | sodium: 243mg

Niçoise Chicken

Prep time: 20 minutes | Cook time: 50 minutes | Serves 6

¼ cup olive oil
3 medium onions, coarsely chopped
3 cloves garlic, minced
4 pounds (1.8 kg) chicken breast from 1 cut-up chicken
5 Roma tomatoes, peeled and chopped
½ cup white wine
1 (14½-ounce / 411-g) can

chicken broth
½ cup black Niçoise olives, pitted
Juice of 1 lemon
¼ cup flat-leaf parsley, chopped
1 tablespoon fresh tarragon leaves, chopped
Sea salt and freshly ground pepper, to taste

1. Heat the olive oil in a deep saucepan or stew pot over medium heat. Cook the onions and garlic 5 minutes, or until tender and translucent. 2. Add the chicken and cook an additional 5 minutes to brown slightly. 3. Add the tomatoes, white wine, and chicken broth, cover, and simmer 30–45 minutes on medium-low heat, or until the chicken is tender and the sauce is thickened slightly. 4. Remove the lid and add the olives and lemon juice. 5. Cook an additional 10–15 minutes to thicken the sauce further. 6. Stir in the parsley and tarragon, and season to taste. Serve immediately with noodles or potatoes and a dark leafy salad.

Per Serving:
calories: 501 | fat: 15g | protein: 74g | carbs: 11g | fiber: 2g | sodium: 451mg

Punjabi Chicken Curry

Prep time: 20 minutes | Cook time: 4 to 6 hours | Serves 6

2 tablespoons vegetable oil
3 onions, finely diced
6 garlic cloves, finely chopped
1 heaped tablespoon freshly grated ginger
1 (14-ounce / 397-g) can plum tomatoes
1 teaspoon salt
1 teaspoon turmeric
1 teaspoon chili powder
Handful coriander stems, finely

chopped
3 fresh green chiles, finely chopped
12 pieces chicken, mixed thighs and drumsticks, or a whole chicken, skinned, trimmed, and chopped
2 teaspoons garam masala
Handful fresh coriander leaves, chopped

1. Heat the oil in a frying pan (or in the slow cooker if you have a sear setting). Add the diced onions and cook for 5 minutes. Add the garlic and continue to cook for 10 minutes until the onions are brown. 2. Heat the slow cooker to high and add the onion-and-garlic mixture. Stir in the ginger, tomatoes, salt, turmeric, chili powder, coriander stems, and chiles. 3. Add the chicken pieces. Cover and cook on low for 6 hours, or on high for 4 hours. 4. Once cooked, check the seasoning, and then stir in the garam masala and coriander leaves.

Per Serving:
calories: 298 | fat: 9g | protein: 35g | carbs: 19g | net carbs: 16g | sugars: 11g | fiber: 3g | sodium: 539mg | cholesterol: 103mg

Grilled Rosemary-Lemon Turkey Cutlets

Prep time: 10 minutes | Cook time: 30 minutes | Serves 4

2 tablespoons olive oil
2 tablespoons fresh lemon juice
1 teaspoon finely chopped fresh rosemary
1 clove garlic, minced
4 turkey cutlets (6 ounces / 170 g each), pounded to ¼' thickness

Kosher salt and ground black pepper, to taste
2 ripe tomatoes, diced
½ red onion, diced
1 tablespoon balsamic vinegar
2 cups (2 ounces / 57 g) baby arugula

1. In a large bowl, combine the oil, lemon juice, rosemary, and garlic. Add the turkey cutlets and let marinate at room temperature while you prepare the grill, about 20 minutes. 2. Coat a grill rack or grill pan with olive oil and prepare the grill to medium-high heat. 3. Season the turkey with the salt and pepper. Grill the cutlets until grill marks form and the turkey is cooked through, about 4 minutes per side. 4. Meanwhile, in a medium bowl, combine the tomatoes, onion, and vinegar and season to taste with the salt and pepper. 5. Top each cutlet with ½ cup baby arugula and a quarter of the tomato mixture.

Per Serving:
calories: 269 | fat: 8g | protein: 43g | carbs: 6g | fiber: 1g | sodium: 398mg

Harissa-Rubbed Cornish Game Hens

Prep time: 30 minutes | Cook time: 21 minutes | Serves 4

Harissa:
½ cup olive oil
6 cloves garlic, minced
2 tablespoons smoked paprika
1 tablespoon ground coriander
1 tablespoon ground cumin
1 teaspoon ground caraway

1 teaspoon kosher salt
½ to 1 teaspoon cayenne pepper
Hens:
½ cup yogurt
2 Cornish game hens, any giblets removed, split in half lengthwise

1. For the harissa: In a medium microwave-safe bowl, combine the oil, garlic, paprika, coriander, cumin, caraway, salt, and cayenne. Microwave on high for 1 minute, stirring halfway through the cooking time. (You can also heat this on the stovetop until the oil is hot and bubbling. Or, if you must use your air fryer for everything, cook it in the air fryer at 350ºF (177ºC) for 5 to 6 minutes, or until the paste is heated through.) 2. For the hens: In a small bowl, combine 1 to 2 tablespoons harissa and the yogurt. Whisk until well combined. Place the hen halves in a resealable plastic bag and pour the marinade over. Seal the bag and massage until all of the pieces are thoroughly coated. Marinate at room temperature for 30 minutes or in the refrigerator for up to 24 hours. 3. Arrange the hen halves in a single layer in the air fryer basket. (If you have a smaller air fryer, you may have to cook this in two batches.) Set the air fryer to 400ºF (204ºC) for 20 minutes. Use a meat thermometer to ensure the game hens have reached an internal temperature of 165ºF (74ºC).

Per Serving:
calories: 421 | fat: 33g | protein: 26g | carbs: 6g | fiber: 2g | sodium: 683mg

Chicken Piccata with Mushrooms

Prep time: 25 minutes | Cook time: 25 minutes | Serves 4

1 pound (454 g) thinly sliced chicken breasts
1½ teaspoons salt, divided
½ teaspoon freshly ground black pepper
¼ cup ground flaxseed
2 tablespoons almond flour
8 tablespoons extra-virgin olive oil, divided
4 tablespoons butter, divided

2 cups sliced mushrooms
½ cup dry white wine or chicken stock
¼ cup freshly squeezed lemon juice
¼ cup roughly chopped capers
Zucchini noodles, for serving
¼ cup chopped fresh flat-leaf Italian parsley, for garnish

1. Season the chicken with 1 teaspoon salt and the pepper. On a plate, combine the ground flaxseed and almond flour and dredge each chicken breast in the mixture. Set aside. 2. In a large skillet, heat 4 tablespoons olive oil and 1 tablespoon butter over medium-high heat. Working in batches if necessary, brown the chicken, 3 to 4 minutes per side. Remove from the skillet and keep warm. 3. Add the remaining 4 tablespoons olive oil and 1 tablespoon butter to the skillet along with mushrooms and sauté over medium heat until just tender, 6 to 8 minutes. 4. Add the white wine, lemon juice, capers, and remaining ½ teaspoon salt to the skillet and bring to a boil, whisking to incorporate any little browned bits that have stuck to the bottom of the skillet. Reduce the heat to low and whisk in the final 2 tablespoons butter. 5. Return the browned chicken to skillet, cover, and simmer over low heat until the chicken is cooked through and the sauce has thickened, 5 to 6 more minutes. 6. Serve chicken and mushrooms warm over zucchini noodles, spooning the mushroom sauce over top and garnishing with chopped parsley.

Per Serving:
calories: 596 | fat: 48g | protein: 30g | carbs: 8g | fiber: 4g | sodium: 862mg

Apricot-Glazed Turkey Tenderloin

Prep time: 20 minutes | Cook time: 30 minutes | Serves 4

Olive oil
¼ cup sugar-free apricot preserves
½ tablespoon spicy brown mustard

1½ pounds (680 g) turkey breast tenderloin
Salt and freshly ground black pepper, to taste

1. Spray the air fryer basket lightly with olive oil. 2. In a small bowl, combine the apricot preserves and mustard to make a paste. 3. Season the turkey with salt and pepper. Spread the apricot paste all over the turkey. 4. Place the turkey in the air fryer basket and lightly spray with olive oil. 5. Air fry at 370ºF (188ºC) for 15 minutes. Flip the turkey over and lightly spray with olive oil. Air fry until the internal temperature reaches at least 170ºF (77ºC), an additional 10 to 15 minutes. 6. Let the turkey rest for 10 minutes before slicing and serving.

Per Serving:
calories: 204 | fat: 3g | protein: 40g | carbs: 3g | fiber: 0g | sodium: 214mg

Chicken Cacciatore

Prep time: 20 minutes | Cook time: 1 hour 10 minutes | Serves 4 to6

2 tablespoons extra-virgin olive oil
½ cup diced carrots
2 garlic cloves, minced
½ cup chopped celery
2 onions, chopped
2 pounds (907 g) chicken tenders
2 (14½-ounce / 411-g) cans Italian seasoned diced tomatoes, drained
2 cups cooked corkscrew pasta, such as whole-grain fusilli

1. In a large saucepan, heat the oil over medium-high heat and sauté the carrots, garlic, celery, and onions for about 5 minutes, until softened. Add the chicken and brown for 4 to 5 minutes on each side. 2. Add the diced tomatoes. Cover and reduce heat to simmer for an hour. Serve over pasta.

Per Serving:
calories: 416 | fat: 3g | protein: 58g | carbs: 38g | fiber: 7g | sodium: 159mg

Crunchy Chicken Tenders

Prep time: 5 minutes | Cook time: 12 minutes | Serves 4

1 egg
¼ cup unsweetened almond milk
¼ cup whole wheat flour
¼ cup whole wheat bread crumbs
½ teaspoon salt
½ teaspoon black pepper
½ teaspoon dried thyme
½ teaspoon dried sage
½ teaspoon garlic powder
1 pound (454 g) chicken tenderloins
1 lemon, quartered

1. Preheat the air fryer to 360°F(182°C). 2. In a shallow bowl, beat together the egg and almond milk until frothy. 3. In a separate shallow bowl, whisk together the flour, bread crumbs, salt, pepper, thyme, sage, and garlic powder. 4. Dip each chicken tenderloin into the egg mixture, then into the bread crumb mixture, coating the outside with the crumbs. Place the breaded chicken tenderloins into the bottom of the air fryer basket in an even layer, making sure that they don't touch each other. 5. Cook for 6 minutes, then turn and cook for an additional 5 to 6 minutes. Serve with lemon slices.

Per Serving:
calories: 224 | fat: 7g | protein: 26g | carbs: 14g | fiber: 2g | sodium: 464mg

Honey-Glazed Chicken Thighs

Prep time: 5 minutes | Cook time: 14 minutes | Serves 4

Oil, for spraying
4 boneless, skinless chicken thighs, fat trimmed
3 tablespoons soy sauce
1 tablespoon balsamic vinegar
2 teaspoons honey
2 teaspoons minced garlic
1 teaspoon ground ginger

1. Preheat the air fryer to 400°F (204°C). Line the air fryer basket with parchment and spray lightly with oil. 2. Place the chicken in the prepared basket. 3. Cook for 7 minutes, flip, and cook for another 7 minutes, or until the internal temperature reaches 165°F (74°C) and the juices run clear. 4. In a small saucepan, combine the soy sauce, balsamic vinegar, honey, garlic, and ginger and cook over low heat for 1 to 2 minutes, until warmed through. 5. Transfer the chicken to a serving plate and drizzle with the sauce just before serving.

Per Serving:
calories: 286 | fat: 10g | protein: 39g | carbs: 7g | fiber: 0g | sodium: 365mg

Savory Chicken Meatballs

Prep time: 20 minutes | Cook time: 20 minutes | Serves 4

2 (1-pound / 454-g) boxes frozen chopped spinach, thawed
1 medium shallot, grated
1 pound (454 g) ground chicken
¾ cup crumbled feta cheese
2 tablespoons za'atar seasoning
¼ cup extra-virgin olive oil
4 whole-wheat pita bread rounds, for serving
Tzatziki, for serving
⅓ seedless cucumber, peeled and chopped, for serving

1. Preheat the oven to 400°F(205°C). 2. While the oven preheats, squeeze all the water out of the spinach until it's completely dry. Use paper towels to blot it if necessary. 3. In a bowl, fluff the spinach with a fork to separate clumps and add the grated shallot to the spinach. Add the chicken, feta, and za'atar seasoning to the spinach and shallots and drizzle with the olive oil. 4. Combine all the ingredients and form the mixture into 10 to 15 meatballs. Lightly flatten the meatballs (just so that they won't roll around) and place on a nonstick baking sheet. 5. Bake for 10 to 12 minutes, or until the meatballs are golden brown and cooked thoroughly. 6. Serve in a pita, topped with tzatziki and cucumbers.

Per Serving:
calories: 514 | fat: 31g | protein: 36g | carbs: 29g | fiber: 9g | sodium: 631mg

Za'atar Chicken

Prep time: 5 minutes | Cook time: 40 minutes | Serves 4 to 6

⅓ cup plus 1 tablespoon za'atar spice
2 tablespoons garlic, minced
⅓ cup lemon juice
⅓ cup extra-virgin olive oil
1 teaspoon salt
8 pieces chicken thighs and drumsticks, skin on

1. Preheat the oven to 400°F(205°C). 2. In a small bowl, combine the ⅓ cup za'atar spice with the garlic, lemon juice, olive oil, and salt. 3. Place the chicken in a baking dish, and pat dry with a paper towel. 4. Pour the za'atar mixture over the chicken, making sure the pieces are completely and evenly coated. 5. Put the chicken in the oven and cook for 40 minutes. 6. Once the chicken is done cooking, sprinkle it with the remaining tablespoon of za'atar spice. Serve with potatoes, rice, or salad.

Per Serving:
calories: 426 | fat: 23g | protein: 51g | carbs: 2g | fiber: 0g | sodium: 633mg

Coconut Chicken Meatballs

Prep time: 10 minutes | Cook time: 14 minutes | Serves 4

1 pound (454 g) ground chicken
2 scallions, finely chopped
1 cup chopped fresh cilantro leaves
¼ cup unsweetened shredded coconut
1 tablespoon hoisin sauce
1 tablespoon soy sauce
2 teaspoons Sriracha or other hot sauce
1 teaspoon toasted sesame oil
½ teaspoon kosher salt
1 teaspoon black pepper

1. In a large bowl, gently mix the chicken, scallions, cilantro, coconut, hoisin, soy sauce, Sriracha, sesame oil, salt, and pepper until thoroughly combined (the mixture will be wet and sticky). 2. Place a sheet of parchment paper in the air fryer basket. Using a small scoop or teaspoon, drop rounds of the mixture in a single layer onto the parchment paper. 3. Set the air fryer to 350ºF (177ºC) for 10 minutes, turning the meatballs halfway through the cooking time. Raise the air fryer temperature to 400ºF (204ºC) and cook for 4 minutes more to brown the outsides of the meatballs. Use a meat thermometer to ensure the meatballs have reached an internal temperature of 165ºF (74ºC). 4. Transfer the meatballs to a serving platter. Repeat with any remaining chicken mixture.
Per Serving:
calories: 213 | fat: 13g | protein: 21g | carbs: 4g | fiber: 1g | sodium: 501mg

Turkey Kofta Casserole

Prep time: 20 minutes | Cook time: 6 to 8 hours | Serves 4

For the Kofta:
2 pounds (907 g) raw ground turkey
1 small onion, diced
3 garlic cloves, minced
2 tablespoons chopped fresh parsley
1 tablespoon ground coriander
2 teaspoons ground cumin
1 teaspoon sea salt
1 teaspoon freshly ground black pepper
½ teaspoon ground nutmeg
½ teaspoon dried mint
½ teaspoon paprika
For the Casserole:
Nonstick cooking spray
4 large (about 2½ pounds / 1.1 kg) potatoes, peeled and cut into ¼-inch-thick rounds
4 large (about 3 pounds / 1.4 kg) tomatoes, cut into ¼-inch-thick rounds
Salt
Freshly ground black pepper
1 (8-ounce / 227-g) can no-salt-added, no-sugar-added tomato sauce

Make the Kofta: 1. In a large bowl, mix together the turkey, onion, garlic, parsley, coriander, cumin, salt, pepper, nutmeg, mint, and paprika until combined. 2. Form the kofta mixture into 13 to 15 equal patties, using about 2 to 3 tablespoons of the meat mixture per patty. Make the Casserole: 1. Coat a slow-cooker insert with cooking spray. 2. Layer the kofta patties, potatoes, and tomatoes in the prepared slow cooker, alternating the ingredients as you go, like a ratatouille. Season with salt and pepper. 3. Spread the tomato sauce over the ingredients. 4. Cover the cooker and cook for 6 to 8 hours on Low heat, or until the potatoes are tender.
Per Serving:
calories: 588 | fat: 17g | protein: 52g | carbs: 61g | fiber: 11g | sodium: 833mg

Chicken and Vegetable Fajitas

Prep time: 15 minutes | Cook time: 23 minutes | Serves 6

Chicken:
1 pound (454 g) boneless, skinless chicken thighs, cut crosswise into thirds
1 tablespoon vegetable oil
4½ teaspoons taco seasoning
Vegetables:
1 cup sliced onion
1 cup sliced bell pepper
1 or 2 jalapeños, quartered
lengthwise
1 tablespoon vegetable oil
½ teaspoon kosher salt
½ teaspoon ground cumin
For Serving:
Tortillas
Sour cream
Shredded cheese
Guacamole
Salsa

1. For the chicken: In a medium bowl, toss together the chicken, vegetable oil, and taco seasoning to coat. 2. For the vegetables: In a separate bowl, toss together the onion, bell pepper, jalapeño(s), vegetable oil, salt, and cumin to coat. 3. Place the chicken in the air fryer basket. Set the air fryer to 375ºF (191ºC) for 10 minutes. Add the vegetables to the basket, toss everything together to blend the seasonings, and set the air fryer for 13 minutes more. Use a meat thermometer to ensure the chicken has reached an internal temperature of 165ºF (74ºC). 4. Transfer the chicken and vegetables to a serving platter. Serve with tortillas and the desired fajita fixings.
Per Serving:
calories: 151 | fat: 8g | protein: 15g | carbs: 4g | fiber: 1g | sodium: 421mg

Tex-Mex Chicken Roll-Ups

Prep time: 10 minutes | Cook time: 14 to 17 minutes | Serves 8

2 pounds (907 g) boneless, skinless chicken breasts or thighs
1 teaspoon chili powder
½ teaspoon smoked paprika
½ teaspoon ground cumin
Sea salt and freshly ground
black pepper, to taste
6 ounces (170 g) Monterey Jack cheese, shredded
4 ounces (113 g) canned diced green chiles
Avocado oil spray

1. Place the chicken in a large zip-top bag or between two pieces of plastic wrap. Using a meat mallet or heavy skillet, pound the chicken until it is about ¼ inch thick. 2. In a small bowl, combine the chili powder, smoked paprika, cumin, and salt and pepper to taste. Sprinkle both sides of the chicken with the seasonings. 3. Sprinkle the chicken with the Monterey Jack cheese, then the diced green chiles. 4. Roll up each piece of chicken from the long side, tucking in the ends as you go. Secure the roll-up with a toothpick. 5. Set the air fryer to 350ºF (177ºC). Spray the outside of the chicken with avocado oil. Place the chicken in a single layer in the basket, working in batches if necessary, and roast for 7 minutes. Flip and cook for another 7 to 10 minutes, until an instant-read thermometer reads 160ºF (71ºC). 6. Remove the chicken from the air fryer and allow it to rest for about 5 minutes before serving.
Per Serving:
calories: 220 | fat: 10g | protein: 31g | carbs: 1g | fiber: 0g | sodium: 355mg

Cashew Chicken and Snap Peas

Prep time: 15 minutes | Cook time: 6 hours | Serves 2

16 ounces (454 g) boneless, skinless chicken breasts, cut into 2-inch pieces
2 cups sugar snap peas, strings removed
1 teaspoon grated fresh ginger
1 teaspoon minced garlic
2 tablespoons low-sodium soy sauce

1 tablespoon ketchup
1 tablespoon rice vinegar
1 teaspoon honey
Pinch red pepper flakes
¼ cup toasted cashews
1 scallion, white and green parts, sliced thin

1. Put the chicken and sugar snap peas into the slow cooker. 2. In a measuring cup or small bowl, whisk together the ginger, garlic, soy sauce, ketchup, vinegar, honey, and red pepper flakes. Pour the mixture over the chicken and snap peas. 3. Cover and cook on low for 6 hours. The chicken should be cooked through, and the snap peas should be tender, but not mushy. 4. Just before serving, stir in the cashews and scallions.

Per Serving:
calories: 463 | fat: 14g | protein: 59g | carbs: 23g | net carbs: 18g | sugars: 6g | fiber: 5g | sodium: 699mg | cholesterol: 126mg

Crispy Mediterranean Chicken Thighs

Prep time: 5 minutes | Cook time: 30 to 35 minutes | Serves 6

2 tablespoons extra-virgin olive oil
2 teaspoons dried rosemary
1½ teaspoons ground cumin
1½ teaspoons ground coriander

¾ teaspoon dried oregano
⅛ teaspoon salt
6 bone-in, skin-on chicken thighs (about 3 pounds / 1.4 kg)

1. Preheat the oven to 450ºF (235ºC). Line a baking sheet with parchment paper. 2. Place the olive oil and spices into a large bowl and mix together, making a paste. Add the chicken and mix together until evenly coated. Place on the prepared baking sheet. 3. Bake for 30 to 35 minutes, or until golden brown and the chicken registers an internal temperature of 165ºF (74ºC).

Per Serving:
calories: 440 | fat: 34g | protein: 30g | carbs: 1g | fiber: 0g | sodium: 180mg

Chapter 6 Beans and Grains

Greek Baked Beans

Prep time: 5 minutes | Cook time: 30 minutes | Serves 4

Olive oil cooking spray
1 (15-ounce/ 425-g) can cannellini beans, drained and rinsed
1 (15-ounce/ 425-g) can great northern beans, drained and rinsed
½ yellow onion, diced
1 (8-ounce/ 227-g) can tomato sauce
1½ tablespoons raw honey

¼ cup olive oil
2 garlic cloves, minced
2 tablespoons chopped fresh dill
½ teaspoon salt
½ teaspoon black pepper
1 bay leaf
1 tablespoon balsamic vinegar
2 ounces (57 g) feta cheese, crumbled, for serving

1. Preheat the air fryer to 360°F(182°C). Lightly coat the inside of a 5-cup capacity casserole dish with olive oil cooking spray. (The shape of the casserole dish will depend upon the size of the air fryer, but it needs to be able to hold at least 5 cups.) 2. In a large bowl, combine all ingredients except the feta cheese and stir until well combined. 3. Pour the bean mixture into the prepared casserole dish. 4. Bake in the air fryer for 30 minutes. 5. Remove from the air fryer and remove and discard the bay leaf. Sprinkle crumbled feta over the top before serving.
Per Serving:
calories: 336 | fat: 19g | protein: 11g | carbs: 34g | fiber: 9.4g | sodium: 497mg

Chicken Artichoke Rice Bake

Prep time: 10 minutes | Cook time: 3 to 5 hours |
Serves 4

Nonstick cooking spray
1 cup raw long-grain brown rice, rinsed
2½ cups low-sodium chicken broth
1 (14-ounce/ 397-g) can artichoke hearts, drained and rinsed
½ small onion, diced

2 garlic cloves, minced
10 ounces (283 g) fresh spinach, chopped
1 teaspoon dried thyme
½ teaspoon sea salt
½ teaspoon freshly ground black pepper
1 pound (454 g) boneless, skinless chicken breast

1. Generously coat a slow-cooker insert with cooking spray. Put the rice, chicken broth, artichoke hearts, onion, garlic, spinach, thyme, salt, and pepper in a slow cooker. Gently stir to mix well. 2. Place the chicken on top of the rice mixture. 3. Cover the cooker and cook for 3 to 5 hours on Low heat. 4. Remove the chicken from the cooker, shred it, and stir it back into the rice in the cooker.
Per Serving:
calories: 323 | fat: 4g | protein: 32g | carbs: 44g | fiber: 6g | sodium: 741mg

Brown Rice with Dried Fruit

Prep time: 15 minutes | Cook time: 20 minutes | Serves 6

2 tablespoons olive oil
2 stalks celery, thinly sliced
2 large carrots, peeled and diced
1 large sweet potato, peeled and diced
1½ cups brown rice
⅓ cup chopped prunes

⅓ cup chopped dried apricots
½ teaspoon ground cinnamon
2 teaspoons grated orange zest
3 cups water
1 bay leaf
½ teaspoon salt

1. Press the Sauté button on the Instant Pot® and heat oil. Add celery, carrots, sweet potato, and rice. Cook until vegetables are just tender, about 3 minutes. Stir in prunes, apricots, cinnamon, and orange zest. Cook until cinnamon is fragrant, about 30 seconds. Add water, bay leaf, and salt. 2. Press the Cancel button, close lid, set steam release to Sealing, press the Manual button, and set time to 16 minutes. When the timer beeps, let pressure release naturally for 10 minutes. Quick-release any remaining pressure until the float valve drops and open the lid. Fluff rice with a fork. 3. Remove and discard bay leaf. Transfer to a serving bowl. Serve hot.
Per Serving:
calories: 192 | fat: 5g | protein: 3g | carbs: 34g | fiber: 4g | sodium: 272mg

Garlicky Split Chickpea Curry

Prep time: 10 minutes | Cook time: 4 to 6 hours |
Serves 6

1½ cups split gram
1 onion, finely chopped
2 tomatoes, chopped
1 tablespoon freshly grated ginger
1 teaspoon cumin seeds, ground or crushed with a mortar and pestle
2 teaspoons turmeric
2 garlic cloves, crushed

1 hot green Thai or other fresh chile, thinly sliced
3 cups hot water
1 teaspoon salt
2 tablespoons rapeseed oil
1 teaspoon cumin seeds, crushed
1 garlic clove, sliced
1 fresh green chile, sliced

1. Heat the slow cooker to high. Add the split gram, onion, tomatoes, ginger, crushed cumin seeds, turmeric, crushed garlic, hot chile, water, and salt, and then stir. 2. Cover and cook on high for 4 hours, or on low for 6 hours, until the split gram is tender. 3. Just before serving, heat the oil in a saucepan. When the oil is hot, add the cumin seeds with the sliced garlic. Cook until the garlic is golden brown, and then pour it over the dhal. 4. To serve, top with the sliced green chile.
Per Serving:
calories: 119 | fat: 5g | protein: 4g | carbs: 15g | net carbs: 12g | sugars: 7g | fiber: 3g | sodium: 503mg | cholesterol: 1mg

Kale with Chickpeas

Prep time: 10 minutes | Cook time: 4 to 6 hours | Serves 6

1 to 2 tablespoons rapeseed oil	1 teaspoon turmeric
½ teaspoon mustard seeds	1 teaspoon salt
1 teaspoon cumin seeds	2 (16-ounce / 454-g) cans
1 large onion, diced	cooked chickpeas, drained and
4 garlic cloves, crushed	rinsed
4 plum tomatoes, finely	¾ cup water
chopped	7 to 8 ounces (198 to 227 g)
1 heaped teaspoon coriander	kale, chopped
seeds, ground	1 fresh green chile, sliced, for
1 fresh green chile, chopped	garnish
1 teaspoon chili powder	

1. Heat the oil in a frying pan (or in the slow cooker if you have a sear setting). When it's hot add the mustard seeds and then the cumin seeds until they pop and become fragrant. 2. Add the diced onion and cook, stirring, for 10 minutes. Add the garlic and cook for a few minutes. Then add the tomatoes. Add the ground coriander seeds, green chile, chili powder, turmeric, and salt. 3. Add the chickpeas and water. Cover and cook on low for 6 hours, or on high for 4 hours. 4. Add the chopped kale, a handful at a time, stirring between. Leave this to cook for another 10 to 15 minutes, until the kale is soft and tender. 5. Top with the sliced chile.

Per Serving:
calories: 202 | fat: 6g | protein: 10g | carbs: 30g | net carbs: 20g | sugars: 8g | fiber: 10g | sodium: 619mg | cholesterol: 0mg

Two-Bean Bulgur Chili

Prep time: 10 minutes | Cook time: 30 minutes | Serves 4 to 5

2 tablespoons olive oil	2 teaspoons dried oregano
1 onion, diced	2 teaspoons ground cumin
2 celery stalks, diced	1 (15-ounce/ 425-g) can black
1 carrot, diced	beans, drained and rinsed
1 jalapeño pepper, seeded and	1 (15-ounce/ 425-g) can
chopped	cannellini beans, drained and
3 garlic cloves, minced	rinsed
1 (28-ounce/ 794-g) can diced	¾ cup dried bulgur
tomatoes	4 cups chicken broth
1 tablespoon tomato paste	Sea salt
1½ teaspoons chili powder	Freshly ground black pepper

1. In a Dutch oven, heat the olive oil over medium-high heat. Add the onion, celery, carrot, jalapeño, and garlic and sauté until the vegetables are tender, about 4 minutes. 2. Reduce the heat to medium and add the diced tomatoes, tomato paste, chili powder, oregano, and cumin. Cook for 3 minutes, then add the black beans, cannellini beans, bulgur, and broth. 3. Increase the heat to high, cover, and bring to a boil. Reduce the heat to low and simmer until the chili is cooked to your desired thickness, about 30 minutes. Season with salt and black pepper and serve.

Per Serving:
calories: 385 | fat: 9g | protein: 16g | carbs: 64g | fiber: 20g | sodium: 325mg

Sweet Potato Black Bean Burgers

Prep time: 10 minutes | Cook time: 10 minutes | Serves 4

1 (15-ounce/ 425-g) can black	¼ to ½ cup whole wheat bread
beans, drained and rinsed	crumbs
1 cup mashed sweet potato	1 tablespoon olive oil
½ teaspoon dried oregano	For serving:
¼ teaspoon dried thyme	Whole wheat buns or whole
¼ teaspoon dried marjoram	wheat pitas
1 garlic clove, minced	Plain Greek yogurt
¼ teaspoon salt	Avocado
¼ teaspoon black pepper	Lettuce
1 tablespoon lemon juice	Tomato
1 cup cooked brown rice	Red onion

1. Preheat the air fryer to 380°F(193ºC). 2. In a large bowl, use the back of a fork to mash the black beans until there are no large pieces left. 3. Add the mashed sweet potato, oregano, thyme, marjoram, garlic, salt, pepper, and lemon juice, and mix until well combined. 4. Stir in the cooked rice. 5. Add in ¼ cup of the whole wheat bread crumbs and stir. Check to see if the mixture is dry enough to form patties. If it seems too wet and loose, add an additional ¼ cup bread crumbs and stir. 6. Form the dough into 4 patties. Place them into the air fryer basket in a single layer, making sure that they don't touch each other. 7. Brush half of the olive oil onto the patties and bake for 5 minutes. 8. Flip the patties over, brush the other side with the remaining oil, and bake for an additional 4 to 5 minutes. 9. Serve on toasted whole wheat buns or whole wheat pitas with a spoonful of yogurt and avocado, lettuce, tomato, and red onion as desired.

Per Serving:
calories: 112 | fat: 4.3g | protein: 2.8g | carbs: 17g | fiber: 3g | sodium: 161mg

Sun-Dried Tomato Rice

Prep time: 10 minutes | Cook time: 30 minutes | Serves 8

2 tablespoons extra-virgin olive	1 tablespoon tomato paste
oil	2 cups brown rice
½ medium yellow onion, peeled	2¼ cups water
and chopped	½ cup chopped fresh basil
2 cloves garlic, peeled and	¼ teaspoon salt
minced	½ teaspoon ground black
1 cup chopped sun-dried	pepper
tomatoes in oil, drained	

1. Press the Sauté button on the Instant Pot® and heat oil. Add onion and cook until soft, about 6 minutes. Add garlic and sun-dried tomatoes and cook until fragrant, about 30 seconds. Add tomato paste, rice, and water, and stir well. Press the Cancel button. 2. Close lid, set steam release to Sealing, press the Manual button, and set time to 22 minutes. When the timer beeps, let pressure release naturally for 10 minutes, then quick-release the remaining pressure. Open lid and fold in basil. Season with salt and pepper. Serve warm.

Per Serving:
calories: 114 | fat: 4g | protein: 2g | carbs: 18g | fiber: 2g | sodium: 112mg

Sweet Potato and Chickpea Moroccan Stew

Prep time: 10 minutes | Cook time: 40 minutes | Serves 4

6 tablespoons extra virgin olive oil

2 medium red or white onions, finely chopped

6 garlic cloves, minced

3 medium carrots (about 8 ounces /227 g), peeled and cubed

1 teaspoon ground cumin

1 teaspoon ground coriander

½ teaspoon smoked paprika

½ teaspoon ground turmeric

1 cinnamon stick

½ pound (227 g) butternut squash, peeled and cut into

½-inch cubes

2 medium sweet potatoes, peeled and cut into ½-inch cubes

4 ounces (113 g) prunes, pitted

4 tomatoes (any variety), chopped, or 20 ounces (567g) canned chopped tomatoes

14 ounces (397 g) vegetable broth

14 ounces (397 g) canned chickpeas

½ cup chopped fresh parsley, for serving

1. Place a deep pan over medium heat and add the olive oil. When the oil is shimmering, add the onions and sauté for 5 minutes, then add the garlic and carrots, and sauté for 1 more minute. 2. Add the cumin, coriander, paprika, turmeric, and cinnamon stick. Continue cooking, stirring continuously, for 1 minute, then add the squash, sweet potatoes, prunes, tomatoes, and vegetable broth. Stir, cover, then reduce the heat to low and simmer for 20 minutes, stirring occasionally and checking the water levels, until the vegetables are cooked through. (If the stew appears to be drying out, add small amounts of hot water until the stew is thick.) 3. Add the chickpeas to the pan, stir, and continue simmering for 10 more minutes, adding more water if necessary. Remove the pan from the heat, discard the cinnamon stick, and set the stew aside to cool for 10 minutes. 4. When ready to serve, sprinkle the chopped parsley over the top of the stew. Store covered in the refrigerator for up to 4 days.

Per Serving:
calories: 471 | fat: 23g | protein: 9g | carbs: 63g | fiber: 12g | sodium: 651mg

Lentils in Tomato Sauce

Prep time: 10 minutes | Cook time: 11 minutes | Serves 6

2 cups red, green, or brown dried lentils, rinsed and drained

½ teaspoon salt

4 cups water

1 (24-ounce / 680-g) jar marinara sauce

1 tablespoon extra-virgin olive oil

1 tablespoon chopped fresh oregano

1 teaspoon ground fennel

¼ teaspoon ground black pepper

½ cup grated Parmesan cheese

½ cup minced fresh flat-leaf parsley

1. Add lentils, salt, and water to the Instant Pot®. Close lid, set steam release to Sealing, press the Manual button, and set time to 6 minutes. When the timer beeps, quick-release the pressure until the float valve drops. Press the Cancel button. Open lid and drain off any excess liquid. 2. Add sauce, oil, oregano, fennel, and pepper to pot and stir well. Close lid, set steam release to Sealing, press the Manual button, and set time to 5 minutes. When the timer beeps, let pressure release naturally for 10 minutes, then quick-release any remaining pressure until the float valve drops. Open lid and top with cheese and parsley.

Per Serving:
calories: 342 | fat: 8g | protein: 21g | carbs: 48g | fiber: 9g | sodium: 640mg

Herbed Wild Rice Dressing

Prep time: 15 minutes | Cook time: 32 minutes | Serves 8

2 tablespoons extra-virgin olive oil

2 stalks celery, chopped

1 medium white onion, peeled and chopped

1 medium carrot, peeled and chopped

2 cups sliced baby bella mushrooms

2 cloves garlic, peeled and minced

1 tablespoon chopped fresh rosemary

1 tablespoon chopped fresh sage

¼ teaspoon salt

½ teaspoon ground black pepper

2 cups wild rice

2½ cups vegetable broth

½ cup dried cranberries

½ cup chopped toasted pecans

1. Press the Sauté button on the Instant Pot® and heat oil. Add celery, onion, carrot, and mushrooms. Cook until soft, about 10 minutes. Add garlic, rosemary, sage, salt, and pepper. Cook until fragrant, about 1 minute. Add rice and mix well. Press the Cancel button. 2. Stir in broth. Close lid, set steam release to Sealing, press the Manual button, and set time to 20 minutes. When the timer beeps, let pressure release naturally for 10 minutes, then quick-release the remaining pressure. Open lid and fold in cranberries and pecans. Serve warm.

Per Serving:
calories: 356 | fat: 13g | protein: 9g | carbs: 50g | fiber: 5g | sodium: 147mg

Asparagus-Spinach Farro

Prep time: 5 minutes | Cook time: 16 minutes | Serves 4

2 tablespoons olive oil

1 cup quick-cooking farro

½ shallot, finely chopped

4 garlic cloves, minced

Sea salt

Freshly ground black pepper

2½ cups water, vegetable broth,

or chicken broth

8 ounces (227 g) asparagus, woody ends trimmed, cut into 2-inch pieces

3 ounces (85 g) fresh baby spinach

½ cup grated Parmesan cheese

1. In a large skillet, heat the olive oil over medium-high heat. Add the farro, shallot, and garlic, season with salt and pepper, and cook for about 4 minutes. Add the water and bring the mixture to a boil. Reduce the heat to low, cover, and simmer for 10 minutes (or for the time recommended on the package of farro). 2. Add the asparagus and cook until tender, about 5 minutes. Add the spinach and cook for 30 seconds more, or until wilted. 3. Top with the Parmesan and serve.

Per Serving:
calories: 277 | fat: 11g | protein: 10g | carbs: 38g | fiber: 7g | sodium: 284mg

Black Beans with Corn and Tomato Relish

Prep time: 20 minutes | Cook time: 30 minutes | Serves 6

½ pound (227 g) dried black beans, soaked overnight and drained
1 medium white onion, peeled and sliced in half
2 cloves garlic, peeled and lightly crushed
8 cups water
1 cup corn kernels
1 large tomato, seeded and chopped
½ medium red onion, peeled and chopped
¼ cup minced fresh cilantro
½ teaspoon ground cumin
¼ teaspoon smoked paprika
¼ teaspoon ground black pepper
¼ teaspoon salt
3 tablespoons extra-virgin olive oil
3 tablespoons lime juice

1. Add beans, white onion, garlic, and water to the Instant Pot®. Close lid, set steam release to Sealing, press the Bean button, and cook for the default time of 30 minutes. When the timer beeps, let pressure release naturally, about 20 minutes. 2. Open lid and remove and discard onion and garlic. Drain beans well and transfer to a medium bowl. Cool to room temperature, about 30 minutes. 3. In a separate small bowl, combine corn, tomato, red onion, cilantro, cumin, paprika, pepper, and salt. Toss to combine. Add to black beans and gently fold to mix. Whisk together olive oil and lime juice in a small bowl and pour over black bean mixture. Gently toss to coat. Serve at room temperature or refrigerate for at least 2 hours.

Per Serving:
calories: 216 | fat: 7g | protein: 8g | carbs: 28g | fiber: 6g | sodium: 192mg

Baked Mushroom-Barley Pilaf

Prep time: 5 minutes | Cook time: 37 minutes | Serves 4

Olive oil cooking spray
2 tablespoons olive oil
8 ounces (227 g) button mushrooms, diced
½ yellow onion, diced
2 garlic cloves, minced
1 cup pearl barley
2 cups vegetable broth
1 tablespoon fresh thyme, chopped
½ teaspoon salt
¼ teaspoon smoked paprika
Fresh parsley, for garnish

1. Preheat the air fryer to 380°F(193°C). Lightly coat the inside of a 5-cup capacity casserole dish with olive oil cooking spray. (The shape of the casserole dish will depend upon the size of the air fryer, but it needs to be able to hold at least 5 cups.) 2. In a large skillet, heat the olive oil over medium heat. Add the mushrooms and onion and cook, stirring occasionally, for 5 minutes, or until the mushrooms begin to brown. 3. Add the garlic and cook for an additional 2 minutes. Transfer the vegetables to a large bowl. 4. Add the barley, broth, thyme, salt, and paprika. 5. Pour the barley-and-vegetable mixture into the prepared casserole dish, and place the dish into the air fryer. Bake for 15 minutes. 6. Stir the barley mixture. Reduce the heat to 360°F(182°C), then return the barley to the air fryer and bake for 15 minutes more. 7. Remove from the air fryer and let sit for 5 minutes before fluffing with a fork and topping with fresh parsley.

Per Serving:
calories: 428 | fat: 9.2g | protein: 10.7g | carbs: 84.7g | fiber: 9.2g | sodium: 775mg

Brown Rice Vegetable Bowl with Roasted Red Pepper Dressing

Prep time: 10 minutes | Cook time: 22 minutes | Serves 2

¼ cup chopped roasted red bell pepper
2 tablespoons extra-virgin olive oil
1 tablespoon red wine vinegar
1 teaspoon honey
2 tablespoons light olive oil
2 cloves garlic, peeled and minced
½ teaspoon ground black pepper
¼ teaspoon salt
1 cup brown rice
1 cup vegetable broth
¼ cup chopped fresh flat-leaf parsley
2 tablespoons chopped fresh chives
2 tablespoons chopped fresh dill
½ cup diced tomato
½ cup chopped red onion
½ cup diced cucumber
½ cup chopped green bell pepper

1. Place roasted red pepper, extra-virgin olive oil, red wine vinegar, and honey in a blender. Purée until smooth, about 1 minute. Refrigerate until ready to serve. 2. Press the Sauté button on the Instant Pot® and heat light olive oil. Add garlic and cook until fragrant, about 30 seconds. Add black pepper, salt, and rice and stir well. Press the Cancel button. 3. Stir in broth. Close lid, set steam release to Sealing, press the Manual button, and set time to 22 minutes.

Per Serving:
calories: 561 | fat: 23g | protein: 10g | carbs: 86g | fiber: 5g | sodium: 505mg

Lentils with Artichoke, Tomato, and Feta

Prep time: 10 minutes | Cook time: 12 minutes | Serves 6

2 cups dried red lentils, rinsed and drained
½ teaspoon salt
4 cups water
1 (12-ounce / 340-g) jar marinated artichokes, drained and chopped
2 medium vine-ripe tomatoes, chopped
½ medium red onion, peeled and diced
½ large English cucumber, diced
½ cup crumbled feta cheese
¼ cup chopped fresh flat-leaf parsley
3 tablespoons extra-virgin olive oil
2 tablespoons balsamic vinegar
½ teaspoon ground black pepper

1. Add lentils, salt, and water to the Instant Pot®. Close lid, set steam release to Sealing, press the Manual button, and set time to 12 minutes. When the timer beeps, quick-release the pressure until the float valve drops. Open lid and drain off any excess liquid. Let lentils cool to room temperature, about 30 minutes. 2. Add artichokes, tomatoes, onion, cucumber, feta, parsley, oil, vinegar, and pepper, and toss to mix. Transfer to a serving bowl. Serve at room temperature or refrigerate for at least 2 hours.

Per Serving:
calories: 332 | fat: 13g | protein: 17g | carbs: 40g | fiber: 6g | sodium: 552mg

Southwestern Rice Casserole

Prep time: 20 minutes | Cook time: 4 to 6 hours | Serves 2

1 teaspoon extra-virgin olive oil	1 teaspoon dried oregano
1 cup brown rice	⅛ teaspoon cayenne pepper
1 cup canned black beans, drained and rinsed	⅛ teaspoon sea salt
1 cup frozen corn, thawed	1½ cups low-sodium vegetable broth or water
1 cup canned fire-roasted diced tomatoes, undrained	¼ cup fresh cilantro
	¼ cup sharp cheddar cheese

1. Grease the inside of the slow cooker with the olive oil. 2. Add the brown rice, beans, corn, tomatoes, oregano, cayenne, and salt. Pour in the broth and stir to mix thoroughly. 3. Cover and cook on low for 4 to 6 hours. 4. Stir in the cilantro and cheddar cheese before serving.

Per Serving:
calories: 681 | fat: 12g | protein: 25g | carbs: 126g | net carbs: 109g | sugars: 11g | fiber: 17g | sodium: 490mg | cholesterol: 140mg

Pesto Rice with Olives and Goat Cheese

Prep time: 5 minutes | Cook time: 22 minutes | Serves 8

2 cups brown basmati rice	½ cup chopped mixed olives
2¼ cups vegetable broth	¼ cup chopped fresh basil
½ cup pesto	¼ cup crumbled goat cheese

1. Place rice, broth, and pesto in the Instant Pot® and stir well. Close lid, set steam release to Sealing, press the Manual button, and set time to 22 minutes. 2. When the timer beeps, let pressure release naturally for 10 minutes, then quick-release the remaining pressure. Open lid, add olives and basil, and fluff rice with a fork. Serve warm, topped with goat cheese.

Per Serving:
calories: 219 | fat: 6g | protein: 6g | carbs: 36g | fiber: 1g | sodium: 148mg

Quinoa Salad in Endive Boats

Prep time: 10 minutes | Cook time: 3 minutes | Serves 4

1 tablespoon walnut oil	½ small red onion, peeled and thinly sliced
1 cup quinoa, rinsed and drained	2 tablespoons olive oil
2½ cups water	1 tablespoon balsamic vinegar
2 cups chopped jarred artichoke hearts	4 large Belgian endive leaves
2 cups diced tomatoes	1 cup toasted pecans

1. Press the Sauté button on the Instant Pot® and heat walnut oil. Add quinoa and toss for 1 minute until slightly browned. Add water and stir. Press the Cancel button. 2. Close lid, set steam release to Sealing, press the Manual button, and set time to 2 minutes. When the timer beeps, let pressure release naturally for 10 minutes. Quick-release any remaining pressure until the float valve drops and open lid. Drain liquid and transfer quinoa to a serving bowl. 3. Add artichoke hearts, tomatoes, onion, olive oil, and vinegar to

quinoa and stir to combine. Cover and refrigerate mixture for 1 hour or up to overnight. 4. Place endive leaves on four plates. Top each with ¼ cup quinoa mixture. Sprinkle toasted pecans over the top of each endive boat and serve.

Per Serving:
calories: 536 | fat: 35g | protein: 13g | carbs: 46g | fiber: 13g | sodium: 657mg

Mediterranean Lentil Casserole

Prep time: 15 minutes | Cook time: 8 to 10 hours | Serves 6

1 pound (454 g) lentils, rinsed well under cold water and picked over to remove debris	1 small onion, diced
	2 garlic cloves, minced
4 cups low-sodium vegetable broth	1 teaspoon sea salt
	1 teaspoon dried basil
3 carrots, diced	1 teaspoon dried oregano
3 cups chopped kale	½ teaspoon dried parsley
	1 lemon, thinly sliced

1. In a slow cooker, combine the lentils, vegetable broth, carrots, kale, onion, garlic, salt, basil, oregano, and parsley. Stir to mix well. 2. Cover the cooker and cook for 8 to 10 hours on Low heat, or until the lentils are tender. 3. Garnish with lemon slices for serving.

Per Serving:
calories: 302 | fat: 2g | protein: 22g | carbs: 54g | fiber: 26g | sodium: 527mg

Lemon Farro Bowl with Avocado

Prep time: 5 minutes | Cook time: 25 minutes | Serves: 6

1 tablespoon plus 2 teaspoons extra-virgin olive oil, divided	added vegetable broth
	1 cup (6 ounces) uncooked pearled or 10-minute farro
1 cup chopped onion (about ½ medium onion)	2 avocados, peeled, pitted, and sliced
2 garlic cloves, minced (about 1 teaspoon)	1 small lemon
1 carrot, shredded (about 1 cup)	¼ teaspoon kosher or sea salt
2 cups low-sodium or no-salt-	

1. In a medium saucepan over medium-high heat, heat 1 tablespoon of oil. Add the onion and cook for 5 minutes, stirring occasionally. Add the garlic and carrot and cook for 1 minute, stirring frequently. Add the broth and farro, and bring to a boil over high heat. Lower the heat to medium-low, cover, and simmer for about 20 minutes or until the farro is plump and slightly chewy (al dente). 2. Pour the farro into a serving bowl, and add the avocado slices. Using a Microplane or citrus zester, zest the peel of the lemon directly into the bowl of farro. Halve the lemon, and squeeze the juice out of both halves using a citrus juicer or your hands. Drizzle the remaining 2 teaspoons of oil over the bowl, and sprinkle with salt. Gently mix all the ingredients and serve.

Per Serving:
calories: 212 | fat: 11.2g | protein: 3.4g | carbs: 28.7g | fiber: 7g | sodium: 147mg

Vegetable Barley Soup

Prep time: 30 minutes | Cook time: 26 minutes | Serves 8

2 tablespoons olive oil
½ medium yellow onion, peeled and chopped
1 medium carrot, peeled and chopped
1 stalk celery, chopped
2 cups sliced button mushrooms
2 cloves garlic, peeled and minced
½ teaspoon dried thyme
½ teaspoon ground black pepper
1 large russet potato, peeled and cut into ½" pieces
1 (14½-ounce / 411-g) can

fire-roasted diced tomatoes, undrained
½ cup medium pearl barley, rinsed and drained
4 cups vegetable broth
2 cups water
1 (15-ounce / 425-g) can corn, drained
1 (15-ounce / 425-g) can cut green beans, drained
1 (15-ounce / 425-g) can Great Northern beans, drained and rinsed
½ teaspoon salt

1. Press the Sauté button on the Instant Pot® and heat oil. Add onion, carrot, celery, and mushrooms. Cook until just tender, about 5 minutes. Add garlic, thyme, and pepper. Cook 30 seconds. Press the Cancel button. 2. Add potato, tomatoes, barley, broth, and water to pot. Close lid, set steam release to Sealing, press the Soup button, and cook for the default time of 20 minutes. 3. When the timer beeps, let pressure release naturally, about 15 minutes. Open lid and stir soup, then add corn, green beans, and Great Northern beans. Close lid and let stand on the Keep Warm setting for 10 minutes. Stir in salt. Serve hot.

Per Serving:
calories: 190 | fat: 4g | protein: 7g | carbs: 34g | fiber: 8g | sodium: 548mg

Quinoa and Artichoke Hearts Salad

Prep time: 10 minutes | Cook time: 5 minutes |
Serves 4

1 cup raw pecan halves
1 cup quinoa, rinsed and drained
2½ cups water
2 cups frozen artichoke hearts, thawed and drained

2 cups halved cherry tomatoes
½ small red onion, peeled and thinly sliced
¼ cup Italian salad dressing
4 large Belgian endive leaves

1. Press the Sauté button on the Instant Pot®. Roughly chop pecans and add them to the Instant Pot®. Dry-roast for several minutes, stirring continuously to prevent burning. Pecans are sufficiently toasted when they're fragrant and slightly brown. Transfer to a medium bowl and set aside to cool. Press the Cancel button. 2. Clean and dry pot. Add quinoa and water to the Instant Pot®. Close lid, set steam release to Sealing, press the Manual button, and set time to 2 minutes. When the timer beeps, let pressure release naturally for 10 minutes. Quick-release any remaining pressure until the float valve drops and open lid. Transfer to a colander, drain excess liquid, and rinse under cold water. Drain well and transfer to a large bowl. 3. While quinoa is cooking, cook artichoke hearts according to package directions and then plunge into cold water to cool and stop the cooking process. Drain and cut into quarters. 4. Stir artichoke hearts into quinoa along with tomatoes and red onion.

Toss with salad dressing. Cover and refrigerate for 1 hour before serving. 5. Place endive leaves on four plates. Top each with ¼ cup quinoa mixture. Sprinkle toasted pecans over the top of each endive boat and serve.

Per Serving:
calories: 414 | fat: 24g | protein: 11g | carbs: 42g | fiber: 10g | sodium: 327mg

Lentils with Cilantro and Lime

Prep time: 15 minutes | Cook time: 20 minutes | Serves 6

2 tablespoons olive oil
1 medium yellow onion, peeled and chopped
1 medium carrot, peeled and chopped
¼ cup chopped fresh cilantro
½ teaspoon ground cumin

½ teaspoon salt
2 cups dried green lentils, rinsed and drained
4 cups low-sodium chicken broth
2 tablespoons lime juice

1. Press the Sauté button on the Instant Pot® and heat oil. Add onion and carrot, and cook until just tender, about 3 minutes. Add cilantro, cumin, and salt, and cook until fragrant, about 30 seconds. Press the Cancel button. 2. Add lentils and broth to pot. Close lid, set steam release to Sealing, press the Manual button, and set time to 15 minutes. 3. When the timer beeps, let pressure release naturally, about 25 minutes. Open lid and stir in lime juice. Serve warm.

Per Serving:
calories: 316 | fat: 5g | protein: 20g | carbs: 44g | fiber: 21g | sodium: 349mg

Vegetarian Dinner Loaf

Prep time: 10 minutes | Cook time: 45 minutes | Serves 6

1 cup dried pinto beans, soaked overnight and drained
8 cups water, divided
1 tablespoon vegetable oil
1 teaspoon salt
1 cup diced onion
1 cup chopped walnuts
½ cup rolled oats

1 large egg, beaten
¾ cup ketchup
1 teaspoon garlic powder
1 teaspoon dried basil
1 teaspoon dried parsley
½ teaspoon salt
½ teaspoon ground black pepper

1. Add beans and 4 cups water to the Instant Pot®. Close lid, set steam release to Sealing, press the Manual button, and set time to 1 minute. When the timer beeps, quick-release the pressure until the float valve drops. Press the Cancel button. 2. Open lid, then drain and rinse beans and return to the pot with remaining 4 cups water. Soak for 1 hour. 3. Preheat oven to 350ºF. 4. Add the oil and salt to pot. Close lid, set steam release to Sealing, press the Manual button, and set time to 11 minutes. When the timer beeps, let pressure release naturally, about 25 minutes, and open lid. Drain beans and pour into a large mixing bowl. 5. Stir in onion, walnuts, oats, egg, ketchup, garlic powder, basil, parsley, salt, and pepper. Spread the mixture into a loaf pan and bake for 30–35 minutes. Cool for 20 minutes in pan before slicing and serving.

Per Serving:
calories: 278 | fat: 17g | protein: 9g | carbs: 27g | fiber: 6g | sodium: 477mg

White Beans with Kale

Prep time: 15 minutes | Cook time: 7½ hours | Serves 2

1 onion, chopped
1 leek, white part only, sliced
2 celery stalks, sliced
2 garlic cloves, minced
1 cup dried white lima beans or cannellini beans, sorted and rinsed

2 cups vegetable broth
½ teaspoon salt
½ teaspoon dried thyme leaves
⅛ teaspoon freshly ground black pepper
3 cups torn kale

1. In the slow cooker, combine all the ingredients except the kale. 2. Cover and cook on low for 7 hours, or until the beans are tender. 3. Add the kale and stir. 4. Cover and cook on high for 30 minutes, or until the kale is tender but still firm, and serve.

Per Serving:
calories: 176 | fat: 1g | protein: 9g | carbs: 36g | net carbs: 27g | sugars: 7g | fiber: 9g | sodium: 616mg | cholesterol: 0mg

Barley Risotto

Prep time: 10 minutes | Cook time: 30 minutes | Serves 6

2 tablespoons olive oil
1 large onion, peeled and diced
1 clove garlic, peeled and minced
1 stalk celery, finely minced
1½ cups pearl barley, rinsed and drained
⅓ cup dried mushrooms

4 cups low-sodium chicken broth
2¼ cups water
1 cup grated Parmesan cheese
2 tablespoons minced fresh parsley
¼ teaspoon salt

1. Press the Sauté button on the Instant Pot® and heat oil. Add onion and sauté 5 minutes. Add garlic and cook 30 seconds. Stir in celery, barley, mushrooms, broth, and water. Press the Cancel button. 2. Close lid, set steam release to Sealing, press the Manual button, and set time to 18 minutes. When the timer beeps, quick-release the pressure until the float valve drops and open the lid. 3. Drain off excess liquid, leaving enough to leave the risotto slightly soupy. Press the Cancel button, then press the Sauté button and cook until thickened, about 5 minutes. Stir in cheese, parsley, and salt. Serve immediately.

Per Serving:
calories: 175 | fat: 9g | protein: 10g | carbs: 13g | fiber: 2g | sodium: 447mg

Crunchy Pea and Barley Salad

Prep time: 10 minutes | Cook time: 15 minutes | Serves 4

2 cups water
1 cup quick-cooking barley
2 cups sugar snap pea pods
Small bunch flat-leaf parsley, chopped

½ small red onion, diced
2 tablespoons olive oil
Juice of 1 lemon
Sea salt and freshly ground pepper, to taste

1. Bring water to boil in a saucepan. Stir in the barley and cover. 2. Simmer for 10 minutes until all water is absorbed, and then let stand about 5 minutes covered. 3. Rinse the barley under cold water and combine it with the peas, parsley, onion, olive oil, and lemon

juice. 4. Season with sea salt and freshly ground pepper to taste.

Per Serving:
calories: 277 | fat: 8g | protein: 8g | carbs: 47g | fiber: 11g | sodium: 19mg

Creamy Yellow Lentil Soup

Prep time: 15 minutes | Cook time: 20 minutes | Serves 6

2 tablespoons olive oil
1 medium yellow onion, peeled and chopped
1 medium carrot, peeled and chopped
2 cloves garlic, peeled and minced

1 teaspoon ground cumin
½ teaspoon ground black pepper
¼ teaspoon salt
2 cups dried yellow lentils, rinsed and drained
6 cups water

1. Press the Sauté button on the Instant Pot® and heat oil. Add onion and carrot and cook until just tender, about 3 minutes. Add garlic, cumin, pepper, and salt and cook until fragrant, about 30 seconds. Press the Cancel button. 2. Add lentils and water, close lid, set steam release to Sealing, press the Manual button, and set time to 15 minutes. When the timer beeps, let pressure release naturally, about 15 minutes. Open lid and purée with an immersion blender or in batches in a blender. Serve warm.

Per Serving:
calories: 248 | fat: 5g | protein: 15g | carbs: 35g | fiber: 8g | sodium: 118mg

Lebanese Rice and Broken Noodles with Cabbage

Prep time: 5 minutes |Cook time: 25 minutes| Serves: 6

1 tablespoon extra-virgin olive oil
1 cup (about 3 ounces / 85 g) uncooked vermicelli or thin spaghetti, broken into 1- to 1½-inch pieces
3 cups shredded cabbage (about half a 14-ounce package of coleslaw mix or half a small head of cabbage)
3 cups low-sodium or no-salt-

added vegetable broth
½ cup water
1 cup instant brown rice
2 garlic cloves
¼ teaspoon kosher or sea salt
⅛ to ¼ teaspoon crushed red pepper
½ cup loosely packed, coarsely chopped cilantro
Fresh lemon slices, for serving (optional)

1. In a large saucepan over medium-high heat, heat the oil. Add the pasta and cook for 3 minutes to toast, stirring often. Add the cabbage and cook for 4 minutes, stirring often. Add the broth, water, rice, garlic, salt, and crushed red pepper, and bring to a boil over high heat. Stir, cover, and reduce the heat to medium-low. Simmer for 10 minutes. 2. Remove the pan from the heat, but do not lift the lid. Let sit for 5 minutes. Fish out the garlic cloves, mash them with a fork, then stir the garlic back into the rice. Stir in the cilantro. Serve with the lemon slices (if using).

Per Serving:
calories: 150 | fat: 3.6g | protein: 3g | carbs: 27g | fiber: 2.8g | sodium: 664mg

Savory Gigantes Plaki (Baked Giant White Beans)

Prep time: 5 minutes | Cook time: 30 minutes | Serves 4

Olive oil cooking spray
1 (15-ounce/ 425-g) can cooked butter beans, drained and rinsed
1 cup diced fresh tomatoes
½ tablespoon tomato paste
2 garlic cloves, minced
½ yellow onion, diced
½ teaspoon salt
¼ cup olive oil
¼ cup fresh parsley, chopped

1. Preheat the air fryer to 380°F(193°C). Lightly coat the inside of a 5-cup capacity casserole dish with olive oil cooking spray. (The shape of the casserole dish will depend upon the size of the air fryer, but it needs to be able to hold at least 5 cups.) 2. In a large bowl, combine the butter beans, tomatoes, tomato paste, garlic, onion, salt, and olive oil, mixing until all ingredients are combined. 3. Pour the mixture into the prepared casserole dish and top with the chopped parsley. 4. Bake in the air fryer for 15 minutes. Stir well, then return to the air fryer and bake for 15 minutes more.

Per Serving:
calories: 199 | fat: 18.6g | protein: 2g | carbs: 8g | fiber: 3g | sodium: 300mg

Spicy Lentil Patties

Prep time: 15 minutes | Cook time: 10 minutes | Serves 4

1 cup cooked brown lentils
¼ cup fresh parsley leaves
½ cup shredded carrots
¼ red onion, minced
¼ red bell pepper, minced
1 jalapeño, seeded and minced
2 garlic cloves, minced
1 egg
2 tablespoons lemon juice
2 tablespoons olive oil, divided
½ teaspoon onion powder
½ teaspoon smoked paprika
½ teaspoon dried oregano
¼ teaspoon salt
¼ teaspoon black pepper
½ cup whole wheat bread crumbs
For serving:
Whole wheat buns or whole wheat pitas
Plain Greek yogurt
Tomato
Lettuce
Red Onion

1. Preheat the air fryer to 380°F(193°C). 2. In a food processor, pulse the lentils and parsley mostly smooth. (You will want some bits of lentils in the mixture.) 3. Pour the lentils into a large bowl, and combine with the carrots, onion, bell pepper, jalapeño, garlic, egg, lemon juice, and 1 tablespoon olive oil. 4. Add the onion powder, paprika, oregano, salt, pepper, and bread crumbs. Stir everything together until the seasonings and bread crumbs are well distributed. 5. Form the dough into 4 patties. Place them into the air fryer basket in a single layer, making sure that they don't touch each other. Brush the remaining 1 tablespoon of olive oil over the patties. 6. Bake for 5 minutes. Flip the patties over and bake for an additional 5 minutes. 7. Serve on toasted whole wheat buns or whole wheat pitas with a spoonful of yogurt and lettuce, tomato, and red onion as desired.

Per Serving:
calories: 225 | fat: 10.3g | protein: 9.3g | carbs: 25g | fiber: 5.7g | sodium: 285mg

Risotto Primavera

Prep time: 20 minutes | Cook time: 20 minutes | Serves 8

2 tablespoons olive oil
2 medium carrots, peeled and finely diced
1 stalk celery, finely diced
2 large shallots, peeled and diced
1 clove garlic, peeled and minced
½ teaspoon dried basil
1 teaspoon dried parsley
2 cups Arborio rice
½ cup dry white wine
5 cups vegetable broth, divided
½ pound (227 g) asparagus, trimmed and chopped into 1" pieces
1 cup frozen green peas, thawed
1 cup shredded snow peas
1 cup diced zucchini
1 cup shredded Fontina cheese
½ cup grated Parmesan cheese

1. Press the Sauté button on the Instant Pot® and heat oil. Add carrots and celery and cook until tender, about 3 minutes. Add shallots and garlic and cook until fragrant, about 30 seconds. Add basil and parsley, and stir well. 2. Stir in rice and cook for 4 minutes or until rice becomes translucent. Add wine. Cook, stirring constantly for 3 minutes or until the liquid is absorbed. Stir in 4½ cups broth. Press the Cancel button. 3. Close lid, set steam release to Sealing, press the Manual button, and set time to 6 minutes. When the timer beeps, quick-release the pressure until the float valve drops and open the lid. 4. Stir in remaining ½ cup broth. Press the Cancel button, then press the Sauté button. Stir until broth is absorbed. Add asparagus, green peas, snow peas, and zucchini. Stir and cook until vegetables are bright green and cooked through, about 5 minutes. Stir in Fontina and Parmesan. Serve immediately.
Per Serving:
calories: 277 | fat: 11g | protein: 13g | carbs: 32g | fiber: 2g | sodium: 706mg

Farro and Mushroom Risotto

Prep time: 10 minutes | Cook time: 20 minutes | Serves 6

2 tablespoons olive oil
1 medium yellow onion, peeled and diced
16 ounces (454 g) sliced button mushrooms
½ teaspoon salt
½ teaspoon ground black pepper
½ teaspoon dried thyme
½ teaspoon dried oregano
1 clove garlic, peeled and minced
1 cup farro, rinsed and drained
1½ cups vegetable broth
¼ cup grated Parmesan cheese
2 tablespoons minced fresh flat-leaf parsley

1. Press the Sauté button on the Instant Pot® and heat oil. Add onion and mushrooms and sauté 8 minutes. Add salt, pepper, thyme, and oregano and cook 30 seconds. Add garlic and cook for 30 seconds. Press the Cancel button. 2. Stir in farro and broth. Close lid, set steam release to Sealing, press the Manual button, and set time to 10 minutes. When timer beeps, let pressure release naturally for 10 minutes, then quick-release the remaining pressure until the float valve drops. 3. Top with cheese and parsley before serving.

Per Serving:
calories: 215 | fat: 8g | protein: 11g | carbs: 24g | fiber: 3g | sodium: 419mg

Brown Rice with Apricots, Cherries, and Toasted Pecans

Prep time: 10 minutes | Cook time: 55 minutes | Serves 2

2 tablespoons olive oil
2 green onions, sliced
½ cup brown rice
1 cup chicken stock
4–5 dried apricots, chopped

2 tablespoons dried cherries
2 tablespoons pecans, toasted and chopped
Sea salt and freshly ground pepper, to taste

1. Heat the olive oil in a medium saucepan, and add the green onions. 2. Sauté for 1–2 minutes, and add the rice. Stir to coat in oil, then add the stock. 3. Bring to a boil, reduce heat, and cover. Simmer for 50 minutes. 4. Remove the lid, add the apricots, cherries, and pecans, and cover for 10 more minutes. 5. Fluff with a fork to mix the fruit into the rice, season with sea salt and freshly ground pepper, and serve.

Lentil Pâté

Prep time: 10 minutes | Cook time: 34 minutes | Serves 12

2 tablespoons olive oil, divided
1 cup diced yellow onion
3 cloves garlic, peeled and minced
1 teaspoon red wine vinegar
2 cups dried green lentils,

rinsed and drained
4 cups water
1 teaspoon salt
¼ teaspoon ground black pepper

1. Press the Sauté button on the Instant Pot® and heat 1 tablespoon oil. Add onion and cook until translucent, about 3 minutes. Add garlic and vinegar, and cook for 30 seconds. Add lentils, water, remaining 1 tablespoon oil, and salt to pot and stir to combine. Press the Cancel button. 2. Close lid, set steam release to Sealing, press the Bean button, and allow to cook for default time of 30 minutes. When the timer beeps, let pressure release naturally for 10 minutes. Quick-release any remaining pressure until the float valve drops, then open lid. 3. Transfer lentil mixture to a food processor or blender, and blend until smooth. Season with pepper and serve warm.

Per Serving:
calories: 138 | fat: 3g | protein: 8g | carbs: 20g | fiber: 10g | sodium: 196mg

South Indian Split Yellow Pigeon Peas with Mixed Vegetables

Prep time: 20 minutes | Cook time: 4½ to 6½ minutes | Serves 6

Sambar Masala:
1 teaspoon rapeseed oil
3 tablespoons coriander seeds
2 tablespoons split gram
1 teaspoon black peppercorns
½ teaspoon fenugreek seeds
½ teaspoon mustard seeds

¼ teaspoon cumin seeds
12 whole dried red chiles
Sambar:
1½ cups split yellow pigeon peas, washed
2 fresh green chiles, sliced lengthwise

2 garlic cloves, chopped
6 pearl onions
4 to 5 tablespoons sambar masala
2 teaspoons salt
1 to 2 carrots, peeled and chopped
1 red potato, peeled and diced
1 white radish (mooli), peeled and chopped into 2¾-inch sticks
1 tomato, roughly chopped
4 cups water

2 to 3 moringa seed pods, or ⅓ pound (151 g) green beans or asparagus, chopped into 2¾-inch lengths
2 tablespoons tamarind paste
½ teaspoon asafetida
2 teaspoons coconut oil
1 teaspoon mustard seeds
20 curry leaves
2 dried red chilies
Handful fresh coriander leaves, chopped (optional)

Make the Sambar Masala: 1. Add the oil to a medium nonstick skillet. Add all of the remaining ingredients and roast for a few minutes until fragrant. The spices will brown a little, but don't let them burn. 2. Remove from the heat and pour onto a plate to cool. Once cooled, place into your spice grinder or mortar and pestle and grind to a powder. Set aside. Make the Sambar: 3. Heat the slow cooker to high and add the pigeon peas, green chiles, garlic, pearl onions, sambar masala, salt, carrots, potatoes, radish, tomato, and water. 4. Cover and cook for 4 hours on high, or for 6 hours on low. 5. Add the moringa (or green beans or asparagus), tamarind paste, and asafetida. Cover and cook for another 30 minutes. 6. When you're ready to serve, heat the coconut oil in a frying pan and pop the mustard seeds with the curry leaves and dried chiles. Pour over the sambar. Top with coriander leaves (if using) and serve.

Per Serving:
calories: 312 | fat: 7g | protein: 12g | carbs: 59g | net carbs: 43g | sugars: 12g | fiber: 16g | sodium: 852mg | cholesterol: 0mg

Fava Beans with Ground Meat

Prep time: 15 minutes | Cook time: 6 to 8 hours | Serves 6

8 ounces (227 g) raw ground meat
1 pound (454 g) dried fava beans, rinsed well under cold water and picked over to remove debris, or 1 (15-ounce/425-g) can fava beans, drained and rinsed
10 cups water or 5 cups water and 5 cups low-sodium vegetable broth
1 small onion, diced

1 bell pepper, any color, seeded and diced
1 teaspoon sea salt
1 teaspoon garlic powder
1 teaspoon dried parsley
1 teaspoon dried oregano
1 teaspoon paprika
1 teaspoon cayenne pepper
½ teaspoon freshly ground black pepper
½ teaspoon dried thyme

1. In a large skillet over medium-high heat, cook the ground meat for 3 to 5 minutes, stirring and breaking it up with a spoon, until it has browned and is no longer pink. Drain any grease and put the meat in a slow cooker. 2. Add the fava beans, water, onion, bell pepper, salt, garlic powder, parsley, oregano, paprika, cayenne pepper, black pepper, and thyme to the meat. Stir to mix well. 3. Cover the cooker and cook for 6 to 8 hours on Low heat, or until the beans are tender.

Per Serving:
calories: 308 | fat: 4g | protein: 26g | carbs: 43g | fiber: 19g | sodium: 417mg

Quinoa Salad with Chicken, Chickpeas, and Spinach

Prep time: 15 minutes | Cook time: 18 minutes | Serves 6

4 tablespoons olive oil, divided
1 medium yellow onion, peeled and chopped
2 cloves garlic, peeled and minced
4 cups fresh baby spinach leaves
½ teaspoon salt
¼ teaspoon ground black pepper
1½ cups quinoa, rinsed and

drained
2 cups vegetable broth
1⅓ cups water
1 tablespoon apple cider vinegar
1 (15-ounce / 425-g) can chickpeas, drained and rinsed
1 (6-ounce / 170-g) boneless, skinless chicken breast, cooked and shredded

1. Press the Sauté button on the Instant Pot® and heat 2 tablespoons olive oil. Add onion and cook until tender, about 3 minutes. Add garlic, spinach, salt, and pepper and cook 3 minutes until spinach has wilted. Transfer spinach mixture to a large bowl. Press the Cancel button. 2. Add quinoa, broth, and water to the Instant Pot®. Close lid, set steam release to Sealing, press the Rice button, and set time to 12 minutes. 3. While quinoa cooks, add remaining 2 tablespoons olive oil, vinegar, chickpeas, and chicken to spinach mixture and toss to coat. Set aside. 4. When the timer beeps, let pressure release naturally, about 20 minutes. 5. Open lid and fluff quinoa with a fork. Press the Cancel button and let quinoa cool 10 minutes, then transfer to the bowl with chicken mixture. Mix well. Serve warm, at room temperature, or cold.

Per Serving:
calories: 232 | fat: 12g | protein: 14g | carbs: 20g | fiber: 6g | sodium: 463mg

Mediterranean Bulgur Medley

Prep time: 15 minutes | Cook time: 20 minutes | Serves 6

2 tablespoons extra-virgin olive oil
1 medium onion, peeled and diced
½ cup chopped button mushrooms
½ cup golden raisins (sultanas)
¼ cup pine nuts
2 cups vegetable stock

1 teaspoon ground cumin
½ teaspoon salt
½ teaspoon ground black pepper
1 cup medium bulgur wheat
1 tablespoon petimezi or honey
12 chestnuts, roasted, peeled, and halved
1 teaspoon sesame seeds

1. Press the Sauté button on the Instant Pot® and heat oil. Add onion and sauté 3 minutes. Add mushrooms, raisins, and pine nuts and cook 2 minutes. 2. Add stock, cumin, salt, pepper, bulgur, and petimezi. Cook, stirring, for 3 minutes. Add chestnuts, then press the Cancel button. 3. Close lid, set steam release to Sealing, press the Rice button, and set time to 12 minutes. When the timer beeps, quick-release the pressure until the float valve drops and open lid. Stir well, then let stand, uncovered, on the Keep Warm setting for 10 minutes. Sprinkle with sesame seeds and serve.

Per Serving:
calories: 129 | fat: 1g | protein: 3g | carbs: 28g | fiber: 2g | sodium: 219mg

Slow Cooker Vegetarian Chili

Prep time: 20 minutes | Cook time: 4 to 6 hours | Serves 4

1 (28-ounce/ 794-g) can chopped whole tomatoes, with the juice
1 medium green bell pepper, chopped
1 (15-ounce / 425-g) can red beans, drained and rinsed
1 (15-ounce / 425-g) can black beans, drained and rinsed
1 yellow onion, chopped

1 tablespoon olive oil
1 tablespoon onion powder
1 teaspoon garlic powder
1 teaspoon cayenne pepper
1 teaspoon paprika
½ teaspoon sea salt
½ teaspoon black pepper
1 large hass avocado, pitted, peeled, and chopped, for garnish

1. Combine the tomatoes, bell pepper, red beans, black beans, and onion in the slow cooker. Sprinkle with the onion powder, garlic powder, cayenne pepper, paprika, ½ teaspoon salt, and ½ teaspoon black pepper. 2. Cover and cook on high for 4 to 6 hours or on low for 8 hours, or until thick. 3. Season with salt and black pepper if needed. Served hot, garnished with some of the avocado.

Per Serving:
calories:446 | fat: 15.4g | protein: 20.9g | carbs: 61g | fiber: 21.5g | sodium: 599mg

Mediterranean Lentils and Rice

Prep time: 5 minutes |Cook time: 25 minutes| Serves: 4

2¼ cups low-sodium or no-salt-added vegetable broth
½ cup uncooked brown or green lentils
½ cup uncooked instant brown rice
½ cup diced carrots (about 1 carrot)
½ cup diced celery (about 1 stalk)
1 (2¼-ounce / 64-g) can sliced olives, drained (about ½ cup)
¼ cup diced red onion (about ⅛

onion)
¼ cup chopped fresh curly-leaf parsley
1½ tablespoons extra-virgin olive oil
1 tablespoon freshly squeezed lemon juice (from about ½ small lemon)
1 garlic clove, minced (about ½ teaspoon)
¼ teaspoon kosher or sea salt
¼ teaspoon freshly ground black pepper

1. In a medium saucepan over high heat, bring the broth and lentils to a boil, cover, and lower the heat to medium-low. Cook for 8 minutes. 2. Raise the heat to medium, and stir in the rice. Cover the pot and cook the mixture for 15 minutes, or until the liquid is absorbed. Remove the pot from the heat and let it sit, covered, for 1 minute, then stir. 3. While the lentils and rice are cooking, mix together the carrots, celery, olives, onion, and parsley in a large serving bowl. 4. In a small bowl, whisk together the oil, lemon juice, garlic, salt, and pepper. Set aside. 5. When the lentils and rice are cooked, add them to the serving bowl. Pour the dressing on top, and mix everything together. Serve warm or cold, or store in a sealed container in the refrigerator for up to 7 days.

Per Serving:
calories: 183 | fat: 6g | protein: 4.9g | carbs: 29.5g | fiber: 3.3g | sodium: 552mg

Earthy Whole Brown Lentil Dhal

Prep time: 10 minutes | Cook time: 6 to 8 hours | Serves 6

6⅓ cups hot water
2 cups whole brown lentils
1 tablespoon ghee
1 teaspoon freshly grated ginger
1 teaspoon sea salt
1 teaspoon turmeric
7 to 8 ounces (198 to 227 g) canned tomatoes

4 garlic cloves, finely chopped
1 or 2 fresh green chiles, finely chopped
1 onion, chopped
1 teaspoon garam masala
Handful fresh coriander leaves, chopped

1. Wash and clean the lentils, then set them aside to drain. 2. Heat the slow cooker to high and add all of the ingredients except the garam masala and coriander leaves. 3. Cover and cook on high for 6 hours, or on low for 8 hours. 4. Add the garam masala and fresh coriander leaves before serving, and enjoy.
Per Serving:
calories: 263 | fat: 3g | protein: 16g | carbs: 44g | net carbs: 36g | sugars: 3g | fiber: 8g | sodium: 401mg | cholesterol: 0mg

Herbed Barley

Prep time: 10 minutes | Cook time: 30 minutes | Serves 4

2 tablespoons olive oil
½ cup diced onion
½ cup diced celery
1 carrot, peeled and diced
3 cups water or chicken broth
1 cup barley

1 bay leaf
½ teaspoon thyme
½ teaspoon rosemary
¼ cup walnuts or pine nuts
Sea salt and freshly ground pepper, to taste

1. Heat the olive oil in a medium saucepan over medium-high heat. Sauté the onion, celery, and carrot over medium heat until they are tender. 2. Add the water or chicken broth, barley, and seasonings, and bring to a boil. Reduce the heat and simmer for 25 minutes, or until tender. 3. Stir in the nuts and season to taste.
Per Serving:
calories: 283 | fat: 11g | protein: 6g | carbs: 43g | fiber: 9g | sodium: 26mg

Fasolakia (Greek Green Beans)

Prep time: 5 minutes | Cook time: 45 minutes | Serves 2

⅓ cup olive oil (any variety)
1 medium onion (red or white), chopped
1 medium russet or white potato, sliced into ¼-inch (.5cm) thick slices
1 pound (454 g) green beans (fresh or frozen)

3 medium tomatoes, grated, or 1 (15-ounce / 425-g) can crushed tomatoes
¼ cup chopped fresh parsley
1 teaspoon granulated sugar
½ teaspoon salt
¼ teaspoon freshly ground black pepper

1. Add the olive oil a medium pot over medium-low heat. When the oil begins to shimmer, add the onions and sauté until soft, about 5 minutes. 2. Add the potatoes to the pot, and sauté for an additional 2–3 minutes. 3. Add the green beans and stir until the beans are thoroughly coated with the olive oil. Add the tomatoes, parsley, sugar, salt, and black pepper. Stir to combine. 4. Add just enough hot water to the pot to cover half the beans. Cover and simmer for 40 minutes or until there is no water left in the pot and the beans are soft. (Do not allow the beans to boil.) 5. Allow the beans to cool until they're warm or until they reach room temperature, but do not serve hot. Store in refrigerator for up to 3 days.
Per Serving:
calories: 536 | fat: 37g | protein: 9g | carbs: 50g | fiber: 11g | sodium: 617mg

Wild Rice Pilaf with Pine Nuts

Prep time: 10 minutes | Cook time: 30 minutes | Serves 8

2 tablespoons extra-virgin olive oil
1 medium white onion, peeled and chopped
2 cups chopped baby bella mushrooms
3 cloves garlic, peeled and minced
2 cups wild rice

2½ cups vegetable broth
½ cup toasted pine nuts
¼ cup chopped fresh flat-leaf parsley
2 tablespoons chopped fresh chives
¼ teaspoon salt
½ teaspoon ground black pepper

1. Press the Sauté button on the Instant Pot® and heat oil. Add onion and mushrooms. Cook until soft, about 8 minutes. Add garlic and cook until fragrant, about 30 seconds. Add rice and press the Cancel button. 2. Stir in broth. Close lid, set steam release to Sealing, press the Manual button, and set time to 20 minutes. When the timer beeps, let pressure release naturally for 10 minutes, then quick-release the remaining pressure. Open lid and fluff rice with a fork. Fold in pine nuts, parsley, and chives. Season with salt and pepper. Serve warm.
Per Serving:
calories: 314 | fat: 18g | protein: 10g | carbs: 41g | fiber: 4g | sodium: 93mg

Skillet Bulgur with Kale and Tomatoes

Prep time: 15 minutes | Cook time: 8 minutes | Serves 2

2 tablespoons olive oil
2 cloves garlic, minced
1 bunch kale, trimmed and cut into bite-sized pieces
Juice of 1 lemon

2 cups cooked bulgur wheat
1 pint cherry tomatoes, halved
Sea salt and freshly ground pepper, to taste

1. Heat the olive oil in a large skillet over medium heat. Add the garlic and sauté for 1 minute. 2. Add the kale leaves and stir to coat. Cook for 5 minutes until leaves are cooked through and thoroughly wilted. 3. Add the lemon juice, then the bulgur and tomatoes. Season with sea salt and freshly ground pepper.
Per Serving:
calories: 311 | fat: 14g | protein: 8g | carbs: 43g | fiber: 10g | sodium: 21mg

Brown Rice and Chickpea Salad

Prep time: 5 minutes | Cook time: 22 minutes | Serves 8

2 cups brown rice
2¼ cups vegetable broth
2 tablespoons light olive oil
1 (15-ounce/ 425-g) can chickpeas, drained and rinsed
½ cup diced tomato
½ cup chopped red onion
½ cup diced cucumber

¼ cup chopped fresh basil
3 tablespoons extra-virgin olive oil
2 tablespoons balsamic vinegar
½ teaspoon ground black pepper
¼ teaspoon salt
¼ cup crumbled feta cheese

1. Place rice, broth, and light oil in the Instant Pot®. Close lid, set steam release to Sealing, press the Manual button, and set time to 22 minutes. 2. When the timer beeps, let pressure release naturally for 10 minutes, then quick-release the remaining pressure. Open lid, transfer rice to a large bowl, and set aside for 20 minutes. Fold in chickpeas, tomato, onion, cucumber, and basil. 3. In a small bowl, whisk together extra-virgin olive oil, balsamic vinegar, pepper, and salt. Pour over rice mixture and toss to coat. Top with feta. Serve at room temperature or refrigerate for at least 2 hours.

Per Serving:
calories: 417 | fat: 21g | protein: 13g | carbs: 45g | fiber: 7g | sodium: 366mg

Lentil and Zucchini Boats

Prep time: 15 minutes | Cook time: 50 minutes | Serves 4

1 cup dried green lentils, rinsed and drained
¼ teaspoon salt
2 cups water
1 tablespoon olive oil
½ medium red onion, peeled and diced
1 clove garlic, peeled and minced

1 cup marinara sauce
¼ teaspoon crushed red pepper flakes
4 medium zucchini, trimmed and cut lengthwise
½ cup shredded part-skim mozzarella cheese
¼ cup chopped fresh flat-leaf parsley

1. Add lentils, salt, and water to the Instant Pot®. Close lid, set steam release to Sealing, press the Manual button, and set time to 12 minutes. When the timer beeps, quick-release the pressure until the float valve drops. Press the Cancel button. Open lid and drain off any excess liquid. Transfer lentils to a medium bowl. Set aside. 2. Press the Sauté button and heat oil. Add onion and cook until tender, about 3 minutes. Add garlic and cook until fragrant, about 30 seconds. Add marinara sauce and crushed red pepper flakes and stir to combine. Press the Cancel button. Stir in lentils. 3. Preheat oven to 350°F (180°C) and spray a 9" × 13" baking dish with nonstick cooking spray. 4. Using a teaspoon, hollow out each zucchini half. Lay zucchini in prepared baking dish. Divide lentil mixture among prepared zucchini. Top with cheese. Bake for 30–35 minutes, or until zucchini are tender and cheese is melted and browned. Top with parsley and serve hot.

Per Serving:
calories: 326 | fat: 10g | protein: 22g | carbs: 39g | fiber: 16g | sodium: 568mg

Creamy Thyme Polenta

Prep time: 5 minutes | Cook time: 10 minutes | Serves 6

3½ cups water
½ cup coarse polenta
½ cup fine cornmeal

1 cup corn kernels
1 teaspoon dried thyme
1 teaspoon salt

1. Add all ingredients to the Instant Pot® and stir. 2. Close lid, set steam release to Sealing, press the Manual button, and set time to 10 minutes. When the timer beeps, quick-release the pressure until the float valve drops and open lid. Serve immediately.

Per Serving:
calories: 74 | fat: 1g | protein: 2g | carbs: 14g | fiber: 2g | sodium: 401mg

Chapter 7 Pasta

Toasted Couscous with Feta, Cucumber, and Tomato

Prep time: 15 minutes | Cook time: 10 minutes | Serves 8

1 tablespoon plus ¼ cup light olive oil, divided
2 cups Israeli couscous
3 cups vegetable broth
2 large tomatoes, seeded and diced
1 large English cucumber, diced
1 medium red onion, peeled and chopped
½ cup crumbled feta cheese
¼ cup red wine vinegar
½ teaspoon ground black pepper
¼ cup chopped flat-leaf parsley
¼ cup chopped fresh basil

1. Press the Sauté button on the Instant Pot® and heat 1 tablespoon oil. Add couscous and cook, stirring frequently, until couscous is light golden brown, about 7 minutes. Press the Cancel button. 2. Add broth and stir. Close lid, set steam release to Sealing, press the Manual button, and set time to 2 minutes. When the timer beeps, let pressure release naturally for 5 minutes, then quick-release the remaining pressure until the float valve drops and open lid. 3. Fluff couscous with a fork, then transfer to a medium bowl and set aside to cool to room temperature, about 30 minutes. Add remaining ¼ cup oil, tomatoes, cucumber, onion, feta, vinegar, pepper, parsley, and basil, and stir until combined. Serve at room temperature or refrigerate for at least 2 hours.

Per Serving:
calories: 286 | fat: 11g | protein: 9g | carbs: 38g | fiber: 3g | sodium: 438mg

Bowtie Pesto Pasta Salad

Prep time: 5 minutes | Cook time: 4 minutes | Serves 8

1 pound (454 g) whole-wheat bowtie pasta
4 cups water
1 tablespoon extra-virgin olive oil
2 cups halved cherry tomatoes
2 cups baby spinach
½ cup chopped fresh basil
½ cup prepared pesto
½ teaspoon ground black pepper
½ cup grated Parmesan cheese

1. Add pasta, water, and olive oil to the Instant Pot®. Close lid, set steam release to Sealing, press the Manual button, and set time to 4 minutes. 2. When the timer beeps, quick-release the pressure until the float valve drops and open lid. Drain off any excess liquid. Allow pasta to cool to room temperature, about 30 minutes. Stir in tomatoes, spinach, basil, pesto, pepper, and cheese. Refrigerate for 2 hours. Stir well before serving.

Per Serving:
calories: 360 | fat: 13g | protein: 16g | carbs: 44g | fiber: 7g | sodium: 372mg

Simple Pesto Pasta

Prep time: 10 minutes | Cook time: 10 minutes |
Serves 4 to 6

1 pound (454 g) spaghetti
4 cups fresh basil leaves, stems removed
3 cloves garlic
1 teaspoon salt
½ teaspoon freshly ground
black pepper
¼ cup lemon juice
½ cup pine nuts, toasted
½ cup grated Parmesan cheese
1 cup extra-virgin olive oil

1. Bring a large pot of salted water to a boil. Add the spaghetti to the pot and cook for 8 minutes. 2. Put basil, garlic, salt, pepper, lemon juice, pine nuts, and Parmesan cheese in a food processor bowl with chopping blade and purée. 3. While the processor is running, slowly drizzle the olive oil through the top opening. Process until all the olive oil has been added. 4. Reserve ½ cup of the pasta water. Drain the pasta and put it into a bowl. Immediately add the pesto and pasta water to the pasta and toss everything together. Serve warm.

Per Serving:
calories: 1067 | fat: 72g | protein: 23g | carbs: 91g | fiber: 6g | sodium: 817mg

Spaghetti with Fresh Mint Pesto and Ricotta Salata

Prep time: 5 minutes | Cook time: 15 minutes | Serves 4

1 pound (454 g) spaghetti
¼ cup slivered almonds
2 cups packed fresh mint leaves, plus more for garnish
3 medium garlic cloves
1 tablespoon lemon juice and
½ teaspoon lemon zest from 1
lemon
⅓ cup olive oil
¼ teaspoon freshly ground black pepper
½ cup freshly grated ricotta salata, plus more for garnish

1. Set a large pot of salted water over high heat to boil for the pasta. 2. In a food processor, combine the almonds, mint leaves, garlic, lemon juice and zest, olive oil, and pepper and pulse to a smooth paste. Add the cheese and pulse to combine. 3. When the water is boiling, add the pasta and cook according to the package instructions. Drain the pasta and return it to the pot. Add the pesto to the pasta and toss until the pasta is well coated. Serve hot, garnished with additional mint leaves and cheese, if desired.

Per Serving:
calories: 619 | fat: 31g | protein: 21g | carbs: 70g | fiber: 4g | sodium: 113mg

Roasted Asparagus Caprese Pasta

Prep time: 10 minutes |Cook time: 15 minutes| Serves: 6

8 ounces (227 g) uncooked small pasta, like orecchiette (little ears) or farfalle (bow ties)
1½ pounds (680 g) fresh asparagus, ends trimmed and stalks chopped into 1-inch pieces (about 3 cups)
1 pint grape tomatoes, halved (about 1½ cups)
2 tablespoons extra-virgin olive
oil
¼ teaspoon freshly ground black pepper
¼ teaspoon kosher or sea salt
2 cups fresh mozzarella, drained and cut into bite-size pieces (about 8 ounces / 227 g)
⅓ cup torn fresh basil leaves
2 tablespoons balsamic vinegar

1. Preheat the oven to 400°F(205ºC). 2. In a large stockpot, cook the pasta according to the package directions. Drain, reserving about ¼ cup of the pasta water. 3. While the pasta is cooking, in a large bowl, toss the asparagus, tomatoes, oil, pepper, and salt together. Spread the mixture onto a large, rimmed baking sheet and bake for 15 minutes, stirring twice as it cooks. 4. Remove the vegetables from the oven, and add the cooked pasta to the baking sheet. Mix with a few tablespoons of pasta water to help the sauce become smoother and the saucy vegetables stick to the pasta. 5. Gently mix in the mozzarella and basil. Drizzle with the balsamic vinegar. Serve from the baking sheet or pour the pasta into a large bowl. 6. If you want to make this dish ahead of time or to serve it cold, follow the recipe up to step 4, then refrigerate the pasta and vegetables. When you are ready to serve, follow step 5 either with the cold pasta or with warm pasta that's been gently reheated in a pot on the stove.

Per Serving:
calories: 317 | fat: 12g | protein: 16g | carbs: 38g | fiber: 7g | sodium: 110mg

Meaty Baked Penne

Prep time: 10 minutes | Cook time: 40 minutes | Serves 8

1 pound (454 g) penne pasta
1 pound (454 g) ground beef
1 teaspoon salt
1 (25-ounce / 709-g) jar marinara sauce
1 (1-pound / 454-g) bag baby spinach, washed
3 cups shredded mozzarella cheese, divided

1. Bring a large pot of salted water to a boil, add the penne, and cook for 7 minutes. Reserve 2 cups of the pasta water and drain the pasta. 2. Preheat the oven to 350°F(180ºC). 3. In a large saucepan over medium heat, cook the ground beef and salt. Brown the ground beef for about 5 minutes. 4. Stir in marinara sauce, and 2 cups of pasta water. Let simmer for 5 minutes. 5. Add a handful of spinach at a time into the sauce, and cook for another 3 minutes. 6. To assemble, in a 9-by-13-inch baking dish, add the pasta and pour the pasta sauce over it. Stir in 1½ cups of the mozzarella cheese. Cover the dish with foil and bake for 20 minutes. 7. After 20 minutes, remove the foil, top with the rest of the mozzarella, and bake for another 10 minutes. Serve warm.

Per Serving:
calories: 454 | fat: 13g | protein: 31g | carbs: 55g | fiber: 9g | sodium: 408mg

Toasted Orzo Salad

Prep time: 15 minutes | Cook time: 8 minutes | Serves 6

2 tablespoons light olive oil
1 clove garlic, peeled and crushed
2 cups orzo
3 cups vegetable broth
½ cup sliced black olives
3 scallions, thinly sliced
1 medium Roma tomato, seeded and diced
1 medium red bell pepper, seeded and diced
¼ cup crumbled feta cheese
1 tablespoon extra-virgin olive oil
1 tablespoon red wine vinegar
½ teaspoon ground black pepper
¼ teaspoon salt

1. Press the Sauté button on the Instant Pot® and heat light olive oil. Add garlic and orzo and cook, stirring frequently, until orzo is light golden brown, about 5 minutes. Press the Cancel button. 2. Add broth and stir. Close lid, set steam release to Sealing, press the Manual button, and set time to 3 minutes. When the timer beeps, let pressure release naturally for 5 minutes, then quick-release the remaining pressure until the float valve drops and open lid. 3. Transfer orzo to a medium bowl, then set aside to cool to room temperature, about 30 minutes. Add olives, scallions, tomato, bell pepper, feta, extra-virgin olive oil, vinegar, black pepper, and salt, and stir until combined. Serve at room temperature or refrigerate for at least 2 hours.

Per Serving:
calories: 120 | fat: 4g | protein: 4g | carbs: 17g | fiber: 1g | sodium: 586mg

Chilled Pearl Couscous Salad

Prep time: 15 minutes | Cook time: 10 minutes | Serves 6

3 tablespoons olive oil, divided
1 cup pearl couscous
1 cup water
1 cup orange juice
1 small cucumber, seeded and diced
1 small yellow bell pepper, seeded and diced
2 small Roma tomatoes, seeded and diced
¼ cup slivered almonds
¼ cup chopped fresh mint leaves
2 tablespoons lemon juice
1 teaspoon grated lemon zest
¼ cup crumbled feta cheese
¼ teaspoon fine sea salt
1 teaspoon smoked paprika
1 teaspoon garlic powder

1. Press the Sauté button and heat 1 tablespoon oil. Add couscous and cook for 2–4 minutes until couscous is slightly browned. Add water and orange juice. Press the Cancel button. 2. Close lid, set steam release to Sealing, press the Manual button, and set time to 5 minutes. When the timer beeps, let pressure release naturally for 5 minutes. Quick-release any remaining pressure until the float valve drops and open lid. Drain any liquid and set aside to cool for 20 minutes. 3. Combine remaining 2 tablespoons oil, cucumber, bell pepper, tomatoes, almonds, mint, lemon juice, lemon zest, cheese, salt, paprika, and garlic powder in a medium bowl. Add couscous and toss ingredients together. Cover and refrigerate overnight before serving.

Per Serving:
calories: 177 | fat: 11g | protein: 5g | carbs: 12g | fiber: 1g | sodium: 319mg

Yogurt and Dill Pasta Salad

Prep time: 10 minutes | Cook time: 4 minutes | Serves 8

½ cup low-fat plain Greek yogurt
1 tablespoon apple cider vinegar
2 tablespoons chopped fresh dill
1 teaspoon honey
1 pound (454 g) whole-wheat elbow macaroni
4 cups water

1 tablespoon extra-virgin olive oil
1 medium red bell pepper, seeded and chopped
1 medium sweet onion, peeled and diced
1 stalk celery, diced
½ teaspoon ground black pepper

1. In a small bowl, combine yogurt and vinegar. Add dill and honey, and mix well. Refrigerate until ready to use. 2. Place pasta, water, and olive oil to the Instant Pot®. Close lid, set steam release to Sealing, press the Manual button, and set time to 4 minutes. 3. When the timer beeps, quick-release the pressure until the float valve drops and open lid. Drain off any excess liquid. Cool pasta to room temperature, about 30 minutes. Add prepared dressing and toss until pasta is well coated. Add bell pepper, onion, celery, and black pepper, and toss to coat. Refrigerate for 2 hours. Stir well before serving.

Per Serving:
calories: 295 | fat: 5g | protein: 19g | carbs: 47g | fiber: 8g | sodium: 51mg

Puglia-Style Pasta with Broccoli Sauce

Prep time: 15 minutes | Cook time: 25 minutes | Serves 3

1 pound (454 g) fresh broccoli, washed and cut into small florets
7 ounces (198 g) uncooked rigatoni pasta
2 tablespoons extra virgin olive oil, plus 1½ tablespoons for serving
3 garlic cloves, thinly sliced
2 tablespoons pine nuts

4 canned packed-in-oil anchovies
½ teaspoon kosher salt
3 teaspoons fresh lemon juice
3 ounces (85 g) grated or shaved Parmesan cheese, divided
½ teaspoon freshly ground black pepper

1. Place the broccoli in a large pot filled with enough water to cover the broccoli. Bring the pot to a boil and cook for 12 minutes or until the stems can be easily pierced with a fork. Use a slotted spoon to transfer the broccoli to a plate, but do not discard the cooking water. Set the broccoli aside. 2. Add the pasta to the pot with the broccoli water and cook according to package instructions. 3. About 3 minutes before the pasta is ready, place a large, deep pan over medium heat and add 2 tablespoons of the olive oil. When the olive oil is shimmering, add the garlic and sauté for 1 minute, stirring continuously, until the garlic is golden, then add the pine nuts and continue sautéing for 1 more minute. 4. Stir in the anchovies, using a wooden spoon to break them into smaller pieces, then add the broccoli. Continue cooking for 1 additional minute, stirring continuously and using the spoon to break the broccoli into smaller pieces. 5. When the pasta is ready, remove the pot from the heat and drain, reserving ¼ cup of the cooking water. 6. Add the pasta and 2 tablespoons of the cooking water to the pan, stirring until all the ingredients are well combined. Cook for 1 minute, then remove the pan from the heat. 7. Promptly divide the pasta among three plates. Top each serving with a pinch of kosher salt, 1 teaspoon of the lemon juice, 1 ounce (28 g) of the Parmesan, 1½ teaspoons of the remaining olive oil, and a pinch of fresh ground pepper. Store covered in the refrigerator for up to 3 days.

Per Serving:
calories: 610 | fat: 31g | protein: 24g | carbs: 66g | fiber: 12g | sodium: 654mg

Rigatoni with Lamb Meatballs

Prep time: 15 minutes | Cook time: 3 to 5 hours | Serves 4

8 ounces (227 g) dried rigatoni pasta
2 (28-ounce / 794-g) cans no-salt-added crushed tomatoes or no-salt-added diced tomatoes
1 small onion, diced
1 bell pepper, any color, seeded and diced
3 garlic cloves, minced, divided

1 pound (454 g) raw ground lamb
1 large egg
2 tablespoons bread crumbs
1 tablespoon dried parsley
1 teaspoon dried oregano
1 teaspoon sea salt
½ teaspoon freshly ground black pepper

1. In a slow cooker, combine the pasta, tomatoes, onion, bell pepper, and 1 clove of garlic. Stir to mix well. 2. In a large bowl, mix together the ground lamb, egg, bread crumbs, the remaining 2 garlic cloves, parsley, oregano, salt, and black pepper until all of the ingredients are evenly blended. Shape the meat mixture into 6 to 9 large meatballs. Nestle the meatballs into the pasta and tomato sauce. 3. Cover the cooker and cook for 3 to 5 hours on Low heat, or until the pasta is tender.

Per Serving:
calories: 653 | fat: 29g | protein: 32g | carbs: 69g | fiber: 10g | sodium: 847mg

Pasta with Marinated Artichokes and Spinach

Prep time: 10 minutes | Cook time: 5 minutes | Serves 6

1 pound (454 g) whole-wheat spaghetti, broken in half
3½ cups water
4 tablespoons extra-virgin olive oil, divided
¼ teaspoon salt
2 cups baby spinach
1 cup drained marinated

artichoke hearts
2 tablespoons chopped fresh oregano
2 tablespoons chopped fresh flat-leaf parsley
1 teaspoon ground black pepper
½ cup grated Parmesan cheese

1. Add pasta, water, 2 tablespoons oil, and salt to the Instant Pot®. Close lid, set steam release to Sealing, press the Manual button, and set time to 5 minutes. 2. When the timer beeps, quick-release the pressure until the float valve drops and open lid. Drain off any excess liquid. Stir in remaining 2 tablespoons oil and spinach. Toss until spinach is wilted. Stir in artichokes, oregano, and parsley until well mixed. Sprinkle with pepper and cheese, and serve immediately.

Per Serving:
calories: 414 | fat: 16g | protein: 16g | carbs: 56g | fiber: 9g | sodium: 467mg

Toasted Orzo with Shrimp and Feta

Prep time: 10 minutes | Cook time: 15 minutes |

Serves 4 to 6

1 pound (454 g) large shrimp (26 to 30 per pound), peeled and deveined	2 cups orzo
1 tablespoon grated lemon zest plus 1 tablespoon juice	2 cups chicken broth, plus extra as needed
¼ teaspoon table salt	1¼ cups water
¼ teaspoon pepper	½ cup pitted kalamata olives, chopped coarse
2 tablespoons extra-virgin olive oil, plus extra for serving	1 ounce (28 g) feta cheese, crumbled (¼ cup), plus extra for serving
1 onion, chopped fine	1 tablespoon chopped fresh dill
2 garlic cloves, minced	

1. Toss shrimp with lemon zest, salt, and pepper in bowl; refrigerate until ready to use. 2. Using highest sauté function, heat oil in Instant Pot until shimmering. Add onion and cook until softened, about 5 minutes. Stir in garlic and cook until fragrant, about 30 seconds. Add orzo and cook, stirring frequently, until orzo is coated with oil and lightly browned, about 5 minutes. Stir in broth and water, scraping up any browned bits. 3. Lock lid in place and close pressure release valve. Select high pressure cook function and cook for 2 minutes. Turn off Instant Pot and quick-release pressure. Carefully remove lid, allowing steam to escape away from you. 4. Stir shrimp, olives, and feta into orzo. Cover and let sit until shrimp are opaque throughout, 5 to 7 minutes. Adjust consistency with extra hot broth as needed. Stir in dill and lemon juice, and season with salt and pepper to taste. Sprinkle individual portions with extra feta and drizzle with extra oil before serving.

Per Serving:
calories: 320 | fat: 8g | protein: 18g | carbs: 46g | fiber: 2g | sodium: 670mg

Creamy Spring Vegetable Linguine

Prep time: 10 minutes | Cook time: 10 minutes |

Serves 4 to 6

1 pound (454 g) linguine	1 cup frozen peas, thawed
5 cups water, plus extra as needed	4 ounces (113 g) finely grated Pecorino Romano (2 cups), plus extra for serving
1 tablespoon extra-virgin olive oil	½ teaspoon pepper
1 teaspoon table salt	2 teaspoons grated lemon zest
1 cup jarred whole baby artichokes packed in water, quartered	2 tablespoons chopped fresh tarragon

1. Loosely wrap half of pasta in dish towel, then press bundle against corner of counter to break noodles into 6-inch lengths; repeat with remaining pasta. 2. Add pasta, water, oil, and salt to Instant Pot, making sure pasta is completely submerged. Lock lid in place and close pressure release valve. Select high pressure cook function and cook for 4 minutes. Turn off Instant Pot and quick-release pressure. Carefully remove lid, allowing steam to escape away from you. 3. Stir artichokes and peas into pasta, cover, and let sit until heated through, about 3 minutes. Gently stir in Pecorino and pepper until cheese is melted and fully combined, 1 to 2 minutes. Adjust consistency with extra hot water as needed. Stir in

lemon zest and tarragon, and season with salt and pepper to taste. Serve, passing extra Pecorino separately.

Per Serving:
calories: 390 | fat: 8g | protein: 17g | carbs: 59g | fiber: 4g | sodium: 680mg

Fettuccine with Tomatoes and Pesto

Prep time: 15 minutes | Cook time: 10 minutes |

Serves 4

1 pound (454 g) whole-grain fettuccine	oregano
4 Roma tomatoes, diced	½ teaspoon salt
2 teaspoons tomato paste	1 packed cup fresh basil leaves
1 cup vegetable broth	¼ cup extra-virgin olive oil
2 garlic cloves, minced	¼ cup grated Parmesan cheese
1 tablespoon chopped fresh	¼ cup pine nuts

1. Bring a large stockpot of water to a boil over high heat, and cook the fettuccine according to the package instructions until al dente (still slightly firm). Drain but do not rinse. 2. Meanwhile, in a large, heavy skillet, combine the tomatoes, tomato paste, broth, garlic, oregano, and salt and stir well. Cook over medium heat for 10 minutes. 3. In a blender or food processor, combine the basil, olive oil, Parmesan cheese, and pine nuts and blend until smooth. 4. Stir the pesto into the tomato mixture. Add the pasta and cook, stirring frequently, just until the pasta is well coated and heated through. 5. Serve immediately.

Per Serving:
calories: 636 | fat: 22g | protein: 11g | carbs: 96g | fiber: 3g | sodium: 741mg

Rotini with Walnut Pesto, Peas, and Cherry Tomatoes

Prep time: 10 minutes | Cook time: 4 minutes | Serves 8

1 cup packed fresh basil leaves	1 pound (454 g) whole-wheat rotini pasta
⅓ cup chopped walnuts	4 cups water
¼ cup grated Parmesan cheese	1 pint cherry tomatoes
¼ cup plus 1 tablespoon extra-virgin olive oil, divided	1 cup fresh or frozen green peas
1 clove garlic, peeled	½ teaspoon ground black pepper
1 tablespoon lemon juice	
¼ teaspoon salt	

1. In a food processor, add basil and walnuts. Pulse until finely chopped, about 12 pulses. Add cheese, ¼ cup oil, garlic, lemon juice, and salt, and pulse until a rough paste forms, about 10 pulses. Refrigerate until ready to use. 2. Add pasta, water, and remaining 1 tablespoon oil to the Instant Pot®. Close lid, set steam release to Sealing, press the Manual button, and set time to 4 minutes. 3. When the timer beeps, quick-release the pressure until the float valve drops and open lid. Drain off any excess liquid. Allow pasta to cool to room temperature, about 30 minutes. Stir in basil mixture until pasta is well coated. Add tomatoes, peas, and pepper and toss to coat. Refrigerate for 2 hours. Stir well before serving.

Per Serving:
calories: 371 | fat: 15g | protein: 12g | carbs: 47g | fiber: 7g | sodium: 205mg

Neapolitan Pasta and Zucchini

Prep time: 5 minutes | Cook time: 28 minutes | Serves 3

⅓ cup extra virgin olive oil
1 large onion (any variety), diced
1 teaspoon fine sea salt, divided
2 large zucchini, quartered lengthwise and cut into ½-inch pieces
10 ounces (283 g) uncooked spaghetti, broken into 1-inch

pieces
2 tablespoons grated Parmesan cheese
2 ounces (57 g) grated or shaved Parmesan cheese for serving
½ teaspoon freshly ground black pepper

1. Add the olive oil to a medium pot over medium heat. When the oil begins to shimmer, add the onions and ¼ teaspoon of the sea salt. Sauté for 3 minutes, add the zucchini, and continue sautéing for 3 more minutes. 2. Add 2 cups of hot water to the pot or enough to just cover the zucchini (the amount of water may vary depending on the size of the pot). Cover, reduce the heat to low, and simmer for 10 minutes. 3. Add the pasta to the pot, stir, then add 2 more cups of hot water. Continue simmering, stirring occasionally, until the pasta is cooked and the mixture has thickened, about 12 minutes. (If the pasta appears to be dry or undercooked, add small amounts of hot water to the pot to ensure the pasta is covered in the water.). When the pasta is cooked, remove the pot from the heat. Add 2 tablespoons of the grated Parmesan and stir. 4. Divide the pasta into three servings and then top each with 1 ounce (28 g) of the grated or shaved Parmesan. Sprinkle the remaining sea salt and black pepper over the top of each serving. Store covered in the refrigerator for up to 3 days.

Per Serving:
calories: 718 | fat: 33g | protein: 24g | carbs: 83g | fiber: 6g | sodium: 815mg

Orzo with Feta and Marinated Peppers

Prep time:1 hour 25 minutes | Cook time: 37 minutes | Serves 2

2 medium red bell peppers
¼ cup extra virgin olive oil
1 tablespoon balsamic vinegar plus 1 teaspoon for serving
¼ teaspoon ground cumin
Pinch of ground cinnamon
Pinch of ground cloves
¼ teaspoon fine sea salt plus a

pinch for the orzo
1 cup uncooked orzo
3 ounces (85 g) crumbled feta
1 tablespoon chopped fresh basil
¼ teaspoon freshly ground black pepper

1. Preheat the oven at 350°F (180°C). Place the peppers on a baking pan and roast in the oven for 25 minutes or until they're soft and can be pierced with a fork. Set aside to cool for 10 minutes. 2. While the peppers are roasting, combine the olive oil, 1 tablespoon of the balsamic vinegar, cumin, cinnamon, cloves, and ¼ teaspoon of the sea salt. Stir to combine, then set aside. 3. Peel the cooled peppers, remove the seeds, and then chop into large pieces. Place the peppers in the olive oil and vinegar mixture and then toss to coat, ensuring the peppers are covered in the marinade. Cover and place in the refrigerator to marinate for 20 minutes. 4. While the peppers are marinating, prepare the orzo by bringing 3 cups of water and a pinch of salt to a boil in a large pot over high heat.

When the water is boiling, add the orzo, reduce the heat to medium, and cook, stirring occasionally, for 10–12 minutes or until soft, then drain and transfer to a serving bowl. 5. Add the peppers and marinade to the orzo, mixing well, then place in the refrigerator and to cool for at least 1 hour. 6. To serve, top with the feta, basil, black pepper, and 1 teaspoon of the balsamic vinegar. Mix well, and serve promptly. Store covered in the refrigerator for up to 3 days.

Per Serving:
calories: 600 | fat: 37g | protein: 15g | carbs: 51g | fiber: 4g | sodium: 690mg

Israeli Pasta Salad

Prep time: 15 minutes | Cook time: 4 minutes | Serves 6

½ pound (227 g) whole-wheat penne pasta
4 cups water
1 tablespoon plus ¼ cup extra-virgin olive oil, divided
1 cup quartered cherry tomatoes
½ English cucumber, chopped
½ medium orange bell pepper, seeded and chopped

½ medium red onion, peeled and chopped
½ cup crumbled feta cheese
1 teaspoon fresh thyme leaves
1 teaspoon chopped fresh oregano
½ teaspoon ground black pepper
¼ cup lemon juice

1. Add pasta, water, and 1 tablespoon oil to the Instant Pot®. Close lid, set steam release to Sealing, press the Manual button, and set time to 4 minutes. 2. When the timer beeps, quick-release the pressure until the float valve drops and open lid. Drain and set aside to cool for 30 minutes. Stir in tomatoes, cucumber, bell pepper, onion, feta, thyme, oregano, black pepper, lemon juice, and remaining ¼ cup oil. Refrigerate for 2 hours.

Per Serving:
calories: 243 | fat: 16g | protein: 7g | carbs: 20g | fiber: 3g | sodium: 180mg

Rotini with Red Wine Marinara

Prep time: 10 minutes | Cook time: 25 minutes | Serves 6

1 pound (454 g) rotini
4 cups water
1 tablespoon olive oil
½ medium yellow onion, peeled and diced
3 cloves garlic, peeled and minced
1 (15-ounce / 425-g) can

crushed tomatoes
½ cup red wine
1 teaspoon sugar
2 tablespoons chopped fresh basil
½ teaspoon salt
¼ teaspoon ground black pepper

1. Add pasta and water to the Instant Pot®. Close lid, set steam release to Sealing, press the Manual button, and set time to 4 minutes. When the timer beeps, quick-release the pressure until the float valve drops and open the lid. Press the Cancel button. Drain pasta and set aside. 2. Clean pot and return to machine. Press the Sauté button and heat oil. Add onion and cook until it begins to caramelize, about 10 minutes. Add garlic and cook 30 seconds. Add tomatoes, red wine, and sugar, and simmer for 10 minutes. Add basil, salt, pepper, and pasta. Serve immediately.

Per Serving:
calories: 320 | fat: 4g | protein: 10g | carbs: 59g | fiber: 4g | sodium: 215mg

Chapter 8 Pizzas, Wraps, and Sandwiches

Croatian Double-Crust Pizza with Greens and Garlic

Prep time: 15 minutes | Cook time: 20 minutes | Serves 4

4½ cups all-purpose flour
1¼ teaspoons salt, divided
1½ cups olive oil, plus 3 tablespoons, divided
1 cup warm water
1 pound (454 g) Swiss chard or kale, tough center ribs removed,

leaves julienned
¼ small head of green cabbage, thinly sliced
¼ teaspoon freshly ground black pepper
4 cloves garlic, minced

1. In a medium bowl, combine the flour and 1 teaspoon salt. Add 1½ cups olive oil and the warm water and stir with a fork until the mixture comes together and forms a ball. Wrap the ball in plastic wrap and refrigerate for at least 30 minutes. 2. While the dough is chilling, in a large bowl, toss together the greens, cabbage, 2 tablespoons olive oil, the remaining ¼ teaspoon salt, and the pepper. 3. Preheat the oven to 400°F(205°C). 4. Halve the dough and place the halves on two sheets of lightly floured parchment paper. Roll or pat the dough out into two ¼-inch-thick, 11-inch-diameter rounds. 5. Spread the greens mixture over one of the dough rounds, leaving about an inch clear around the edge. Place the second dough round over the greens and fold the edges together to seal the two rounds together. Bake in the preheated oven until the crust is golden brown, about 20 minutes. 6. While the pizza is in the oven, combine 1 tablespoon of olive oil with the garlic. When the pizza is done, remove it from the oven and immediately brush the garlic-oil mixture over the crust. Cut into wedges and serve hot.

Per Serving:
calories: 670 | fat: 45g | protein: 10g | carbs: 62g | fiber: 5g | sodium: 504mg

Sautéed Mushroom, Onion, and Pecorino Romano Panini

Prep time: 10 minutes | Cook time: 20 minutes | Serves 4

3 tablespoons olive oil, divided
1 small onion, diced
10 ounces (283 g) button or cremini mushrooms, sliced
½ teaspoon salt

¼ teaspoon freshly ground black pepper
4 crusty Italian sandwich rolls
4 ounces (113 g) freshly grated Pecorino Romano

1. Heat 1 tablespoon of the olive oil in a skillet over medium-high heat. Add the onion and cook, stirring, until it begins to soften, about 3 minutes. Add the mushrooms, season with salt and pepper, and cook, stirring, until they soften and the liquid they release evaporates, about 7 minutes. 2. To make the panini, heat a skillet or grill pan over high heat and brush with 1 tablespoon olive oil. Brush the inside of the rolls with the remaining 1 tablespoon olive oil. Divide the mushroom mixture evenly among the rolls and top each with ¼ of the grated cheese. 3. Place the sandwiches in the hot pan and place another heavy pan, such as a cast-iron skillet, on top to weigh them down. Cook for about 3 to 4 minutes, until crisp and golden on the bottom, and then flip over and repeat on the second side, cooking for an additional 3 to 4 minutes until golden and crisp. Slice each sandwich in half and serve hot.

Per Serving:
calories: 348 | fat: 20g | protein: 14g | carbs: 30g | fiber: 2g | sodium: 506mg

Grilled Eggplant and Chopped Greek Salad Wraps

Prep time: 10 minutes | Cook time: 20 minutes | Serves 4

15 small tomatoes, such as cherry or grape tomatoes, halved
10 pitted Kalamata olives, chopped
1 medium red onion, halved and thinly sliced
¾ cup crumbled feta cheese (about 4 ounces / 113 g)
2 tablespoons balsamic vinegar
1 tablespoon chopped fresh parsley
1 clove garlic, minced

2 tablespoons olive oil, plus 2 teaspoons, divided
¾ teaspoon salt, divided
1 medium cucumber, peeled, halved lengthwise, seeded, and diced
1 large eggplant, sliced ½-inch thick
½ teaspoon freshly ground black pepper
4 whole-wheat sandwich wraps or whole-wheat flour tortillas

1. In a medium bowl, toss together the tomatoes, olives, onion, cheese, vinegar, parsley, garlic, 2 teaspoons olive oil, and ¼ teaspoon of salt. Let sit at room temperature for 20 minutes. Add the cucumber, toss to combine, and let sit another 10 minutes. 2. While the salad is resting, grill the eggplant. Heat a grill or grill pan to high heat. Brush the remaining 2 tablespoons olive oil onto both sides of the eggplant slices. Grill for about 8 to 10 minutes per side, until grill marks appear and the eggplant is tender and cooked through. Transfer to a plate and season with the remaining ½ teaspoon of salt and the pepper. 3. Heat the wraps in a large, dry skillet over medium heat just until warm and soft, about 1 minute on each side. Place 2 or 3 eggplant slices down the center of each wrap. Spoon some of the salad mixture on top of the eggplant, using a slotted spoon so that any excess liquid is drained off. Fold in the sides of the wrap and roll up like a burrito. Serve immediately.

Per Serving:
calories: 233 | fat: 10g | protein: 8g | carbs: 29g | fiber: 7g | sodium: 707mg

Bocadillo with Herbed Tuna and Piquillo Peppers

Prep time: 5 minutes | Cook time: 20 minutes | Serves 4

2 tablespoons olive oil, plus more for brushing
1 medium onion, finely chopped
2 leeks, white and tender green parts only, finely chopped
1 teaspoon chopped thyme
½ teaspoon dried marjoram
½ teaspoon salt
¼ teaspoon freshly ground black pepper

3 tablespoons sherry vinegar
1 carrot, finely diced
2 (8-ounce / 227-g) jars Spanish tuna in olive oil
4 crusty whole-wheat sandwich rolls, split
1 ripe tomato, grated on the large holes of a box grater
4 piquillo peppers, cut into thin strips

1. Heat 2 tablespoons olive oil in a medium skillet over medium heat. Add the onion, leeks, thyme, marjoram, salt, and pepper. Stir frequently until the onions are softened, about 10 minutes. Stir in the vinegar and carrot and cook until the liquid has evaporated, 5 minutes. Transfer the mixture to a bowl and let cool to room temperature or refrigerate for 15 minutes or so. 2. In a medium bowl, combine the tuna, along with its oil, with the onion mixture, breaking the tuna chunks up with a fork. 3. Brush the rolls lightly with oil and toast under the broiler until lightly browned, about 2 minutes. Spoon the tomato pulp onto the bottom half of each roll, dividing equally and spreading it with the back of the spoon. Divide the tuna mixture among the rolls and top with the piquillo pepper slices. Serve immediately.

Per Serving:
calories: 416 | fat: 18g | protein: 35g | carbs: 30g | fiber: 5g | sodium: 520mg

Herbed Focaccia Panini with Anchovies and Burrata

Prep time: 5 minutes | Cook time: 8 minutes | Serves 4

8 ounces (227 g) burrata cheese, chilled and sliced
1 pound (454 g) whole-wheat herbed focaccia, cut crosswise into 4 rectangles and split horizontally

1 can anchovy fillets packed in oil, drained
8 slices tomato, sliced
2 cups arugula
1 tablespoon olive oil

1. Divide the cheese evenly among the bottom halves of the focaccia rectangles. Top each with 3 or 4 anchovy fillets, 2 slices of tomato, and ½ cup arugula. Place the top halves of the focaccia on top of the sandwiches. 2. To make the panini, heat a skillet or grill pan over high heat and brush with the olive oil. 3. Place the sandwiches in the hot pan and place another heavy pan, such as a cast-iron skillet, on top to weigh them down. Cook for about 3 to 4 minutes, until crisp and golden on the bottom, and then flip over and repeat on the second side, cooking for an additional 3 to 4 minutes until golden and crisp. Slice each sandwich in half and serve hot.

Per Serving:
calories: 596 | fat: 30g | protein: 27g | carbs: 58g | fiber: 5g | sodium: 626mg

Pesto Chicken Mini Pizzas

Prep time: 5 minutes | Cook time: 10 minutes | Serves 4

2 cups shredded cooked chicken
¾ cup pesto
4 English muffins, split

2 cups shredded Mozzarella cheese

1. In a medium bowl, toss the chicken with the pesto. Place one-eighth of the chicken on each English muffin half. Top each English muffin with ¼ cup of the Mozzarella cheese. 2. Put four pizzas at a time in the air fryer and air fry at 350ºF (177ºC) for 5 minutes. Repeat this process with the other four pizzas.

Per Serving:
calories: 617 | fat: 36g | protein: 45g | carbs: 29g | fiber: 3g | sodium: 544mg

Avocado and Asparagus Wraps

Prep time: 10 minutes | Cook time: 10 minutes | Serves 6

12 spears asparagus
1 ripe avocado, mashed slightly
Juice of 1 lime
2 cloves garlic, minced
2 cups brown rice, cooked and chilled

3 tablespoons Greek yogurt
Sea salt and freshly ground pepper, to taste
3 (8-inch) whole-grain tortillas
½ cup cilantro, diced
2 tablespoons red onion, diced

1. Steam asparagus in microwave or stove top steamer until tender. Mash the avocado, lime juice, and garlic in a medium mixing bowl. In a separate bowl, mix the rice and yogurt. 2. Season both mixtures with sea salt and freshly ground pepper to taste. Heat the tortillas in a dry nonstick skillet. 3. Spread each tortilla with the avocado mixture, and top with the rice, cilantro, and onion, followed by the asparagus. 4. Fold up both sides of the tortilla, and roll tightly to close. Cut in half diagonally before serving.

Per Serving:
calories: 361 | fat: 9g | protein: 9g | carbs: 63g | fiber: 7g | sodium: 117mg

Mediterranean-Pita Wraps

Prep time: 5 minutes | Cook time: 14 minutes | Serves 4

1 pound (454 g) mackerel fish fillets
2 tablespoons olive oil
1 tablespoon Mediterranean seasoning mix
½ teaspoon chili powder

Sea salt and freshly ground black pepper, to taste
2 ounces (57 g) feta cheese, crumbled
4 tortillas

1. Toss the fish fillets with the olive oil; place them in the lightly oiled air fryer basket. 2. Air fry the fish fillets at 400ºF (204ºC) for about 14 minutes, turning them over halfway through the cooking time. 3. Assemble your pitas with the chopped fish and remaining ingredients and serve warm.

Per Serving:
calories: 275 | fat: 13g | protein: 27g | carbs: 13g | fiber: 2g | sodium: 322mg

Greek Salad Pita

1 cup chopped romaine lettuce	1 tablespoon crumbled feta
1 tomato, chopped and seeded	cheese
½ cup baby spinach leaves	½ tablespoon red wine vinegar
½ small red onion, thinly sliced	1 teaspoon Dijon mustard
½ small cucumber, chopped and	Sea salt and freshly ground
deseeded	pepper, to taste
2 tablespoons olive oil	1 whole-wheat pita

1. Combine everything except the sea salt, freshly ground pepper, and pita bread in a medium bowl. 2. Toss until the salad is well combined. 3. Season with sea salt and freshly ground pepper to taste. Fill the pita with the salad mixture, serve, and enjoy!

Per Serving:
calories: 123 | fat: 8g | protein: 3g | carbs: 12g | fiber: 2g | sodium: 125mg

Za'atar Pizza

1 sheet puff pastry	⅓ cup za'atar seasoning
¼ cup extra-virgin olive oil	

1. Preheat the oven to 350°F(180°C). 2. Put the puff pastry on a parchment-lined baking sheet. Cut the pastry into desired slices. 3. Brush the pastry with olive oil. Sprinkle with the za'atar. 4. Put the pastry in the oven and bake for 10 to 12 minutes or until edges are lightly browned and puffed up. Serve warm or at room temperature.

Per Serving:
calories: 374 | fat: 30g | protein: 3g | carbs: 20g | fiber: 1g | sodium: 166mg

Margherita Open-Face Sandwiches

2 (6- to 7-inch) whole-wheat	¼ teaspoon dried oregano
submarine or hoagie rolls,	1 cup fresh mozzarella (about 4
sliced open horizontally	ounces / 113 g), patted dry and
1 tablespoon extra-virgin olive	sliced
oil	¼ cup lightly packed fresh basil
1 garlic clove, halved	leaves, torn into small pieces
1 large ripe tomato, cut into 8	¼ teaspoon freshly ground
slices	black pepper

1. Preheat the broiler to high with the rack 4 inches under the heating element. 2. Place the sliced bread on a large, rimmed baking sheet. Place under the broiler for 1 minute, until the bread is just lightly toasted. Remove from the oven. 3. Brush each piece of the toasted bread with the oil, and rub a garlic half over each piece. 4. Place the toasted bread back on the baking sheet. Evenly distribute the tomato slices on each piece, sprinkle with the oregano, and layer the cheese on top. 5. Place the baking sheet under the broiler. Set the timer for 1½ minutes, but check after 1 minute. When the cheese is melted and the edges are just starting to get dark brown, remove the sandwiches from the oven (this can take anywhere from 1½ to 2 minutes). 6. Top each sandwich with the fresh basil and pepper.

Per Serving:
calories: 176 | fat: 9g | protein: 10g | carbs: 14g | fiber: 2g | sodium: 119mg

Dill Salmon Salad Wraps

1 pound (454 g) salmon	2 tablespoons capers
filet, cooked and flaked, or 3	1½ tablespoons extra-virgin
(5-ounce / 142-g) cans salmon	olive oil
½ cup diced carrots (about 1	1 tablespoon aged balsamic
carrot)	vinegar
½ cup diced celery (about 1	½ teaspoon freshly ground
celery stalk)	black pepper
3 tablespoons chopped fresh	¼ teaspoon kosher or sea salt
dill	4 whole-wheat flatbread wraps
3 tablespoons diced red onion (a	or soft whole-wheat tortillas
little less than ⅛ onion)	

1. In a large bowl, mix together the salmon, carrots, celery, dill, red onion, capers, oil, vinegar, pepper, and salt. 2. Divide the salmon salad among the flatbreads. Fold up the bottom of the flatbread, then roll up the wrap and serve.

Per Serving:
calories: 185 | fat: 8g | protein: 17g | carbs: 12g | fiber: 2g | sodium: 237mg

Flatbread Pizza with Roasted Cherry Tomatoes, Artichokes, and Feta

1½ pounds (680 g) cherry or	1 can artichoke hearts, rinsed,
grape tomatoes, halved	well drained, and cut into thin
3 tablespoons olive oil, divided	wedges
½ teaspoon salt	8 ounces (227 g) crumbled feta
½ teaspoon freshly ground	cheese
black pepper	¼ cup chopped fresh Greek
4 Middle Eastern–style	oregano
flatbread rounds	

1. Preheat the oven to 500°F(260°C). 2. In a medium bowl, toss the tomatoes with 1 tablespoon olive oil, the salt, and the pepper. Spread out on a large baking sheet. Roast in the preheated oven until the tomato skins begin to blister and crack, about 10 to 12 minutes. Remove the tomatoes from the oven and reduce the heat to 450°F(235°C). 3. Place the flatbreads on a large baking sheet (or two baking sheets if necessary) and brush the tops with the remaining 2 tablespoons of olive oil. Top with the artichoke hearts, roasted tomatoes, and cheese, dividing equally. 4. Bake the flatbreads in the oven for about 8 to 10 minutes, until the edges are lightly browned and the cheese is melted. Sprinkle the oregano over the top and serve immediately.

Per Serving:
calories: 436 | fat: 27g | protein: 16g | carbs: 34g | fiber: 6g | sodium: 649mg

Chicken and Goat Cheese Pizza

Prep time: 10 minutes | Cook time: 10 minutes | Serves 4

All-purpose flour, for dusting
1 pound (454 g) premade pizza dough
2 tablespoons olive oil
1 cup shredded cooked chicken

3 ounces (85 g) goat cheese, crumbled
Sea salt
Freshly ground black pepper

1. Preheat the oven to 475°F (245°C) . 2. On a floured surface, roll out the dough to a 12-inch round and place it on a lightly floured pizza pan or baking sheet. Drizzle the dough with the olive oil and spread it out evenly. Top the dough with the chicken and goat cheese. 3. Bake the pizza for 8 to 10 minutes, until the crust is cooked through and golden. 4. Season with salt and pepper and serve.

Per Serving:
calories: 555 | fat: 23g | protein: 24g | carbs: 60g | fiber: 2g | sodium: 660mg

Mediterranean Tuna Salad Sandwiches

Prep time: 10 minutes | Cook time: 5 minutes | Serves 2

1 can white tuna, packed in water or olive oil, drained
1 roasted red pepper, diced
½ small red onion, diced
10 low-salt olives, pitted and finely chopped
¼ cup plain Greek yogurt

1 tablespoon flat-leaf parsley, chopped
Juice of 1 lemon
Sea salt and freshly ground pepper, to taste
4 whole-grain pieces of bread

1. In a small bowl, combine all of the ingredients except the bread, and mix well. 2. Season with sea salt and freshly ground pepper to taste. Toast the bread or warm in a pan. 3. Make the sandwich and serve immediately.

Per Serving:
calories: 307 | fat: 7g | protein: 30g | carbs: 31g | fiber: 5g | sodium: 564mg

Roasted Vegetable Bocadillo with Romesco Sauce

Prep time: 10 minutes | Cook time: 20 minutes | Serves 4

2 small yellow squash, sliced lengthwise
2 small zucchini, sliced lengthwise
1 medium red onion, thinly sliced
4 large button mushrooms, sliced
2 tablespoons olive oil
1 teaspoon salt, divided
½ teaspoon freshly ground

black pepper, divided
2 roasted red peppers from a jar, drained
2 tablespoons blanched almonds
1 tablespoon sherry vinegar
1 small clove garlic
4 crusty multigrain rolls
4 ounces (113 g) goat cheese, at room temperature
1 tablespoon chopped fresh basil

1. Preheat the oven to 400°F(205°C). 2. In a medium bowl, toss the yellow squash, zucchini, onion, and mushrooms with the olive oil,

½ teaspoon salt, and ¼ teaspoon pepper. Spread on a large baking sheet. Roast the vegetables in the oven for about 20 minutes, until softened. 3. Meanwhile, in a food processor, combine the roasted peppers, almonds, vinegar, garlic, the remaining ½ teaspoon salt, and the remaining ¼ teaspoon pepper and process until smooth. 4. Split the rolls and spread ¼ of the goat cheese on the bottom of each. Place the roasted vegetables on top of the cheese, dividing equally. Top with chopped basil. Spread the top halves of the rolls with the roasted red pepper sauce and serve immediately.

Per Serving:
calories: 379 | fat: 21g | protein: 17g | carbs: 32g | fiber: 4g | sodium: 592mg

Moroccan Lamb Flatbread with Pine Nuts, Mint, and Ras Al Hanout

Prep time: 10 minutes | Cook time: 20 minutes | Serves 4

1⅓ cups plain Greek yogurt
Juice of 1½ lemons, divided
1¼ teaspoons salt, divided
1 pound (454 g) ground lamb
1 medium red onion, diced
1 clove garlic, minced
1 tablespoon ras al hanout
¼ cup chopped fresh mint

leaves
Freshly ground black pepper
4 Middle Eastern-style flatbread rounds
2 tablespoons toasted pine nuts
16 cherry tomatoes, halved
2 tablespoons chopped cilantro

1. Preheat the oven to 450°F(235°C). 2. In a small bowl, stir together the yogurt, the juice of ½ lemon, and ¼ teaspoon salt. 3. Heat a large skillet over medium-high heat. Add the lamb and cook, stirring frequently, until browned, about 5 minutes. Drain any excess rendered fat from the pan and then stir in the onion and garlic and cook, stirring, until softened, about 3 minutes more. Stir in the ras al hanout, mint, the remaining teaspoon of salt, and pepper. 4. Place the flatbread rounds on a baking sheet (or two if necessary) and top with the lamb mixture, pine nuts, and tomatoes, dividing equally. Bake in the preheated oven until the crust is golden brown and the tomatoes have softened, about 10 minutes. Scatter the cilantro over the flatbreads and squeeze the remaining lemon juice over them. Cut into wedges and serve dolloped with the yogurt sauce.

Per Serving:
calories: 463 | fat: 22g | protein: 34g | carbs: 34g | fiber: 3g | sodium: 859mg

Cucumber Basil Sandwiches

Prep time: 10 minutes | Cook time: 0 minutes | Serves 2

Cucumber Basil Sandwiches
Prep time: 10 minutes | Cook time: 0 minutes | Serves 2
4 slices whole-grain bread
¼ cup hummus

1 large cucumber, thinly sliced
4 whole basil leaves

1. Spread the hummus on 2 slices of bread, and layer the cucumbers onto it. Top with the basil leaves and close the sandwiches. 2. Press down lightly and serve immediately.

Per Serving:
calories: 209 | fat: 5g | protein: 9g | carbs: 32g | fiber: 6g | sodium: 275mg

Greek Salad Wraps

Prep time: 15 minutes |Cook time: 0 minutes| Serves: 4

1½ cups seedless cucumber, peeled and chopped (about 1 large cucumber)
1 cup chopped tomato (about 1 large tomato)
½ cup finely chopped fresh mint
1 (2¼-ounce / 64-g) can sliced black olives (about ½ cup), drained
¼ cup diced red onion (about ¼ onion)

2 tablespoons extra-virgin olive oil
1 tablespoon red wine vinegar
¼ teaspoon freshly ground black pepper
¼ teaspoon kosher or sea salt
½ cup crumbled goat cheese (about 2 ounces / 57 g)
4 whole-wheat flatbread wraps or soft whole-wheat tortillas

1. In a large bowl, mix together the cucumber, tomato, mint, olives, and onion until well combined. 2. In a small bowl, whisk together the oil, vinegar, pepper, and salt. Drizzle the dressing over the salad, and mix gently. 3. With a knife, spread the goat cheese evenly over the four wraps. Spoon a quarter of the salad filling down the middle of each wrap. 4. Fold up each wrap: Start by folding up the bottom, then fold one side over and fold the other side over the top. Repeat with the remaining wraps and serve.

Per Serving:
calories: 217 | fat: 14g | protein: 7g | carbs: 17g | fiber: 3g | sodium: 329mg

Classic Margherita Pizza

Prep time: 10 minutes | Cook time: 10 minutes | Serves 4

All-purpose flour, for dusting
1 pound (454 g) premade pizza dough
1 (15-ounce / 425-g) can crushed San Marzano tomatoes, with their juices
2 garlic cloves

1 teaspoon Italian seasoning
Pinch sea salt, plus more as needed
1½ teaspoons olive oil, for drizzling
10 slices mozzarella cheese
12 to 15 fresh basil leaves

1. Preheat the oven to 475ºF (245ºC). 2. On a floured surface, roll out the dough to a 12-inch round and place it on a lightly floured pizza pan or baking sheet. 3. In a food processor, combine the tomatoes with their juices, garlic, Italian seasoning, and salt and process until smooth. Taste and adjust the seasoning. 4. Drizzle the olive oil over the pizza dough, then spoon the pizza sauce over the dough and spread it out evenly with the back of the spoon, leaving a 1-inch border. Evenly distribute the mozzarella over the pizza. 5. Bake until the crust is cooked through and golden, 8 to 10 minutes. Remove from the oven and let sit for 1 to 2 minutes. Top with the basil right before serving.

Per Serving:
calories: 570 | fat: 21g | protein: 28g | carbs: 66g | fiber: 4g | sodium: 570mg

Chapter 9 Snacks and Appetizers

Crispy Green Bean Fries with Lemon-Yogurt Sauce

Prep time: 5 minutes | Cook time: 5 minutes | Serves 4

Green Beans:
1 egg
2 tablespoons water
1 tablespoon whole wheat flour
¼ teaspoon paprika
½ teaspoon garlic powder
½ teaspoon salt
¼ cup whole wheat bread crumbs
½ pound (227 g) whole green beans
Lemon-Yogurt Sauce:
½ cup nonfat plain Greek yogurt
1 tablespoon lemon juice
¼ teaspoon salt
⅛ teaspoon cayenne pepper

Make the Green Beans: 1. Preheat the air fryer to 380°F(193ºC). 2. In a medium shallow bowl, beat together the egg and water until frothy. 3. In a separate medium shallow bowl, whisk together the flour, paprika, garlic powder, and salt, then mix in the bread crumbs. 4. Spray the bottom of the air fryer with cooking spray. 5. Dip each green bean into the egg mixture, then into the bread crumb mixture, coating the outside with the crumbs. Place the green beans in a single layer in the bottom of the air fryer basket. 6. Fry in the air fryer for 5 minutes, or until the breading is golden brown. Make the Lemon-Yogurt Sauce: 7. In a small bowl, combine the yogurt, lemon juice, salt, and cayenne. 8. Serve the green bean fries alongside the lemon-yogurt sauce as a snack or appetizer.

Per Serving:
calories: 86 | fat: 2g | protein: 5g | carbs: 13g | fiber: 2g | sodium: 529mg

Goat'S Cheese & Hazelnut Dip

Prep time: 10 minutes | Cook time: 0 minutes | Serves 8

2 heads yellow chicory or endive
Enough ice water to cover the leaves
Pinch of salt
Dip:
12 ounces (340 g) soft goat's cheese
3 tablespoons extra-virgin olive oil
1 tablespoon fresh lemon juice
1 teaspoon lemon zest (about ½ lemon)
1 clove garlic, minced
Freshly ground black pepper, to taste
Salt, if needed, to taste
Topping:
2 tablespoons chopped fresh chives
¼ cup crushed hazelnuts, pecans, or walnuts
1 tablespoon extra-virgin olive oil
Chile flakes or black pepper, to taste

1. Cut off the bottom of the chicory and trim the leaves to get rid of any that are limp or brown. Place the leaves in salted ice water for 10 minutes. This will help the chicory leaves to become crisp.

Drain and leave in the strainer. 2. To make the dip: Place the dip ingredients in a bowl and use a fork or spatula to mix until smooth and creamy. 3. Stir in the chives. Transfer to a serving bowl and top with the crushed hazelnuts, olive oil, and chile flakes. Serve with the crisp chicory leaves. Store in a sealed jar in the fridge for up to 5 days.

Per Serving:
calories: 219 | fat: 18g | protein: 10g | carbs: 5g | fiber: 4g | sodium: 224mg

Citrus-Marinated Olives

Prep time: 10 minutes | Cook time: 0 minutes |
Makes 2 cups

2 cups mixed green olives with pits
¼ cup red wine vinegar
¼ cup extra-virgin olive oil
4 garlic cloves, finely minced
Zest and juice of 2 clementines
or 1 large orange
1 teaspoon red pepper flakes
2 bay leaves
½ teaspoon ground cumin
½ teaspoon ground allspice

1. In a large glass bowl or jar, combine the olives, vinegar, oil, garlic, orange zest and juice, red pepper flakes, bay leaves, cumin, and allspice and mix well. Cover and refrigerate for at least 4 hours or up to a week to allow the olives to marinate, tossing again before serving.

Per Serving:
¼ cup: calories: 112 | fat: 10g | protein: 1g | carbs: 5g | fiber: 2g | sodium: 248mg

Tirokafteri (Spicy Feta and Yogurt Dip)

Prep time: 10 minutes | Cook time: 0 minutes | Serves 8

1 teaspoon red wine vinegar
1 small green chili, seeded and sliced
2 teaspoons extra virgin olive
oil
9 ounces (255 g) full-fat feta
¾ cup full-fat Greek yogurt

1. Combine the vinegar, chili, and olive oil in a food processor. Blend until smooth. 2. In a small bowl, combine the feta and Greek yogurt, and use a fork to mash the ingredients until a paste is formed. Add the pepper mixture and stir until blended. 3. Cover and transfer to the refrigerator to chill for at least 1 hour before serving. Store covered in the refrigerator for up to 3 days.

Per Serving:
calories: 109 | fat: 8g | protein: 6g | carbs: 4g | fiber: 0g | sodium: 311mg

Sea Salt Potato Chips

Prep time: 30 minutes | Cook time: 27 minutes | Serves 4

Oil, for spraying
4 medium yellow potatoes

1 tablespoon oil
⅛ to ¼ teaspoon fine sea salt

1. Line the air fryer basket with parchment and spray lightly with oil. 2. Using a mandoline or a very sharp knife, cut the potatoes into very thin slices. 3. Place the slices in a bowl of cold water and let soak for about 20 minutes. 4. Drain the potatoes, transfer them to a plate lined with paper towels, and pat dry. 5. Drizzle the oil over the potatoes, sprinkle with the salt, and toss to combine. Transfer to the prepared basket. 6. Air fry at 200°F (93°C) for 20 minutes. Toss the chips, increase the heat to 400°F (204°C), and cook for another 5 to 7 minutes, until crispy.
Per Serving:
calories: 194 | fat: 4g | protein: 4g | carbs: 37g | fiber: 5g | sodium: 90mg

Warm Olives with Rosemary and Garlic

Prep time: 5 minutes | Cook time: 3 minutes | Serves 4

1 tablespoon olive oil
1 clove garlic, chopped
2 sprigs fresh rosemary

¼ teaspoon salt
1 cup whole cured black olives, such as Kalamata

1. Heat the olive oil in a medium saucepan over medium heat. Add the garlic, rosemary, and salt. Reduce the heat to low and cook, stirring, for 1 minute. 2. Add the olives and cook, stirring occasionally, for about 2 minutes, until the olives are warm. 3. To serve, scoop the olives from the pan using a slotted spoon into a serving bowl. Pour the rosemary and garlic over the olives and serve warm.
Per Serving:
calories: 71 | fat: 7g | protein: 1g | carbs: 3g | fiber: 1g | sodium: 441mg

Garlic-Roasted Tomatoes and Olives

Prep time: 5 minutes | Cook time: 20 minutes | Serves 6

2 cups cherry tomatoes
4 garlic cloves, roughly chopped
½ red onion, roughly chopped
1 cup black olives
1 cup green olives

1 tablespoon fresh basil, minced
1 tablespoon fresh oregano, minced
2 tablespoons olive oil
¼ to ½ teaspoon salt

1. Preheat the air fryer to 380°F(193°C). 2. In a large bowl, combine all of the ingredients and toss together so that the tomatoes and olives are coated well with the olive oil and herbs. 3. Pour the mixture into the air fryer basket, and roast for 10 minutes. Stir the mixture well, then continue roasting for an additional 10 minutes. 4. Remove from the air fryer, transfer to a serving bowl, and enjoy.
Per Serving:
calories: 107 | fat: 9g | protein: 1g | carbs: 6g | fiber: 2g | sodium: 429mg

Garlic-Mint Yogurt Dip

Prep time: 5 minutes | Cook time: 0 minutes | Serves 4 to 6

1 cup plain Greek yogurt
Zest and juice of 1 lemon
1 garlic clove, minced
3 tablespoons chopped fresh mint

¼ teaspoon Aleppo pepper or cayenne pepper
¼ teaspoon salt
Freshly ground black pepper (optional)

1. In a small bowl, stir together all the ingredients until well combined. Season with black pepper, if desired. Refrigerate until ready to serve.
Per Serving:
1 cup: calories: 52 | fat: 2g | protein: 2g | carbs: 7g | fiber: 0g | sodium: 139mg

Romesco Dip

Prep time: 10 minutes |Cook time:minutes| Serves: 10

1 (12-ounce / 340-g) jar roasted red peppers, drained
1 (14½-ounce / 411-g) can diced tomatoes, undrained
½ cup dry-roasted almonds
2 garlic cloves
2 teaspoons red wine vinegar
1 teaspoon smoked paprika or
½ teaspoon cayenne pepper
¼ teaspoon kosher or sea salt

¼ teaspoon freshly ground black pepper
¼ cup extra-virgin olive oil
⅔ cup torn, day-old bread or toast (about 2 slices)
Assortment of sliced raw vegetables such as carrots, celery, cucumber, green beans, and bell peppers, for serving

1. In a high-powered blender or food processor, combine the roasted peppers, tomatoes and their juices, almonds, garlic, vinegar, smoked paprika, salt, and pepper. 2. Begin puréeing the ingredients on medium speed, and slowly drizzle in the oil with the blender running. Continue to purée until the dip is thoroughly mixed. 3. Add the bread and purée. 4. Serve with raw vegetables for dipping, or store in a jar with a lid for up to one week in the refrigerator.
Per Serving:
calories: 133 | fat: 10g | protein: 3g | carbs: 10g | fiber: 2g | sodium: 515mg

Mediterranean Trail Mix

Prep time: 5 minutes | Cook time: 0 minutes | Serves 6

1 cup roughly chopped unsalted walnuts
½ cup roughly chopped salted almonds

½ cup shelled salted pistachios
½ cup roughly chopped apricots
½ cup roughly chopped dates
⅓ cup dried figs, sliced in half

1. In a large zip-top bag, combine the walnuts, almonds, pistachios, apricots, dates, and figs and mix well.
Per Serving:
calories: 348 | fat: 24g | protein: 9g | carbs: 33g | fiber: 7g | sodium: 95mg

Roasted Za'atar Chickpeas

Prep time: 5 minutes | Cook time: 1 hour | Serves 8

3 tablespoons za'atar
2 tablespoons extra-virgin olive oil
½ teaspoon kosher salt
¼ teaspoon freshly ground

black pepper
4 cups cooked chickpeas, or 2 (15-ounce / 425-g) cans, drained and rinsed

1. Preheat the oven to 400ºF (205ºC). Line a baking sheet with foil or parchment paper. 2. In a large bowl, combine the za'atar, olive oil, salt, and black pepper. Add the chickpeas and mix thoroughly. 3. Spread the chickpeas in a single layer on the prepared baking sheet. Bake for 45 to 60 minutes, or until golden brown and crispy. Cool and store in an airtight container at room temperature for up to 1 week.

Per Serving:
calories: 150 | fat: 6g | protein: 6g | carbs: 17g | fiber: 6g | sodium: 230mg

Spiced Roasted Cashews

Prep time: 5 minutes | Cook time: 10 minutes | Serves 4

2 cups raw cashews
2 tablespoons olive oil
¼ teaspoon salt

¼ teaspoon chili powder
⅛ teaspoon garlic powder
⅛ teaspoon smoked paprika

1. Preheat the air fryer to 360°F(182ºC). 2. In a large bowl, toss all of the ingredients together. 3. Pour the cashews into the air fryer basket and roast them for 5 minutes. Shake the basket, then cook for 5 minutes more. 4. Serve immediately.

Per Serving:
calories: 453 | fat: 38g | protein: 13g | carbs: 22g | fiber: 2g | sodium: 159mg

Grilled Halloumi with Watermelon, Cherry Tomatoes, Olives, and Herb Oil

Prep time: 5 minutes | Cook time: 5 minutes | Serves 4

½ cup coarsely chopped fresh basil
3 tablespoons coarsely chopped fresh mint leaves, plus thinly sliced mint for garnish
1 clove garlic, coarsely chopped
½ cup olive oil, plus more for brushing
½ teaspoon salt, plus a pinch
½ teaspoon freshly ground

black pepper, plus a pinch
¾ pound (340 g) cherry tomatoes
8 ounces (227 g) Halloumi cheese, cut crosswise into 8 slices
2 cups thinly sliced watermelon, rind removed
¼ cup sliced, pitted Kalamata olives

1. Heat a grill or grill pan to high. 2. In a food processor or blender, combine the basil, chopped mint, and garlic and pulse to chop. While the machine is running, add the olive oil in a thin stream. Strain the oil through a fine-meshed sieve and discard the solids. Stir in ½ teaspoon of salt and ½ teaspoon of pepper. 3. Brush the grill rack with olive oil. Drizzle 2 tablespoons of the herb oil over the tomatoes and cheese and season them with pinches of salt and pepper. Place the tomatoes on the grill and cook, turning occasionally, until their skins become blistered and begin to burst, about 4 minutes. Place the cheese on the grill and cook until grill marks appear and the cheese begins to get melty, about 1 minute per side. 4. Arrange the watermelon on a serving platter. Arrange the grilled cheese and tomatoes on top of the melon. Drizzle the herb oil over the top and garnish with the olives and sliced mint. Serve immediately.

Per Serving:
calories: 535 | fat: 50g | protein: 14g | carbs: 12g | fiber: 2g | sodium: 663mg

Roasted Mushrooms with Garlic

Prep time: 3 minutes | Cook time: 22 to 27 minutes | Serves 4

16 garlic cloves, peeled
2 teaspoons olive oil, divided
16 button mushrooms
½ teaspoon dried marjoram

⅛ teaspoon freshly ground black pepper
1 tablespoon white wine or low-sodium vegetable broth

1. In a baking pan, mix the garlic with 1 teaspoon of olive oil. Roast in the air fryer at 350ºF (177ºC) for 12 minutes. 2. Add the mushrooms, marjoram, and pepper. Stir to coat. Drizzle with the remaining 1 teaspoon of olive oil and the white wine. 3. Return to the air fryer and roast for 10 to 15 minutes more, or until the mushrooms and garlic cloves are tender. Serve.

Per Serving:
calories: 57 | fat: 3g | protein: 3g | carbs: 7g | fiber: 1g | sodium: 6mg

Turmeric-Spiced Crunchy Chickpeas

Prep time: 15 minutes | Cook time: 30 minutes | Serves 4

2 (15-ounce / 425-g) cans organic chickpeas, drained and rinsed
3 tablespoons extra-virgin olive oil
2 teaspoons Turkish or smoked paprika

2 teaspoons turmeric
½ teaspoon dried oregano
½ teaspoon salt
¼ teaspoon ground ginger
⅛ teaspoon ground white pepper (optional)

1. Preheat the oven to 400°F(205ºC). Line a baking sheet with parchment paper and set aside. 2. Completely dry the chickpeas. Lay the chickpeas out on a baking sheet, roll them around with paper towels, and allow them to air-dry. I usually let them dry for at least 2½ hours, but can also be left to dry overnight. 3. In a medium bowl, combine the olive oil, paprika, turmeric, oregano, salt, ginger, and white pepper (if using). 4. Add the dry chickpeas to the bowl and toss to combine. 5. Put the chickpeas on the prepared baking sheet and cook for 30 minutes, or until the chickpeas turn golden brown. At 15 minutes, move the chickpeas around on the baking sheet to avoid burning. Check every 10 minutes in case the chickpeas begin to crisp up before the full cooking time has elapsed. 6. Remove from the oven and set them aside to cool.

Per Serving:
½ cup: calories: 308 | fat: 13g | protein: 11g | carbs: 40g | fiber: 11g | sodium: 292mg

Seared Halloumi with Pesto and Tomato

Prep time: 2 minutes | Cook time: 5 minutes | Serves 2

3 ounces (85 g) Halloumi cheese, cut crosswise into 2 thinner, rectangular pieces
2 teaspoons prepared pesto

sauce, plus additional for drizzling if desired
1 medium tomato, sliced

1. Heat a nonstick skillet over medium-high heat and place the slices of Halloumi in the hot pan. After about 2 minutes, check to see if the cheese is golden on the bottom. If it is, flip the slices, top each with 1 teaspoon of pesto, and cook for another 2 minutes, or until the second side is golden. 2. Serve with slices of tomato and a drizzle of pesto, if desired, on the side.

Per Serving:
calories: 177 | fat: 14g | protein: 10g | carbs: 4g | fiber: 1g | sodium: 233mg

Stuffed Fried Mushrooms

Prep time: 20 minutes | Cook time: 10 to 11 minutes | Serves 10

½ cup panko bread crumbs
½ teaspoon freshly ground black pepper
½ teaspoon onion powder
½ teaspoon cayenne pepper
1 (8-ounce / 227-g) package

cream cheese, at room temperature
20 cremini or button mushrooms, stemmed
1 to 2 tablespoons oil

1. In a medium bowl, whisk the bread crumbs, black pepper, onion powder, and cayenne until blended. 2. Add the cream cheese and mix until well blended. Fill each mushroom top with 1 teaspoon of the cream cheese mixture 3. Preheat the air fryer to 360ºF (182ºC). Line the air fryer basket with a piece of parchment paper. 4. Place the mushrooms on the parchment and spritz with oil. 5. Cook for 5 minutes. Shake the basket and cook for 5 to 6 minutes more until the filling is firm and the mushrooms are soft.

Per Serving:
calories: 120 | fat: 9g | protein: 3g | carbs: 7g | fiber: 1g | sodium: 125mg

Lemon Shrimp with Garlic Olive Oil

Prep time: 5 minutes | Cook time: 6 minutes | Serves 4

1 pound (454 g) medium shrimp, cleaned and deveined
¼ cup plus 2 tablespoons olive oil, divided
Juice of ½ lemon
3 garlic cloves, minced and divided

½ teaspoon salt
¼ teaspoon red pepper flakes
Lemon wedges, for serving (optional)
Marinara sauce, for dipping (optional)

1. Preheat the air fryer to 380ºF(193ºC). 2. In a large bowl, combine the shrimp with 2 tablespoons of the olive oil, as well as the lemon juice, ⅓ of the minced garlic, salt, and red pepper flakes. Toss to coat the shrimp well. 3. In a small ramekin, combine the remaining ¼ cup of olive oil and the remaining minced garlic. 4. Tear off a

12-by-12-inch sheet of aluminum foil. Pour the shrimp into the center of the foil, then fold the sides up and crimp the edges so that it forms an aluminum foil bowl that is open on top. Place this packet into the air fryer basket. 5. Roast the shrimp for 4 minutes, then open the air fryer and place the ramekin with oil and garlic in the basket beside the shrimp packet. Cook for 2 more minutes. 6. Transfer the shrimp on a serving plate or platter with the ramekin of garlic olive oil on the side for dipping. You may also serve with lemon wedges and marinara sauce, if desired.

Per Serving:
calories: 283 | fat: 21g | protein: 23g | carbs: 1g | fiber: 0g | sodium: 427mg

Asiago Shishito Peppers

Prep time: 5 minutes | Cook time: 10 minutes | Serves 4

Oil, for spraying
6 ounces (170 g) shishito peppers
1 tablespoon olive oil

½ teaspoon salt
½ teaspoon lemon pepper
⅓ cup grated Asiago cheese, divided

1. Line the air fryer basket with parchment and spray lightly with oil. 2. Rinse the shishitos and pat dry with paper towels. 3. In a large bowl, mix together the shishitos, olive oil, salt, and lemon pepper. Place the shishitos in the prepared basket. 4. Roast at 350ºF (177ºC) for 10 minutes, or until blistered but not burned. 5. Sprinkle with half of the cheese and cook for 1 more minute. 6. Transfer to a serving plate. Immediately sprinkle with the remaining cheese and serve.

Per Serving:
calories: 81 | fat: 6g | protein: 3g | carbs: 5g | fiber: 1g | sodium 443mg

Crunchy Orange-Thyme Chickpeas

Prep time: 5 minutes |Cook time: 20 minutes| Serves: 4

1 (15-ounce / 425-g) can chickpeas, drained and rinsed
2 teaspoons extra-virgin olive oil
¼ teaspoon dried thyme or ½

teaspoon chopped fresh thyme leaves
⅛ teaspoon kosher or sea salt
Zest of ½ orange (about ½ teaspoon)

1. Preheat the oven to 450°F (235°C). 2. Spread the chickpeas on a clean kitchen towel, and rub gently until dry. 3. Spread the chickpeas on a large, rimmed baking sheet. Drizzle with the oil and sprinkle with the thyme and salt. Using a Microplane or citrus zester, zest about half of the orange over the chickpeas. Mix well using your hands. 4. Bake for 10 minutes, then open the oven door and, using an oven mitt, give the baking sheet a quick shake. (Do not remove the sheet from the oven.) Bake for 10 minutes more. Taste the chickpeas (carefully!). If they are golden but you think they could be a bit crunchier, bake for 3 minutes more before serving.

Per Serving:
calories: 167 | fat: 5g | protein: 7g | carbs: 24g | fiber: 7g | sodium 303mg

Sfougato

Prep time: 10 minutes | Cook time: 8 minutes | Serves 4

½ cup crumbled feta cheese
¼ cup bread crumbs
1 medium onion, peeled and minced
4 tablespoons all-purpose flour
2 tablespoons minced fresh mint

½ teaspoon salt
½ teaspoon ground black pepper
1 tablespoon dried thyme
6 large eggs, beaten
1 cup water

1. In a medium bowl, mix cheese, bread crumbs, onion, flour, mint, salt, pepper, and thyme. Stir in eggs. 2. Spray an 8" round baking dish with nonstick cooking spray. Pour egg mixture into dish. 3. Place rack in the Instant Pot® and add water. Fold a long piece of foil in half lengthwise. Lay foil over rack to form a sling and top with dish. Cover loosely with foil. Close lid, set steam release to Sealing, press the Manual button, and set time to 8 minutes. 4. When the timer beeps, quick-release the pressure until the float valve drops. Open lid. Let stand 5 minutes, then remove dish from pot.

Per Serving:
calories: 226 | fat: 12g | protein: 14g | carbs: 15g | fiber: 1g | sodium: 621mg

Black Olive and Lentil Pesto

Prep time: 10 minutes | Cook time: 20 minutes | Serves 10 to 12

¾ cup green lentils, rinsed
¼ teaspoon salt
½ cup pitted Kalamata olives
2 tablespoons fresh Greek oregano

2 garlic cloves, minced
2 tablespoons coarsely chopped fresh parsley
3 tablespoons fresh lemon juice
5 tablespoons olive oil

1. Place the lentils in a large saucepan and add cold water to cover by 1 inch. Bring the water to a boil; cover and simmer for 20 minutes, or until the lentils are soft but not disintegrating. Drain and let cool. 2. Shake the colander a few times to remove any excess water, then transfer the lentils to a blender or food processor. Add the salt, olives, oregano, garlic, and parsley. With the machine running, add the lemon juice, then the olive oil, and blend until smooth. 3. Serve with pita chips, pita bread, or as a dip for fresh vegetables.

Per Serving:
1 cup: calories: 70 | fat: 7g | protein: 1g | carbs: 2g | fiber: 1g | sodium: 99mg

Spiced Maple Nuts

Prep time: 5 minutes | Cook time:10 minutes | Makes about 2 cups

2 cups raw walnuts or pecans (or a mix of nuts)
1 teaspoon extra-virgin olive oil
1 teaspoon ground sumac

½ teaspoon pure maple syrup
¼ teaspoon kosher salt
¼ teaspoon ground ginger
2 to 4 rosemary sprigs

1. Preheat the oven to 350ºF (180°C). Line a baking sheet with parchment paper or foil. 2. In a large bowl, combine the nuts, olive oil, sumac, maple syrup, salt, and ginger; mix together. Spread in a single layer on the prepared baking sheet. Add the rosemary. Roast for 8 to 10 minutes, or until golden and fragrant. 3. Remove the rosemary leaves from the stems and place in a serving bowl. Add the nuts and toss to combine before serving.

Per Serving:
¼ cup: calories: 175 | fat: 18g | protein: 3g | carbs: 4g | fiber: 2g | sodium: 35mg

Ultimate Nut Butter

Prep time: 5 minutes | Cook time: 30 minutes | Makes about 2 cups

1½ cups macadamia nuts
1 cup pecans
½ cup coconut butter
5 tablespoons light tahini
2 teaspoons cinnamon

1 teaspoon vanilla powder or 1 tablespoon unsweetened vanilla extract
¼ teaspoon salt

1. Preheat the oven to 285°F (140°C) fan assisted or 320°F (160°C) conventional. Line a baking tray with parchment. 2. Place the macadamias and pecans on the baking tray, transfer to the oven, and bake for about 30 minutes. Remove the nuts from the oven, let cool for about 10 minutes, and then transfer to a food processor while still warm. 3. Add the remaining ingredients. Blend until smooth and creamy, 2 to 3 minutes, scraping down the sides as needed with a spatula. Transfer to a jar and store at room temperature for up to 1 week or in the fridge for up to 1 month.

Per Serving:
¼ cup: calories: 374 | fat: 39g | protein: 3g | carbs: 6g | fiber: 4g | sodium: 76mg

Mediterranean-Style Stuffed Mushrooms

Prep time: 10 minutes | Cook time: 20 minutes | Serves 4

2 ounces (57 g) feta
1 tablespoon cream cheese
2 teaspoons dried oregano
1 tablespoon finely chopped fresh parsley
2 tablespoons finely chopped fresh basil
2 tablespoons finely chopped fresh mint

¼ teaspoon freshly ground black pepper
3 tablespoons unseasoned breadcrumbs, divided
2 tablespoons extra virgin olive oil, divided
20 medium button mushrooms, washed, dried, and stems removed

1. Preheat the oven to 400°F (205°C). Line a large baking pan with foil. 2. In a medium bowl, combine the feta, cream cheese, oregano, parsley, basil, mint, black pepper, 2 tablespoons of the breadcrumbs, and 1 tablespoon of the olive oil. Use a fork to mash the ingredients until they're combined and somewhat creamy. 3. Stuff the mushrooms with the filling and then place them in the prepared pan. 4. Sprinkle the remaining 1 tablespoon of breadcrumbs over the mushrooms and then drizzle the remaining olive oil over the top. 5. Bake for 15–20 minutes or until the tops are golden brown. Serve promptly.

Per Serving:
calories: 151 | fat: 12g | protein: 6g | carbs: 8g | fiber: 1g | sodium: 186mg

Crunchy Tex-Mex Tortilla Chips

Prep time: 5 minutes | Cook time: 5 minutes | Serves 4

Olive oil
½ teaspoon salt
½ teaspoon ground cumin
½ teaspoon chili powder

½ teaspoon paprika
Pinch cayenne pepper
8 (6-inch) corn tortillas, each
cut into 6 wedges

1. Spray fryer basket lightly with olive oil. 2. In a small bowl, combine the salt, cumin, chili powder, paprika, and cayenne pepper. 3. Place the tortilla wedges in the air fryer basket in a single layer. Spray the tortillas lightly with oil and sprinkle with some of the seasoning mixture. You will need to cook the tortillas in batches. 4. Air fry at 375ºF (191ºC) for 2 to 3 minutes. Shake the basket and cook until the chips are light brown and crispy, an additional 2 to 3 minutes. Watch the chips closely so they do not burn.

Per Serving:
calories: 118 | fat: 1g | protein: 3g | carbs: 25g | fiber: 3g | sodium: 307mg

Zucchini Feta Roulades

Prep time: 10 minutes | Cook time: 10 minutes |

Serves 6

½ cup feta
1 garlic clove, minced
2 tablespoons fresh basil, minced
1 tablespoon capers, minced

⅛ teaspoon salt
⅛ teaspoon red pepper flakes
1 tablespoon lemon juice
2 medium zucchini
12 toothpicks

1. Preheat the air fryer to 360ºF (182ºC).(If using a grill attachment, make sure it is inside the air fryer during preheating.) 2. In a small bowl, combine the feta, garlic, basil, capers, salt, red pepper flakes, and lemon juice. 3. Slice the zucchini into ⅛-inch strips lengthwise. (Each zucchini should yield around 6 strips.) 4. Spread 1 tablespoon of the cheese filling onto each slice of zucchini, then roll it up and secure it with a toothpick through the middle. 5. Place the zucchini roulades into the air fryer basket in a single layer, making sure that they don't touch each other. 6. Bake or grill in the air fryer for 10 minutes. 7. Remove the zucchini roulades from the air fryer and gently remove the toothpicks before serving.

Per Serving:
calories: 36 | fat: 3g | protein: 2g | carbs: 1g | fiber: 0g | sodium: 200mg

Red Lentils with Sumac

Prep time: 5 minutes | Cook time: 20 minutes |

Serves 6 to 8

1 cup red lentils, picked through and rinsed
1 teaspoon ground sumac

½ teaspoon salt
Pita chips, warm pita bread, or raw vegetables, for serving

1. In a medium saucepan, combine the lentils, sumac, and 2 cups water. Bring the water to a boil. Reduce the heat to maintain a simmer and cook for 15 minutes, or until the lentils are softened and most of the water has been absorbed. Stir in the salt and cook until the lentils have absorbed all the water, about 5 minutes more. 2. Serve with pita chips, warm pita bread, or as a dip for raw vegetables.

Per Serving:
1 cup: calories: 162 | fat: 1g | protein: 11g | carbs: 30g | fiber: 9g | sodium: 219mg

Pita Pizza with Olives, Feta, and Red Onion

Prep time: 15 minutes | Cook time: 10 minutes | Serves 4

4 (6-inch) whole-wheat pitas
1 tablespoon extra-virgin olive oil
½ cup hummus
½ bell pepper, julienned
½ red onion, julienned
¼ cup olives, pitted and

chopped
¼ cup crumbled feta cheese
¼ teaspoon red pepper flakes
¼ cup fresh herbs, chopped (mint, parsley, oregano, or a mix)

1. Preheat the broiler to low. Line a baking sheet with parchment paper or foil. 2. Place the pitas on the prepared baking sheet and brush both sides with the olive oil. Broil 1 to 2 minutes per side until starting to turn golden brown. 3. Spread 2 tablespoons hummus on each pita. Top the pitas with bell pepper, onion, olives, feta cheese, and red pepper flakes. Broil again until the cheese softens and starts to get golden brown, 4 to 6 minutes, being careful not to burn the pitas. 4. Remove from broiler and top with the herbs.

Per Serving:
calories: 185 | fat: 11g | protein: 5g | carbs: 17g | fiber: 3g | sodium: 285mg

Black-Eyed Pea "Caviar"

Prep time: 10 minutes | Cook time: 30 minutes |

Makes 5 cups

1 cup dried black-eyed peas
4 cups water
1 pound (454 g) cooked corn kernels
½ medium red onion, peeled and diced
½ medium green bell pepper, seeded and diced
2 tablespoons minced pickled jalapeño pepper

1 medium tomato, diced
2 tablespoons chopped fresh cilantro
¼ cup red wine vinegar
2 tablespoons extra-virgin olive oil
1 teaspoon salt
½ teaspoon ground black pepper
½ teaspoon ground cumin

1. Add black-eyed peas and water to the Instant Pot®. Close lid, set steam release to Sealing, press the Manual button, and set time to 30 minutes. 2. When the timer beeps, let pressure release naturally, about 25 minutes, and open lid. Drain peas and transfer to a large mixing bowl. Add all remaining ingredients and stir until thoroughly combined. Cover and refrigerate for 2 hours before serving.

Per Serving:
½ cup: calories: 28 | fat: 1g | protein: 1g | carbs: 4 | fiber: 1g | sodium: 51mg

Shrimp and Chickpea Fritters

Prep time: 5 minutes | Cook time: 10 minutes | Serves 6

2 tablespoons olive oil, plus ¼ cup, divided
½ small yellow onion, finely chopped
12 ounces (340 g) raw medium shrimp, peeled, deveined, and finely chopped
¼ cup chickpea flour

2 tablespoon all-purpose flour
2 tablespoons roughly chopped parsley
1 teaspoon baking powder
½ teaspoon hot or sweet paprika
¾ teaspoon salt, plus additional to sprinkle over finished dish
½ lemon

1. Heat 2 tablespoons of the olive oil in a large skillet over medium-high heat. Add the onion and cook, stirring frequently, until softened, about 5 minutes. Using a slotted spoon, transfer the cooked onions to a medium bowl. Add the shrimp, chickpea flour, all-purpose flour, parsley, baking powder, paprika, and salt and mix well. Let sit for 10 minutes. 2. Heat the remaining ¼ cup olive oil in the same skillet set over medium-high heat. When the oil is very hot, add the batter, about 2 tablespoons at a time. Cook for about 2 minutes, until the bottom turns golden and the edges are crisp. Flip over and cook for another minute or two until the second side is golden and crisp. Drain on paper towels. Serve hot, with lemon squeezed over the top. Season with salt just before serving.

Per Serving:
calories: 148 | fat: 6g | protein: 15g | carbs: 9g | fiber: 3g | sodium: 435mg

Baked Italian Spinach and Ricotta Balls

Prep time: 15 minutes | Cook time: 2 minutes | Serves 4

1½ tablespoons extra virgin olive oil
1 garlic clove
9 ounces (255 g) fresh baby leaf spinach, washed
3 spring onions (white parts only), thinly sliced
9 ounces (255 g) ricotta, drained
1¾ ounces (50 g) grated Parmesan cheese

2 tablespoons chopped fresh basil
¾ teaspoon salt, divided
¼ teaspoon plus a pinch of freshly ground black pepper, divided
4½ tablespoons plus ⅓ cup unseasoned breadcrumbs, divided
1 egg

1. Preheat the oven to 400°F (205°C). Line a large baking pan with parchment paper. 2. Add the olive oil and garlic clove to a large pan over medium heat. When the oil begins to shimmer, add the spinach and sauté, tossing continuously, until the spinach starts to wilt, then add the spring onions. Continue tossing and sautéing until most of the liquid has evaporated, about 6 minutes, then transfer the spinach and onion mixture to a colander to drain and cool for 10 minutes. 3. When the spinach mixture has cooled, discard the garlic clove and squeeze the spinach to remove as much of the liquid as possible. Transfer the spinach mixture to a cutting board and finely chop. 4. Combine the ricotta, Parmesan, basil, ½ teaspoon of the salt, and ¼ teaspoon of the black pepper in a large bowl. Use a fork to mash the ingredients together, then add the spinach and continue mixing until the ingredients are combined. Add 4½ tablespoons of the breadcrumbs and mix until all ingredients are well combined. 5. In a small bowl, whisk the egg with the remaining ¼ teaspoon salt and a pinch of the black pepper. Place the remaining ⅓ cup of breadcrumbs on a small plate. Scoop out 1 tablespoon of the spinach mixture and roll it into a smooth ball, then dip it in the egg mixture and then roll it in the breadcrumbs. Place the ball on the prepared baking pan and continue the process with the remaining spinach mixture. 6. Bake for 16–20 minutes or until the balls turn a light golden brown. Remove the balls from the oven and serve promptly. Store covered in the refrigerator for up to 1 day. (Reheat before serving.)

Per Serving:
calories: 311 | fat: 19g | protein: 18g | carbs: 18g | fiber: 3g | sodium: 684mg

Smoky Baba Ghanoush

Prep time: 50 minutes | Cook time: 40 minutes | Serves 6

2 large eggplants, washed
¼ cup lemon juice
1 teaspoon garlic, minced
1 teaspoon salt

½ cup tahini paste
3 tablespoons extra-virgin olive oil

1. Grill the whole eggplants over a low flame using a gas stovetop or grill. Rotate the eggplant every 5 minutes to make sure that all sides are cooked evenly. Continue to do this for 40 minutes. 2. Remove the eggplants from the stove or grill and put them onto a plate or into a bowl; cover with plastic wrap. Let sit for 5 to 10 minutes. 3. Using your fingers, peel away and discard the charred skin of the eggplants. Cut off the stem. 4. Put the eggplants into a food processor fitted with a chopping blade. Add the lemon juice, garlic, salt, and tahini paste, and pulse the mixture 5 to 7 times. 5. Pour the eggplant mixture onto a serving plate. Drizzle with the olive oil. Serve chilled or at room temperature.

Per Serving:
calories: 230 | fat: 18g | protein: 5g | carbs: 16g | fiber: 7g | sodium: 416mg

Nutty Apple Salad

Prep time: 25 minutes | Cook time: 0 minutes | Serves 4

6 firm apples, such as Gala or Golden Delicious, peeled, cored, and sliced
1 tablespoon freshly squeezed lemon juice
2 kiwis, peeled and diced
½ cup sliced strawberries
½ cup packaged shredded coleslaw mix, without dressing

½ cup walnut halves
¼ cup slivered almonds
¼ cup balsamic vinegar
¼ cup extra-virgin olive oil
2 tablespoons sesame seeds, plus more for garnish (optional)
¼ teaspoon salt
¼ teaspoon freshly ground black pepper

1. In a medium bowl, toss the apple slices with the lemon juice to prevent browning. Add the kiwis, strawberries, coleslaw mix, walnuts, and almonds and toss well to mix. 2. In a small bowl, whisk together the balsamic vinegar, olive oil, and sesame seeds and season with salt and pepper. 3. Pour the dressing over the salad and toss to coat. 4. To serve, spoon into small bowls and top with additional sesame seeds if desired.

Per Serving:
calories: 371 | fat: 21g | protein: 3g | carbs: 49g | fiber: 9g | sodium: 155mg

Classic Hummus with Tahini

Prep time: 5 minutes | Cook time: 0 minutes | Makes about 2 cups

2 cups drained canned chickpeas, liquid reserved
½ cup tahini
¼ cup olive oil, plus more for garnish
2 cloves garlic, peeled, or to taste
Juice of 1 lemon, plus more as needed

1 tablespoon ground cumin
Salt
Freshly ground black pepper
1 teaspoon paprika, for garnish
2 tablespoons chopped flat-leaf parsley, for garnish
4 whole-wheat pita bread or flatbread rounds, warmed

1. In a food processor, combine the chickpeas, tahini, oil, garlic, lemon juice, and cumin. Season with salt and pepper, and process until puréed. With the food processor running, add the reserved chickpea liquid until the mixture is smooth and reaches the desired consistency. 2. Spoon the hummus into a serving bowl, drizzle with a bit of olive oil, and sprinkle with the paprika and parsley. 3. Serve immediately, with warmed pita bread or flatbread, or cover and refrigerate for up to 2 days. Bring to room temperature before serving.

Per Serving:
¼ cup: calories: 309 | fat: 16g | protein: 9g | carbs: 36g | fiber: 7g | sodium: 341mg

Garlic-Parmesan Croutons

Prep time: 3 minutes | Cook time: 12 minutes | Serves 4

Oil, for spraying
4 cups cubed French bread
1 tablespoon grated Parmesan cheese

3 tablespoons olive oil
1 tablespoon granulated garlic
½ teaspoon unsalted salt

1. Line the air fryer basket with parchment and spray lightly with oil. 2. In a large bowl, mix together the bread, Parmesan cheese, olive oil, garlic, and salt, tossing with your hands to evenly distribute the seasonings. Transfer the coated bread cubes to the prepared basket. 3. Air fry at 350ºF (177ºC) for 10 to 12 minutes, stirring once after 5 minutes, or until crisp and golden brown.

Per Serving:
calories: 220 | fat: 12g | protein: 5g | carbs: 23g | fiber: 1g | sodium: 285mg

Croatian Red Pepper Dip

Prep time: 10 minutes | Cook time: 30 minutes | Serves 4 to 6

4 or 5 medium red bell peppers
1 medium eggplant (about ¾ pound / 340 g)
¼ cup olive oil, divided
1 teaspoon salt, divided

½ teaspoon freshly ground black pepper, divided
4 cloves garlic, minced
1 tablespoon white vinegar

1. Preheat the broiler to high. 2. Line a large baking sheet with aluminum foil. 3. Brush the peppers and eggplant all over with 2 tablespoons of the olive oil and sprinkle with ½ teaspoon of the salt and ¼ teaspoon of the pepper. Place the peppers and the eggplant on the prepared baking sheet and broil, turning every few minutes until the skins are charred on all sides. The peppers will take about 10 minutes and the eggplant will take about 20 minutes. 4. When the peppers are fully charred, remove them from the baking sheet, place them in a bowl, cover with plastic wrap, and let them steam while the eggplant continues to cook. When the eggplant is fully charred and soft in the center, remove it from the oven and set aside to cool. 5. When the peppers are cool enough to handle, slip the charred skins off. Discard the charred skins. Seed the peppers and place them in a food processor. 6. Add the garlic to the food processor and pulse until the vegetables are coarsely chopped. Add the rest of the olive oil, the vinegar, and remaining ½ teaspoon of salt and process to a smooth purée. 7. Transfer the vegetable mixture to a medium saucepan and bring to a simmer over medium-high heat. Lower the heat to medium-low and let simmer, stirring occasionally, for 30 minutes. Remove from the heat and cool to room temperature. Serve at room temperature.

Per Serving:
calories: 144 | fat: 11g | protein: 2g | carbs: 12g | fiber: 5g | sodium: 471mg

Sweet Potato Fries

Prep time: 15 minutes | Cook time: 40 minutes | Serves 4

4 large sweet potatoes, peeled and cut into finger-like strips
2 tablespoons extra-virgin olive oil

½ teaspoon salt
½ teaspoon freshly ground black pepper

1. Preheat the oven to 350°F(180ºC). Line a baking sheet with aluminum foil. Toss the potatoes in a large bowl with the olive oil, salt, and pepper. 2. Arrange the potatoes in a single layer on the baking sheet and bake until brown at the edges, about 40 minutes. Serve piping hot.

Per Serving:
calories: 171 | fat: 7g | protein: 2g | carbs: 26g | fiber: 4g | sodium: 362mg

Mini Lettuce Wraps

Prep time: 10 minutes | Cook time: 0 minutes | Makes about 1 dozen wraps

1 tomato, diced
1 cucumber, diced
1 red onion, sliced
1 ounce (28 g) low-fat feta cheese, crumbled
Juice of 1 lemon

1 tablespoon olive oil
Sea salt and freshly ground pepper, to taste
12 small, intact iceberg lettuce leaves

1. Combine the tomato, cucumber, onion, and feta in a bowl with the lemon juice and olive oil. 2. Season with sea salt and freshly ground pepper. 3. Without tearing the leaves, gently fill each leaf with a tablespoon of the veggie mixture. 4. Roll them as tightly as you can, and lay them seam-side-down on a serving platter.

Per Serving:
1 wrap: calories: 26 | fat: 2g | protein: 1g | carbs: 2g | fiber: 1g | sodium: 20mg

Roasted Rosemary Olives

Prep time: 5 minutes | Cook time: 25 minutes | Serves 4

1 cup mixed variety olives, pitted and rinsed
2 tablespoons lemon juice
1 tablespoon extra-virgin olive

oil
6 garlic cloves, peeled
4 rosemary sprigs

1. Preheat the oven to 400ºF (205ºC). Line the baking sheet with parchment paper or foil. 2. Combine the olives, lemon juice, olive oil, and garlic in a medium bowl and mix together. Spread in a single layer on the prepared baking sheet. Sprinkle on the rosemary. Roast for 25 minutes, tossing halfway through. 3. Remove the rosemary leaves from the stem and place in a serving bowl. Add the olives and mix before serving.

Per Serving:
calories: 100 | fat: 9g | protein: 0g | carbs: 4g | fiber: 0g | sodium: 260mg

Honey-Rosemary Almonds

Prep time: 5 minutes |Cook time: 10 minutes| Serves: 6

1 cup raw, whole, shelled almonds
1 tablespoon minced fresh rosemary

¼ teaspoon kosher or sea salt
1 tablespoon honey
Nonstick cooking spray

1. In a large skillet over medium heat, combine the almonds, rosemary, and salt. Stir frequently for 1 minute. 2. Drizzle in the honey and cook for another 3 to 4 minutes, stirring frequently, until the almonds are coated and just starting to darken around the edges. 3. Remove from the heat. Using a spatula, spread the almonds onto a pan coated with nonstick cooking spray. Cool for 10 minutes or so. Break up the almonds before serving.

Per Serving:
calories: 149 | fat: 12g | protein: 5g | carbs: 8g | fiber: 3g | sodium: 97mg

Parmesan French Fries

Prep time: 10 minutes | Cook time: 25 minutes |
Serves 2 to 3

2 to 3 large russet potatoes, peeled and cut into ½-inch sticks
2 teaspoons vegetable or canola oil
¾ cup grated Parmesan cheese

½ teaspoon salt
Freshly ground black pepper, to taste
1 teaspoon fresh chopped parsley

1. Bring a large saucepan of salted water to a boil on the stovetop while you peel and cut the potatoes. Blanch the potatoes in the boiling salted water for 4 minutes while you preheat the air fryer to 400ºF (204ºC). Strain the potatoes and rinse them with cold water. Dry them well with a clean kitchen towel. 2. Toss the dried potato sticks gently with the oil and place them in the air fryer basket. Air fry for 25 minutes, shaking the basket a few times while the fries cook to help them brown evenly. 3. Combine the Parmesan cheese,

salt and pepper. With 2 minutes left on the air fryer cooking time, sprinkle the fries with the Parmesan cheese mixture. Toss the fries to coat them evenly with the cheese mixture and continue to air fry for the final 2 minutes, until the cheese has melted and just starts to brown. Sprinkle the finished fries with chopped parsley, a little more grated Parmesan cheese if you like, and serve.

Per Serving:
calories: 252 | fat: 11g | protein: 13g | carbs: 27g | fiber: 2g | sodium: 411mg

Flatbread with Ricotta and Orange-Raisin Relish

Prep time: 5 minutes | Cook time: 8 minutes | Serves
4 to 6

¾ cup golden raisins, roughly chopped
1 shallot, finely diced
1 tablespoon olive oil
1 tablespoon red wine vinegar
1 tablespoon honey
1 tablespoon chopped flat-leaf parsley
1 tablespoon fresh orange zest

strips
Pinch of salt
1 oval prebaked whole-wheat flatbread, such as naan or pocketless pita
8 ounces (227 g) whole-milk ricotta cheese
½ cup baby arugula

1. Preheat the oven to 450°F(235ºC). 2. In a small bowl, stir together the raisins, shallot, olive oil, vinegar, honey, parsley, orange zest, and salt. 3. Place the flatbread on a large baking sheet and toast in the preheated oven until the edges are lightly browned, about 8 minutes. 4. Spoon the ricotta cheese onto the flatbread, spreading with the back of the spoon. Scatter the arugula over the cheese. Cut the flatbread into triangles and top each piece with a dollop of the relish. Serve immediately.

Per Serving:
calories: 195 | fat: 9g | protein: 6g | carbs: 25g | fiber: 1g | sodium: 135mg

Pesto Cucumber Boats

Prep time: 10 minutes | Cook time: 0 minutes |
Serves 4 to 6

3 medium cucumbers
¼ teaspoon salt
1 packed cup fresh basil leaves
1 garlic clove, minced

¼ cup walnut pieces
¼ cup grated Parmesan cheese
¼ cup extra-virgin olive oil
½ teaspoon paprika

1. Cut each cucumber in half lengthwise and again in half crosswise to make 4 stocky pieces. Use a spoon to remove the seeds and hollow out a shallow trough in each piece. Lightly salt each piece and set aside on a platter. 2. In a blender or food processor, combine the basil, garlic, walnuts, Parmesan cheese, and olive oil and blend until smooth. 3. Use a spoon to spread pesto into each cucumber "boat" and sprinkle each with paprika. Serve.

Per Serving:
calories: 143 | fat: 14g | protein: 3g | carbs: 4g | fiber: 1g | sodium: 175mg

Citrus-Kissed Melon

Prep time: 5 minutes | Cook time: 0 minutes | Serves 4

2 cups cubed melon, such as Crenshaw, Sharlyn, or honeydew
2 cups cubed cantaloupe
½ cup freshly squeezed orange juice
¼ cup freshly squeezed lime juice
1 tablespoon orange zest

1. In a large bowl, combine the melon cubes. In a small bowl, whisk together the orange juice, lime juice, and orange zest and pour over the fruit. 2. Cover and refrigerate for at least 4 hours, stirring occasionally. Serve chilled.

Per Serving:
calories: 80 | fat: 0g | protein: 2g | carbs: 20g | fiber: 2g | sodium: 30mg

Asian Five-Spice Wings

Prep time: 30 minutes | Cook time: 13 to 15 minutes | Serves 4

2 pounds (907 g) chicken wings
½ cup Asian-style salad dressing
2 tablespoons Chinese five-spice powder

1. Cut off wing tips and discard or freeze for stock. Cut remaining wing pieces in two at the joint. 2. Place wing pieces in a large sealable plastic bag. Pour in the Asian dressing, seal bag, and massage the marinade into the wings until well coated. Refrigerate for at least an hour. 3. Remove wings from bag, drain off excess marinade, and place wings in air fryer basket. 4. Air fry at 360°F (182°C) for 13 to 15 minutes or until juices run clear. About halfway through cooking time, shake the basket or stir wings for more even cooking. 5. Transfer cooked wings to plate in a single layer. Sprinkle half of the Chinese five-spice powder on the wings, turn, and sprinkle other side with remaining seasoning.

Per Serving:
calories: 357 | fat: 12g | protein: 51g | carbs: 9g | fiber: 2g | sodium: 591mg

Mexican Potato Skins

Prep time: 10 minutes | Cook time: 55 minutes | Serves 6

Olive oil
6 medium russet potatoes, scrubbed
Salt and freshly ground black pepper, to taste
1 cup fat-free refried black beans
1 tablespoon taco seasoning
½ cup salsa
¾ cup reduced-fat shredded Cheddar cheese

1. Spray the air fryer basket lightly with olive oil. 2. Spray the potatoes lightly with oil and season with salt and pepper. Pierce each potato a few times with a fork. 3. Place the potatoes in the air fryer basket. Air fry at 400°F (204°C) until fork-tender, 30 to 40 minutes. The cooking time will depend on the size of the potatoes. You can cook the potatoes in the microwave or a standard oven, but they won't get the same lovely crispy skin they will get in the air fryer. 4. While the potatoes are cooking, in a small bowl, mix together the beans and taco seasoning. Set aside until the potatoes are cool enough to handle. 5. Cut each potato in half lengthwise. Scoop out most of the insides, leaving about ¼ inch in the skins so the potato skins hold their shape. 6. Season the insides of the potato skins with salt and black pepper. Lightly spray the insides of the potato skins with oil. You may need to cook them in batches. 7. Place them into the air fryer basket, skin-side down, and air fry until crisp and golden, 8 to 10 minutes. 8. Transfer the skins to a work surface and spoon ½ tablespoon of seasoned refried black beans into each one. Top each with 2 teaspoons salsa and 1 tablespoon shredded Cheddar cheese. 9. Place filled potato skins in the air fryer basket in a single layer. Lightly spray with oil. 10. Air fry until the cheese is melted and bubbly, 2 to 3 minutes.

Per Serving:
calories: 239 | fat: 2g | protein: 10g | carbs: 46g | fiber: 5g | sodium: 492mg

Fried Baby Artichokes with Lemon-Garlic Aioli

Prep time: 5 minutes | Cook time: 50 minutes | Serves 10

Artichokes:
15 baby artichokes
½ lemon
3 cups olive oil
Kosher salt, to taste
Aioli:
1 egg
2 cloves garlic, chopped
1 tablespoon fresh lemon juice
½ teaspoon Dijon mustard
½ cup olive oil
Kosher salt and ground black pepper, to taste

1. Make the Artichokes: Wash and drain the artichokes. With a paring knife, strip off the coarse outer leaves around the base and stalk, leaving the softer leaves on. Carefully peel the stalks and trim off all but 2' below the base. Slice off the top ½' of the artichokes. Cut each artichoke in half. Rub the cut surfaces with a lemon half to keep from browning. 2. In a medium saucepan fitted with a deep-fry thermometer over medium heat, warm the oil to about 280°F(138°C). Working in batches, cook the artichokes in the hot oil until tender, about 15 minutes. Using a slotted spoon, remove and drain on a paper towel–lined plate. Repeat with all the artichoke halves. 3. Increase the heat of the oil to 375°F(190°C). In batches, cook the precooked baby artichokes until browned at the edges and crisp, about 1 minute. Transfer to a paper towel–lined plate. Season with the salt to taste. Repeat with the remaining artichokes. 4. Make the aioli: In a blender, pulse together the egg, garlic, lemon juice, and mustard until combined. With the blender running, slowly drizzle in the oil a few drops at a time until the mixture thickens like mayonnaise, about 2 minutes. Transfer to a bowl and season to taste with the salt and pepper. 5. Serve the warm artichokes with the aioli on the side.

Per Serving:
calories: 236 | fat: 17g | protein: 6g | carbs: 21g | fiber: 10g | sodium: 283mg

Ranch Oyster Snack Crackers

Prep time: 3 minutes | Cook time: 12 minutes | Serves 6

Oil, for spraying
¼ cup olive oil
2 teaspoons dry ranch seasoning
1 teaspoon chili powder

½ teaspoon dried dill
½ teaspoon granulated garlic
½ teaspoon salt
1 (9-ounce / 255-g) bag oyster crackers

1. Preheat the air fryer to 325°F (163°C). Line the air fryer basket with parchment and spray lightly with oil. 2. In a large bowl, mix together the olive oil, ranch seasoning, chili powder, dill, garlic, and salt. Add the crackers and toss until evenly coated. 3. Place the mixture in the prepared basket. 4. Cook for 10 to 12 minutes, shaking or stirring every 3 to 4 minutes, or until crisp and golden brown.

Per Serving:
calories: 261 | fat: 13g | protein: 4g | carbs: 32g | fiber: 1g | sodium: 621mg

Cinnamon-Apple Chips

Prep time: 10 minutes | Cook time: 32 minutes | Serves 4

Oil, for spraying
2 Red Delicious or Honeycrisp apples

¼ teaspoon ground cinnamon, divided

1. Line the air fryer basket with parchment and spray lightly with oil. 2. Trim the uneven ends off the apples. Using a mandoline on the thinnest setting or a sharp knife, cut the apples into very thin slices. Discard the cores. 3. Place half of the apple slices in a single layer in the prepared basket and sprinkle with half of the cinnamon. 4. Place a metal air fryer trivet on top of the apples to keep them from flying around while they are cooking. 5. Air fry at 300°F (149°C) for 16 minutes, flipping every 5 minutes to ensure even cooking. Repeat with the remaining apple slices and cinnamon. 6. Let cool to room temperature before serving. The chips will firm up as they cool.

Per Serving:
calories: 63 | fat: 0g | protein: 0g | carbs: 15g | fiber: 3g | sodium: 1mg

Chapter 10 Vegetarian Mains

Baked Falafel Sliders

Prep time: 10 minutes | Cook time: 30 minutes | Makes 6 sliders

Olive oil cooking spray
1 (15-ounce / 425-g) can no-salt-added or low-sodium chickpeas, drained and rinsed
1 onion, roughly chopped
2 garlic cloves, peeled
2 tablespoons fresh parsley, chopped
2 tablespoons whole-wheat flour
½ teaspoon ground coriander
½ teaspoon ground cumin
½ teaspoon baking powder
½ teaspoon kosher salt
¼ teaspoon freshly ground black pepper

1. Preheat the oven to 350ºF (180ºC). Line a baking sheet with parchment paper or foil and lightly spray with olive oil cooking spray. 2. In a food processor, add the chickpeas, onion, garlic, parsley, flour, coriander, cumin, baking powder, salt, and black pepper. Process until smooth, stopping to scrape down the sides of the bowl. 3. Make 6 slider patties, each with a heaping ¼ cup of mixture, and arrange on the prepared baking sheet. Bake for 30 minutes, turning over halfway through.

Per Serving:
1 slider: calories: 90 | fat: 1g | protein: 4g | carbs:17 g | fiber: 3g | sodium: 110mg

Greek Frittata with Tomato-Olive Salad

Prep time: 10 minutes | Cook time: 25 minutes | Serves 4 to 6

Frittata:
2 tablespoons olive oil
6 scallions, thinly sliced
4 cups (about 5 ounces / 142 g) baby spinach leaves
8 eggs
¼ cup whole-wheat breadcrumbs, divided
1 cup (about 3 ounces / 85 g) crumbled feta cheese
¾ teaspoon salt
¼ teaspoon freshly ground black pepper

Tomato-Olive Salad:
2 tablespoons olive oil
1 tablespoon lemon juice
¼ teaspoon dried oregano
½ teaspoon salt
¼ teaspoon freshly ground black pepper
1 pint cherry, grape, or other small tomatoes, halved
3 pepperoncini, stemmed and chopped
½ cup coarsely chopped pitted Kalamata olives

1. Preheat the oven to 450°F(235ºC). 2. Heat the olive oil in an oven-safe skillet set over medium-high heat. Add the scallions and spinach and cook, stirring frequently, for about 4 minutes, until the spinach wilts. 3. In a medium bowl, whisk together the eggs, 2 tablespoons breadcrumbs, cheese, ¾ cup water, salt, and pepper. Pour the egg mixture into the skillet with the spinach and onions and stir to mix. Sprinkle the remaining 2 tablespoons of breadcrumbs evenly over the top. Bake the frittata in the preheated oven for about 20 minutes, until the egg is set and the top is lightly browned. 4. While the frittata is cooking, make the salad. In a medium bowl, whisk together the olive oil, lemon juice, oregano, salt, and pepper. Add the tomatoes, pepperoncini, and olives and toss to mix well. 5. Invert the frittata onto a serving platter and slice it into wedges. Serve warm or at room temperature with the tomato-olive salad.

Per Serving:
calories: 246 | fat: 19g | protein: 11g | carbs: 8g | fiber: 1g | sodium: 832mg

Baked Mediterranean Tempeh with Tomatoes and Garlic

Prep time: 25 minutes | Cook time: 35 minutes | Serves 4

For the Tempeh:
12 ounces (340 g) tempeh
¼ cup white wine
2 tablespoons extra-virgin olive oil
2 tablespoons lemon juice
Zest of 1 lemon
¼ teaspoon kosher salt
¼ teaspoon freshly ground black pepper
For the Tomatoes and Garlic Sauce:
1 tablespoon extra-virgin olive

oil
1 onion, diced
3 garlic cloves, minced
1 (14½-ounce / 411-g) can no-salt-added crushed tomatoes
1 beefsteak tomato, diced
1 dried bay leaf
1 teaspoon white wine vinegar
1 teaspoon lemon juice
1 teaspoon dried oregano
1 teaspoon dried thyme
¾ teaspoon kosher salt
¼ cup basil, cut into ribbons

Make the Tempeh: 1. Place the tempeh in a medium saucepan. Add enough water to cover it by 1 to 2 inches. Bring to a boil over medium-high heat, cover, and lower heat to a simmer. Cook for 10 to 15 minutes. Remove the tempeh, pat dry, cool, and cut into 1-inch cubes. 2. In a large bowl, combine the white wine, olive oil, lemon juice, lemon zest, salt, and black pepper. Add the tempeh, cover the bowl, and put in the refrigerator for 4 hours, or up to overnight. 3. Preheat the oven to 375ºC (190ºC). Place the marinated tempeh and the marinade in a baking dish and cook for 15 minutes. Make the Tomatoes and Garlic Sauce: 4. Heat the olive oil in a large skillet over medium heat. Add the onion and sauté until transparent, 3 to 5 minutes. Add the garlic and sauté for 30 seconds. Add the crushed tomatoes, beefsteak tomato, bay leaf, vinegar, lemon juice, oregano, thyme, and salt. Mix well. Simmer for 15 minutes. 5. Add the baked tempeh to the tomato mixture and gently mix together. Garnish with the basil.

Per Serving:
calories: 330 | fat: 20g | protein: 18g | carbs: 22g | fiber: 4g | sodium: 305mg

Pesto Vegetable Skewers

Prep time: 30 minutes | Cook time: 8 minutes |
Makes 8 skewers

1 medium zucchini, trimmed and cut into ½-inch slices
½ medium yellow onion, peeled and cut into 1-inch squares
1 medium red bell pepper, seeded and cut into 1-inch squares
16 whole cremini mushrooms
⅓ cup basil pesto
½ teaspoon salt
¼ teaspoon ground black pepper

1. Divide zucchini slices, onion, and bell pepper into eight even portions. Place on 6-inch skewers for a total of eight kebabs. Add 2 mushrooms to each skewer and brush kebabs generously with pesto. 2. Sprinkle each kebab with salt and black pepper on all sides, then place into ungreased air fryer basket. Adjust the temperature to 375ºF (191ºC) and air fry for 8 minutes, turning kebabs halfway through cooking. Vegetables will be browned at the edges and tender-crisp when done. Serve warm.

Per Serving:
calories: 75 | fat: 6g | protein: 3g | carbs: 4g | fiber: 1g | sodium: 243mg

Roasted Ratatouille Pasta

Prep time: 10 minutes | Cook time: 20 minutes | Serves 2

1 small eggplant (about 8 ounces / 227 g)
1 small zucchini
1 portobello mushroom
1 Roma tomato, halved
½ medium sweet red pepper, seeded
½ teaspoon salt, plus additional for the pasta water
1 teaspoon Italian herb seasoning
1 tablespoon olive oil
2 cups farfalle pasta (about 8 ounces / 227 g)
2 tablespoons minced sun-dried tomatoes in olive oil with herbs
2 tablespoons prepared pesto

1. Slice the ends off the eggplant and zucchini. Cut them lengthwise into ½-inch slices. 2. Place the eggplant, zucchini, mushroom, tomato, and red pepper in a large bowl and sprinkle with ½ teaspoon of salt. Using your hands, toss the vegetables well so that they're covered evenly with the salt. Let them rest for about 10 minutes. 3. While the vegetables are resting, preheat the oven to 400°F (205ºC) and set the rack to the bottom position. Line a baking sheet with parchment paper. 4. When the oven is hot, drain off any liquid from the vegetables and pat them dry with a paper towel. Add the Italian herb seasoning and olive oil to the vegetables and toss well to coat both sides. 5. Lay the vegetables out in a single layer on the baking sheet. Roast them for 15 to 20 minutes, flipping them over after about 10 minutes or once they start to brown on the underside. When the vegetables are charred in spots, remove them from the oven. 6. While the vegetables are roasting, fill a large saucepan with water. Add salt and cook the pasta according to package directions. Drain the pasta, reserving ½ cup of the pasta water. 7. When cool enough to handle, cut the vegetables into large chunks (about 2 inches) and add them to the hot pasta. 8. Stir in the sun-dried tomatoes and pesto and toss everything well.

Per Serving:
calories: 612 | fat: 16g | protein: 23g | carbs: 110g | fiber: 23g | sodium: 776mg

Roasted Veggie Bowl

Prep time: 10 minutes | Cook time: 15 minutes | Serves 2

1 cup broccoli florets
1 cup quartered Brussels sprouts
½ cup cauliflower florets
¼ medium white onion, peeled and sliced ¼ inch thick
½ medium green bell pepper, seeded and sliced ¼ inch thick
1 tablespoon coconut oil
2 teaspoons chili powder
½ teaspoon garlic powder
½ teaspoon cumin

1. Toss all ingredients together in a large bowl until vegetables are fully coated with oil and seasoning. 2. Pour vegetables into the air fryer basket. 3. Adjust the temperature to 360ºF (182ºC) and roast for 15 minutes. 4. Shake two or three times during cooking. Serve warm.

Per Serving:
calories: 112 | fat: 7.68g | protein: 3.64g | carbs: 10.67g | sugars: 3.08g | fiber: 4.6g | sodium: 106mg

Farro with Roasted Tomatoes and Mushrooms

Prep time: 20 minutes | Cook time: 1 hour | Serves 4

For the Tomatoes:
2 pints cherry tomatoes
1 teaspoon extra-virgin olive oil
¼ teaspoon kosher salt
For the Farro:
3 to 4 cups water
½ cup farro
¼ teaspoon kosher salt
For the Mushrooms:
2 tablespoons extra-virgin olive oil
1 onion, julienned
½ teaspoon kosher salt
¼ teaspoon freshly ground black pepper
10 ounces (283 g) baby bella (crimini) mushrooms, stemmed and thinly sliced
½ cup no-salt-added vegetable stock
1 (15-ounce / 425-g) can no-salt-added or low-sodium cannellini beans, drained and rinsed
1 cup baby spinach
2 tablespoons fresh basil, cut into ribbons
¼ cup pine nuts, toasted
Aged balsamic vinegar (optional)

Make the Tomatoes: Preheat the oven to 400ºF (205ºC). Line a baking sheet with parchment paper or foil. Toss the tomatoes, olive oil, and salt together on the baking sheet and roast for 30 minutes. Make the Farro: Bring the water, farro, and salt to a boil in a medium saucepan or pot over high heat. Cover, reduce the heat to low, and simmer, and cook for 30 minutes, or until the farro is al dente. Drain and set aside. Make the Mushrooms: 1. Heat the olive oil in a large skillet or sauté pan over medium-low heat. Add the onions, salt, and black pepper and sauté until golden brown and starting to caramelize, about 15 minutes. Add the mushrooms, increase the heat to medium, and sauté until the liquid has evaporated and the mushrooms brown, about 10 minutes. Add the vegetable stock and deglaze the pan, scraping up any brown bits, and reduce the liquid for about 5 minutes. Add the beans and warm through, about 3 minutes. 2. Remove from the heat and mix in the spinach, basil, pine nuts, roasted tomatoes, and farro. Garnish with a drizzle of balsamic vinegar, if desired.

Per Serving:
calories: 375 | fat: 15g | protein: 14g | carbs: 48g | fiber: 10g | sodium: 305mg

Cauliflower Steak with Gremolata

Prep time: 15 minutes | Cook time: 25 minutes | Serves 4

2 tablespoons olive oil
1 tablespoon Italian seasoning
1 large head cauliflower, outer leaves removed and sliced lengthwise through the core into thick "steaks"
Salt and freshly ground black pepper, to taste
¼ cup Parmesan cheese

Gremolata:
1 bunch Italian parsley (about 1 cup packed)
2 cloves garlic
Zest of 1 small lemon, plus 1 to 2 teaspoons lemon juice
½ cup olive oil
Salt and pepper, to taste

1. Preheat the air fryer to 400°F (204°C). 2. In a small bowl, combine the olive oil and Italian seasoning. Brush both sides of each cauliflower "steak" generously with the oil. Season to taste with salt and black pepper. 3. Working in batches if necessary, arrange the cauliflower in a single layer in the air fryer basket. Pausing halfway through the cooking time to turn the "steaks," air fry for 15 to 20 minutes until the cauliflower is tender and the edges begin to brown. Sprinkle with the Parmesan and air fry for 5 minutes longer. 4. To make the gremolata: In a food processor fitted with a metal blade, combine the parsley, garlic, and lemon zest and juice. With the motor running, add the olive oil in a steady stream until the mixture forms a bright green sauce. Season to taste with salt and black pepper. Serve the cauliflower steaks with the gremolata spooned over the top.

Per Serving:
calories: 336 | fat: 30g | protein: 7g | carbs: 15g | fiber: 5g | sodium: 340mg

Quinoa Lentil "Meatballs" with Quick Tomato Sauce

Prep time: 25 minutes | Cook time: 45 minutes | Serves 4

For the Meatballs:
Olive oil cooking spray
2 large eggs, beaten
1 tablespoon no-salt-added tomato paste
½ teaspoon kosher salt
½ cup grated Parmesan cheese
½ onion, roughly chopped
¼ cup fresh parsley
1 garlic clove, peeled
1½ cups cooked lentils
1 cup cooked quinoa

For the Tomato Sauce:
1 tablespoon extra-virgin olive oil
1 onion, minced
½ teaspoon dried oregano
½ teaspoon kosher salt
2 garlic cloves, minced
1 (28-ounce / 794-g) can no-salt-added crushed tomatoes
½ teaspoon honey
¼ cup fresh basil, chopped

Make the Meatballs: 1. Preheat the oven to 400°F (205°C). Lightly grease a 12-cup muffin pan with olive oil cooking spray. 2. In a large bowl, whisk together the eggs, tomato paste, and salt until fully combined. Mix in the Parmesan cheese. 3. In a food processor, add the onion, parsley, and garlic. Process until minced. Add to the egg mixture and stir together. Add the lentils to the food processor and process until puréed into a thick paste. Add to the large bowl and mix together. Add the quinoa and mix well. 4. Form balls, slightly larger than a golf ball, with ¼ cup of the quinoa mixture. Place each ball in a muffin pan cup. Note: The mixture will be somewhat soft but should hold together. 5. Bake 25 to 30 minutes, until golden brown. Make the Tomato Sauce: 6. Heat the olive oil in a large saucepan over medium heat. Add the onion, oregano, and salt and sauté until light golden brown, about 5 minutes. Add the garlic and cook for 30 seconds. 7. Stir in the tomatoes and honey. Increase the heat to high and cook, stirring often, until simmering, then decrease the heat to medium-low and cook for 10 minutes. Remove from the heat and stir in the basil. Serve with the meatballs.

Per Serving:
3 meatballs: calories: 360 | fat: 10g | protein: 20g | carbs: 48g | fiber: 14g | sodium: 520mg

Freekeh, Chickpea, and Herb Salad

Prep time: 15 minutes | Cook time: 10 minutes | Serves 4 to 6

1 (15-ounce / 425-g) can chickpeas, rinsed and drained
1 cup cooked freekeh
1 cup thinly sliced celery
1 bunch scallions, both white and green parts, finely chopped
½ cup chopped fresh flat-leaf parsley
¼ cup chopped fresh mint

3 tablespoons chopped celery leaves
½ teaspoon kosher salt
⅓ cup extra-virgin olive oil
¼ cup freshly squeezed lemon juice
¼ teaspoon cumin seeds
1 teaspoon garlic powder

1. In a large bowl, combine the chickpeas, freekeh, celery, scallions, parsley, mint, celery leaves, and salt and toss lightly. 2. In a small bowl, whisk together the olive oil, lemon juice, cumin seeds, and garlic powder. Once combined, add to freekeh salad.

Per Serving:
calories: 350 | fat: 19g | protein: 9g | carbs: 38g | fiber: 9g | sodium: 329mg

Herbed Ricotta–Stuffed Mushrooms

Prep time: 10 minutes | Cook time: 30 minutes | Serves 4

6 tablespoons extra-virgin olive oil, divided
4 portobello mushroom caps, cleaned and gills removed
1 cup whole-milk ricotta cheese
⅓ cup chopped fresh herbs

(such as basil, parsley, rosemary, oregano, or thyme)
2 garlic cloves, finely minced
½ teaspoon salt
¼ teaspoon freshly ground black pepper

1. Preheat the oven to 400°F (205°C). 2. Line a baking sheet with parchment or foil and drizzle with 2 tablespoons olive oil, spreading evenly. Place the mushroom caps on the baking sheet, gill-side up. 3. In a medium bowl, mix together the ricotta, herbs, 2 tablespoons olive oil, garlic, salt, and pepper. Stuff each mushroom cap with one-quarter of the cheese mixture, pressing down if needed. Drizzle with remaining 2 tablespoons olive oil and bake until golden brown and the mushrooms are soft, 30 to 35 minutes, depending on the size of the mushrooms.

Per Serving:
calories: 308 | fat: 29g | protein: 9g | carbs: 6g | fiber: 1g | sodium: 351mg

Broccoli Crust Pizza

Prep time: 15 minutes | Cook time: 12 minutes | Serves 4

3 cups riced broccoli, steamed and drained well
1 large egg
½ cup grated vegetarian Parmesan cheese
3 tablespoons low-carb Alfredo sauce
½ cup shredded Mozzarella cheese

1. In a large bowl, mix broccoli, egg, and Parmesan. 2. Cut a piece of parchment to fit your air fryer basket. Press out the pizza mixture to fit on the parchment, working in two batches if necessary. Place into the air fryer basket. 3. Adjust the temperature to 370°F (188°C) and air fry for 5 minutes. 4. The crust should be firm enough to flip. If not, add 2 additional minutes. Flip crust. 5. Top with Alfredo sauce and Mozzarella. Return to the air fryer basket and cook an additional 7 minutes or until cheese is golden and bubbling. Serve warm.

Per Serving:
calories: 87 | fat: 2g | protein: 11g | carbs: 5g | fiber: 1g | sodium: 253mg

Crustless Spinach Cheese Pie

Prep time: 10 minutes | Cook time: 20 minutes | Serves 4

6 large eggs
¼ cup heavy whipping cream
1 cup frozen chopped spinach, drained
1 cup shredded sharp Cheddar cheese
¼ cup diced yellow onion

1. In a medium bowl, whisk eggs and add cream. Add remaining ingredients to bowl. 2. Pour into a round baking dish. Place into the air fryer basket. 3. Adjust the temperature to 320°F (160°C) and bake for 20 minutes. 4. Eggs will be firm and slightly browned when cooked. Serve immediately.

Per Serving:
calories: 263 | fat: 20g | protein: 18g | carbs: 4g | fiber: 1g | sodium: 321mg

Linguine and Brussels Sprouts

Prep time: 10 minutes | Cook time: 25 minutes | Serves 4

8 ounces (227 g) whole-wheat linguine
⅓ cup, plus 2 tablespoons extra-virgin olive oil, divided
1 medium sweet onion, diced
2 to 3 garlic cloves, smashed
8 ounces (227 g) Brussels
sprouts, chopped
½ cup chicken stock, as needed
⅓ cup dry white wine
½ cup shredded Parmesan cheese
1 lemon, cut in quarters

1. Bring a large pot of water to a boil and cook the pasta according to package directions. Drain, reserving 1 cup of the pasta water. Mix the cooked pasta with 2 tablespoons of olive oil, then set aside. 2. In a large sauté pan or skillet, heat the remaining ⅓ cup of olive oil on medium heat. Add the onion to the pan and cook for about 5 minutes, until softened. Add the smashed garlic cloves and cook for 1 minute, until fragrant. 3. Add the Brussels sprouts and cook covered for 15 minutes. Add chicken stock as needed to prevent

burning. Once Brussels sprouts have wilted and are fork-tender, add white wine and cook down for about 7 minutes, until reduced. 4. Add the pasta to the skillet and add the pasta water as needed. 5. Serve with the Parmesan cheese and lemon for squeezing over the dish right before eating.

Per Serving:
calories: 502 | fat: 31g | protein: 15g | carbs: 50g | fiber: 9g | sodium: 246mg

One-Pan Mushroom Pasta with Mascarpone

Prep time: 10 minutes | Cook time: 20 minutes | Serves 2

2 tablespoons olive oil
1 large shallot, minced
8 ounces (227 g) baby bella (cremini) mushrooms, sliced
¼ cup dry sherry
1 teaspoon dried thyme
2 cups low-sodium vegetable
stock
6 ounces (170 g) dry pappardelle pasta
2 tablespoons mascarpone cheese
Salt
Freshly ground black pepper

1. Heat olive oil in a large sauté pan over medium-high heat. Add the shallot and mushrooms and sauté for 10 minutes, or until the mushrooms have given up much of their liquid. 2. Add the sherry, thyme, and vegetable stock. Bring the mixture to a boil. 3. Add the pasta, breaking it up as needed so it fits into the pan and is covered by the liquid. Return the mixture to a boil. Cover, and reduce the heat to medium-low. Let the pasta cook for 10 minutes, or until al dente. Stir it occasionally so it doesn't stick. If the sauce gets too dry, add some water or additional chicken stock. 4. When the pasta is tender, stir in the mascarpone cheese and season with salt and pepper. 5. The sauce will thicken up a bit when it's off the heat.

Per Serving:
calories: 517 | fat: 18g | protein: 16g | carbs: 69g | fiber: 3g | sodium: 141mg

Pistachio Mint Pesto Pasta

Prep time: 10 minutes | Cook time: 10 minutes | Serves 4

8 ounces (227 g) whole-wheat pasta
1 cup fresh mint
½ cup fresh basil
⅓ cup unsalted pistachios,
shelled
1 garlic clove, peeled
½ teaspoon kosher salt
Juice of ½ lime
⅓ cup extra-virgin olive oil

1. Cook the pasta according to the package directions. Drain, reserving ½ cup of the pasta water, and set aside. 2. In a food processor, add the mint, basil, pistachios, garlic, salt, and lime juice. Process until the pistachios are coarsely ground. Add the olive oil in a slow, steady stream and process until incorporated. 3. In a large bowl, mix the pasta with the pistachio pesto; toss well to incorporate. If a thinner, more saucy consistency is desired, add some of the reserved pasta water and toss well.

Per Serving:
calories: 420 | fat: 3g | protein: 11g | carbs: 48g | fiber: 2g | sodium: 150mg

Baked Tofu with Sun-Dried Tomatoes and Artichokes

Prep time: 15 minutes | Cook time: 30 minutes | Serves 4

1 (16-ounce / 454-g) package extra-firm tofu, drained and patted dry, cut into 1-inch cubes
2 tablespoons extra-virgin olive oil, divided
2 tablespoons lemon juice, divided
1 tablespoon low-sodium soy sauce or gluten-free tamari
1 onion, diced
½ teaspoon kosher salt
2 garlic cloves, minced

1 (14-ounce / 397-g) can artichoke hearts, drained
8 sun-dried tomato halves packed in oil, drained and chopped
¼ teaspoon freshly ground black pepper
1 tablespoon white wine vinegar
Zest of 1 lemon
¼ cup fresh parsley, chopped

1. Preheat the oven to 400ºF (205ºC). Line a baking sheet with foil or parchment paper. 2. In a bowl, combine the tofu, 1 tablespoon of the olive oil, 1 tablespoon of the lemon juice, and the soy sauce. Allow to sit and marinate for 15 to 30 minutes. Arrange the tofu in a single layer on the prepared baking sheet and bake for 20 minutes, turning once, until light golden brown. 3. Heat the remaining 1 tablespoon olive oil in a large skillet or sauté pan over medium heat. Add the onion and salt; sauté until translucent, 5 to 6 minutes. Add the garlic and sauté for 30 seconds. Add the artichoke hearts, sun-dried tomatoes, and black pepper and sauté for 5 minutes. Add the white wine vinegar and the remaining 1 tablespoon lemon juice and deglaze the pan, scraping up any brown bits. Remove the pan from the heat and stir in the lemon zest and parsley. Gently mix in the baked tofu.

Per Serving:
calories: 230 | fat: 14g | protein: 14g | carbs: 13g | fiber: 5g | sodium: 500mg

Cauliflower Steaks with Olive Citrus Sauce

Prep time: 15 minutes | Cook time: 30 minutes | Serves 4

1 or 2 large heads cauliflower (at least 2 pounds / 907 g, enough for 4 portions)
⅓ cup extra-virgin olive oil
¼ teaspoon kosher salt
⅛ teaspoon ground black pepper
Juice of 1 orange

Zest of 1 orange
¼ cup black olives, pitted and chopped
1 tablespoon Dijon or grainy mustard
1 tablespoon red wine vinegar
½ teaspoon ground coriander

1. Preheat the oven to 400ºF (205ºC). Line a baking sheet with parchment paper or foil. 2. Cut off the stem of the cauliflower so it will sit upright. Slice it vertically into four thick slabs. Place the cauliflower on the prepared baking sheet. Drizzle with the olive oil, salt, and black pepper. Bake for about 30 minutes, turning over once, until tender and golden brown. 3. In a medium bowl, combine the orange juice, orange zest, olives, mustard, vinegar, and coriander; mix well. 4. Serve the cauliflower warm or at room temperature with the sauce.

Per Serving:
calories: 265 | fat: 21g | protein: 5g | carbs: 19g | fiber: 4g | sodium: 310mg

Grilled Eggplant Stacks

Prep time: 20 minutes | Cook time: 10 minutes | Serves 2

1 medium eggplant, cut crosswise into 8 slices
¼ teaspoon salt
1 teaspoon Italian herb seasoning mix

2 tablespoons olive oil
1 large tomato, cut into 4 slices
4 (1-ounce / 28-g) slices of buffalo mozzarella
Fresh basil, for garnish

1. Place the eggplant slices in a colander set in the sink or over a bowl. Sprinkle both sides with the salt. Let the eggplant sit for 15 minutes. 2. While the eggplant is resting, heat the grill to medium-high heat (about 350ºF / 180ºC). 3. Pat the eggplant dry with paper towels and place it in a mixing bowl. Sprinkle it with the Italian herb seasoning mix and olive oil. Toss well to coat. 4. Grill the eggplant for 5 minutes, or until it has grill marks and is lightly charred. Flip each eggplant slice over, and grill on the second side for another 5 minutes. 5. Flip the eggplant slices back over and top four of the slices with a slice of tomato and a slice of mozzarella. Top each stack with one of the remaining four slices of eggplant. 6. Turn the grill down to low and cover it to let the cheese melt. Check after 30 seconds and remove when the cheese is soft and mostly melted. 7. Sprinkle with fresh basil slices.

Per Serving:
calories: 354 | fat: 29g | protein: 13g | carbs: 19g | fiber: 9g | sodium: 340mg

Creamy Chickpea Sauce with Whole-Wheat Fusilli

Prep time: 15 minutes | Cook time: 20 minutes | Serves 4

¼ cup extra-virgin olive oil
½ large shallot, chopped
5 garlic cloves, thinly sliced
1 (15-ounce / 425-g) can chickpeas, drained and rinsed, reserving ½ cup canning liquid
Pinch red pepper flakes
1 cup whole-grain fusilli pasta
¼ teaspoon salt

⅛ teaspoon freshly ground black pepper
¼ cup shaved fresh Parmesan cheese
¼ cup chopped fresh basil
2 teaspoons dried parsley
1 teaspoon dried oregano
Red pepper flakes

1. In a medium pan, heat the oil over medium heat, and sauté the shallot and garlic for 3 to 5 minutes, until the garlic is golden. Add ¾ of the chickpeas plus 2 tablespoons of liquid from the can, and bring to a simmer. 2. Remove from the heat, transfer into a standard blender, and blend until smooth. At this point, add the remaining chickpeas. Add more reserved chickpea liquid if it becomes thick. 3. Bring a large pot of salted water to a boil and cook pasta until al dente, about 8 minutes. Reserve ½ cup of the pasta water, drain the pasta, and return it to the pot. 4. Add the chickpea sauce to the hot pasta and add up to ¼ cup of the pasta water. You may need to add more pasta water to reach your desired consistency. 5. Place the pasta pot over medium heat and mix occasionally until the sauce thickens. Season with salt and pepper. 6. Serve, garnished with Parmesan, basil, parsley, oregano, and red pepper flakes.

Per Serving:
1 cup pasta: calories: 310 | fat: 17g | protein: 10g | carbs: 33g | fiber: 7g | sodium: 243mg

Root Vegetable Soup with Garlic Aioli

Prep time: 10 minutes | Cook time 25 minutes | Serves 4

For the Soup:	1 pound (454 g) turnips, peeled
8 cups vegetable broth	and cut into 1-inch cubes
½ teaspoon salt	1 red bell pepper, cut into strips
1 medium leek, cut into thick	2 tablespoons fresh oregano
rounds	For the Aioli:
1 pound (454 g) carrots, peeled	5 garlic cloves, minced
and diced	¼ teaspoon salt
1 pound (454 g) potatoes,	⅔ cup olive oil
peeled and diced	1 drop lemon juice

1. Bring the broth and salt to a boil and add the vegetables one at a time, letting the water return to a boil after each addition. Add the carrots first, then the leeks, potatoes, turnips, and finally the red bell peppers. Let the vegetables cook for about 3 minutes after adding the green beans and bringing to a boil. The process will take about 20 minutes in total. 2. Meanwhile, make the aioli. In a mortar and pestle, grind the garlic to a paste with the salt. Using a whisk and whisking constantly, add the olive oil in a thin stream. Continue whisking until the mixture thickens to the consistency of mayonnaise. Add the lemon juice. 3. Serve the vegetables in the broth, dolloped with the aioli and garnished with the fresh oregano.

Per Serving:
calories: 538 | fat: 37g | protein: 5g | carbs: 50g | fiber: 9g | sodium: 773mg

Zucchini Lasagna

Prep time: 15 minutes | Cook time: 1 hour | Serves 8

½ cup extra-virgin olive oil,	1 teaspoon garlic powder
divided	½ teaspoon freshly ground
4 to 5 medium zucchini squash	black pepper
1 teaspoon salt	2 cups shredded fresh whole-
8 ounces (227 g) frozen	milk mozzarella cheese
spinach, thawed and well	1¾ cups shredded Parmesan
drained (about 1 cup)	cheese
2 cups whole-milk ricotta	½ (24-ounce / 680-g) jar low-
cheese	sugar marinara sauce (less than
¼ cup chopped fresh basil or 2	5 grams sugar)
teaspoons dried basil	

1. Preheat the oven to 425ºF (220ºC). 2. Line two baking sheets with parchment paper or aluminum foil and drizzle each with 2 tablespoons olive oil, spreading evenly. 3. Slice the zucchini lengthwise into ¼-inch-thick long slices and place on the prepared baking sheet in a single layer. Sprinkle with ½ teaspoon salt per sheet. Bake until softened, but not mushy, 15 to 18 minutes. Remove from the oven and allow to cool slightly before assembling the lasagna. 4. Reduce the oven temperature to 375ºF (190ºC). 5. While the zucchini cooks, prep the filling. In a large bowl, combine the spinach, ricotta, basil, garlic powder, and pepper. In a small bowl, mix together the mozzarella and Parmesan cheeses. In a medium bowl, combine the marinara sauce and remaining ¼ cup olive oil and stir to fully incorporate the oil into sauce. 6. To assemble the lasagna, spoon a third of the marinara sauce mixture into the bottom of a 9-by-13-inch glass baking dish and spread evenly. Place 1 layer of softened zucchini slices to fully cover the sauce, then add a third of the ricotta-spinach mixture and spread evenly on top of the zucchini. Sprinkle a third of the mozzarella-Parmesan mixture on top of the ricotta. Repeat with 2 more cycles of these layers: marinara, zucchini, ricotta-spinach, then cheese blend. 7. Bake until the cheese is bubbly and melted, 30 to 35 minutes. Turn the broiler to low and broil until the top is golden brown, about 5 minutes. Remove from the oven and allow to cool slightly before slicing.

Per Serving:
calories: 473 | fat: 36g | protein: 23g | carbs: 17g | fiber: 3g | sodium: 868mg

Fava Bean Purée with Chicory

Prep time: 5 minutes | Cook time: 2 hours 10 minutes | Serves 4

½ pound (227 g) dried fava	¼ cup olive oil
beans, soaked in water	1 small onion, chopped
overnight and drained	1 clove garlic, minced
1 pound (454 g) chicory leaves	Salt

1. In a saucepan, cover the fava beans by at least an inch of water and bring to a boil over medium-high heat. Reduce the heat to low, cover, and simmer until very tender, about 2 hours. Check the pot from time to time to make sure there is enough water and add more as needed. 2. Drain off any excess water and then mash the beans with a potato masher. 3. While the beans are cooking, bring a large pot of salted water to a boil. Add the chicory and cook for about 3 minutes, until tender. Drain. 4. In a medium skillet, heat the olive oil over medium-high heat. Add the onion and a pinch of salt and cook, stirring frequently, until softened and beginning to brown, about 5 minutes. Add the garlic and cook, stirring, for another minute. Transfer half of the onion mixture, along with the oil, to the bowl with the mashed beans and stir to mix. Taste and add salt as needed. 5. Serve the purée topped with some of the remaining onions and oil, with the chicory leaves on the side.

Per Serving:
calories: 336 | fat: 14g | protein: 17g | carbs: 40g | fiber: 19g | sodium: 59mg

Mediterranean Baked Chickpeas

Prep time: 15 minutes | Cook time: 15 minutes | Serves 4

1 tablespoon extra-virgin olive	4 cups halved cherry tomatoes
oil	2 (15-ounce / 425-g) cans
½ medium onion, chopped	chickpeas, drained and rinsed
3 garlic cloves, chopped	½ cup plain, unsweetened, full-
2 teaspoons smoked paprika	fat Greek yogurt, for serving
¼ teaspoon ground cumin	1 cup crumbled feta, for serving

1. Preheat the oven to 425ºF (220ºC). 2. In an oven-safe sauté pan or skillet, heat the oil over medium heat and sauté the onion and garlic. Cook for about 5 minutes, until softened and fragrant. Stir in the paprika and cumin and cook for 2 minutes. Stir in the tomatoes and chickpeas. 3. Bring to a simmer for 5 to 10 minutes before placing in the oven. 4. Roast in oven for 25 to 30 minutes, until bubbling and thickened. To serve, top with Greek yogurt and feta.

Per Serving:
calories: 412 | fat: 15g | protein: 20g | carbs: 51g | fiber: 13g | sodium: 444mg

Crispy Tofu

Prep time: 30 minutes | Cook time: 15 to 20 minutes | Serves 4

1 (16-ounce / 454-g) block extra-firm tofu
2 tablespoons coconut aminos
1 tablespoon toasted sesame oil
1 tablespoon olive oil
1 tablespoon chili-garlic sauce
1½ teaspoons black sesame seeds
1 scallion, thinly sliced

1. Press the tofu for at least 15 minutes by wrapping it in paper towels and setting a heavy pan on top so that the moisture drains. 2. Slice the tofu into bite-size cubes and transfer to a bowl. Drizzle with the coconut aminos, sesame oil, olive oil, and chili-garlic sauce. Cover and refrigerate for 1 hour or up to overnight. 3. Preheat the air fryer to 400ºF (204ºC). 4. Arrange the tofu in a single layer in the air fryer basket. Pausing to shake the pan halfway through the cooking time, air fry for 15 to 20 minutes until crisp. Serve with any juices that accumulate in the bottom of the air fryer, sprinkled with the sesame seeds and sliced scallion.

Per Serving:
calories: 173 | fat: 14g | protein: 12g | carbs: 3g | fiber: 1g | sodium: 49mg

Stuffed Portobellos

Prep time: 10 minutes | Cook time: 8 minutes | Serves 4

3 ounces (85 g) cream cheese, softened
½ medium zucchini, trimmed and chopped
¼ cup seeded and chopped red bell pepper
1½ cups chopped fresh spinach
leaves
4 large portobello mushrooms, stems removed
2 tablespoons coconut oil, melted
½ teaspoon salt

1. In a medium bowl, mix cream cheese, zucchini, pepper, and spinach. 2. Drizzle mushrooms with coconut oil and sprinkle with salt. Scoop ¼ zucchini mixture into each mushroom. 3. Place mushrooms into ungreased air fryer basket. Adjust the temperature to 400ºF (204ºC) and air fry for 8 minutes. Portobellos will be tender and tops will be browned when done. Serve warm.

Per Serving:
calories: 151 | fat: 13g | protein: 4g | carbs: 6g | fiber: 2g | sodium: 427mg

Cauliflower Rice-Stuffed Peppers

Prep time: 10 minutes | Cook time: 15 minutes | Serves 4

2 cups uncooked cauliflower rice
¾ cup drained canned petite diced tomatoes
2 tablespoons olive oil
1 cup shredded Mozzarella
cheese
¼ teaspoon salt
¼ teaspoon ground black pepper
4 medium green bell peppers, tops removed, seeded

1. In a large bowl, mix all ingredients except bell peppers. Scoop mixture evenly into peppers. 2. Place peppers into ungreased air

fryer basket. Adjust the temperature to 350ºF (177ºC) and air fry for 15 minutes. Peppers will be tender and cheese will be melted when done. Serve warm.

Per Serving:
calories: 144 | fat: 7g | protein: 11g | carbs: 11g | fiber: 5g | sodium: 380mg

Crustless Spanakopita

Prep time: 15 minutes | Cook time: 45 minutes | Serves 6

12 tablespoons extra-virgin olive oil, divided
1 small yellow onion, diced
1 (32-ounce / 907-g) bag frozen chopped spinach, thawed, fully drained, and patted dry (about 4 cups)
4 garlic cloves, minced
½ teaspoon salt
½ teaspoon freshly ground black pepper
1 cup whole-milk ricotta cheese
4 large eggs
¾ cup crumbled traditional feta cheese
¼ cup pine nuts

1. Preheat the oven to 375ºF (190ºC). 2. In a large skillet, heat 4 tablespoons olive oil over medium-high heat. Add the onion and sauté until softened, 6 to 8 minutes. 3. Add the spinach, garlic, salt, and pepper and sauté another 5 minutes. Remove from the heat and allow to cool slightly. 4. In a medium bowl, whisk together the ricotta and eggs. Add to the cooled spinach and stir to combine. 5. Pour 4 tablespoons olive oil in the bottom of a 9-by-13-inch glass baking dish and swirl to coat the bottom and sides. Add the spinach-ricotta mixture and spread into an even layer. 6. Bake for 20 minutes or until the mixture begins to set. Remove from the oven and crumble the feta evenly across the top of the spinach. Add the pine nuts and drizzle with the remaining 4 tablespoons olive oil. Return to the oven and bake for an additional 15 to 20 minutes, or until the spinach is fully set and the top is starting to turn golden brown. Allow to cool slightly before cutting to serve.

Per Serving:
calories: 497 | fat: 44g | protein: 18g | carbs: 11g | fiber: 5g | sodium: 561mg

Quinoa with Almonds and Cranberries

Prep time: 15 minutes | Cook time: 0 minutes | Serves 4

2 cups cooked quinoa
⅓ teaspoon cranberries or currants
¼ cup sliced almonds
2 garlic cloves, minced
1¼ teaspoons salt
½ teaspoon ground cumin
½ teaspoon turmeric
¼ teaspoon ground cinnamon
¼ teaspoon freshly ground black pepper

1. In a large bowl, toss the quinoa, cranberries, almonds, garlic, salt, cumin, turmeric, cinnamon, and pepper and stir to combine. Enjoy alone or with roasted cauliflower.

Per Serving:
calories: 194 | fat: 6g | protein: 7g | carbs: 31g | fiber: 4g | sodium: 727mg

Provençal Ratatouille with Herbed Breadcrumbs and Goat Cheese

Prep time: 10 minutes | Cook time: 1 hour 5 minutes | Serves 4

6 tablespoons olive oil, divided	tomatoes, drained
2 medium onions, diced	1 teaspoon salt
2 cloves garlic, minced	½ teaspoon freshly ground
2 medium eggplants, halved	black pepper
lengthwise and cut into ¾-inch	8 ounces (227 g) fresh
thick half rounds	breadcrumbs
3 medium zucchini, halved	1 tablespoon chopped fresh
lengthwise and cut into ¾-inch	parsley
thick half rounds	1 tablespoon chopped fresh
2 red bell peppers, seeded and	basil
cut into 1½-inch pieces	1 tablespoon chopped fresh
1 green bell pepper, seeded and	chives
cut into 1½-inch pieces	6 ounces (170 g) soft, fresh goat
1 (14-ounce / 397-g) can diced	cheese

1. Preheat the oven to 375°F(190°C). 2. Heat 5 tablespoons of the olive oil in a large skillet over medium heat. Add the onions and garlic and cook, stirring frequently, until the onions are soft and beginning to turn golden, about 8 minutes. Add the eggplant, zucchini, and bell peppers and cook, turning the vegetables occasionally, for another 10 minutes. Stir in the tomatoes, salt, and pepper and let simmer for 15 minutes. 3. While the vegetables are simmering, stir together the breadcrumbs, the remaining tablespoon of olive oil, the parsley, basil, and chives. 4. Transfer the vegetable mixture to a large baking dish, spreading it out into an even layer. Crumble the goat cheese over the top, then sprinkle the breadcrumb mixture evenly over the top. Bake in the preheated oven for about 30 minutes, until the topping is golden brown and crisp. Serve hot.
Per Serving:
calories: 644 | fat: 37g | protein: 21g | carbs: 63g | fiber: 16g | sodium: 861mg

Tangy Asparagus and Broccoli

Prep time: 25 minutes | Cook time: 22 minutes | Serves 4

½ pound (227 g) asparagus, cut	Salt and white pepper, to taste
into 1½-inch pieces	½ cup vegetable broth
½ pound (227 g) broccoli, cut	2 tablespoons apple cider
into 1½-inch pieces	vinegar
2 tablespoons olive oil	

1. Place the vegetables in a single layer in the lightly greased air fryer basket. Drizzle the olive oil over the vegetables. 2. Sprinkle with salt and white pepper. 3. Cook at 380°F (193°C) for 15 minutes, shaking the basket halfway through the cooking time. 4. Add ½ cup of vegetable broth to a saucepan; bring to a rapid boil and add the vinegar. Cook for 5 to 7 minutes or until the sauce has reduced by half. 5. Spoon the sauce over the warm vegetables and serve immediately. Bon appétit!
Per Serving:
calories: 93 | fat: 7g | protein: 3g | carbs: 6g | fiber: 3g | sodium: 89mg

Asparagus and Mushroom Farrotto

Prep time: 20 minutes | Cook time: 45 minutes | Serves 2

1½ ounces (43 g) dried porcini	4 ounces / 113-g)
mushrooms	¾ cup farro
1 cup hot water	½ cup dry white wine
3 cups low-sodium vegetable	½ teaspoon dried thyme
stock	4 ounces (113 g) asparagus,
2 tablespoons olive oil	cut into ½-inch pieces (about 1
½ large onion, minced (about 1	cup)
cup)	2 tablespoons grated Parmesan
1 garlic clove	cheese
1 cup diced mushrooms (about	Salt

1. Soak the dried mushrooms in the hot water for about 15 minutes. When they're softened, drain the mushrooms, reserving the liquid. (I like to strain the liquid through a coffee filter in case there's any grit.) Mince the porcini mushrooms. 2. Add the mushroom liquid and vegetable stock to a medium saucepan and bring it to a boil. Reduce the heat to low just to keep it warm. 3. Heat the olive oil in a Dutch oven over high heat. Add the onion, garlic, and mushrooms, and sauté for 10 minutes. 4. Add the farro to the Dutch oven and sauté it for 3 minutes to toast. 5. Add the wine, thyme, and one ladleful of the hot mushroom and chicken stock. Bring it to a boil while stirring the farro. Do not cover the pot while the farro is cooking. 6. Reduce the heat to medium. When the liquid is absorbed, add another ladleful or two at a time to the pot, stirring occasionally, until the farro is cooked through. Keep an eye on the heat, to make sure it doesn't cook too quickly. 7. When the farro is al dente, add the asparagus and another ladleful of stock. Cook for another 3 to 5 minutes, or until the asparagus is softened. 8. Stir in Parmesan cheese and season with salt.
Per Serving:
calories: 341 | fat: 16g | protein: 13g | carbs: 26g | fiber: 5g | sodium: 259mg

Ricotta, Basil, and Pistachio-Stuffed Zucchini

Prep time: 15 minutes | Cook time: 25 minutes | Serves 4

2 medium zucchini, halved	¾ cup ricotta cheese
lengthwise	¼ cup unsalted pistachios,
1 tablespoon extra-virgin olive	shelled and chopped
oil	¼ cup fresh basil, chopped
1 onion, diced	1 large egg, beaten
1 teaspoon kosher salt	¼ teaspoon freshly ground
2 garlic cloves, minced	black pepper

1. Preheat the oven to 425°F (220°C). Line a baking sheet with parchment paper or foil. 2. Scoop out the seeds/pulp from the zucchini, leaving ¼-inch flesh around the edges. Transfer the pulp to a cutting board and chop the pulp. 3. Heat the olive oil in a large skillet or sauté pan over medium heat. Add the onion, pulp, and salt and sauté about 5 minutes. Add the garlic and sauté 30 seconds. 4. In a medium bowl, combine the ricotta cheese, pistachios, basil, egg, and black pepper. Add the onion mixture and mix together well. 5. Place the 4 zucchini halves on the prepared baking sheet. Fill the zucchini halves with the ricotta mixture. Bake for 20 minutes, or until golden brown.
Per Serving:
calories: 200 | fat: 12g | protein: 11g | carbs: 14g | fiber: 3g | sodium: 360mg

Prep time: 15 minutes | Cook time: 20 minutes | Serves 4

Nonstick cooking spray
2 cups broccoli florets
2 cups cauliflower florets
1 (15-ounce / 425-g) can
chickpeas, drained and rinsed
1 cup carrots sliced 1 inch thick
2 to 3 tablespoons extra-virgin
olive oil, divided
Salt
Freshly ground black pepper

2 to 3 tablespoons sesame
seeds, for garnish
2 cups cooked brown rice
For the Dressing:
3 to 4 tablespoons tahini
2 tablespoons honey
1 lemon, juiced
1 garlic clove, minced
Salt
Freshly ground black pepper

1. Preheat the oven to 400ºF (205ºC). Spray two baking sheets with cooking spray. 2. Cover the first baking sheet with the broccoli and cauliflower and the second with the chickpeas and carrots. Toss each sheet with half of the oil and season with salt and pepper before placing in oven. 3. Cook the carrots and chickpeas for 10 minutes, leaving the carrots still just crisp, and the broccoli and cauliflower for 20 minutes, until tender. Stir each halfway through cooking. 4. To make the dressing, in a small bowl, mix the tahini, honey, lemon juice, and garlic. Season with salt and pepper and set aside. 5. Divide the rice into individual bowls, then layer with vegetables and drizzle dressing over the dish.

Per Serving:
calories: 454 | fat: 18g | protein: 12g | carbs: 62g | fiber: 11g | sodium: 61mg

Prep time: 15 minutes | Cook time: 30 minutes | Serves 2

1 tablespoon olive oil
1 small zucchini, minced
½ medium onion, minced
1 garlic clove, minced
⅔ cup cooked orzo (from ¼
cup dry orzo, cooked according

to package instructions, or
precooked)
½ teaspoon salt
2 teaspoons dried oregano
6 medium round tomatoes (not
Roma)

1. Preheat the oven to 350ºF (180ºC). 2. Heat the olive oil in a large sauté pan over medium-high heat. Add the zucchini, onion, and garlic and sauté for 15 minutes, or until the vegetables turn golden. 3. Add the orzo, salt, and oregano and stir to heat through. Remove the pan from the heat and set aside. 4. Cut about ½ inch from the top of each tomato. With a paring knife, cut around the inner core of the tomato to remove about half of the flesh. Reserve for another recipe or a salad. 5. Stuff each tomato with the orzo mixture. 6. If serving hot, put the tomatoes in a baking dish, or, if they'll fit, a muffin tin. Roast the tomatoes for about 15 minutes, or until they're soft. Don't overcook them or they won't hold together. If desired, this can also be served without roasting the tomatoes.

Per Serving:
calories: 241 | fat: 8g | protein: 7g | carbs: 38g | fiber: 6g | sodium: 301mg

Prep time: 15 minutes | Cook time: 10 minutes | Serves 4

1 large eggplant, ends trimmed,
cut into ½-inch slices
½ teaspoon salt
2 ounces (57 g) Parmesan 100%

cheese crisps, finely ground
½ teaspoon paprika
¼ teaspoon garlic powder
1 large egg

1. Sprinkle eggplant rounds with salt. Place rounds on a kitchen towel for 30 minutes to draw out excess water. Pat rounds dry. 2. In a medium bowl, mix cheese crisps, paprika, and garlic powder. In a separate medium bowl, whisk egg. Dip each eggplant round in egg, then gently press into cheese crisps to coat both sides. 3. Place eggplant rounds into ungreased air fryer basket. Adjust the temperature to 400ºF (204ºC) and air fry for 10 minutes, turning rounds halfway through cooking. Eggplant will be golden and crispy when done. Serve warm.

Per Serving:
calories: 113 | fat: 5g | protein: 7g | carbs: 10g | fiber: 4g | sodium: 567mg

Prep time: 20 minutes | Cook time: 30 minutes | Serves 2

½ ounce (14 g) dried porcini
mushrooms (optional but
recommended)
2 tablespoons olive oil
1 pound (454 g) baby bella
(cremini) mushrooms, quartered
1 large shallot, minced (about
⅓ cup)
1 garlic clove, minced
1 tablespoon flour
2 teaspoons tomato paste
½ cup red wine

1 cup mushroom stock (or
reserved liquid from soaking
the porcini mushrooms, if
using)
½ teaspoon dried thyme
1 fresh rosemary sprig
1½ cups water
½ teaspoon salt
⅓ cup instant polenta
2 tablespoons grated Parmesan
cheese

1. If using the dried porcini mushrooms, soak them in 1 cup of hot water for about 15 minutes to soften them. When they're softened, scoop them out of the water, reserving the soaking liquid. (I strain it through a coffee filter to remove any possible grit.) Mince the porcini mushrooms. 2. Heat the olive oil in a large sauté pan over medium-high heat. Add the mushrooms, shallot, and garlic, and sauté for 10 minutes, or until the vegetables are wilted and starting to caramelize. 3. Add the flour and tomato paste, and cook for another 30 seconds. Add the red wine, mushroom stock or porcini soaking liquid, thyme, and rosemary. Bring the mixture to a boil, stirring constantly until it thickens. Reduce the heat and let it simmer for 10 minutes. 4. While the mushrooms are simmering, bring the water to a boil in a saucepan and add salt. 5. Add the instant polenta and stir quickly while it thickens. Stir in the Parmesan cheese. Taste and add additional salt if needed.

Per Serving:
calories: 451 | fat: 16g | protein: 14g | carbs: 58g | fiber: 5g | sodium: 165mg

Beet and Carrot Fritters with Yogurt Sauce

Prep time: 15 minutes | Cook time: 15 minutes | Serves 2

For the Yogurt Sauce:
⅓ cup plain Greek yogurt
1 tablespoon freshly squeezed lemon juice
Zest of ½ lemon
¼ teaspoon garlic powder
¼ teaspoon salt
For the Fritters:
1 large carrot, peeled
1 small potato, peeled
1 medium golden or red beet, peeled

1 scallion, minced
2 tablespoons fresh minced parsley
¼ cup brown rice flour or unseasoned bread crumbs
¼ teaspoon garlic powder
¼ teaspoon salt
1 large egg, beaten
¼ cup feta cheese, crumbled
2 tablespoons olive oil (more if needed)

Make the Yogurt Sauce: In a small bowl, mix together the yogurt, lemon juice and zest, garlic powder, and salt. Set aside. Make the Fritters: 1. Shred the carrot, potato, and beet in a food processor with the shredding blade. You can also use a mandoline with a julienne shredding blade or a vegetable peeler. Squeeze out any moisture from the vegetables and place them in a large bowl. 2. Add the scallion, parsley, rice flour, garlic powder, salt, and egg. Stir the mixture well to combine. Add the feta cheese and stir briefly, leaving chunks of feta cheese throughout. 3. Heat a large nonstick sauté pan over medium-high heat and add 1 tablespoon of the olive oil. 4. Make the fritters by scooping about 3 tablespoons of the vegetable mixture into your hands and flattening it into a firm disc about 3 inches in diameter. 5. Place 2 fritters at a time in the pan and let them cook for about two minutes. Check to see if the underside is golden, and then flip and repeat on the other side. Remove from the heat, add the rest of the olive oil to the pan, and repeat with the remaining vegetable mixture. 6. To serve, spoon about 1 tablespoon of the yogurt sauce on top of each fritter.

Per Serving:
calories: 295 | fat: 14g | protein: 6g | carbs: 44g | fiber: 5g | sodium: 482mg

Broccoli-Cheese Fritters

Prep time: 5 minutes | Cook time: 20 to 25 minutes | Serves 4

1 cup broccoli florets
1 cup shredded Mozzarella cheese
¾ cup almond flour
½ cup flaxseed meal, divided
2 teaspoons baking powder

1 teaspoon garlic powder
Salt and freshly ground black pepper, to taste
2 eggs, lightly beaten
½ cup ranch dressing

1. Preheat the air fryer to 400ºF (204ºC). 2. In a food processor fitted with a metal blade, pulse the broccoli until very finely chopped. 3. Transfer the broccoli to a large bowl and add the Mozzarella, almond flour, ¼ cup of the flaxseed meal, baking powder, and garlic powder. Stir until thoroughly combined. Season to taste with salt and black pepper. Add the eggs and stir again to form a sticky dough. Shape the dough into 1¼-inch fritters. 4. Place the remaining ¼ cup flaxseed meal in a shallow bowl and roll the fritters in the meal to form an even coating. 5. Working in batches if necessary, arrange the fritters in a single layer in the basket of the air fryer and spray generously with olive oil. Pausing halfway through the cooking time to shake the basket, air fry for 20 to 25 minutes until the fritters are golden brown and crispy. Serve with the ranch dressing for dipping.

Per Serving:
calories: 388 | fat: 30g | protein: 19g | carbs: 14g | fiber: 7g | sodium: 526mg

Sheet Pan Roasted Chickpeas and Vegetables with Harissa Yogurt

Prep time: 10 minutes | Cook time: 30 minutes | Serves 2

4 cups cauliflower florets (about ½ small head)
2 medium carrots, peeled, halved, and then sliced into quarters lengthwise
2 tablespoons olive oil, divided
½ teaspoon garlic powder, divided

½ teaspoon salt, divided
2 teaspoons za'atar spice mix, divided
1 (15-ounce / 425-g) can chickpeas, drained, rinsed, and patted dry
¾ cup plain Greek yogurt
1 teaspoon harissa spice paste

1. Preheat the oven to 400ºF (205ºC) and set the rack to the middle position. Line a sheet pan with foil or parchment paper. 2. Place the cauliflower and carrots in a large bowl. Drizzle with 1 tablespoon olive oil and sprinkle with ¼ teaspoon of garlic powder, ¼ teaspoon of salt, and 1 teaspoon of za'atar. Toss well to combine. 3. Spread the vegetables onto one half of the sheet pan in a single layer. 4. Place the chickpeas in the same bowl and season with the remaining 1 tablespoon of oil, ¼ teaspoon of garlic powder, and ¼ teaspoon of salt, and the remaining za'atar. Toss well to combine. 5. Spread the chickpeas onto the other half of the sheet pan. 6. Roast for 30 minutes, or until the vegetables are tender and the chickpeas start to turn golden. Flip the vegetables halfway through the cooking time, and give the chickpeas a stir so they cook evenly. 7. The chickpeas may need an extra few minutes if you like them crispy. If so, remove the vegetables and leave the chickpeas in until they're cooked to desired crispiness. 8. While the vegetables are roasting, combine the yogurt and harissa in a small bowl. Taste, and add additional harissa as desired.

Per Serving:
calories: 467 | fat: 23g | protein: 18g | carbs: 54g | fiber: 15g | sodium: 632mg

Chapter 11 Vegetables and Sides

Toasted Grain and Almond Pilaf

Prep time: 15 minutes | Cook time: 35 minutes | Serves 2

1 tablespoon olive oil
1 garlic clove, minced
3 scallions, minced
2 ounces (57 g) mushrooms, sliced
¼ cup sliced almonds
½ cup uncooked pearled barley

1½ cups low-sodium chicken stock
½ teaspoon dried thyme
1 tablespoon fresh minced parsley
Salt

1. Heat the oil in a saucepan over medium-high heat. Add the garlic, scallions, mushrooms, and almonds, and sauté for 3 minutes. 2. Add the barley and cook, stirring, for 1 minute to toast it. 3. Add the chicken stock and thyme and bring the mixture to a boil. 4. Cover and reduce the heat to low. Simmer the barley for 30 minutes, or until the liquid is absorbed and the barley is tender. 5. Sprinkle with fresh parsley and season with salt before serving.

Per Serving:
calories: 333 | fat: 14g | protein: 10g | carbs: 46g | fiber: 10g | sodium: 141mg

Superflax Tortillas

Prep time: 5 minutes | Cook time: 10 minutes | Serves 6

1 packed cup flax meal
⅓ cup coconut flour
¼ cup ground chia seeds
2 tablespoons whole psyllium husks

1 teaspoon salt, or to taste
1 cup lukewarm water
2 tablespoons extra-virgin avocado oil or ghee

1. Place all the dry ingredients in a bowl and mix to combine. (For ground chia seeds, simply place whole seeds into a coffee grinder or food processor and pulse until smooth.) Add the water and mix until well combined. Place the dough in the refrigerator to rest for about 30 minutes. 2. When ready, remove the dough from the fridge and cut it into 4 equal pieces. You will make the remaining 2 tortillas using the excess dough. Place one piece of dough between two pieces of parchment paper and roll it out until very thin. Alternatively, use a silicone roller and a silicone mat. Remove the top piece of parchment paper. Press a large 8-inch (20 cm) lid into the dough (or use a piece of parchment paper cut into a circle of the same size). Press the lid into the dough or trace around it with your knife to cut out the tortilla. 3. Repeat for the remaining pieces of dough. Add the cut-off excess dough to the last piece and create the remaining 2 tortillas from it. If you have any dough left over, simply roll it out and cut it into tortilla-chip shapes. 4. Grease a large pan with the avocado oil and cook 1 tortilla at a time for 2 to 3 minutes on each side over medium heat until lightly browned. Don't overcook: the tortillas should be flexible, not too crispy. 5.

Once cool, store the tortillas in a sealed container for up to 1 week and reheat them in a dry pan, if needed.

Per Serving:
calories: 182 | fat: 16g | protein: 4g | carbs: 8g | fiber: 7g | sodium: 396mg

Crispy Green Beans

Prep time: 5 minutes | Cook time: 8 minutes | Serves 4

2 teaspoons olive oil
½ pound (227 g) fresh green beans, ends trimmed

¼ teaspoon salt
¼ teaspoon ground black pepper

1. In a large bowl, drizzle olive oil over green beans and sprinkle with salt and pepper. 2. Place green beans into ungreased air fryer basket. Adjust the temperature to 350ºF (177ºC) and set the timer for 8 minutes, shaking the basket two times during cooking. Green beans will be dark golden and crispy at the edges when done. Serve warm.

Per Serving:
calories: 33 | fat: 3g | protein: 1g | carbs: 3g | fiber: 1g | sodium: 147mg

Baba Ghanoush

Prep time: 15 minutes | Cook time: 2 to 4 hours | Serves 6

1 large eggplant (2 to 4 pounds / 907 g to 1.8 kg), peeled and diced
¼ cup freshly squeezed lemon juice
2 garlic cloves, minced
2 tablespoons tahini
1 teaspoon extra-virgin olive

oil, plus more as needed
¼ teaspoon sea salt, plus more as needed
⅛ teaspoon freshly ground black pepper, plus more as needed
2 tablespoons chopped fresh parsley

1. In a slow cooker, combine the eggplant, lemon juice, garlic, tahini, olive oil, salt, and pepper. Stir to mix well. 2. Cover the cooker and cook for 2 to 4 hours on Low heat. 3. Using a spoon or potato masher, mash the mixture. If you prefer a smoother texture, transfer it to a food processor and blend to your desired consistency. Taste and season with olive oil, salt, and pepper as needed. 4. Garnish with fresh parsley for serving.

Per Serving:
calories: 81 | fat: 4g | protein: 3g | carbs: 12g | fiber: 4g | sodium: 108mg

Warm Beets with Hazelnuts and Spiced Yogurt

Prep time: 5 minutes | Cook time: 40 minutes | Serves 4

4 or 5 beets, peeled
¼ cup hazelnuts
½ cup low-fat plain Greek yogurt
1 tablespoon honey
1 tablespoon chopped fresh
mint
1 teaspoon ground cinnamon
¼ teaspoon ground cumin
⅛ teaspoon ground black pepper

1. Place racks in the upper and lower thirds of the oven. Preheat the oven to 400°F(205°C). 2. Place the beets on a 12' × 12' piece of foil. Fold the foil over the beets, and seal the sides. Bake until the beets are tender enough to be pierced by a fork, about 40 minutes. Remove from the oven, carefully open the packet, and let cool slightly. When cool enough to handle, slice the beets into ¼'-thick rounds. 3. Meanwhile, toast the hazelnuts on a small baking sheet until browned and fragrant, about 5 minutes. Using a paper towel or kitchen towel, rub the skins off. Coarsely chop the nuts and set aside. 4. In a medium bowl, stir together the yogurt, honey, mint, cinnamon, cumin, and pepper. 5. Serve the beets with a dollop of the spiced yogurt and a sprinkle of the nuts.

Per Serving:
calories: 126 | fat: 6g | protein: 5g | carbs: 15g | fiber: 4g | sodium: 74mg

Roasted Brussels Sprouts with Delicata Squash and Balsamic Glaze

Prep time: 10 minutes | Cook time: 30 minutes | Serves 2

½ pound (227 g) Brussels sprouts, ends trimmed and outer leaves removed
1 medium delicata squash, halved lengthwise, seeded, and cut into 1-inch pieces
1 cup fresh cranberries
2 teaspoons olive oil
Salt
Freshly ground black pepper
½ cup balsamic vinegar
2 tablespoons roasted pumpkin seeds
2 tablespoons fresh pomegranate arils (seeds)

1. Preheat oven to 400°F (205°C) and set the rack to the middle position. Line a sheet pan with parchment paper. 2. Combine the Brussels sprouts, squash, and cranberries in a large bowl. Drizzle with olive oil, and season liberally with salt and pepper. Toss well to coat and arrange in a single layer on the sheet pan. 3. Roast for 30 minutes, turning vegetables halfway through, or until Brussels sprouts turn brown and crisp in spots and squash has golden-brown spots. 4. While vegetables are roasting, prepare the balsamic glaze by simmering the vinegar for 10 to 12 minutes, or until mixture has reduced to about ¼ cup and turns a syrupy consistency. 5. Remove the vegetables from the oven, drizzle with balsamic syrup, and sprinkle with pumpkin seeds and pomegranate arils before serving.

Per Serving:
calories: 201 | fat: 7g | protein: 6g | carbs: 21g | fiber: 8g | sodium: 34mg

Sheet Pan Cauliflower with Parmesan and Garlic

Prep time: 5 minutes | Cook time: 40 minutes | Serves 4

1 large head cauliflower (about 6–7 inches/15.25–17.5cm] in diameter), washed and cut into medium florets
2 garlic cloves, minced
⅓ cup extra virgin olive oil
1 teaspoon kosher salt
¼ cup grated Parmesan cheese
Freshly ground black pepper to taste

1. Preheat the oven to 400°F (205°C). 2. In a large bowl, combine the cauliflower and garlic. Toss to combine, then add the olive oil and mix well, ensuring the florets are thoroughly coated in the oil. 3. Spread the cauliflower florets in a single layer on a large sheet pan, and drizzle any remaining olive oil over the florets. (Make sure the florets are closely grouped.) 4. Transfer to the oven. Bake for 30–40 minutes or until the florets are golden brown and tender, then carefully remove the pan from the oven. 5. Promptly sprinkle the kosher salt, Parmesan cheese, and black pepper over the top of the florets. Store in the refrigerator for up to 4 days.

Per Serving:
calories: 251 | fat: 20g | protein: 7g | carbs: 11g | fiber: 4g | sodium: 649mg

Braised Radishes with Sugar Snap Peas and Dukkah

Prep time: 20 minutes | Cook time: 5 minutes | Serves 4

¼ cup extra-virgin olive oil, divided
1 shallot, sliced thin
3 garlic cloves, sliced thin
1½ pounds (680 g) radishes, 2 cups greens reserved, radishes trimmed and halved if small or quartered if large
½ cup water
½ teaspoon table salt
8 ounces (227 g) sugar snap
peas, strings removed, sliced thin on bias
8 ounces (227 g) cremini mushrooms, trimmed and sliced thin
2 teaspoons grated lemon zest plus 1 teaspoon juice
1 cup plain Greek yogurt
½ cup fresh cilantro leaves
3 tablespoons dukkah

1. Using highest sauté function, heat 2 tablespoons oil in Instant Pot until shimmering. Add shallot and cook until softened, about 2 minutes. Stir in garlic and cook until fragrant, about 30 seconds. Stir in radishes, water, and salt. Lock lid in place and close pressure release valve. Select high pressure cook function and cook for 1 minute. 2. Turn off Instant Pot and quick-release pressure. Carefully remove lid, allowing steam to escape away from you. Stir in snap peas, cover, and let sit until heated through, about 3 minutes. Add radish greens, mushrooms, lemon zest and juice, and remaining 2 tablespoons oil and gently toss to combine. Season with salt and pepper to taste. 3. Spread ¼ cup yogurt over bottom of 4 individual serving plates. Using slotted spoon, arrange vegetable mixture on top and sprinkle with cilantro and dukkah. Serve.

Per Serving:
calories: 310 | fat: 23g | protein: 10g | carbs: 17g | fiber: 5g | sodium: 320mg

Ratatouille

Prep time: 15 minutes | Cook time: 20 minutes | Serves 2 to 3

2 cups ¾-inch cubed peeled eggplant
1 small red, yellow, or orange bell pepper, stemmed, seeded, and diced
1 cup cherry tomatoes
6 to 8 cloves garlic, peeled and halved lengthwise
3 tablespoons olive oil
1 teaspoon dried oregano
½ teaspoon dried thyme
1 teaspoon kosher salt
½ teaspoon black pepper

1. In a medium bowl, combine the eggplant, bell pepper, tomatoes, garlic, oil, oregano, thyme, salt, and pepper. Toss to combine. 2. Place the vegetables in the air fryer basket. Set the air fryer to 400ºF (204ºC) for 20 minutes, or until the vegetables are crisp-tender.

Per Serving:
calories: 161 | fat: 14g | protein: 2g | carbs: 9g | fiber: 3g | sodium: 781mg

Parmesan and Herb Sweet Potatoes

Prep time: 10 minutes | Cook time: 18 minutes | Serves 4

2 large sweet potatoes, peeled and cubed
¼ cup olive oil
1 teaspoon dried rosemary
½ teaspoon salt
2 tablespoons shredded Parmesan

1. Preheat the air fryer to 360°F(182°C). 2. In a large bowl, toss the sweet potatoes with the olive oil, rosemary, and salt. 3. Pour the potatoes into the air fryer basket and roast for 10 minutes, then stir the potatoes and sprinkle the Parmesan over the top. Continue roasting for 8 minutes more. 4. Serve hot and enjoy.

Per Serving:
calories: 186 | fat: 14g | protein: 2g | carbs: 13g | fiber: 2g | sodium: 369mg

Sesame-Ginger Broccoli

Prep time: 10 minutes | Cook time: 15 minutes | Serves 4

3 tablespoons toasted sesame oil
2 teaspoons sesame seeds
1 tablespoon chili-garlic sauce
2 teaspoons minced fresh ginger
½ teaspoon kosher salt
½ teaspoon black pepper
1 (16-ounce / 454-g) package frozen broccoli florets (do not thaw)

1. In a large bowl, combine the sesame oil, sesame seeds, chili-garlic sauce, ginger, salt, and pepper. Stir until well combined. Add the broccoli and toss until well coated. 2. Arrange the broccoli in the air fryer basket. Set the air fryer to 325ºF (163ºC) for 15 minutes, or until the broccoli is crisp, tender, and the edges are lightly browned, gently tossing halfway through the cooking time.

Per Serving:
calories: 143 | fat: 11g | protein: 4g | carbs: 9g | fiber: 4g | sodium: 385mg

Blackened Zucchini with Kimchi-Herb Sauce

Prep time: 10 minutes | Cook time: 15 minutes | Serves 2

2 medium zucchini, ends trimmed (about 6 ounces / 170 g each)
2 tablespoons olive oil
½ cup kimchi, finely chopped
¼ cup finely chopped fresh cilantro
¼ cup finely chopped fresh
flat-leaf parsley, plus more for garnish
2 tablespoons rice vinegar
2 teaspoons Asian chili-garlic sauce
1 teaspoon grated fresh ginger
Kosher salt and freshly ground black pepper, to taste

1. Brush the zucchini with half of the olive oil, place in the air fryer and air fry at 400ºF (204ºC), turning halfway through, until lightly charred on the outside and tender, about 15 minutes. 2. Meanwhile in a small bowl, combine the remaining 1 tablespoon olive oil, the kimchi, cilantro, parsley, vinegar, chili-garlic sauce, and ginger 3. Once the zucchini is finished cooking, transfer it to a colander and let it cool for 5 minutes. Using your fingers, pinch and break the zucchini into bite-size pieces, letting them fall back into the colander. Season the zucchini with salt and pepper, toss to combine then let sit a further 5 minutes to allow some of its liquid to drain Pile the zucchini atop the kimchi sauce on a plate and sprinkle with more parsley to serve.

Per Serving:
calories: 172 | fat: 15g | protein: 4g | carbs: 8g | fiber: 3g | sodium 102mg

Garlic Cauliflower with Tahini

Prep time: 10 minutes | Cook time: 20 minutes | Serves 4

Cauliflower:
5 cups cauliflower florets (about 1 large head)
6 garlic cloves, smashed and cut into thirds
3 tablespoons vegetable oil
½ teaspoon ground cumin
½ teaspoon ground coriander
½ teaspoon kosher salt
Sauce:
2 tablespoons tahini (sesame paste)
2 tablespoons hot water
1 tablespoon fresh lemon juice
1 teaspoon minced garlic
½ teaspoon kosher salt

1. For the cauliflower: In a large bowl, combine the cauliflower florets and garlic. Drizzle with the vegetable oil. Sprinkle with the cumin, coriander, and salt. Toss until well coated. 2. Place the cauliflower in the air fryer basket. Set the air fryer to 400ºF (204ºC) for 20 minutes, turning the cauliflower halfway through the cooking time. 3. Meanwhile, for the sauce: In a small bowl combine the tahini, water, lemon juice, garlic, and salt. (The sauce will appear curdled at first, but keep stirring until you have a thick creamy, smooth mixture.) 4. Transfer the cauliflower to a large serving bowl. Pour the sauce over and toss gently to coat. Serve immediately.

Per Serving:
calories: 176 | fat: 15g | protein: 4g | carbs: 10g | fiber: 4g | sodium 632mg

Stuffed Red Peppers with Herbed Ricotta and Tomatoes

Prep time: 10 minutes | Cook time: 20 minutes | Serves 4

2 red bell peppers
1 cup cooked brown rice
2 Roma tomatoes, diced
1 garlic clove, minced
¼ teaspoon salt
¼ teaspoon black pepper
4 ounces (113 g) ricotta

3 tablespoons fresh basil, chopped
3 tablespoons fresh oregano, chopped
¼ cup shredded Parmesan, for topping

1. Preheat the air fryer to 360°F(182°C). 2. Cut the bell peppers in half and remove the seeds and stem. 3. In a medium bowl, combine the brown rice, tomatoes, garlic, salt, and pepper. 4. Distribute the rice filling evenly among the four bell pepper halves. 5. In a small bowl, combine the ricotta, basil, and oregano. Put the herbed cheese over the top of the rice mixture in each bell pepper. 6. Place the bell peppers into the air fryer and roast for 20 minutes. 7. Remove and serve with shredded Parmesan on top.

Per Serving:
calories: 152 | fat: 6g | protein: 7g | carbs: 18g | fiber: 3g | sodium: 261mg

Roasted Garlic

Prep time: 5 minutes | Cook time: 20 minutes | Makes 12 cloves

1 medium head garlic   2 teaspoons avocado oil

1. Remove any hanging excess peel from the garlic but leave the cloves covered. Cut off ¼ of the head of garlic, exposing the tips of the cloves. 2. Drizzle with avocado oil. Place the garlic head into a small sheet of aluminum foil, completely enclosing it. Place it into the air fryer basket. 3. Adjust the temperature to 400°F (204°C) and air fry for 20 minutes. If your garlic head is a bit smaller, check it after 15 minutes. 4. When done, garlic should be golden brown and very soft. 5. To serve, cloves should pop out and easily be spread or sliced. Store in an airtight container in the refrigerator up to 5 days. You may also freeze individual cloves on a baking sheet, then store together in a freezer-safe storage bag once frozen.

Per Serving:
calories: 8 | fat: 1g | protein: 0g | carbs: 0g | fiber: 0g | sodium: 0mg

Braised Fennel

Prep time: 10 minutes | Cook time: 50 minutes | Serves 4

2 large fennel bulbs
¼ cup extra-virgin avocado oil or ghee, divided
1 small shallot or red onion
1 clove garlic, sliced
4 to 6 thyme sprigs
1 small bunch fresh parsley,

leaves and stalks separated
1 cup water
3 tablespoons fresh lemon juice
Salt and black pepper, to taste
¼ cup extra-virgin olive oil, to drizzle

1. Cut off the fennel stalks where they attach to the bulb. Reserve the stalks. Cut the fennel bulb in half, trim the hard bottom part,

and cut into wedges. 2. Heat a saucepan greased with 2 tablespoons of the avocado oil over medium-high heat. Sauté the shallot, garlic, thyme sprigs, parsley stalks, and hard fennel stalks for about 5 minutes. Add the water, bring to a boil, and simmer over medium heat for 10 minutes. Remove from the heat, set aside for 10 minutes, and then strain the stock, discarding the aromatics. 3. Preheat the oven to 350°F (180°C) fan assisted or 400°F (205°C) conventional. 4. Heat an ovenproof skillet greased with the remaining 2 tablespoons of avocado oil over medium-high heat and add the fennel wedges. Sear until caramelized, about 5 minutes, turning once. Pour the stock and the lemon juice over the fennel wedges, and season with salt and pepper. Loosely cover with a piece of aluminum foil. Bake for about 30 minutes. When done, the fennel should be easy to pierce with the tip of a knife. 5. Remove from the oven and scatter with the chopped parsley leaves and drizzle with the olive oil. To store, let cool and refrigerate for up to 5 days.

Per Serving:
calories: 225 | fat: 20g | protein: 2g | carbs: 12g | fiber: 5g | sodium: 187mg

Roasted Beets with Oranges and Onions

Prep time: 10 minutes | Cook time: 40 minutes | Serves 6

4 medium beets, trimmed and scrubbed
Juice and zest of 2 oranges
1 red onion, thinly sliced
2 tablespoons olive oil

1 tablespoon red wine vinegar
Juice of 1 lemon
Sea salt and freshly ground pepper, to taste

1. Preheat oven to 400°F (205°C). 2. Wrap the beets in a foil pack and close tightly. Place them on a baking sheet and roast 40 minutes until tender enough to be pierced easily with a knife. 3. Cool until easy to handle. 4. Combine the beets with the orange juice and zest, red onion, olive oil, vinegar, and lemon juice. 5. Season with sea salt and freshly ground pepper to taste, and toss lightly. Allow to sit for about 15 minutes for the flavors to meld before serving.

Per Serving:
calories: 86 | fat: 5g | protein: 1g | carbs: 10g | fiber: 2g | sodium: 44mg

Rustic Cauliflower and Carrot Hash

Prep time: 10 minutes | Cook time: 10 minutes | Serves 4

3 tablespoons extra-virgin olive oil
1 large onion, chopped
1 tablespoon garlic, minced
2 cups carrots, diced

4 cups cauliflower pieces, washed
1 teaspoon salt
½ teaspoon ground cumin

1. In a large skillet over medium heat, cook the olive oil, onion, garlic, and carrots for 3 minutes. 2. Cut the cauliflower into 1-inch or bite-size pieces. Add the cauliflower, salt, and cumin to the skillet and toss to combine with the carrots and onions. 3. Cover and cook for 3 minutes. 4. Toss the vegetables and continue to cook uncovered for an additional 3 to 4 minutes. 5. Serve warm.

Per Serving:
calories: 159 | fat: 11g | protein: 3g | carbs: 15g | fiber: 5g | sodium: 657mg

Coriander-Cumin Roasted Carrots

Prep time: 10 minutes | Cook time: 20 minutes | Serves 2

½ pound (227 g) rainbow carrots (about 4)
2 tablespoons fresh orange juice
1 tablespoon honey
½ teaspoon coriander
Pinch salt

1. Preheat oven to 400°F(205°C) and set the oven rack to the middle position. 2. Peel the carrots and cut them lengthwise into slices of even thickness. Place them in a large bowl. 3. In a small bowl, mix together the orange juice, honey, coriander, and salt. 4. Pour the orange juice mixture over the carrots and toss well to coat. 5. Spread carrots onto a baking dish in a single layer. 6. Roast for 15 to 20 minutes, or until fork-tender.

Per Serving:
calories: 85 | fat: 0g | protein: 1g | carbs: 21g | fiber: 3g | sodium: 156mg

Maple-Roasted Tomatoes

Prep time: 15 minutes | Cook time: 20 minutes | Serves 2

10 ounces (283 g) cherry tomatoes, halved
Kosher salt, to taste
2 tablespoons maple syrup
1 tablespoon vegetable oil
2 sprigs fresh thyme, stems removed
1 garlic clove, minced
Freshly ground black pepper

1. Place the tomatoes in a colander and sprinkle liberally with salt. Let stand for 10 minutes to drain. 2. Transfer the tomatoes cut-side up to a cake pan, then drizzle with the maple syrup, followed by the oil. Sprinkle with the thyme leaves and garlic and season with pepper. Place the pan in the air fryer and roast at 325°F (163°C) until the tomatoes are soft, collapsed, and lightly caramelized on top, about 20 minutes. 3. Serve straight from the pan or transfer the tomatoes to a plate and drizzle with the juices from the pan to serve.

Per Serving:
calories: 139 | fat: 7g | protein: 1g | carbs: 20g | fiber: 2g | sodium: 10mg

Cucumbers with Feta, Mint, and Sumac

Prep time: 15 minutes | Cook time: 0 minutes | Serves 4

1 tablespoon extra-virgin olive oil
1 tablespoon lemon juice
2 teaspoons ground sumac
½ teaspoon kosher salt
2 hothouse or English cucumbers, diced
¼ cup crumbled feta cheese
1 tablespoon fresh mint, chopped
1 tablespoon fresh parsley, chopped
⅛ teaspoon red pepper flakes

1. In a large bowl, whisk together the olive oil, lemon juice, sumac, and salt. Add the cucumber and feta cheese and toss well. 2. Transfer to a serving dish and sprinkle with the mint, parsley, and red pepper flakes.

Per Serving:
calories: 85 | fat: 6g | protein: 3g | carbs: 8g | fiber: 1g | sodium: 230mg

Mediterranean Lentil Sloppy Joes

Prep time: 5 minutes |Cook time: 15 minutes| Serves: 4

1 tablespoon extra-virgin olive oil
1 cup chopped onion (about ½ medium onion)
1 cup chopped bell pepper, any color (about 1 medium bell pepper)
2 garlic cloves, minced (about 1 teaspoon)
1 (15-ounce / 425-g) can lentils, drained and rinsed
1 (14½-ounce / 411-g) can low-
sodium or no-salt-added diced tomatoes, undrained
1 teaspoon ground cumin
1 teaspoon dried thyme
¼ teaspoon kosher or sea salt
4 whole-wheat pita breads, split open
1½ cups chopped seedless cucumber (1 medium cucumber)
1 cup chopped romaine lettuce

1. In a medium saucepan over medium-high heat, heat the oil. Add the onion and bell pepper and cook for 4 minutes, stirring frequently. Add the garlic and cook for 1 minute, stirring frequently. Add the lentils, tomatoes (with their liquid), cumin, thyme, and salt. Turn the heat to medium and cook, stirring occasionally, for 10 minutes, or until most of the liquid has evaporated. 2. Stuff the lentil mixture inside each pita. Lay the cucumbers and lettuce on top of the lentil mixture and serve.

Per Serving:
calories: 530 | fat: 6g | protein: 31g | carbs: 93g | fiber: 17g | sodium: 292mg

Potatoes with Cumin

Prep time: 10 minutes | Cook time: 2 to 4 hours | Serves 6

2 teaspoons cumin seeds, divided
1 tablespoon coriander seeds
2 tablespoons vegetable oil
1 onion, sliced
2 fresh green chiles, sliced lengthwise
1-inch piece fresh ginger, sliced very thinly
¼ teaspoon turmeric
1 teaspoon chili powder
Sea salt
6 large potatoes, peeled and chopped into 1½-inch chunks
½ cup hot water
2 teaspoons mango powder (amchoor), or a squeeze of lemon juice
Handful fresh coriander leaves, chopped

1. Preheat the slow cooker on high. 2. Meanwhile, in a dry frying pan toast 1 teaspoon of the cumin seeds along with all of the coriander seeds. Once fragrant, remove from the heat and crush in a mortar and pestle or spice grinder. 3. To the hot slow cooker, add the oil, onion, sliced green chiles, ginger, and remaining 1 teaspoon of cumin seeds. Stir, and then add the roasted spice powder, turmeric, chili powder, and salt. 4. Add the cubed potatoes and mix well. Then add the water. Cover and cook on high for 2 to 3 hours, or on low for 4 hours. 5. Stir in the mango powder and garnish with coriander leaves to serve.

Per Serving:
calories: 332 | fat: 5g | protein: 8g | carbs: 66g | net carbs: 57g | sugars: 3g | fiber: 9g | sodium: 37mg | cholesterol: 0mg

Gorgonzola Sweet Potato Burgers

Prep time: 10 minutes |Cook time: 15 minutes| Serves: 4

1 large sweet potato (about 8 ounces / 227 g)
2 tablespoons extra-virgin olive oil, divided
1 cup chopped onion (about ½ medium onion)
1 cup old-fashioned rolled oats
1 large egg
1 tablespoon balsamic vinegar

1 tablespoon dried oregano
1 garlic clove
¼ teaspoon kosher or sea salt
½ cup crumbled Gorgonzola or blue cheese (about 2 ounces / 57 g)
Salad greens or 4 whole-wheat rolls, for serving (optional)

1. Using a fork, pierce the sweet potato all over and microwave on high for 4 to 5 minutes, until tender in the center. Cool slightly, then slice in half. 2. While the sweet potato is cooking, in a large skillet over medium-high heat, heat 1 tablespoon of oil. Add the onion and cook for 5 minutes, stirring occasionally. 3. Using a spoon, carefully scoop the sweet potato flesh out of the skin and put the flesh in a food processor. Add the onion, oats, egg, vinegar, oregano, garlic, and salt. Process until smooth. Add the cheese and pulse four times to barely combine. With your hands, form the mixture into four (½-cup-size) burgers. Place the burgers on a plate, and press to flatten each to about ¾-inch thick. 4. Wipe out the skillet with a paper towel, then heat the remaining 1 tablespoon of oil over medium-high heat until very hot, about 2 minutes. Add the burgers to the hot oil, then turn the heat down to medium. Cook the burgers for 5 minutes, flip with a spatula, then cook an additional 5 minutes. Enjoy as is or serve on salad greens or whole-wheat rolls.

Per Serving:
calories: 337 | fat: 16g | protein: 13g | carbs: 38g | fiber: 6g | sodium: 378mg

Saffron Couscous with Almonds, Currants, and Scallions

Prep time: 5 minutes | Cook time: 35 minutes | Serves 8

2 cups whole wheat couscous
1 tablespoon olive oil
5 scallions, thinly sliced, whites and greens kept separate
1 large pinch saffron threads, crumbled

3 cups low-sodium chicken broth or vegetable broth
½ cup slivered almonds
¼ cup dried currants
Kosher salt and ground black pepper, to taste

1. In a medium saucepan over medium heat, toast the couscous, stirring occasionally, until lightly browned, about 5 minutes. Transfer to a bowl. 2. In the same saucepan, add the oil and scallion whites. Cook, stirring, until lightly browned, about 5 minutes. Sprinkle in the saffron and stir to combine. Pour in the broth and bring to a boil. 3. Remove the saucepan from the heat, stir in the couscous, cover, and let sit until all the liquid is absorbed and the couscous is tender, about 15 minutes. 4. Fluff the couscous with a fork. Fluff in the scallion greens, almonds, and currants. Season to taste with the salt and pepper.

Per Serving:
calories: 212 | fat: 6g | protein: 8g | carbs: 34g | fiber: 4g | sodium: 148mg

Zesty Cabbage Soup

Prep time: 25 minutes | Cook time: 30 minutes | Serves 8

2 tablespoons extra-virgin olive oil
3 medium onions, peeled and chopped
1 large carrot, peeled, quartered, and sliced
1 stalk celery, chopped
3 bay leaves
1 teaspoon smoked paprika
3 cups sliced white cabbage
1 teaspoon fresh thyme leaves
3 cloves garlic, peeled and minced
½ cup chopped roasted red

pepper
1 (15-ounce / 425-g) can white navy beans, drained and rinsed
1½ cups low-sodium vegetable cocktail beverage
7 cups low-sodium vegetable stock
1 dried chili pepper
2 medium zucchini, trimmed, halved lengthwise, and thinly sliced
1 teaspoon salt
½ teaspoon ground black pepper

1. Press the Sauté button on the Instant Pot® and heat oil. Add onions, carrot, celery, and bay leaves. Cook for 7–10 minutes or until vegetables are soft. 2. Add paprika, cabbage, thyme, garlic, roasted red pepper, and beans. Stir to combine and cook for 2 minutes. Add vegetable cocktail beverage, stock, and chili pepper. Press the Cancel button. 3. Close lid, set steam release to Sealing, press the Soup button, and cook for default time of 20 minutes. When the timer beeps, quick-release the pressure until the float valve drops and open lid. 4. Remove and discard bay leaves. Add zucchini, close lid, and let stand on the Keep Warm setting for 15 minutes. Season with salt and pepper. Serve hot.

Per Serving:
calories: 157 | fat: 4g | protein: 7g | carbs: 25g | fiber: 8g | sodium: 360mg

Herb Vinaigrette Potato Salad

Prep time: 10 minutes | Cook time: 4 minutes | Serves 10

¼ cup olive oil
3 tablespoons red wine vinegar
¼ cup chopped fresh flat-leaf parsley
2 tablespoons chopped fresh dill
2 tablespoons chopped fresh chives
1 clove garlic, peeled and

minced
½ teaspoon dry mustard powder
¼ teaspoon ground black pepper
2 pounds (907 g) baby Yukon Gold potatoes
1 cup water
1 teaspoon salt

1. Whisk together oil, vinegar, parsley, dill, chives, garlic, mustard, and pepper in a small bowl. Set aside. 2. Place potatoes in a steamer basket. Place the rack in the Instant Pot®, add water and salt, then top with the steamer basket. Close lid, set steam release to Sealing, press the Manual button, and set time to 4 minutes. When the timer beeps, quick-release the pressure until the float valve drops. Press the Cancel button and open lid. 3. Transfer hot potatoes to a serving bowl. Pour dressing over potatoes and gently toss to coat. Serve warm or at room temperature.

Per Serving:
calories: 116 | fat: 6g | protein: 2g | carbs: 16g | fiber: 1g | sodium: 239mg

Vibrant Green Beans

Prep time: 10 minutes | Cook time: 15 minutes | Serves 6

2 tablespoons olive oil
2 leeks, white parts only, sliced
Sea salt and freshly ground
pepper, to taste
1 pound (454 g) fresh green

string beans, trimmed
1 tablespoon Italian seasoning
2 tablespoons white wine
Zest of 1 lemon

1. Heat the olive oil over medium heat in a large skillet. 2. Add leeks and cook, stirring often, until they start to brown and become lightly caramelized. 3. Season with sea salt and freshly ground pepper. 4. Add green beans and Italian seasoning, cooking for a few minutes until beans are tender but still crisp to the bite. 5. Add the wine and continue cooking until beans are done to your liking and leeks are crispy and browned. 6. Sprinkle with lemon zest before serving.

Per Serving:
calories: 87 | fat: 5g | protein: 2g | carbs: 11g | fiber: 3g | sodium: 114mg

Root Vegetable Hash

Prep time: 20 minutes | Cook time: 8 hours | Makes 9 (¾-cup) servings

4 carrots, peeled and cut into
1-inch cubes
3 large russet potatoes, peeled
and cut into 1-inch cubes
1 onion, diced
3 garlic cloves, minced
½ teaspoon salt

⅛ teaspoon freshly ground
black pepper
½ teaspoon dried thyme leaves
1 sprig rosemary
½ cup vegetable broth
3 plums, cut into 1-inch pieces

1. In the slow cooker, combine the carrots, potatoes, onion, and garlic. Sprinkle with the salt, pepper, and thyme, and stir. 2. Imbed the rosemary sprig in the vegetables. 3. Pour the broth over everything. 4. Cover and cook on low for 7½ hours, or until the vegetables are tender. 5. Stir in the plums, cover, and cook on low for 30 minutes, until tender. 6. Remove and discard the rosemary sprig, and serve.

Per Serving:
calories: 137 | fat: 0g | protein: 3g | carbs: 32g | net carbs: 28g | sugars: 6g | fiber: 4g | sodium: 204mg | cholesterol: 0mg

Crispy Roasted Red Potatoes with Garlic, Rosemary, and Parmesan

Prep time: 10 minutes | Cook time: 55 minutes | Serves 2

12 ounces (340 g) red potatoes
(3 to 4 small potatoes)
1 tablespoon olive oil
½ teaspoon garlic powder
¼ teaspoon salt

1 tablespoon grated Parmesan
cheese
1 teaspoon minced fresh
rosemary (from 1 sprig)

1. Preheat the oven to 425°F(220°C) and set the rack to the bottom position. Line a baking sheet with parchment paper. (Do not use foil, as the potatoes will stick.) 2. Scrub the potatoes and dry them well. Dice into 1-inch pieces. 3. In a mixing bowl, combine the potatoes, olive oil, garlic powder, and salt. Toss well to coat. 4. Lay the potatoes on the parchment paper and roast for 10 minutes. Flip the potatoes over and return to the oven for 10 more minutes. 5. Check the potatoes to make sure they are golden brown on the top and bottom. Toss them again, turn the heat down to 350°F(180°C), and roast for 30 minutes more. 6. When the potatoes are golden, crispy, and cooked through, sprinkle the Parmesan cheese over them and toss again. Return to the oven for 3 minutes to let the cheese melt a bit. 7. Remove from the oven and sprinkle with the fresh rosemary.

Per Serving:
calories: 193 | fat: 8g | protein: 5g | carbs: 28g | fiber: 3g | sodium: 334mg

Mashed Sweet Potato Tots

Prep time: 10 minutes | Cook time: 12 to 13 minutes per batch | Makes 18 to 24 tots

1 cup cooked mashed sweet
potatoes
1 egg white, beaten
⅛ teaspoon ground cinnamon
1 dash nutmeg

2 tablespoons chopped pecans
1½ teaspoons honey
Salt, to taste
½ cup panko bread crumbs
Oil for misting or cooking spray

1. Preheat the air fryer to 390ºF (199ºC). 2. In a large bowl, mix together the potatoes, egg white, cinnamon, nutmeg, pecans, honey, and salt to taste. 3. Place panko crumbs on a sheet of wax paper. 4. For each tot, use about 2 teaspoons of sweet potato mixture. To shape, drop the measure of potato mixture onto panko crumbs and push crumbs up and around potatoes to coat edges. Then turn to over to coat other side with crumbs. 5. Mist tots with oil or cooking spray and place in air fryer basket in single layer. 6. Air fry at 390ºF (199ºC) for 12 to 13 minutes, until browned and crispy. 7. Repeat steps 5 and 6 to cook remaining tots.

Per Serving:
calories: 51 | fat: 1g | protein: 1g | carbs: 9g | fiber: 1g | sodium: 45mg

Root Vegetable Tagine

Prep time: 30 minutes | Cook time: 9 hours | Serves 8

1 pound parsnips, peeled and
chopped into bite-size pieces
1 pound turnips, peeled and
chopped into bite-size pieces
2 medium yellow onions,
chopped into bite-size pieces
1 pound carrots, peeled and
chopped into bite-size pieces
6 dried apricots, chopped
6 figs, chopped

1 teaspoon ground turmeric
1 teaspoon ground cumin
½ teaspoon ground ginger
½ teaspoon ground cinnamon
¼ teaspoon cayenne pepper
1 tablespoon dried parsley
1 tablespoon dried cilantro (or
2 tablespoons chopped fresh
cilantro)
1¾ cups vegetable stock

1. Combine the parsnips, turnips, onions, carrots, apricots, and figs in the slow cooker. Sprinkle with the turmeric, cumin, ginger, cinnamon, cayenne pepper, parsley, and cilantro. 2. Pour in the vegetable stock. Cover and cook for 9 hours on low. the vegetables will be very tender. Serve hot.

Beet and Watercress Salad with Orange and Dill

Prep time: 20 minutes | Cook time: 8 minutes | Serves 4

2 pounds (907 g) beets, scrubbed, trimmed, and cut into ¾-inch pieces
½ cup water
1 teaspoon caraway seeds
½ teaspoon table salt
1 cup plain Greek yogurt
1 small garlic clove, minced to paste
5 ounces (142 g) watercress, torn into bite-size pieces
1 tablespoon extra-virgin olive

oil, divided, plus extra for drizzling
1 tablespoon white wine vinegar, divided
1 teaspoon grated orange zest plus 2 tablespoons juice
¼ cup hazelnuts, toasted, skinned, and chopped
¼ cup coarsely chopped fresh dill
Coarse sea salt

1. Combine beets, water, caraway seeds, and table salt in Instant Pot. Lock lid in place and close pressure release valve. Select high pressure cook function and cook for 8 minutes. Turn off Instant Pot and quick-release pressure. Carefully remove lid, allowing steam to escape away from you. 2. Using slotted spoon, transfer beets to plate; set aside to cool slightly. Combine yogurt, garlic, and 3 tablespoons beet cooking liquid in bowl; discard remaining cooking liquid. In large bowl toss watercress with 2 teaspoons oil and 1 teaspoon vinegar. Season with table salt and pepper to taste. 3. Spread yogurt mixture over surface of serving dish. Arrange watercress on top of yogurt mixture, leaving 1-inch border of yogurt mixture. Add beets to now-empty large bowl and toss with orange zest and juice, remaining 2 teaspoons vinegar, and remaining 1 teaspoon oil. Season with table salt and pepper to taste. Arrange beets on top of watercress mixture. Drizzle with extra oil and sprinkle with hazelnuts, dill, and sea salt. Serve.
Per Serving:
calories: 240 | fat: 15g | protein: 9g | carbs: 19g | fiber: 5g | sodium: 440mg

Tahini-Lemon Kale

Prep time: 5 minutes | Cook time: 15 minutes | Serves 2 to 4

¼ cup tahini
¼ cup fresh lemon juice
2 tablespoons olive oil
1 teaspoon sesame seeds
½ teaspoon garlic powder
¼ teaspoon cayenne pepper

4 cups packed torn kale leaves (stems and ribs removed and leaves torn into palm-size pieces; about 4 ounces / 113 g)
Kosher salt and freshly ground black pepper, to taste

1. In a large bowl, whisk together the tahini, lemon juice, olive oil, sesame seeds, garlic powder, and cayenne until smooth. Add the kale leaves, season with salt and black pepper, and toss in the dressing until completely coated. Transfer the kale leaves to a cake pan. 2. Place the pan in the air fryer and roast at 350ºF (177ºC), stirring every 5 minutes, until the kale is wilted and the top is lightly browned, about 15 minutes. Remove the pan from the air fryer and serve warm.
Per Serving:
calories: 221 | fat: 21g | protein: 5g | carbs: 8g | fiber: 3g | sodium: 32mg

Swiss Chard with White Beans and Bell Peppers

Prep time: 15 minutes | Cook time: 15 minutes | Serves 4

2 tablespoons olive oil
1 medium onion, chopped
1 bell pepper, diced
2 cloves garlic, minced
1 large bunch of Swiss chard,

tough stems removed, cut into bite-size pieces
2 cups white beans, cooked
Sea salt and freshly ground pepper, to taste

1. Heat the oil in a large skillet over medium-high heat. Add the onion and pepper and cook for 5 minutes until soft. 2. Add the garlic, stir, and add the Swiss chard. Cook for 10 minutes until greens are tender. 3. Add the beans, stir until heated through, and season with sea salt and freshly ground pepper. 4. Serve immediately.
Per Serving:
calories: 212 | fat: 7g | protein: 10g | carbs: 28g | fiber: 7g | sodium: 66mg

Zucchini Casserole

Prep time: 20 minutes | Cook time: 3 hours | Serves 4

1 medium red onion, sliced
1 green bell pepper, cut into thin strips
4 medium zucchini, sliced
1 (15-ounce / 425-g) can diced tomatoes, with the juice

1 teaspoon sea salt
½ teaspoon black pepper
½ teaspoon basil
1 tablespoon extra-virgin olive oil
¼ cup grated Parmesan cheese

1. Combine the onion slices, bell pepper strips, zucchini slices, and tomatoes in the slow cooker. Sprinkle with the salt, pepper, and basil. 2. Cover and cook on low for 3 hours. 3. Drizzle the olive oil over the casserole and sprinkle with the Parmesan. Cover and cook on low for 1½ hours more. Serve hot.
Per Serving:
calories: 124 | fat: 6g | protein: 6g | carbs: 15g | fiber: 5g | sodium: 723mg

Glazed Sweet Potato Bites

Prep time: 10 minutes | Cook time: 25 minutes | Serves 4

Oil, for spraying
3 medium sweet potatoes, peeled and cut into 1-inch pieces

2 tablespoons honey
1 tablespoon olive oil
2 teaspoons ground cinnamon

1. Line the air fryer basket with parchment and spray lightly with oil. 2. In a large bowl, toss together the sweet potatoes, honey, olive oil, and cinnamon until evenly coated. 3. Place the potatoes in the prepared basket. 4. Air fry at 400ºF (204ºC) for 20 to 25 minutes, or until crispy and easily pierced with a fork.
Per Serving:
calories: 149 | fat: 3g | protein: 2g | carbs: 29g | fiber: 4g | sodium: 54mg

Dill-and-Garlic Beets

Prep time: 10 minutes | Cook time: 30 minutes | Serves 4

4 beets, cleaned, peeled, and sliced	dill
1 garlic clove, minced	¼ teaspoon salt
2 tablespoons chopped fresh	¼ teaspoon black pepper
	3 tablespoons olive oil

1. Preheat the air fryer to 380°F(193°C). 2. In a large bowl, mix together all of the ingredients so the beets are well coated with the oil. 3. Pour the beet mixture into the air fryer basket, and roast for 15 minutes before stirring, then continue roasting for 15 minutes more.

Per Serving:
calories: 136 | fat: 2g | protein: 2g | carbs: 10g | fiber: 3g | sodium: 210mg

Roasted Salsa

Prep time: 15 minutes | Cook time: 30 minutes | Makes 2 cups

2 large San Marzano tomatoes, cored and cut into large chunks	2 cloves garlic, peeled and diced
½ medium white onion, peeled and large-diced	½ teaspoon salt
½ medium jalapeño, seeded and large-diced	1 tablespoon coconut oil
	¼ cup fresh lime juice

1. Place tomatoes, onion, and jalapeño into an ungreased round nonstick baking dish. Add garlic, then sprinkle with salt and drizzle with coconut oil. 2. Place dish into air fryer basket. Adjust the temperature to 300°F (149°C) and bake for 30 minutes. Vegetables will be dark brown around the edges and tender when done. 3. Pour mixture into a food processor or blender. Add lime juice. Process on low speed 30 seconds until only a few chunks remain. 4. Transfer salsa to a sealable container and refrigerate at least 1 hour. Serve chilled.

Per Serving:
calories: 115 | fat: 7g | protein: 2g | carbs: 13g | fiber: 3g | sodium: 593mg

Radish Chips

Prep time: 10 minutes | Cook time: 5 minutes | Serves 4

2 cups water	½ teaspoon garlic powder
1 pound (454 g) radishes	2 tablespoons coconut oil,
¼ teaspoon onion powder	melted
¼ teaspoon paprika	

1. Place water in a medium saucepan and bring to a boil on stovetop. 2. Remove the top and bottom from each radish, then use a mandoline to slice each radish thin and uniformly. You may also use the slicing blade in the food processor for this step. 3. Place the radish slices into the boiling water for 5 minutes or until translucent. Remove them from the water and place them into a clean kitchen towel to absorb excess moisture. 4. Toss the radish chips in a large bowl with remaining ingredients until fully coated

in oil and seasoning. Place radish chips into the air fryer basket. 5. Adjust the temperature to 320°F (160°C) and air fry for 5 minutes. 6. Shake the basket two or three times during the cooking time. Serve warm.

Per Serving:
calories: 81 | fat: 7g | protein: 1g | carbs: 5g | fiber: 2g | sodium: 27mg

Chermoula-Roasted Beets

Prep time: 15 minutes | Cook time: 25 minutes | Serves 4

Chermoula:	½ cup extra-virgin olive oil
1 cup packed fresh cilantro leaves	Kosher salt, to taste
½ cup packed fresh parsley leaves	Beets:
6 cloves garlic, peeled	3 medium beets, trimmed, peeled, and cut into 1-inch chunks
2 teaspoons smoked paprika	2 tablespoons chopped fresh cilantro
2 teaspoons ground cumin	
1 teaspoon ground coriander	2 tablespoons chopped fresh parsley
½ to 1 teaspoon cayenne pepper	
Pinch crushed saffron (optional)	

1. For the chermoula: In a food processor, combine the cilantro, parsley, garlic, paprika, cumin, coriander, and cayenne. Pulse until coarsely chopped. Add the saffron, if using, and process until combined. With the food processor running, slowly add the olive oil in a steady stream; process until the sauce is uniform. Season to taste with salt. 2. For the beets: In a large bowl, drizzle the beets with ½ cup of the chermoula, or enough to coat. Arrange the beets in the air fryer basket. Set the air fryer to 375°F (191°C) for 25 to minutes, or until the beets are tender. 3. Transfer the beets to a serving platter. Sprinkle with chopped cilantro and parsley and serve.

Per Serving:
calories: 61 | fat: 2g | protein: 2g | carbs: 9g | fiber: 3g | sodium: 59mg

Herbed Shiitake Mushrooms

Prep time: 10 minutes | Cook time: 5 minutes | Serves 4

8 ounces (227 g) shiitake mushrooms, stems removed and caps roughly chopped	1 teaspoon chopped fresh thyme leaves
1 tablespoon olive oil	1 teaspoon chopped fresh oregano
½ teaspoon salt	1 tablespoon chopped fresh parsley
Freshly ground black pepper, to taste	

1. Preheat the air fryer to 400°F (204°C). 2. Toss the mushrooms with the olive oil, salt, pepper, thyme and oregano. Air fry for 5 minutes, shaking the basket once or twice during the cooking process. The mushrooms will still be somewhat chewy with a meaty texture. If you'd like them a little more tender, add a couple of minutes to this cooking time. 3. Once cooked, add the parsley to the mushrooms and toss. Season again to taste and serve.

Per Serving:
calories: 50 | fat: 4g | protein: 1g | carbs: 4g | fiber: 2g | sodium: 296mg

Potato Vegetable Hash

Prep time: 20 minutes | Cook time: 5 to 7 hours | Serves 4

1½ pounds (680 g) red potatoes, diced
8 ounces (227 g) green beans, trimmed and cut into ½-inch pieces
4 ounces (113 g) mushrooms, chopped
1 large tomato, chopped
1 large zucchini, diced
1 small onion, diced
1 red bell pepper, seeded and chopped
⅓ cup low-sodium vegetable broth
1 teaspoon sea salt
½ teaspoon garlic powder
½ teaspoon freshly ground black pepper
¼ teaspoon red pepper flakes
¼ cup shredded cheese of your choice (optional)

1. In a slow cooker, combine the potatoes, green beans, mushrooms, tomato, zucchini, onion, bell pepper, vegetable broth, salt, garlic powder, black pepper, and red pepper flakes. Stir to mix well. 2. Cover the cooker and cook for 5 to 7 hours on Low heat. 3. Garnish with cheese for serving (if using).
Per Serving:
calories: 183 | fat: 1g | protein: 7g | carbs: 41g | fiber: 8g | sodium: 642mg

Parmesan-Rosemary Radishes

Prep time: 5 minutes | Cook time: 15 to 20 minutes | Serves 4

1 bunch radishes, stemmed, trimmed, and quartered
1 tablespoon avocado oil
2 tablespoons finely grated fresh Parmesan cheese
1 tablespoon chopped fresh rosemary
Sea salt and freshly ground black pepper, to taste

1. Place the radishes in a medium bowl and toss them with the avocado oil, Parmesan cheese, rosemary, salt, and pepper. 2. Set the air fryer to 375°F (191°C). Arrange the radishes in a single layer in the air fryer basket. Roast for 15 to 20 minutes, until golden brown and tender. Let cool for 5 minutes before serving.
Per Serving:
calories: 58 | fat: 4g | protein: 1g | carbs: 4g | fiber: 2g | sodium: 53mg

Sweet-and-Sour Brussels Sprouts

Prep time: 10 minutes | Cook time: 20 minutes | Serves 2

¼ cup Thai sweet chili sauce
2 tablespoons black vinegar or balsamic vinegar
½ teaspoon hot sauce, such as Tabasco
8 ounces (227 g) Brussels sprouts, trimmed (large sprouts halved)
2 small shallots, cut into ¼-inch-thick slices
Kosher salt and freshly ground black pepper, to taste
2 teaspoons lightly packed fresh cilantro leaves

1. In a large bowl, whisk together the chili sauce, vinegar, and hot sauce. Add the Brussels sprouts and shallots, season with salt and pepper, and toss to combine. Scrape the Brussels sprouts and sauce into a cake pan. 2. Place the pan in the air fryer and roast at 375°F (191°C), stirring every 5 minutes, until the Brussels sprouts are tender and the sauce is reduced to a sticky glaze, about 20 minutes. 3. Remove the pan from the air fryer and transfer the Brussels sprouts to plates. Sprinkle with the cilantro and serve warm.
Per Serving:
calories: 106 | fat: 0g | protein: 5g | carbs: 21g | fiber: 7g | sodium: 498mg

Spicy Grilled Veggie Pita

Prep time: 10 minutes | Cook time: 15 minutes | Serves 4

4 pita breads
2 tablespoons olive oil
2 garlic cloves, minced
1 zucchini, sliced
1 red bell pepper, cut into strips
½ red onion, sliced
½ cup plain full-fat Greek yogurt
1 teaspoon harissa
1 large tomato, sliced
Sea salt
Freshly ground black pepper

1. Toast the pitas in a skillet over medium-high heat for 3 to 4 minutes per side, then remove from the heat and set aside. 2. In the same skillet, combine the olive oil and garlic and sauté over medium-high heat for 2 minutes. Add the zucchini, bell pepper, and onion and sauté for 5 to 6 minutes, until softened. Remove from the heat. 3. While the vegetables are cooking, in a small bowl, mix the yogurt and harissa. 4. Halve the pitas crosswise and open each half to form a pocket. Add 1 tablespoon of the yogurt mixture to each pita pocket and spread it over the inside. Spoon the cooked vegetable mixture into the pockets and top with the tomatoes. Season with salt and black pepper. 5. Serve the pitas with the extra sauce on the side.
Per Serving:
calories: 215 | fat: 10g | protein: 5g | carbs: 27g | fiber: 5g | sodium: 244mg

Roasted Fennel with Parmesan

Prep time: 5 minutes | Cook time: 30 minutes | Serves 4

2 fennel bulbs (about 2 pounds / 907 g), cored and cut into 8 wedges each (reserve fronds for garnish)
¼ cup olive oil
Salt
Freshly ground black pepper
1¼ teaspoons red pepper flakes
½ cup freshly grated Parmesan cheese

1. Preheat the oven to 350°F (180°C). 2. Arrange the fennel wedges on a large, rimmed baking sheet and drizzle the oil over the top. 3. Sprinkle each wedge with a pinch each of salt, black pepper, and red pepper flakes. Sprinkle the cheese over the top. 4. Bake in the preheated oven for about 30 minutes, until the fennel is tender and the cheese is golden brown. Remove from the oven and let cool in the oil until just warm. Using a slotted metal spatula, transfer the fennel to plates and garnish with the reserved fennel fronds.
Per Serving:
calories: 237 | fat: 19g | protein: 11g | carbs: 10g | fiber: 4g | sodium: 363mg

Turkish Stuffed Eggplant

Prep time: 10 minutes | Cook time: 2 hours 10 minutes | Serves 6

½ cup extra-virgin olive oil
3 small eggplants
1 teaspoon sea salt
½ teaspoon black pepper
1 large yellow onion, finely chopped
4 garlic cloves, minced
1 (15-ounce / 425-g) can diced tomatoes, with the juice
¼ cup finely chopped fresh flat-leaf parsley
6 (8-inch) round pita breads, quartered and toasted
1 cup plain Greek yogurt

1. Pour ¼ cup of the olive oil into the slow cooker, and generously coat the interior of the crock. 2. Cut each eggplant in half lengthwise. You can leave the stem on. Score the cut side of each half every ¼ inch, being careful not to cut through the skin. 3. Arrange the eggplant halves, skin-side down, in the slow cooker. Sprinkle with 1 teaspoon salt and ½ teaspoon pepper. 4. In a large skillet, heat the remaining ¼ cup olive oil over medium-high heat. Sauté the onion and garlic for 3 minutes, or until the onion begins to soften. 5. Add the tomatoes and parsley to the skillet. Season with salt and pepper. Sauté for another 5 minutes, until the liquid has almost evaporated. 6. Using a large spoon, spoon the tomato mixture over the eggplants, covering each half with some of the mixture. 7. Cover and cook on high for 2 hours or on low for 4 hours. When the dish is finished, the eggplant should feel very tender when you insert the tip of a sharp knife into the thickest part. 8. Uncover the slow cooker, and let the eggplant rest for 10 minutes. Then transfer the eggplant to a serving dish. If there is any juice in the bottom of the cooker, spoon it over the eggplant. Serve hot with toasted pita wedges and yogurt on the side.

Per Serving:
calories: 449 | fat: 22g | protein: 11g | carbs: 59g | fiber: 15g | sodium: 706mg

Hearty Minestrone Soup

Prep time: 20 minutes | Cook time: 20 minutes | Serves 8

2 cups dried Great Northern beans, soaked overnight and drained
1 cup orzo
2 large carrots, peeled and diced
1 bunch Swiss chard, ribs removed and roughly chopped
1 medium zucchini, trimmed and diced
2 stalks celery, diced
1 medium onion, peeled and
diced
1 teaspoon minced garlic
1 tablespoon Italian seasoning
1 teaspoon salt
½ teaspoon ground black pepper
2 bay leaves
1 (14½-ounce / 411-g) can diced tomatoes, including juice
4 cups vegetable broth
1 cup tomato juice

1. Place all ingredients in the Instant Pot® and stir to combine. Close lid, set steam release to Sealing, press the Soup button, and cook for the default time of 20 minutes. 2. When the timer beeps, let pressure release naturally for 10 minutes. Quick-release any remaining pressure until the float valve drops and open lid. Remove and discard bay leaves. 3. Ladle into bowls and serve warm.

Per Serving:
calories: 207 | fat: 1g | protein: 12g | carbs: 47g | fiber: 10g | sodium: 814mg

Garlic-Parmesan Crispy Baby Potatoes

Prep time: 10 minutes | Cook time: 15 minutes | Serves 4

Oil, for spraying
1 pound (454 g) baby potatoes
½ cup grated Parmesan cheese, divided
3 tablespoons olive oil
2 teaspoons granulated garlic
½ teaspoon onion powder
½ teaspoon salt
¼ teaspoon freshly ground black pepper
¼ teaspoon paprika
2 tablespoons chopped fresh parsley, for garnish

1. Line the air fryer basket with parchment and spray lightly with oil. 2. Rinse the potatoes, pat dry with paper towels, and place in a large bowl. 3. In a small bowl, mix together ¼ cup of Parmesan cheese, the olive oil, garlic, onion powder, salt, black pepper, and paprika. Pour the mixture over the potatoes and toss to coat. 4. Transfer the potatoes to the prepared basket and spread them out in an even layer, taking care to keep them from touching. You may need to work in batches, depending on the size of your air fryer. 5. Air fry at 400ºF (204ºC) for 15 minutes, stirring after 7 to 8 minutes, or until easily pierced with a fork. Continue to cook for another 1 to 2 minutes, if needed. 6. Sprinkle with the parsley and the remaining Parmesan cheese and serve.

Per Serving:
calories: 234 | fat: 14g | protein: 6g | carbs: 22g | fiber: 3g | sodium: 525mg

Melitzanes Yiahni (Braised Eggplant)

Prep time: 15 minutes | Cook time: 30 minutes | Serves 6

2 large eggplants, cut into 1" pieces
1¾ teaspoons salt, divided
3 tablespoons extra-virgin olive oil, divided
1 medium yellow onion, peeled and diced
3 cloves garlic, peeled and
minced
2 cups diced fresh tomatoes
1 cup water
1 tablespoon dried oregano
½ teaspoon ground black pepper
2 tablespoons minced fresh basil

1. Place eggplant in a colander and sprinkle with 1½ teaspoon salt. Place colander over a plate. Let stand 30 minutes to drain. 2. Press the Sauté button on the Instant Pot® and heat 2 tablespoons oil. Add onion and cook until soft, about 5 minutes. Add garlic and cook until fragrant, about 30 seconds. Add tomatoes and water. Press the Cancel button. 3. Rinse eggplant well and drain. Add to pot. Close lid, set steam release to Sealing, press the Manual button, and set time to 8 minutes. Once timer beeps, quick-release the pressure until the float valve drops, press the Cancel button, and open lid. Add oregano, pepper, and remaining ¼ teaspoon salt. 4. Add remaining 1 tablespoon oil to pot and stir well. Press the Sauté button and simmer for 15 minutes to thicken. Add basil and serve hot.

Per Serving:
calories: 121 | fat: 7g | protein: 2g | carbs: 14g | fiber: 7g | sodium: 107mg

Tingly Chili-Roasted Broccoli

Prep time: 5 minutes | Cook time: 10 minutes | Serves 2

12 ounces (340 g) broccoli florets
2 tablespoons Asian hot chili oil
1 teaspoon ground Sichuan peppercorns (or black pepper)

2 garlic cloves, finely chopped
1 (2-inch) piece fresh ginger, peeled and finely chopped
Kosher salt and freshly ground black pepper, to taste

1. In a bowl, toss together the broccoli, chili oil, Sichuan peppercorns, garlic, ginger, and salt and black pepper to taste. 2. Transfer to the air fryer and roast at 375°F (191°C), shaking the basket halfway through, until lightly charred and tender, about 10 minutes. Remove from the air fryer and serve warm.

Per Serving:
calories: 141 | fat: 9g | protein: 5g | carbs: 13g | fiber: 5g | sodium: 57mg

Spicy Creamer Potatoes

Prep time: 10 minutes | Cook time: 8 hours | Makes 7 (1-cup) servings

2 pounds (907 g) creamer potatoes
1 onion, chopped
3 garlic cloves, minced
1 chipotle chile in adobo sauce, minced
2 tablespoons freshly squeezed

lemon juice
2 tablespoons water
1 tablespoon chili powder
½ teaspoon ground cumin
½ teaspoon salt
⅛ teaspoon freshly ground black pepper

1. In the slow cooker, combine all the ingredients and stir. 2. Cover and cook on low for 7 to 8 hours, or until the potatoes are tender, and serve.

Per Serving:
calories: 113 | fat: 0g | protein: 3g | carbs: 25g | net carbs: 21g | sugars: 2g | fiber: 4g | sodium: 208mg | cholesterol: 0mg

Sautéed Kale with Tomato and Garlic

Prep time: 5 minutes | Cook time: 10 minutes | Serves 4

1 tablespoon extra-virgin olive oil
4 garlic cloves, sliced
¼ teaspoon red pepper flakes
2 bunches kale, stemmed and

chopped or torn into pieces
1 (14½-ounce / 411-g) can no-salt-added diced tomatoes
½ teaspoon kosher salt

1. Heat the olive oil in a wok or large skillet over medium-high heat. Add the garlic and red pepper flakes, and sauté until fragrant, about 30 seconds. Add the kale and sauté, about 3 to 5 minutes, until the kale shrinks down a bit. 2. Add the tomatoes and the salt, stir together, and cook for 3 to 5 minutes, or until the liquid reduces and the kale cooks down further and becomes tender.

Per Serving:
calories: 110 | fat: 5g | protein: 6g | carbs: 15g | fiber: 6g | sodium: 222mg

Sautéed Garlic Spinach

Prep time: 5 minutes | Cook time: 10 minutes | Serves 4

¼ cup extra-virgin olive oil
1 large onion, thinly sliced
3 cloves garlic, minced
6 (1-pound / 454-g) bags of

baby spinach, washed
½ teaspoon salt
1 lemon, cut into wedges

1. Cook the olive oil, onion, and garlic in a large skillet for 2 minutes over medium heat. 2. Add one bag of spinach and ½ teaspoon of salt. Cover the skillet and let the spinach wilt for 30 seconds. Repeat (omitting the salt), adding 1 bag of spinach at a time. 3. Once all the spinach has been added, remove the cover and cook for 3 minutes, letting some of the moisture evaporate. 4. Serve warm with a generous squeeze of lemon over the top.

Per Serving:
calories: 301 | fat: 14g | protein: 17g | carbs: 29g | fiber: 17g | sodium: 812mg

Corn on the Cob

Prep time: 5 minutes | Cook time: 12 to 15 minutes | Serves 4

2 large ears fresh corn
Olive oil for misting

Salt, to taste (optional)

1. Shuck corn, remove silks, and wash. 2. Cut or break each ear in half crosswise. 3. Spray corn with olive oil. 4. Air fry at 390°F (199°C) for 12 to 15 minutes or until browned as much as you like. 5. Serve plain or with coarsely ground salt.

Per Serving:
calories: 67 | fat: 1g | protein: 2g | carbs: 14g | fiber: 2g | sodium: 156mg

Green Beans with Pine Nuts and Garlic

Prep time: 10 minutes | Cook time: 20 minutes | Serves 4 to 6

1 pound (454 g) green beans, trimmed
1 head garlic (10 to 12 cloves), smashed
2 tablespoons extra-virgin olive oil

½ teaspoon kosher salt
¼ teaspoon red pepper flakes
1 tablespoon white wine vinegar
¼ cup pine nuts, toasted

1. Preheat the oven to 425°F (220°C). Line a baking sheet with parchment paper or foil. 2. In a large bowl, combine the green beans, garlic, olive oil, salt, and red pepper flakes and mix together. Arrange in a single layer on the baking sheet. Roast for 10 minutes, stir, and roast for another 10 minutes, or until golden brown. 3. Mix the cooked green beans with the vinegar and top with the pine nuts.

Per Serving:
calories: 165 | fat: 13g | protein: 4g | carbs: 12g | fiber: 4g | sodium: 150mg

Spiced Winter Squash with Halloumi and Shaved Brussels Sprouts

Prep time: 20 minutes | Cook time: 15 minutes | Serves 4

3 tablespoons extra-virgin olive oil, divided
2 tablespoons lemon juice
2 garlic cloves, minced, divided
⅛ teaspoon plus ½ teaspoon table salt, divided
8 ounces (227 g) Brussels sprouts, trimmed, halved, and sliced very thin
1 (8-ounce / 227-g) block halloumi cheese, sliced crosswise into ¾-inch-thick slabs

4 scallions, white parts minced, green parts sliced thin on bias
½ teaspoon ground cardamom
¼ teaspoon ground cumin
⅛ teaspoon cayenne pepper
2 pounds (907 g) butternut squash, peeled, seeded, and cut into 1-inch pieces
½ cup chicken or vegetable broth
2 teaspoons honey
¼ cup dried cherries
2 tablespoons roasted pepitas

1. Whisk 1 tablespoon oil, lemon juice, ¼ teaspoon garlic, and ⅛ teaspoon salt together in bowl. Add Brussels sprouts and toss to coat; let sit until ready to serve. 2. Using highest sauté function, heat remaining 2 tablespoons oil in Instant Pot until shimmering. Arrange halloumi around edges of pot and cook until browned, about 3 minutes per side; transfer to plate. Add scallion whites to fat left in pot and cook until softened, about 2 minutes. Stir in remaining garlic, cardamom, cumin, and cayenne and cook until fragrant, about 30 seconds. Stir in squash, broth, and remaining ½ teaspoon salt. Lock lid in place and close pressure release valve. Select high pressure cook function and cook for 6 minutes. 3. Turn off Instant Pot and quick-release pressure. Carefully remove lid, allowing steam to escape away from you. Using highest sauté function, continue to cook squash mixture, stirring occasionally until liquid is almost completely evaporated, about 5 minutes. Turn off Instant Pot. Using potato masher, mash squash until mostly smooth. Season with salt and pepper to taste. 4. Spread portion of squash over bottom of individual serving plates. Top with Brussels sprouts and halloumi. Drizzle with honey and sprinkle with cherries, pepitas, and scallion greens. Serve.

Per Serving:
calories: 337 | fat: 13g | protein: 24g | carbs: 38g | fiber: 8g | sodium: 534mg

Cretan Roasted Zucchini

Prep time: 15 minutes | Cook time: 1 hour 15 minutes | Serves 2

6 small zucchini (no longer than 6 inches), washed and ends trimmed
3 garlic cloves, thinly sliced
2 medium tomatoes, chopped, or 1 (15-ounce / 425-g) can crushed tomatoes
⅓ cup extra virgin olive oil

½ teaspoon salt
½ teaspoon freshly ground black pepper
2 tablespoons chopped fresh parsley, divided
Coarse sea salt, for serving (optional)

1. Preheat the oven to 350°F (180°C). 2. Make a long, lengthwise slit in each zucchini that reaches about halfway through. (Do not cut the zucchini all the way through.) Stuff each zucchini with the sliced garlic. 3. Transfer the tomatoes to an oven-safe casserole dish, and nestle the zucchini between the tomatoes. Drizzle the olive oil over the zucchini and tomatoes. 4. Sprinkle the salt, black pepper, and 1 tablespoon of the parsley over the zucchini and tomatoes. Turn the zucchini gently so they are covered in the olive oil. 5. Transfer to the oven and cook for 1 hour 15 minutes or until the skins are soft and the edges have browned. 6. Carefully remove the dish from the oven and sprinkle the remaining parsley and sea salt, if using, over the top. Store covered in the refrigerator for up to 3 days.

Per Serving:
calories: 406 | fat: 37g | protein: 6g | carbs: 18g | fiber: 5g | sodium: 619mg

Caramelized Root Vegetables

Prep time: 20 minutes | Cook time: 40 minutes | Serves 6

2 medium carrots, peeled and cut into chunks
2 medium red or gold beets, cut into chunks
2 turnips, peeled and cut into chunks
2 tablespoons olive oil

1 teaspoon cumin
1 teaspoon sweet paprika
Sea salt and freshly ground pepper, to taste
Juice of 1 lemon
1 small bunch flat-leaf parsley, chopped

1. Preheat oven to 400°F (205°C). 2. Toss the vegetables with the olive oil and seasonings. 3. Lay in a single layer on a sheet pan, cover with lemon juice, and roast for 30–40 minutes, until veggies are slightly browned and crisp. 4. Serve warm, topped with the chopped parsley.

Per Serving:
calories: 79 | fat: 5g | protein: 1g | carbs: 9g | fiber: 3g | sodium: 69mg

Nordic Stone Age Bread

Prep time: 10 minutes | Cook time: 1 hour | Serves 14

½ cup flaxseeds
½ cup chia seeds
½ cup sesame seeds
¼ cup pumpkin seeds
¼ cup sunflower seeds
½ cup whole almonds, chopped
½ cup blanched hazelnuts,

chopped
½ cup pecans or walnuts
1 teaspoon salt, or to taste
1 teaspoon coarse black pepper
4 large eggs
½ cup extra-virgin olive oil or melted ghee

1. Preheat the oven to 285°F (140°C) fan assisted or 320°F (160°C) conventional. Line a loaf pan with parchment paper. 2. In a mixing bowl, combine all of the dry ingredients. Add the eggs and olive oil and stir through until well combined. Pour the dough into the loaf pan. Transfer to the oven and bake for about 1 hour or until the top is crisp. 3. Remove from the oven and let cool slightly in the pan before transferring to a wire rack to cool completely before slicing. Store at room temperature for up to 3 days loosely covered with a kitchen towel, refrigerate for up to 10 days, or freeze for up to 3 months.

Per Serving:
calories: 251 | fat: 23g | protein: 7g | carbs: 7g | fiber: 5g | sodium: 192mg

Sweet and Crispy Roasted Pearl Onions

Prep time: 5 minutes | Cook time: 18 minutes | Serves 3

1 (14½-ounce / 411-g) package frozen pearl onions (do not thaw)
2 tablespoons extra-virgin olive oil
2 tablespoons balsamic vinegar
2 teaspoons finely chopped fresh rosemary
½ teaspoon kosher salt
¼ teaspoon black pepper

1. In a medium bowl, combine the onions, olive oil, vinegar, rosemary, salt, and pepper until well coated. 2. Transfer the onions to the air fryer basket. Set the air fryer to 400°F (204°C) for 18 minutes, or until the onions are tender and lightly charred, stirring once or twice during the cooking time.

Per Serving:
calories: 145 | fat: 9g | protein: 2g | carbs: 15g | fiber: 2g | sodium: 396mg

Mini Moroccan Pumpkin Cakes

Prep time: 10 minutes | Cook time: 10 minutes | Serves 6

2 cups cooked brown rice
1 cup pumpkin purée
½ cup finely chopped walnuts
3 tablespoons olive oil, divided
½ medium onion, diced
½ red bell pepper, diced
1 teaspoon ground cumin
Sea salt and freshly ground pepper, to taste
1 teaspoon hot paprika or a pinch of cayenne

1. Combine the rice, pumpkin, and walnuts in a large bowl; set aside. 2. In a medium skillet, heat the olive oil over medium heat, add the onion and bell pepper, and cook until soft, about 5 minutes. 3. Add the cumin to the onions and bell peppers. Add onion mixture to the rice mixture. 4. Mix thoroughly and season with sea salt, freshly ground pepper, and paprika or cayenne. 5. In a large skillet, heat 2 tablespoons of olive oil over medium heat. 6. Form the rice mixture into 1-inch patties and add them to the skillet. Cook until both sides are browned and crispy. 7. Serve with Greek yogurt or tzatziki on the side.

Per Serving:
calories: 193 | fat: 12g | protein: 3g | carbs: 20g | fiber: 3g | sodium: 6mg

Roasted Cauliflower and Tomatoes

Prep time: 5 minutes | Cook time: 25 minutes | Serves 4

4 cups cauliflower, cut into 1-inch pieces
6 tablespoons extra-virgin olive oil, divided
1 teaspoon salt, divided
4 cups cherry tomatoes
½ teaspoon freshly ground black pepper
½ cup grated Parmesan cheese

1. Preheat the oven to 425°F (220°C). 2. Add the cauliflower, 3 tablespoons of olive oil, and ½ teaspoon of salt to a large bowl and toss to evenly coat. Pour onto a baking sheet and spread the cauliflower out in an even layer. 3. In another large bowl, add the tomatoes, remaining 3 tablespoons of olive oil, and ½ teaspoon of salt, and toss to coat evenly. Pour onto a different baking sheet. 4. Put the sheet of cauliflower and the sheet of tomatoes in the oven to roast for 17 to 20 minutes until the cauliflower is lightly browned and tomatoes are plump. 5. Using a spatula, spoon the cauliflower into a serving dish, and top with tomatoes, black pepper, and Parmesan cheese. Serve warm.

Per Serving:
calories: 294 | fat: 26g | protein: 9g | carbs: 13g | fiber: 4g | sodium: 858mg

Mushroom-Stuffed Zucchini

Prep time: 15 minutes | Cook time: 46 minutes | Serves 2

2 tablespoons olive oil
2 cups button mushrooms, finely chopped
2 cloves garlic, finely chopped
2 tablespoons chicken broth
1 tablespoon flat-leaf parsley, finely chopped
1 tablespoon Italian seasoning
Sea salt and freshly ground pepper, to taste
2 medium zucchini, cut in half lengthwise

1. Preheat oven to 350°F (180°C). 2. Heat a large skillet over medium heat, and add the olive oil. Add the mushrooms and cook until tender, about 4 minutes. Add the garlic and cook for 2 more minutes. 3. Add the chicken broth and cook another 3–4 minutes. 4. Add the parsley and Italian seasoning, and season with sea salt and freshly ground pepper. 5. Stir and remove from heat. 6. Scoop out the insides of the halved zucchini and stuff with mushroom mixture. 7. Place zucchini in a casserole dish, and drizzle a tablespoon of water or broth in the bottom. 8. Cover with foil and bake for 30–40 minutes until zucchini are tender. Serve immediately.

Per Serving:
calories: 189 | fat: 14g | protein: 5g | carbs: 12g | fiber: 3g | sodium: 335mg

Vegetable Tagine

Prep time: 15 minutes | Cook time: 45 minutes | Serves 4

3 tablespoons olive oil
1 onion, thinly sliced
5 garlic cloves, minced
2 carrots, cut into long ribbons
2 red bell peppers, coarsely chopped
1 (15-ounce / 425-g) can diced tomatoes
½ cup chopped dried apricots
1 to 2 tablespoons harissa
1 teaspoon ground coriander
½ teaspoon ground turmeric
½ teaspoon ground cinnamon
3 cups vegetable broth
1 sweet potato, peeled and cubed
1 (15-ounce / 425-g) can chickpeas, drained and rinsed
Sea salt
Freshly ground black pepper

1. In a large stockpot, heat the olive oil over medium-high heat. Add the onion and garlic and sauté for 5 minutes. Add the carrots and bell peppers and sauté for 7 to 10 minutes, until the vegetables are tender. 2. Add the tomatoes, apricots, harissa, coriander, turmeric, and cinnamon and cook for 5 minutes. Add the broth and sweet potato and bring to a boil. Reduce the heat to low, cover, and simmer for 20 minutes, or until the sweet potato is tender. 3. Add the chickpeas and simmer for 3 minutes to heat through. Season with salt and black pepper and serve.

Per Serving:
calories: 324 | fat: 12g | protein: 9g | carbs: 48g | fiber: 12g | sodium: 210mg

Brussels Sprouts with Pecans and Gorgonzola

Prep time: 10 minutes | Cook time: 25 minutes | Serves 4

½ cup pecans
1½ pounds (680 g) fresh Brussels sprouts, trimmed and quartered
2 tablespoons olive oil

Salt and freshly ground black pepper, to taste
¼ cup crumbled Gorgonzola cheese

1. Spread the pecans in a single layer of the air fryer and set the heat to 350ºF (177ºC). Air fry for 3 to 5 minutes until the pecans are lightly browned and fragrant. Transfer the pecans to a plate and continue preheating the air fryer, increasing the heat to 400ºF (204ºC). 2. In a large bowl, toss the Brussels sprouts with the olive oil and season with salt and black pepper to taste. 3. Working in batches if necessary, arrange the Brussels sprouts in a single layer in the air fryer basket. Pausing halfway through the baking time to shake the basket, air fry for 20 to 25 minutes until the sprouts are tender and starting to brown on the edges. 4. Transfer the sprouts to a serving bowl and top with the toasted pecans and Gorgonzola. Serve warm or at room temperature.

Per Serving:
calories: 253 | fat: 18g | protein: 9g | carbs: 17g | fiber: 8g | sodium: 96mg

Easy Greek Briami (Ratatouille)

Prep time: 15 minutes | Cook time: 40 minutes | Serves 6

2 russet potatoes, cubed
½ cup Roma tomatoes, cubed
1 eggplant, cubed
1 zucchini, cubed
1 red onion, chopped
1 red bell pepper, chopped
2 garlic cloves, minced
1 teaspoon dried mint
1 teaspoon dried parsley

1 teaspoon dried oregano
½ teaspoon salt
½ teaspoon black pepper
¼ teaspoon red pepper flakes
⅓ cup olive oil
1 (8-ounce / 227-g) can tomato paste
¼ cup vegetable broth
¼ cup water

1. Preheat the air fryer to 320°F(160ºC). 2. In a large bowl, combine the potatoes, tomatoes, eggplant, zucchini, onion, bell pepper, garlic, mint, parsley, oregano, salt, black pepper, and red pepper flakes. 3. In a small bowl, mix together the olive oil, tomato paste, broth, and water. 4. Pour the oil-and-tomato-paste mixture over the vegetables and toss until everything is coated. 5. Pour the coated vegetables into the air fryer basket in an even layer and roast for 20 minutes. After 20 minutes, stir well and spread out again. Roast for an additional 10 minutes, then repeat the process and cook for another 10 minutes.

Per Serving:
calories: 239 | fat: 13g | protein: 5g | carbs: 31g | fiber: 7g | sodium: 250mg

Citrus-Roasted Broccoli Florets

Prep time: 5 minutes | Cook time: 12 minutes | Serves 6

4 cups broccoli florets (approximately 1 large head)
2 tablespoons olive oil
½ teaspoon salt

½ cup orange juice
1 tablespoon raw honey
Orange wedges, for serving (optional)

1. Preheat the air fryer to 360°F(182ºC). 2. In a large bowl, combine the broccoli, olive oil, salt, orange juice, and honey. Toss the broccoli in the liquid until well coated. 3. Pour the broccoli mixture into the air fryer basket and roast for 6 minutes. Stir and roast for 6 minutes more. 4. Serve alone or with orange wedges for additional citrus flavor, if desired.

Per Serving:
calories: 73 | fat: 5g | protein: 2g | carbs: 8g | fiber: 0g | sodium: 207mg

Garlicky Broccoli Rabe with Artichokes

Prep time: 5 minutes | Cook time: 10 minutes | Serves 4

2 pounds (907 g) fresh broccoli rabe
½ cup extra-virgin olive oil, divided
3 garlic cloves, finely minced
1 teaspoon salt
1 teaspoon red pepper flakes

1 (13¾-ounce / 390-g) can artichoke hearts, drained and quartered
1 tablespoon water
2 tablespoons red wine vinegar
Freshly ground black pepper

1. Trim away any thick lower stems and yellow leaves from the broccoli rabe and discard. Cut into individual florets with a couple inches of thin stem attached. 2. In a large skillet, heat ¼ cup olive oil over medium-high heat. Add the trimmed broccoli, garlic, salt, and red pepper flakes and sauté for 5 minutes, until the broccoli begins to soften. Add the artichoke hearts and sauté for another 2 minutes. 3. Add the water and reduce the heat to low. Cover and simmer until the broccoli stems are tender, 3 to 5 minutes. 4. In a small bowl, whisk together remaining ¼ cup olive oil and the vinegar. Drizzle over the broccoli and artichokes. Season with ground black pepper, if desired.

Per Serving:
calories: 341 | fat: 28g | protein: 11g | carbs: 18g | fiber: 12g | sodium: 750mg

Chapter 12 Salads

Bacalhau and Black-Eyed Pea Salad

Prep time: 10 minutes | Cook time: 10 minutes | Serves 4

1 pound (454 g) bacalhau (salt cod) fillets	black pepper
¼ cup olive oil, plus 1 tablespoon, divided	1 (15-ounce / 425-g) can black-eyed peas, drained and rinsed
3 tablespoons white wine vinegar	1 small yellow onion, halved and thinly sliced crosswise
1 teaspoon salt	1 small clove garlic, minced
¼ teaspoon freshly ground	¼ cup chopped fresh flat-leaf parsley leaves, divided

1. Rinse the cod under cold running water to remove any surface salt. Place the fish pieces in a large nonreactive pot, cover with water and refrigerate (covered) for 24 hours, changing the water several times. 2. Pour off the water, refill the pot with clean water and gently boil the cod until it flakes easily with a fork, about 7 to 10 minutes (or longer), depending on the thickness. Drain and set aside to cool. 3. To make the dressing, whisk together the oil, vinegar, salt, and pepper in a small bowl. 4. In a large bowl, combine the beans, onion, garlic, and ¾ of the parsley. Add the dressing and mix to coat well. Stir in the salt cod, cover, and chill in the refrigerator for at least 2 hours to let the flavors meld. Let sit on the countertop for 30 minutes before serving. 5. Serve garnished with the remaining parsley.

Per Serving:
calories: 349 | fat: 18g | protein: 32g | carbs: 16g | fiber: 4g | sodium: 8mg

Garden Salad with Sardine Fillets

Prep time: 20 minutes | Cook time: 0 minutes | Serves 6

½ cup olive oil	1 pound (454 g) arugula, trimmed and chopped
Juice of 1 medium lemon	1 small red onion, thinly sliced
1 teaspoon Dijon mustard	1 small bunch flat-leaf parsley, chopped
Sea salt and freshly ground pepper, to taste	4 whole sardine fillets packed in olive oil, drained and chopped
4 medium tomatoes, diced	
1 large cucumber, peeled and diced	

1. For the dressing, whisk together the olive oil, lemon juice, and mustard, and season with sea salt and pepper. Set aside. 2. In a large bowl, combine all the vegetables with the parsley, and toss. Add the sardine fillets on top of the salad. 3. Drizzle the dressing over the salad just before serving.

Per Serving:
calories: 226 | fat: 20g | protein: 5g | carbs: 9g | fiber: 3g | sodium: 66mg

Citrus Fennel Salad

Prep time: 15 minutes | Cook time: 0 minutes | Serves 2

For the Dressing:	2 cups packed baby kale
2 tablespoons fresh orange juice	1 medium navel or blood orange, segmented
3 tablespoons olive oil	½ small fennel bulb, stems and leaves removed, sliced into matchsticks
1 tablespoon blood orange vinegar, other orange vinegar, or cider vinegar	3 tablespoons toasted pecans, chopped
1 tablespoon honey	2 ounces (57 g) goat cheese, crumbled
Salt	
Freshly ground black pepper	
For the Salad:	

Make the Dressing: Combine the orange juice, olive oil, vinegar, and honey in a small bowl and whisk to combine. Season with salt and pepper. Set the dressing aside. Make the Salad: 1. Divide the baby kale, orange segments, fennel, pecans, and goat cheese evenly between two plates. 2. Drizzle half of the dressing over each salad.

Per Serving:
calories: 502 | fat: 39g | protein: 13g | carbs: 31g | fiber: 6g | sodium: 158mg

Greek Potato Salad

Prep time: 15 minutes | Cook time: 15 to 18 minutes | Serves 6

1½ pounds (680 g) small red or new potatoes	cheese (for a less salty option)
½ cup olive oil	1 green bell pepper, seeded and chopped (1¼ cups)
⅓ cup red wine vinegar	1 small red onion, halved and thinly sliced (generous 1 cup)
1 teaspoon fresh Greek oregano	½ cup Kalamata olives, pitted and halved
4 ounces (113 g) feta cheese, crumbled, if desired, or 4 ounces (113 g) grated Swiss	

1. Put the potatoes in a large saucepan and add water to cover. Bring the water to a boil and cook until tender, 15 to 18 minutes. Drain and set aside until cool enough to handle. 2. Meanwhile, in a large bowl, whisk together the olive oil, vinegar, and oregano. 3. When the potatoes are just cool enough to handle, cut them into 1-inch pieces and add them to the bowl with the dressing. Toss to combine. Add the cheese, bell pepper, onion, and olives and toss gently. Let stand for 30 minutes before serving.

Per Serving:
calories: 315 | fat: 23g | protein: 5g | carbs: 21g | fiber: 3g | sodium: 360mg

Tuscan Kale Salad with Anchovies

Prep time: 15 minutes | Cook time: 0 minutes | Serves 4

1 large bunch lacinato or dinosaur kale
¼ cup toasted pine nuts
1 cup shaved or coarsely shredded fresh Parmesan cheese
¼ cup extra-virgin olive oil
8 anchovy fillets, roughly

chopped
2 to 3 tablespoons freshly squeezed lemon juice (from 1 large lemon)
2 teaspoons red pepper flakes (optional)

1. Remove the rough center stems from the kale leaves and roughly tear each leaf into about 4-by-1-inch strips. Place the torn kale in a large bowl and add the pine nuts and cheese. 2. In a small bowl, whisk together the olive oil, anchovies, lemon juice, and red pepper flakes (if using). Drizzle over the salad and toss to coat well. Let sit at room temperature 30 minutes before serving, tossing again just prior to serving.

Per Serving:
calories: 333 | fat: 27g | protein: 16g | carbs: 12g | fiber: 4g | sodium: 676mg

Double-Apple Spinach Salad

Prep time: 15 minutes | Cook time: 0 minutes | Serves 4

8 cups baby spinach
1 medium Granny Smith apple, diced
1 medium red apple, diced
½ cup toasted walnuts

2 ounces (57 g) low-fat, sharp white cheddar cheese, cubed
3 tablespoons olive oil
1 tablespoon red wine vinegar or apple cider vinegar

1. Toss the spinach, apples, walnuts, and cubed cheese together. Lightly drizzle olive oil and vinegar over top and serve.

Per Serving:
calories: 275 | fat: 22g | protein: 7g | carbs: 16g | fiber: 4g | sodium: 140mg

Arugula and Fennel Salad with Fresh Basil

Prep time: 5 minutes | Cook time: 0 minutes | Serves 4

3 tablespoons olive oil
3 tablespoons lemon juice
1 teaspoon honey
½ teaspoon salt
1 medium bulb fennel, very thinly sliced
1 small cucumber, very thinly

sliced
2 cups arugula
¼ cup toasted pine nuts
½ cup crumbled feta cheese
¼ cup julienned fresh basil leaves

1. In a medium bowl, whisk together the olive oil, lemon juice, honey, and salt. Add the fennel and cucumber and toss to coat and let sit for 10 minutes or so. 2. Put the arugula in a large salad bowl. Add the marinated cucumber and fennel, along with the dressing, to the bowl and toss well. Serve immediately, sprinkled with pine nuts, feta cheese, and basil.

Per Serving:
calories: 237 | fat: 21g | protein: 6g | carbs: 11g | fiber: 3g | sodium: 537mg

Roasted Cauliflower "Steak" Salad

Prep time: 10 minutes | Cook time: 50 minutes | Serves 4

2 tablespoons olive oil, divided
2 large heads cauliflower (about 3 pounds / 1.4 kg each), trimmed of outer leaves
2 teaspoons za'atar
1½ teaspoons kosher salt, divided
1¼ teaspoons ground black pepper, divided
1 teaspoon ground cumin

2 large carrots
8 ounces (227 g) dandelion greens, tough stems removed
½ cup low-fat plain Greek yogurt
2 tablespoons tahini
2 tablespoons fresh lemon juice
1 tablespoon water
1 clove garlic, minced

1. Preheat the oven to 450°F(235°C). Brush a large baking sheet with some of the oil. 2. Place the cauliflower on a cutting board, stem side down. Cut down the middle, through the core and stem, and then cut two 1'-thick "steaks" from the middle. Repeat with the other cauliflower head. Set aside the remaining cauliflower for another use. Brush both sides of the steaks with the remaining oil and set on the baking sheet. 3. Combine the za'atar, 1 teaspoon of the salt, 1 teaspoon of the pepper, and the cumin. Sprinkle on the cauliflower steaks. Bake until the bottom is deeply golden, about 30 minutes. Flip and bake until tender, 10 to 15 minutes. 4. Meanwhile, set the carrots on a cutting board and use a vegetable peeler to peel them into ribbons. Add to a large bowl with the dandelion greens. 5. In a small bowl, combine the yogurt, tahini, lemon juice, water, garlic, the remaining ½ teaspoon salt, and the remaining ¼ teaspoon pepper. 6. Dab 3 tablespoons of the dressing onto the carrot-dandelion mix. With a spoon or your hands, massage the dressing into the mix for 5 minutes. 7. Remove the steaks from the oven and transfer to individual plates. Drizzle each with 2 tablespoons of the dressing and top with 1 cup of the salad.

Per Serving:
calories: 214 | fat: 12g | protein: 9g | carbs: 21g | fiber: 7g | sodium: 849mg

Mediterranean Quinoa and Garbanzo Salad

Prep time: 10 minutes | Cook time: 30 minutes | Serves 8

4 cups water
2 cups red or yellow quinoa
2 teaspoons salt, divided
1 cup thinly sliced onions (red or white)
1 (16-ounce / 454-g) can

garbanzo beans, rinsed and drained
⅓ cup extra-virgin olive oil
¼ cup lemon juice
1 teaspoon freshly ground black pepper

1. In a 3-quart pot over medium heat, bring the water to a boil. 2. Add the quinoa and 1 teaspoon of salt to the pot. Stir, cover, and let cook over low heat for 15 to 20 minutes. 3. Turn off the heat, fluff the quinoa with a fork, cover again, and let stand for 5 to 10 more minutes. 4. Put the cooked quinoa, onions, and garbanzo beans in a large bowl. 5. In a separate small bowl, whisk together the olive oil, lemon juice, remaining 1 teaspoon of salt, and black pepper. 6. Add the dressing to the quinoa mixture and gently toss everything together. Serve warm or cold.

Per Serving:
calories: 318 | fat: 13g | protein: 9g | carbs: 43g | fiber: 6g | sodium: 585mg

Fruited Chicken Salad

Prep time: 10 minutes | Cook time: 0 minutes | Serves 2

2 cups chopped cooked chicken breast	2 tablespoons honey Dijon mustard
2 Granny Smith apples, peeled, cored, and diced	1 tablespoon olive oil mayonnaise
½ cup dried cranberries	½ teaspoon salt
¼ cup diced red onion	¼ teaspoon freshly ground black pepper
¼ cup diced celery	

1. In a medium bowl, combine the chicken, apples, cranberries, onion, and celery and mix well. 2. In a small bowl, combine the mustard, mayonnaise, salt, and pepper and whisk together until well blended. 3. Stir the dressing into the chicken mixture until thoroughly combined.

Per Serving:
calories: 384 | fat: 9g | protein: 45g | carbs: 28g | fiber: 7g | sodium: 638mg

Four-Bean Salad

Prep time: 20 minutes | Cook time: 0 minutes | Serves 4

½ cup white beans, cooked	chopped
½ cup black-eyed peas, cooked	2 tablespoons olive oil
½ cup fava beans, cooked	1 teaspoon ground cumin
½ cup lima beans, cooked	Juice of 1 lemon
1 red bell pepper, diced	Sea salt and freshly ground
1 small bunch flat-leaf parsley,	pepper, to taste

1. You can cook the beans a day or two in advance to speed up the preparation of this dish. 2. Combine all ingredients in a large bowl and mix well. Season to taste. 3. Allow to sit for 30 minutes, so the flavors can come together before serving.

Per Serving:
calories: 189 | fat: 7g | protein: 8g | carbs: 24g | fiber: 7g | sodium: 14mg

Warm Fennel, Cherry Tomato, and Spinach Salad

Prep time: 15 minutes | Cook time: 0 minutes | Serves 2

4 tablespoons chicken broth	pepper, to taste
4 cups baby spinach leaves	1 fennel bulb, sliced
10 cherry tomatoes, halved	¼ cup olive oil
Sea salt and freshly ground	Juice of 2 lemons

1. In a large sauté pan, heat the chicken broth over medium heat. Add the spinach and tomatoes and cook until spinach is wilted. Season with sea salt and freshly ground pepper to taste. 2. Remove from heat and toss fennel slices in with the spinach and tomatoes. Let the fennel warm in the pan, then transfer to a large bowl. 3. Drizzle with the olive oil and lemon juice, and serve immediately.

Per Serving:
calories: 319 | fat: 28g | protein: 5g | carbs: 18g | fiber: 6g | sodium: 123mg

Pear-Fennel Salad with Pomegranate

Prep time: 15 minutes | Cook time: 5 minutes | Serves 6

Dressing:	chopped, or pine nuts
2 tablespoons red wine vinegar	2 red pears, halved, cored, and very thinly sliced
1½ tablespoons pomegranate molasses	1 bulb fennel, halved, cored, and very thinly sliced, fronds reserved
2 teaspoons finely chopped shallot	1 tablespoon fresh lemon juice
½ teaspoon Dijon mustard	4 cups baby arugula
½ teaspoon kosher salt	½ cup pomegranate seeds
¼ teaspoon ground black pepper	⅓ cup crumbled feta cheese or shaved Parmigiano-Reggiano cheese
¼ cup extra-virgin olive oil	
Salad:	
¼ cup walnuts, coarsely	

1. Make the Dressing: In a small bowl or jar with a lid, combine the vinegar, pomegranate molasses, shallot, mustard, salt, and pepper. Add the oil and whisk until emulsified (or cap the jar and shake vigorously). Set aside. 2. Make the Salad: In a small skillet over medium heat, toast the nuts until golden and fragrant, 4 to 5 minutes. Remove from the skillet to cool. 3. In a large bowl, combine the pears and fennel. Sprinkle with the lemon juice and toss gently. 4. Add the arugula and toss again to evenly distribute. Pour over 3 to 4 tablespoons of the dressing, just enough to moisten the arugula, and toss. Add the pomegranate seeds, cheese, and nuts and toss again. Add more dressing, if necessary, or store remainder in the refrigerator for up to 1 week. Serve the salad topped with the reserved fennel fronds.

Per Serving:
calories: 165 | fat: 10g | protein:31g | carbs: 18g | fiber: 4g | sodium: 215mg

Arugula Spinach Salad with Shaved Parmesan

Prep time: 10 minutes | Cook time: 2 minutes | Serves 3

3 tablespoons raw pine nuts	For the Dressing:
3 cups arugula	4 teaspoons balsamic vinegar
3 cups baby leaf spinach	1 teaspoon Dijon mustard
5 dried figs, pitted and chopped	1 teaspoon honey
2½ ounces (71 g) shaved Parmesan cheese	5 tablespoons extra virgin olive oil

1. In a small pan over low heat, toast the pine nuts for 2 minutes or until they begin to brown. Promptly remove them from the heat and transfer to a small bowl. 2. Make the dressing by combining the balsamic vinegar, Dijon mustard, and honey in a small bowl. Using a fork to whisk, gradually add the olive oil while continuously mixing. 3. In a large bowl, toss the arugula and baby spinach and then top with the figs, Parmesan cheese, and toasted pine nuts. Drizzle the dressing over the top and toss until the ingredients are thoroughly coated with the dressing. Serve promptly. (This salad is best served fresh.)

Per Serving:
calories: 416 | fat: 35g | protein: 10g | carbs: 18g | fiber: 3g | sodium: 478mg

Tossed Green Mediterranean Salad

Prep time: 15 minutes | Cook time: 0 minutes | Serves 4

1 medium head romaine lettuce, washed, dried, and chopped into bite-sized pieces	½ cup finely chopped fresh dill
	⅓ cup extra virgin olive oil
2 medium cucumbers, peeled and sliced	2 tablespoons fresh lemon juice
	¼ teaspoon fine sea salt
3 spring onions (white parts only), sliced	4 ounces (113 g) crumbled feta
	7 Kalamata olives, pitted

1. Add the lettuce, cucumber, spring onions, and dill to a large bowl. Toss to combine. 2. In a small bowl, whisk together the olive oil and lemon juice. Pour the dressing over the salad, toss, then sprinkle the sea salt over the top. 3. Sprinkle the feta and olives over the top and then gently toss the salad one more time. Serve promptly. (This recipe is best served fresh.)

Per Serving:
calories: 284 | fat: 25g | protein: 7g | carbs: 10g | fiber: 5g | sodium: 496mg

Easy Greek Salad

Prep time: 10 minutes | Cook time: 0 minutes | Serves 4 to 6

1 head iceberg lettuce	1 teaspoon salt
1 pint (2 cups) cherry tomatoes	1 clove garlic, minced
1 large cucumber	1 cup Kalamata olives, pitted
1 medium onion	1 (6-ounce / 170-g) package feta cheese, crumbled
½ cup extra-virgin olive oil	
¼ cup lemon juice	

1. Cut the lettuce into 1-inch pieces and put them in a large salad bowl. 2. Cut the tomatoes in half and add them to the salad bowl. 3. Slice the cucumber into bite-size pieces and add them to the salad bowl. 4. Thinly slice the onion and add it to the salad bowl. 5. In another small bowl, whisk together the olive oil, lemon juice, salt, and garlic. Pour the dressing over the salad and gently toss to evenly coat. 6. Top the salad with the Kalamata olives and feta cheese and serve.

Per Serving:
calories: 297 | fat: 27g | protein: 6g | carbs: 11g | fiber: 3g | sodium: 661mg

Classic Tabouli

Prep time: 30 minutes | Cook time: 0 minutes | Serves 8 to 10

1 cup bulgur wheat, grind	chopped
4 cups Italian parsley, finely chopped	½ cup lemon juice
	½ cup extra-virgin olive oil
2 cups ripe tomato, finely diced	1½ teaspoons salt
1 cup green onion, finely	1 teaspoon dried mint

1. Before you chop the vegetables, put the bulgur in a small bowl. Rinse with water, drain, and let stand in the bowl while you prepare the other ingredients. 2. Put the parsley, tomatoes, green onion,

and bulgur into a large bowl. 3. In a small bowl, whisk together the lemon juice, olive oil, salt, and mint. 4. Pour the dressing over the tomato, onion, and bulgur mixture, tossing everything together. Add additional salt to taste. Serve immediately or store in the fridge for up to 2 days.

Per Serving:
calories: 207 | fat: 14g | protein: 4g | carbs: 20g | fiber: 5g | sodium: 462mg

Tomato and Pepper Salad

Prep time: 10 minutes | Cook time: 0 minutes | Serves 6

3 large yellow peppers	4 large tomatoes, seeded and diced
¼ cup olive oil	
1 small bunch fresh basil leaves	Sea salt and freshly ground pepper, to taste
2 cloves garlic, minced	

1. Preheat broiler to high heat and broil the peppers until blackened on all sides. 2. Remove from heat and place in a paper bag. Seal and allow peppers to cool. 3. Once cooled, peel the skins off the peppers, then seed and chop them. 4. Add half of the peppers to a food processor along with the olive oil, basil, and garlic, and pulse several times to make the dressing. 5. Combine the rest of the peppers with the tomatoes and toss with the dressing. 6. Season the salad with sea salt and freshly ground pepper. Allow salad to come to room temperature before serving.

Per Serving:
calories: 129 | fat: 9g | protein: 2g | carbs: 11g | fiber: 2g | sodium: 8mg

Quinoa with Zucchini, Mint, and Pistachios

Prep time: 20 to 30 minutes | Cook time: 20 minutes | Serves 4

For the Quinoa:	¾ teaspoon kosher salt
1½ cups water	¼ teaspoon freshly ground black pepper
1 cup quinoa	
¼ teaspoon kosher salt	2 garlic cloves, sliced
For the Salad:	Zest of 1 lemon
2 tablespoons extra-virgin olive oil	2 tablespoons lemon juice
	¼ cup fresh mint, chopped
1 zucchini, thinly sliced into rounds	¼ cup fresh basil, chopped
	¼ cup pistachios, shelled and toasted
6 small radishes, sliced	
1 shallot, julienned	

Make the Quinoa: Bring the water, quinoa, and salt to a boil in a medium saucepan. Reduce to a simmer, cover, and cook for 10 to 12 minutes. Fluff with a fork. Make the Salad: 1. Heat the olive oil in a large skillet or sauté pan over medium-high heat. Add the zucchini, radishes, shallot, salt, and black pepper, and sauté for 7 to 8 minutes. Add the garlic and cook 30 seconds to 1 minute more. 2. In a large bowl, combine the lemon zest and lemon juice. Add the quinoa and mix well. Add the cooked zucchini mixture and mix well. Add the mint, basil, and pistachios and gently mix.

Per Serving:
calories: 220 | fat: 12g | protein: 6g | carbs: 25g | fiber: 5g | sodium: 295mg

Roasted Golden Beet, Avocado, and Watercress Salad

Prep time: 15 minutes | Cook time: 1 hour | Serves 4

1 bunch (about 1½ pounds / 680 g) golden beets	1 bunch (about 4 ounces / 113 g) watercress
1 tablespoon extra-virgin olive oil	1 avocado, peeled, pitted, and diced
1 tablespoon white wine vinegar	¼ cup crumbled feta cheese
½ teaspoon kosher salt	¼ cup walnuts, toasted
¼ teaspoon freshly ground black pepper	1 tablespoon fresh chives, chopped

1. Preheat the oven to 425°F (220°C). Wash and trim the beets (cut an inch above the beet root, leaving the long tail if desired), then wrap each beet individually in foil. Place the beets on a baking sheet and roast until fully cooked, 45 to 60 minutes depending on the size of each beet. Start checking at 45 minutes; if easily pierced with a fork, the beets are cooked. 2. Remove the beets from the oven and allow them to cool. Under cold running water, slough off the skin. Cut the beets into bite-size cubes or wedges. 3. In a large bowl, whisk together the olive oil, vinegar, salt, and black pepper. Add the watercress and beets and toss well. Add the avocado, feta, walnuts, and chives and mix gently.

Per Serving:
calories: 235 | fat: 16g | protein: 6g | carbs: 21g | fiber: 8g | sodium: 365mg

Powerhouse Arugula Salad

Prep time: 10 minutes | Cook time: 0 minutes | Serves 4

4 tablespoons extra-virgin olive oil	¼ teaspoon freshly ground black pepper
Zest and juice of 2 clementines or 1 orange (2 to 3 tablespoons)	8 cups baby arugula
	1 cup coarsely chopped walnuts
1 tablespoon red wine vinegar	1 cup crumbled goat cheese
½ teaspoon salt	½ cup pomegranate seeds

1. In a small bowl, whisk together the olive oil, zest and juice, vinegar, salt, and pepper and set aside. 2. To assemble the salad for serving, in a large bowl, combine the arugula, walnuts, goat cheese, and pomegranate seeds. Drizzle with the dressing and toss to coat.

Per Serving:
calories: 448 | fat: 41g | protein: 11g | carbs: 13g | fiber: 4g | sodium: 647mg

Pipirrana (Spanish Summer Salad)

Prep time: 15 minutes | Cook time: 0 minutes | Serves 2

1 medium red onion, diced	Pinch of ground cumin
2 large tomatoes, cut into small cubes	½ teaspoon salt plus a pinch for the garlic paste
1 large Persian or mini cucumber, cut into small cubes	3 tablespoons extra virgin olive oil plus a few drops for the garlic paste
1 large green bell pepper, seeded and diced	2 tablespoons red wine vinegar
2 garlic cloves, minced	

1. Place the onions in a small bowl filled with water. Set aside to soak. 2. Place the tomatoes, cucumber, and bell pepper in a medium bowl. Drain the onions and then combine them with the rest of the vegetables. Mix well. 3. In a mortar or small bowl, combine the garlic, cumin, a pinch of salt, and a few drops of olive oil, then roll or mash the ingredients until a paste is formed. 4. In another small bowl, combine 3 tablespoons of the olive oil, vinegar, and ½ teaspoon of the salt. Add the garlic paste and mix well. 5. Add the dressing to the salad and mix well. 6. Cover and refrigerate for 30 minutes before serving. Store in the refrigerator for up to 2 days.

Per Serving:
calories: 274 | fat: 21g | protein: 4g | carbs: 20g | fiber: 6g | sodium: 600mg

Tuna Niçoise

Prep time: 15 minutes | Cook time: 20 minutes | Serves 4

1 pound (454 g) small red or fingerling potatoes, halved	8 radishes, thinly sliced
	½ cup olives, pitted (any kind you like)
1 pound (454 g) green beans or haricots verts, trimmed	2 (5-ounce / 142-g) cans no-salt-added tuna packed in olive oil, drained
1 head romaine lettuce, chopped or torn into bite-size pieces	
½ pint cherry tomatoes, halved	8 anchovies (optional)

1. Fill a large pot fitted with a steamer basket with 2 to 3 inches of water. Put the potatoes in the steamer basket and lay the green beans on top of the potatoes. Bring the water to a boil over high heat, lower the heat to low and simmer, cover, and cook for 7 minutes, or until the green beans are tender but crisp. Remove the green beans and continue to steam the potatoes for an additional 10 minutes. 2. Place the romaine lettuce on a serving platter. Group the potatoes, green beans, tomatoes, radishes, olives, and tuna in different areas of the platter. If using the anchovies, place them around the platter.

Per Serving:
calories: 315 | fat: 9g | protein: 28g | carbs: 33g | fiber: 9g | sodium: 420mg

Arugula and Artichokes

Prep time: 20 minutes | Cook time: 0 minutes | Serves 6

4 tablespoons olive oil	6 low-salt olives, pitted and chopped
2 tablespoons balsamic vinegar	
1 teaspoon Dijon mustard	1 cup cherry tomatoes, sliced in half
1 clove garlic, minced	
6 cups baby arugula leaves	4 fresh basil leaves, thinly sliced
6 oil-packed artichoke hearts, sliced	

1. Make the dressing by whisking together the olive oil, vinegar, Dijon, and garlic until you have a smooth emulsion. Set aside. 2. Toss the arugula, artichokes, olives, and tomatoes together. 3. Drizzle the salad with the dressing, garnish with the fresh basil, and serve.

Per Serving:
calories: 133 | fat: 12g | protein: 2g | carbs: 6g | fiber: 3g | sodium: 75mg

Italian Coleslaw

Prep time: 10 minutes | Cook time: 0 minutes | Serves 6

1 cup shredded green cabbage
½ cup shredded red cabbage
½ cup shredded carrot
1 small yellow bell pepper, seeded and cut into thin strips

¼ cup sliced red onion or shallot
2 tablespoons olive oil
3 tablespoons red wine vinegar
¼ teaspoon celery seeds

1. In a large bowl, mix all the ingredients. Refrigerate until chilled before serving.

Per Serving:
calories: 62 | fat: 4g | protein: 1g | carbs: 5g | fiber: 1g | sodium: 14mg

Italian White Bean Salad with Bell Peppers

Prep time: 15 minutes | Cook time: 0 minutes | Serves 4

2 tablespoons extra-virgin olive oil
2 tablespoons white wine vinegar
½ shallot, minced
½ teaspoon kosher salt
¼ teaspoon freshly ground black pepper
3 cups cooked cannellini beans,

or 2 (15-ounce / 425-g) cans no-salt-added or low-sodium cannellini beans, drained and rinsed
2 celery stalks, diced
½ red bell pepper, diced
¼ cup fresh parsley, chopped
¼ cup fresh mint, chopped

1. In a large bowl, whisk together the olive oil, vinegar, shallot, salt, and black pepper. 2. Add the beans, celery, red bell pepper, parsley, and mint; mix well.

Per Serving:
calories: 300 | fat: 8g | protein: 15g | carbs: 46g | fiber: 11g | sodium: 175mg

Panzanella (Tuscan Tomato and Bread Salad)

Prep time: 1 hour 5 minutes | Cook time: 0 minutes | Serves 2

3 tablespoons white wine vinegar, divided
1 small red onion, thinly sliced
4 ounces (113 g) stale, dense bread, such as French baguette or Italian (Vienna-style)
1 large tomato (any variety), chopped into bite-sized pieces

1 large Persian (or mini) cucumber, sliced
¼ cup chopped fresh basil
2 tablespoons extra virgin olive oil, divided
Pinch of kosher salt
⅛ teaspoon freshly ground black pepper

1. Add 2 tablespoons of the vinegar to a small bowl filled with water. Add the onion and then set aside. 2. In a medium bowl, combine the remaining tablespoon of vinegar and 2 cups of water. Add the bread to the bowl and soak for 2–3 minutes (depending on how hard the bread is) until the bread has softened on the outside but is not falling apart. Place the bread in a colander and gently squeeze out any excess water and then chop into bite-sized pieces. Arrange the bread pieces on a large plate. 3. Drain the onion and

add it to plate with the bread. Add the tomato, cucumber, basil, 1 tablespoon of the olive oil, kosher salt, and black pepper. Toss the ingredients carefully, then cover and transfer to the refrigerator to chill for a minimum of 1 hour. 4. When ready to serve, drizzle the remaining 1 tablespoon of olive oil over the top of the salad and serve promptly. This salad can be stored in the refrigerator for up to 5 hours, but should be consumed on the same day it is prepared.

Per Serving:
calories: 325 | fat: 16g | protein: 7g | carbs: 38g | fiber: 4g | sodium: 358mg

No-Mayo Florence Tuna Salad

Prep time: 10 minutes | Cook time: 0 minutes | Serves 4

4 cups spring mix greens
1 (15-ounce / 425-g) can cannellini beans, drained
2 (5-ounce / 142-g) cans water-packed, white albacore tuna, drained (I prefer Wild Planet brand)
⅔ cup crumbled feta cheese
½ cup thinly sliced sun-dried tomatoes
¼ cup sliced pitted kalamata

olives
¼ cup thinly sliced scallions, both green and white parts
3 tablespoons extra-virgin olive oil
½ teaspoon dried cilantro
2 or 3 leaves thinly chopped fresh sweet basil
1 lime, zested and juiced
Kosher salt
Freshly ground black pepper

1. In a large bowl, combine greens, beans, tuna, feta, tomatoes, olives, scallions, olive oil, cilantro, basil, and lime juice and zest. Season with salt and pepper, mix, and enjoy!

Per Serving:
1 cup: calories: 355 | fat: 19g | protein: 22g | carbs: 25g | fiber: 8g | sodium: 744mg

Citrus Avocado Salad

Prep time: 5 minutes | Cook time: 0 minutes | Serves 2

½ medium orange (any variety), peeled and cut into bite-sized chunks
1 medium tangerine, peeled and sectioned
½ medium white grapefruit, peeled and cut into bite-sized chunks
2 thin slices red onion
1 medium avocado, peeled, pitted, and sliced

Pinch of freshly ground black pepper
For the Dressing:
3 tablespoons extra virgin olive oil
1 tablespoon fresh lemon juice
½ teaspoon ground cumin
½ teaspoon coarse sea salt
Pinch of freshly ground black pepper

1. Make the dressing by combining the olive oil, lemon juice, cumin, sea salt, and black pepper in a small jar or bowl. Whisk or shake to combine. 2. Toss the orange, tangerine, and grapefruit in a medium bowl, then place the sliced onion on top. Drizzle half the dressing over the salad. 3. Fan the avocado slices over the top of the salad. Drizzle the remaining dressing over the salad and then sprinkle a pinch of black pepper over the top. 4. Toss gently before serving. (This salad is best eaten fresh, but can be stored in the refrigerator for up to 1 day.)

Per Serving:
calories: 448 | fat: 36g | protein: 4g | carbs: 35g | fiber: 11g | sodium: 595mg

Cabbage and Carrot Salad

Prep time: 10 minutes | Cook time: 0 minutes | Serves 3

½ medium head cabbage, thinly sliced, rinsed, and drained	3 tablespoons fresh lemon juice
3 medium carrots, peeled and shredded	½ teaspoon salt
4 tablespoons extra virgin olive oil	¼ teaspoon freshly ground black pepper
	1 garlic clove, minced
	8 Kalamata olives, pitted

1. Place the cabbage and carrots in a large bowl and toss. 2. In a jar or small bowl, combine the olive oil, lemon juice, salt, black pepper, and garlic. Whisk or shake to combine. 3. Pour the dressing over the salad and toss. (Note that it will reduce in volume.) 4. Scatter the olives over the salad just before serving. Store covered in the refrigerator for up to 2 days.

Per Serving:
calories: 237 | fat: 19g | protein: 3g | carbs: 16g | fiber: 6g | sodium: 570mg

Riviera Tuna Salad

Prep time: 15 minutes | Cook time: 0 minutes | Serves 4

¼ cup olive oil	1 (6-ounce / 170-g) can solid white albacore tuna, drained
¼ cup balsamic vinegar	
½ teaspoon minced garlic	1 cup canned garbanzo beans, rinsed and drained
¼ teaspoon dried oregano	
Sea salt and freshly ground pepper, to taste	¼ cup low-salt olives, pitted and quartered
2 tablespoons capers, drained	2 Roma tomatoes, chopped
4–6 cups baby greens	

1. To make the vinaigrette, whisk together the olive oil, balsamic vinegar, garlic, oregano, sea salt, and pepper until emulsified. 2. Stir in the capers. Refrigerate for up to 6 hours before serving. 3. Place the baby greens in a salad bowl or on individual plates, and top with the tuna, beans, olives, and tomatoes. 4. Drizzle the vinaigrette over all, and serve immediately.

Per Serving:
calories: 300 | fat: 19g | protein: 16g | carbs: 17g | fiber: 5g | sodium: 438mg

Israeli Salad with Nuts and Seeds

Prep time: 15 minutes | Cook time: 0 minutes | Serves 4

¼ cup pine nuts	chopped
¼ cup shelled pistachios	½ cup finely chopped fresh flat-leaf Italian parsley
¼ cup coarsely chopped walnuts	
	¼ cup extra-virgin olive oil
¼ cup shelled pumpkin seeds	2 to 3 tablespoons freshly squeezed lemon juice (from 1 lemon)
¼ cup shelled sunflower seeds	
2 large English cucumbers, unpeeled and finely chopped	
	1 teaspoon salt
1 pint cherry tomatoes, finely chopped	¼ teaspoon freshly ground black pepper
½ small red onion, finely	4 cups baby arugula

1. In a large dry skillet, toast the pine nuts, pistachios, walnuts, pumpkin seeds, and sunflower seeds over medium-low heat until golden and fragrant, 5 to 6 minutes, being careful not to burn them. Remove from the heat and set aside. 2. In a large bowl, combine the cucumber, tomatoes, red onion, and parsley. 3. In a small bowl, whisk together olive oil, lemon juice, salt, and pepper. Pour over the chopped vegetables and toss to coat. 4. Add the toasted nuts and seeds and arugula and toss with the salad to blend well. Serve at room temperature or chilled.

Per Serving:
calories: 404 | fat: 36g | protein: 10g | carbs: 16g | fiber: 5g | sodium: 601mg

Greek Black-Eyed Pea Salad

Prep time: 10 minutes | Cook time: 0 minutes | Serves 4

2 tablespoons olive oil	1 shallot, finely chopped
Juice of 1 lemon (about 2 tablespoons)	2 scallions (green onions), chopped
1 garlic clove, minced	2 tablespoons chopped fresh dill
1 teaspoon ground cumin	
1 (15½-ounce / 439-g) can no-salt-added black-eyed peas, drained and rinsed	¼ cup chopped fresh parsley
	½ cup pitted Kalamata olives, sliced
1 red bell pepper, seeded and chopped	½ cup crumbled feta cheese (optional)

1. In a large bowl, whisk together the olive oil, lemon juice, garlic, and cumin. 2. Add the black-eyed peas, bell pepper, shallot, scallions, dill, parsley, olives, and feta (if using) and toss to combine. Serve.

Per Serving:
calories: 213 | fat: 14g | protein: 7g | carbs: 16g | fiber: 5g | sodium: 426mg

Beets with Goat Cheese and Chermoula

Prep time: 10 minutes | Cook time: 40 minutes | Serves 4

6 beets, trimmed	1 teaspoon smoked paprika
Chermoula:	½ teaspoon kosher salt
1 cup fresh cilantro leaves	¼ teaspoon chili powder (optional)
1 cup fresh flat-leaf parsley leaves	
	¼ cup extra-virgin olive oil
¼ cup fresh lemon juice	2 ounces (57 g) goat cheese, crumbled
3 cloves garlic, minced	
2 teaspoons ground cumin	

1. Preheat the oven to 400°F(205°C). 2. Wrap the beets in a piece of foil and place on a baking sheet. Roast until the beets are tender enough to be pierced with a fork, 30 to 40 minutes. When cool enough to handle, remove the skins and slice the beets into ¼' rounds. Arrange the beet slices on a large serving platter. 3. To make the chermoula: In a food processor, pulse the cilantro, parsley, lemon juice, garlic, cumin, paprika, salt, and chili powder (if using) until the herbs are just coarsely chopped and the ingredients are combined. Stir in the oil. 4. To serve, dollop the chermoula over the beets and scatter the cheese on top.

Per Serving:
calories: 249 | fat: 19g | protein: 6g | carbs: 15g | fiber: 5g | sodium: 472mg

Spanish Potato Salad

Prep time: 10 minutes | Cook time: 10 minutes |
Serves 6 to 8

4 russet potatoes, peeled and chopped	olives
3 large hard-boiled eggs, chopped	½ teaspoon freshly ground black pepper
1 cup frozen mixed vegetables, thawed	½ teaspoon dried mustard seed
½ cup plain, unsweetened, full-fat Greek yogurt	½ tablespoon freshly squeezed lemon juice
5 tablespoons pitted Spanish	½ teaspoon dried dill
	Salt
	Freshly ground black pepper

1. Boil potatoes for 5 to 7 minutes, until just fork-tender, checking periodically for doneness. You don't want to overcook them. 2. While the potatoes are cooking, in a large bowl, mix the eggs, vegetables, yogurt, olives, pepper, mustard, lemon juice, and dill. Season with salt and pepper. Once the potatoes are cooled somewhat, add them to the large bowl, then mix well and serve.

Per Serving:
calories: 192 | fat: 5g | protein: 9g | carbs: 30g | fiber: 2g | sodium: 59mg

Wilted Kale Salad

Prep time: 10 minutes | Cook time: 5 minutes | Serves 4

2 heads kale	1 cup cherry tomatoes, sliced
1 tablespoon olive oil, plus 1 teaspoon	Sea salt and freshly ground pepper, to taste
2 cloves garlic, minced	Juice of 1 lemon

1. Rinse and dry kale. 2. Tear the kale into bite-sized pieces. 3. Heat 1 tablespoon of the olive oil in a large skillet, and add the garlic. Cook for 1 minute and then add the kale. 4. Cook just until wilted, then add the tomatoes. 5. Cook until tomatoes are softened, then remove from heat. 6. Place tomatoes and kale in a bowl, and season with sea salt and freshly ground pepper. 7. Drizzle with remaining olive oil and lemon juice, serve, and enjoy.

Per Serving:
calories: 153 | fat: 6g | protein: 10g | carbs: 23g | fiber: 9g | sodium: 88mg

Moroccan Chickpea and Green Bean Salad with Ras el Hanout

Prep time: 10 minutes | Cook time: 10 minutes |
Serves 6 to 8

1 pound (454 g) green beans, trimmed	1 (15½-ounce / 439-g) can no-salt-added chickpeas, drained and rinsed
2 tablespoons olive oil	
2 tablespoons red wine vinegar	1 shallot, finely chopped
1 garlic clove, minced	3 tablespoons chopped fresh parsley
2 teaspoons ras el hanout	

1. Bring a large saucepan of water to a boil. Add the green beans and cook just until crisp-tender. Drain the green beans into a colander and rinse under cool running water to stop the cooking. 2. In a large bowl, whisk together the olive oil, vinegar, garlic, and ras el hanout. 3. Add the chickpeas, green beans, shallot, and parsley and toss to combine. Serve.

Per Serving:
1 cup: calories: 68 | fat: 4g | protein: 2g | carbs: 7g | fiber: 3g | sodium: 16mg

Red Pepper, Pomegranate, and Walnut Salad

Prep time: 5 minutes | Cook time: 40 minutes | Serves 4

2 red bell peppers, halved and seeded	⅛ teaspoon ground black pepper
1 teaspoon plus 2 tablespoons olive oil	4 plum tomatoes, halved, seeded, and chopped
4 teaspoons pomegranate molasses, divided	¼ cup walnut halves, chopped
2 teaspoons fresh lemon juice	¼ cup chopped fresh flat-leaf parsley
¼ teaspoon kosher salt	

1. Preheat the oven to 450°F(235°C). 2. Brush the bell peppers all over with 1 teaspoon of the oil and place cut side up on a large rimmed baking sheet. Drizzle 2 teaspoons of the pomegranate molasses in the cavities of the bell peppers. Roast the bell peppers until they have softened and the skins have charred, turning once during cooking, 30 to 40 minutes. Remove from the oven and cool to room temperature. Remove the skins and chop the peppers coarsely. 3. In a large bowl, whisk together the lemon juice, salt, black pepper, the remaining 2 tablespoons oil, and the remaining 2 teaspoons pomegranate molasses. Add the bell peppers, tomatoes, walnuts, and parsley and toss gently to combine. Serve at room temperature.

Per Serving:
calories: 166 | fat: 13g | protein: 2g | carbs: 11g | fiber: 3g | sodium: 153mg

Turkish Shepherd'S Salad

Prep time: 15 minutes | Cook time: 0 minutes | Serves 6

¼ cup extra-virgin olive oil	chopped
2 tablespoons apple cider vinegar	1 green bell pepper, seeded and chopped
2 tablespoons lemon juice	1 small red onion, chopped
½ teaspoon kosher salt	⅓ cup pitted black olives (such as kalamata), halved
¼ teaspoon ground black pepper	½ cup chopped fresh flat-leaf parsley
3 plum tomatoes, seeded and chopped	¼ cup chopped fresh mint
2 cucumbers, seeded and chopped	¼ cup chopped fresh dill
1 red bell pepper, seeded and	6 ounces (170 g) feta cheese, cubed

1. In a small bowl, whisk together the oil, vinegar, lemon juice, salt, and black pepper. 2. In a large serving bowl, combine the tomatoes, cucumber, bell peppers, onion, olives, parsley, mint, and dill. Pour the dressing over the salad, toss gently, and sprinkle with the cheese.

Per Serving:
calories: 238 | fat: 20g | protein: 6g | carbs: 10g | fiber: 2g | sodium: 806mg

Dakos (Cretan Salad)

Prep time: 7 minutes | Cook time: 00 minutes | Serves 1

1 medium ripe tomato (any variety)
2 whole-grain crispbreads or rusks (or 1 slice toasted whole-grain, wheat, or barley bread)
1 tablespoon plus 1 teaspoon extra virgin olive oil
Pinch of kosher salt

1½ ounces (43 g) crumbled feta
2 teaspoons capers, drained
2 Kalamata olives, pitted
Pinch of dried oregano

1. Slice a thin round off the bottom of the tomato. Hold the tomato from the stem side and begin grating the tomato over a plate, using the largest holes of the grater. Grate until only the skin of the tomato remains, then discard the skin. Use a fine mesh strainer to drain the liquid from the grated tomato. 2. Place the crisps on a plate, one next to the other, and sprinkle with a few drops of water. Drizzle 1 tablespoon of the olive oil over the crisps and then top the crisps with the grated tomato, ensuring the crisps are thoroughly covered with the tomato. 3. Sprinkle the kosher salt over the tomato, then layer the crumbled feta over the top. Top with the capers and olives, and sprinkle the oregano over the top and drizzle with the remaining 1 teaspoon of olive oil. Serve promptly. (This salad is best served fresh.)

Per Serving:
calories: 346 | fat: 24g | protein: 12g | carbs: 21g | fiber: 4g | sodium: 626mg

Chapter 13 Desserts

Cocoa and Coconut Banana Slices

Prep time: 10 minutes | Cook time: 0 minutes | Serves 1

1 banana, peeled and sliced
2 tablespoons unsweetened, shredded coconut

1 tablespoon unsweetened cocoa powder
1 teaspoon honey

1. Lay the banana slices on a parchment-lined baking sheet in a single layer. Put in the freezer for about 10 minutes, until firm but not frozen solid. Mix the coconut with the cocoa powder in a small bowl. 2. Roll the banana slices in honey, followed by the coconut mixture. 3. You can either eat immediately or put back in the freezer for a frozen, sweet treat.

Per Serving:
calories: 187 | fat: 4g | protein: 3g | carbs: 41g | fiber: 6g | sodium: 33mg

Date and Nut Balls

Prep time: 10 minutes | Cook time: 10 minutes |

Serves 6 to 8

»1 cup walnuts or pistachios
»1 cup unsweetened shredded coconut
»14 medjool dates, pits

removed
»8 tablespoons (1 stick) butter, melted

1. Preheat the oven to 350°F. 2. Put the nuts on a baking sheet. Toast the nuts for 5 minutes. 3. Put the shredded coconut on a clean baking sheet; toast just until it turns golden brown, about 3 to 5 minutes (coconut burns fast so keep an eye on it). Once done, remove it from the oven and put it in a shallow bowl. 4. In a food processor fitted with a chopping blade, process the nuts until they have a medium chop. Put the chopped nuts into a medium bowl. 5. Add the dates and melted butter to the food processor and blend until the dates become a thick paste. Pour the chopped nuts into the food processor with the dates and pulse just until the mixture is combined, about 5 to 7 pulses. 6. Remove the mixture from the food processor and scrape it into a large bowl. 7. To make the balls, spoon 1 to 2 tablespoons of the date mixture into the palm of your hand and roll around between your hands until you form a ball. Put the ball on a clean, lined baking sheet. Repeat until all the mixture is formed into balls. 8. Roll each ball in the toasted coconut until the outside of the ball is coated, put the ball back on the baking sheet, and repeat. 9. Put all the balls into the fridge for 20 minutes before serving so that they firm up. You can also store any leftovers in the fridge in an airtight container.

Per Serving:
calories: 489 | fat: 35g | protein: 5g | carbs: 48g | fiber: 7g | sodium: 114mg

Baklava and Honey

Prep time: 40 minutes | Cook time: 1 hour | Serves 6 to 8

2 cups very finely chopped walnuts or pecans
1 teaspoon cinnamon
1 cup (2 sticks) of unsalted

butter, melted
1 (16-ounce / 454-g) package phyllo dough, thawed
1 (12-ounce / 340-g) jar honey

1. Preheat the oven to 350°F(180ºC). 2. In a bowl, combine the chopped nuts and cinnamon. 3. Using a brush, butter the sides and bottom of a 9-by-13-inch inch baking dish. 4. Remove the phyllo dough from the package and cut it to the size of the baking dish using a sharp knife. 5. Place one sheet of phyllo dough on the bottom of the dish, brush with butter, and repeat until you have 8 layers. 6. Sprinkle ⅓ cup of the nut mixture over the phyllo layers. Top with a sheet of phyllo dough, butter that sheet, and repeat until you have 4 sheets of buttered phyllo dough. 7. Sprinkle ⅓ cup of the nut mixture for another layer of nuts. Repeat the layering of nuts and 4 sheets of buttered phyllo until all the nut mixture is gone. The last layer should be 8 buttered sheets of phyllo. 8. Before you bake, cut the baklava into desired shapes; traditionally this is diamonds, triangles, or squares. 9. Bake the baklava for 1 hour or until the top layer is golden brown. 10. While the baklava is baking, heat the honey in a pan just until it is warm and easy to pour. 11. Once the baklava is done baking, immediately pour the honey evenly over the baklava and let it absorb it, about 20 minutes. Serve warm or at room temperature.

Per Serving:
calories: 1235 | fat: 89g | protein: 18g | carbs: 109g | fiber: 7g | sodium: 588mg

Creamy Spiced Almond Milk

Prep time: 5 minutes | Cook time: 1 minute | Serves 6

1 cup raw almonds
5 cups filtered water, divided

1 teaspoon vanilla bean paste
½ teaspoon pumpkin pie spice

1. Add almonds and 1 cup water to the Instant Pot®. Close lid, set steam release to Sealing, press the Manual button, and set time to 1 minute. 2. When the timer beeps, quick-release the pressure until the float valve drops. Press the Cancel button and open lid. Strain almonds and rinse under cool water. Transfer to a high-powered blender with remaining 3.cups water. Purée for 2 minutes on high speed. 4. Pour mixture into a nut milk bag set over a large bowl. Squeeze bag to extract all liquid. Stir in vanilla and pumpkin pie spice. Transfer to a Mason jar or sealed jug and refrigerate for 8 hours. Stir or shake gently before serving.

Per Serving:
calories: 86 | fat: 8g | protein: 3g | carbs: 3g | fiber: 2g | sodium: 0mg

Date and Honey Almond Milk Ice Cream

Prep time: 10 minutes | Cook time: 5 minutes | Serves 4

¾ cup (about 4 ounces/ 113 g) pitted dates
¼ cup honey
½ cup water

2 cups cold unsweetened almond milk
2 teaspoons vanilla extract

1. Combine the dates and water in a small saucepan and bring to a boil over high heat. Remove the pan from the heat, cover, and let stand for 15 minutes. 2. In a blender, combine the almond milk, dates, the date soaking water, honey, and the vanilla and process until very smooth. 3. Cover the blender jar and refrigerate the mixture until cold, at least 1 hour. 4. Transfer the mixture to an electric ice cream maker and freeze according to the manufacturer's instructions. 5. Serve immediately or transfer to a freezer-safe storage container and freeze for 4 hours (or longer). Serve frozen.

Per Serving:
calories: 106 | fat: 2g | protein: 1g | carbs: 23g | fiber: 3g | sodium: 92mg

Grilled Peaches with Greek Yogurt

Prep time: 5 minutes | Cook time: 30 minutes | Serves 4

4 ripe peaches, halved and pitted
2 tablespoons olive oil
1 teaspoon ground cinnamon,

plus extra for topping
2 cups plain full-fat Greek yogurt
¼ cup honey, for drizzling

1. Preheat the oven to 350°F (180°C). 2. Place the peaches in a baking dish, cut-side up. 3. In a small bowl, stir together the olive oil and cinnamon, then brush the mixture over the peach halves. 4. Bake the peaches for about 30 minutes, until they are soft. 5. Top the peaches with the yogurt and drizzle them with the honey, then serve.

Per Serving:
calories: 259 | fat: 11g | protein: 6g | carbs: 38g | fiber: 3g | sodium: 57mg

Dried Fruit Compote

Prep time: 15 minutes | Cook time: 8 minutes | Serves 6

8 ounces (227 g) dried apricots, quartered
8 ounces (227 g) dried peaches, quartered

1 cup golden raisins
1½ cups orange juice
1 cinnamon stick
4 whole cloves

1. Place all ingredients in the Instant Pot®. Stir to combine. Close lid, set steam release to Sealing, press the Manual button, and set time to 3 minutes. When the timer beeps, let pressure release naturally, about 20 minutes. Press the Cancel button and open lid. 2. Remove and discard cinnamon stick and cloves. Press the Sauté button and simmer for 5–6 minutes. Serve warm or allow to cool, and then cover and refrigerate for up to a week.

Per Serving:
calories: 258 | fat: 0g | protein: 4g | carbs: 63g | fiber: 5g | sodium: 7mg

Nut Butter Cup Fat Bomb

Prep time: 5 minutes | Cook time: 0 minutes | Serves 8

½ cup crunchy almond butter (no sugar added)
½ cup light fruity extra-virgin olive oil
¼ cup ground flaxseed
2 tablespoons unsweetened

cocoa powder
1 teaspoon vanilla extract
1 teaspoon ground cinnamon (optional)
1 to 2 teaspoons sugar-free sweetener of choice (optional)

1. In a mixing bowl, combine the almond butter, olive oil, flaxseed, cocoa powder, vanilla, cinnamon (if using), and sweetener (if using) and stir well with a spatula to combine. Mixture will be a thick liquid. 2. Pour into 8 mini muffin liners and freeze until solid, at least 12 hours. Store in the freezer to maintain their shape.

Per Serving:
calories: 239 | fat: 24g | protein: 4g | carbs: 5g | fiber: 3g | sodium: 3mg

Lightened-Up Baklava Rolls

Prep time: 2 minutes | Cook time: 1 hour 15 minutes | Serves 12
4 ounces (113 g) shelled walnuts
1¼ teaspoons ground cinnamon
1½ teaspoons granulated sugar
5 teaspoons unseasoned breadcrumbs
1 teaspoon extra virgin olive oil

plus 2 tablespoons for brushing
6 phyllo sheets, defrosted
Syrup:
¼ cup water
½ cup granulated sugar
1½ tablespoons fresh lemon juice

1. Preheat the oven to 350°F (180°C). 2. Make the syrup by combining the water and sugar in a small pan placed over medium heat. Bring to a boil, cook for 2 minutes, then remove the pan from the heat. Add the lemon juice, and stir. Set aside to cool. 3. In a food processor, combine the walnuts, cinnamon, sugar, breadcrumbs, and 1 teaspoon of the olive oil. Pulse until combined and grainy, but not chunky. 4. Place 1 phyllo sheet on a clean working surface and brush with the olive oil. Place a second sheet on top of the first sheet, brush with olive oil, and repeat the process with a third sheet. Cut the sheets in half crosswise, and then cut each half into 3 pieces crosswise. 5. Scatter 1 tablespoon of the walnut mixture over the phyllo sheet. Start rolling the phyllo and filling into a log shape while simultaneously folding the sides in (like a burrito) until the filling is encased in each piece of dough. The rolls should be about 3½ inches long. Place the rolls one next to the other in a large baking pan, then repeat the process with the remaining 3 phyllo sheets. You should have a total of 12 rolls. 6. Lightly brush the rolls with the remaining olive oil. Place in the oven to bake for 30 minutes or until the rolls turn golden brown, then remove from the oven and promptly drizzle the cold syrup over the top. 7. Let the rolls sit for 20 minutes, then flip them over and let them sit for an additional 20 minutes. Turn them over once more and sprinkle any remining walnut mixture over the rolls before serving. Store uncovered at room temperature for 2 days (to retain crispiness) and then cover with plastic wrap and store at room temperature for up to 10 days.

Per Serving:
calories: 148 | fat: 9g | protein: 2g | carbs: 16g | fiber: 1g | sodium: 53mg

Creamy Rice Pudding

Prep time: 5 minutes | Cook time: 45 minutes | Serves 6

1¼ cups long-grain rice
5 cups whole milk
1 cup sugar

1 tablespoon rose water or
orange blossom water
1 teaspoon cinnamon

1. Rinse the rice under cold water for 30 seconds. 2. Put the rice, milk, and sugar in a large pot. Bring to a gentle boil while continually stirring. 3. Turn the heat down to low and let simmer for 40 to 45 minutes, stirring every 3 to 4 minutes so that the rice does not stick to the bottom of the pot. 4. Add the rose water at the end and simmer for 5 minutes. 5. Divide the pudding into 6 bowls. Sprinkle the top with cinnamon. Cool for at least 1 hour before serving. Store in the fridge.
Per Serving:
calories: 394 | fat: 7g | protein: 9g | carbs: 75g | fiber: 1g | sodium: 102mg

Cherry-Stuffed Apples

Prep time: 15 minutes | Cook time: 4 hours | Serves 2

3 apples
1 tablespoon freshly squeezed
lemon juice
⅓ cup dried cherries

2 tablespoons apple cider
2 tablespoons honey
¼ cup water

1. Cut about half an inch off the top of each of the apples, and peel a small strip of the skin away around the top. 2. Using a small serrated spoon or melon baller, core the apples, making sure not to go through the bottom. Drizzle with the lemon juice. 3. Fill the apples with the dried cherries. Carefully spoon the cider and honey into the apples. 4. Place the apples in the slow cooker. Pour the water around the apples. 5. Cover and cook on low for 4 hours, or until the apples are soft, and serve.
Per Serving:
calories: 227 | fat: 1g | protein: 1g | carbs: 60g | net carbs: 53g | sugars: 49g | fiber: 7g | sodium: 6mg | cholesterol: 0mg

S'mores

Prep time: 5 minutes | Cook time: 30 seconds |
Makes 8 s'mores

Oil, for spraying
8 graham cracker squares
2 (1½-ounce / 43-g) chocolate

bars
4 large marshmallows

1. Line the air fryer basket with parchment and spray lightly with oil. 2. Place 4 graham cracker squares in the prepared basket. 3. Break the chocolate bars in half and place 1 piece on top of each graham cracker. Top with 1 marshmallow. 4. Air fry at 370°F (188°C) for 30 seconds, or until the marshmallows are puffed and golden brown and slightly melted. 5. Top with the remaining graham cracker squares and serve.
Per Serving:
calories: 154 | fat: 7g | protein: 2g | carbs: 22g | fiber: 2g | sodium: 75mg

Honey Ricotta with Espresso and Chocolate Chips

Prep time: 5 minutes | Cook time: 0 minutes | Serves 2

8 ounces (227 g) ricotta cheese
2 tablespoons honey
2 tablespoons espresso, chilled

or room temperature
1 teaspoon dark chocolate chips
or chocolate shavings

1. In a medium bowl, whip together the ricotta cheese and honey until light and smooth, 4 to 5 minutes. 2. Spoon the ricotta cheese honey mixture evenly into 2 dessert bowls. Drizzle 1 tablespoon espresso into each dish and sprinkle with chocolate chips or shavings.
Per Serving:
calories: 235 | fat: 10g | protein: 13g | carbs: 25g | fiber: 0g | sodium: 115mg

Red-Wine Poached Pears

Prep time: 10 minutes | Cook time: 20 minutes | Serves 2

2 cups red wine, such as Merlot
or Zinfandel, more if necessary
2 firm pears, peeled
2 to3 cardamom pods, split

1 cinnamon stick
2 peppercorns
1 bay leaf

1. Put all ingredients in a large pot and bring to a boil. Make sure the pears are submerged in the wine. 2. Reduce heat and simmer for 15–20 minutes until the pears are tender when poked with a fork. 3. Remove the pears from the wine, and allow to cool. 4. Bring the wine to a boil, and cook until it reduces to a syrup. 5. Strain and drizzle the pears with the warmed syrup before serving.
Per Serving:
calories: 268 | fat: 0g | protein: 1g | carbs: 22g | fiber: 6g | sodium: 0mg

Grilled Fruit Kebabs with Honey Labneh

Prep time: 15 minutes | Cook time: 10 minutes | Serves 2

⅔ cup prepared labneh, or, if
making your own, ⅔ cup full-
fat plain Greek yogurt
2 tablespoons honey
1 teaspoon vanilla extract

Pinch salt
3 cups fresh fruit cut into 2-inch
chunks (pineapple, cantaloupe,
nectarines, strawberries, plums,
or mango)

1. If making your own labneh, place a colander over a bowl and line it with cheesecloth. Place the Greek yogurt in the cheesecloth and wrap it up. Put the bowl in the refrigerator and let sit for at least 12 to 24 hours, until it's thick like soft cheese. 2. Mix honey, vanilla, and salt into labneh. Stir well to combine and set it aside. 3. Heat the grill to medium (about 300°F/ 150°C) and oil the grill grate. Alternatively, you can cook these on the stovetop in a heavy grill pan (cast iron works well). 4. Thread the fruit onto skewers and grill for 4 minutes on each side, or until fruit is softened and has grill marks on each side. 5. Serve the fruit with labneh to dip.
Per Serving:
calories: 292 | fat: 6g | protein: 5g | carbs: 60g | fiber: 4g | sodium: 131mg

Golden Coconut Cream Pops

Prep time: 5 minutes | Cook time: 0 minutes | Makes 8 cream pops

1½ cups coconut cream
½ cup coconut milk
4 egg yolks
2 teaspoons ground turmeric
1 teaspoon ground ginger
1 teaspoon cinnamon
1 teaspoon vanilla powder or 1

tablespoon unsweetened vanilla extract
¼ teaspoon ground black pepper
Optional: low-carb sweetener, to taste

1. Place all of the ingredients in a blender (including the optional sweetener) and process until well combined. Pour into eight ⅓-cup (80 ml) ice pop molds. Freeze until solid for 3 hours, or until set. 2. To easily remove the ice pops from the molds, fill a pot as tall as the ice pops with warm (not hot) water and dip the ice pop molds in for 15 to 20 seconds. Remove the ice pops from the molds and then freeze again. Store in the freezer in a resealable bag for up to 3 months.

Per Serving:
calories: 219 | fat: 21g | protein: 3g | carbs: 5g | fiber: 2g | sodium: 9mg

Lemon Coconut Cake

Prep time: 5 minutes | Cook time: 40 minutes | Serves 9

Base:
6 large eggs, separated
⅓ cup melted ghee or virgin coconut oil
1 tablespoon fresh lemon juice
Zest of 2 lemons
2 cups almond flour
½ cup coconut flour
¼ cup collagen powder
1 teaspoon baking soda
1 teaspoon vanilla powder or 1 tablespoon unsweetened vanilla extract

Optional: low-carb sweetener, to taste
Topping:
½ cup unsweetened large coconut flakes
1 cup heavy whipping cream or coconut cream
¼ cup mascarpone, more heavy whipping cream, or coconut cream
½ teaspoon vanilla powder or 1½ teaspoons unsweetened vanilla extract

1. Preheat the oven to 285°F (140°C) fan assisted or 320°F (160°C) conventional. Line a baking tray with parchment paper (or use a silicone tray). A square 8 × 8–inch (20 × 20 cm) or a rectangular tray of similar size will work best. 2. To make the base: Whisk the egg whites in a bowl until stiff peaks form. In a separate bowl, whisk the egg yolks, melted ghee, lemon juice, and lemon zest. In a third bowl, mix the almond flour, coconut flour, collagen, baking soda, vanilla and optional sweetener. 3. Add the whisked egg yolk–ghee mixture into the dry mixture and combine well. Gently fold in the egg whites, trying not to deflate them. 4. Pour into the baking tray. Bake for 35 to 40 minutes, until lightly golden on top and set inside. Remove from the oven and let cool completely before adding the topping. 5. To make the topping: Preheat the oven to 350°F (175°C) fan assisted or 380°F (195°C) conventional. Place the coconut flakes on a baking tray and bake for 2 to 3 minutes. Remove from the oven and set aside to cool. 6. Once the cake is cool, place the cream, mascarpone, and vanilla in a bowl. Whip until soft peaks form. Spread on top of the cooled cake and top with the toasted coconut flakes. 7. To store, refrigerate for up to 5 days or freeze for up to 3 months. Coconut flakes will soften in the fridge. If you want to keep them crunchy, sprinkle on top of each slice before serving.

Per Serving:
calories: 342 | fat: 31g | protein: 9g | carbs: 10g | fiber: 4g | sodium: 208mg

Toasted Almonds with Honey

Prep time: 15 minutes | Cook time: 5 minutes | Serves 4

½ cup raw almonds
3 tablespoons good-quality

honey, plus more if desired

1. Fill a medium saucepan three-quarters full with water and bring to a boil over high heat. Add the almonds and cook for 1 minute. Drain the almonds in a fine-mesh sieve and rinse them under cold water to cool and stop the cooking. Remove the skins from the almonds by rubbing them in a clean kitchen towel. Place the almonds on a paper towel to dry. 2. In the same saucepan, combine the almonds and honey and cook over medium heat until the almonds get a little golden, 4 to 5 minutes. Remove from the heat and let cool completely, about 15 minutes, before serving or storing.

Per Serving:
calories: 151 | fat: 9g | protein: 4g | carbs: 17g | fiber: 2g | sodium: 1mg

Apricot and Mint No-Bake Parfait

Prep time: 10 minutes | Cook time: 0 minutes | Serves 6

4 ounces (113 g) Neufchâtel or other light cream cheese
1 (7-ounce / 198-g) container 2% Greek yogurt
½ cup plus 2 tablespoons sugar
2 teaspoons vanilla extract
1 tablespoon fresh lemon juice

1 pound (454 g) apricots, rinsed, pitted, and cut into bite-size pieces
2 tablespoons finely chopped fresh mint, plus whole leaves for garnish if desired

1. In the bowl of a stand mixer fitted with the paddle attachment, beat the Neufchâtel cheese and yogurt on low speed until well combined, about 2 minutes, scraping down the bowl as needed. Add ½ cup of the sugar, the vanilla, and the lemon juice. Mix until smooth and free of lumps, 2 to 3 minutes; set aside. 2. In a medium bowl, combine the apricots, mint, and remaining 2 tablespoons sugar. Stir occasionally, waiting to serve until after the apricots have released their juices and have softened. 3. Line up six 6-to 8-ounce (170-to 227-g) glasses. Using an ice cream scoop, spoon 3 to 4 tablespoons of the cheesecake mixture evenly into the bottom of each glass. (Alternatively, transfer the cheesecake mixture to a piping bag or a small zip-top bag with one corner snipped and pipe the mixture into the glasses.) Add a layer of the same amount of apricots to each glass. Repeat so you have two layers of cheesecake mixture and two layers of the apricots, ending with the apricots.) Garnish with the mint, if desired, and serve.

Per Serving:
calories: 132 | fat: 2g | protein: 5g | carbs: 23g | fiber: 2g | sodium: 35mg

Tahini Baklava Cups

Prep time: 10 minutes | Cook time: 25 minutes | Serves 8

1 box (about 16) mini phyllo dough cups, thawed	garnish
⅓ cup tahini	4 tablespoons honey, divided
¼ cup shelled pistachios or walnuts, chopped, plus more for	1 teaspoon ground cinnamon
	Pinch of kosher salt
	½ teaspoon rosewater (optional)

1. Preheat the oven to 350°F(180ºC). Remove the phyllo cups from the packaging and place on a large rimmed baking sheet. 2. In a small bowl, stir together the tahini, nuts, 1 tablespoon of the honey, the cinnamon, and salt. Divide this mixture among the phyllo cups and top each with a few more nuts. Bake until golden and warmed through, 10 minutes. Remove from the oven and cool for 5 minutes. 3. Meanwhile, in a small saucepan or in a microwaveable bowl, stir together the remaining 3 tablespoons honey and the rosewater, if using, and heat until warmed, about 5 minutes over medium heat o

Per Serving:
calories: 227 | fat: 9g | protein: 5g | carbs: 32g | fiber: 2g | sodium: 195mg

Figs with Mascarpone and Honey

Prep time: 5 minutes | Cook time: 5 minutes | Serves 4

⅓ cup walnuts, chopped	1 tablespoon honey
8 fresh figs, halved	¼ teaspoon flaked sea salt
¼ cup mascarpone cheese	

1. In a skillet over medium heat, toast the walnuts, stirring often, 3 to 5 minutes. 2. Arrange the figs cut-side up on a plate or platter. Using your finger, make a small depression in the cut side of each fig and fill with mascarpone cheese. Sprinkle with a bit of the walnuts, drizzle with the honey, and add a tiny pinch of sea salt.

Per Serving:
calories: 200 | fat: 13g | protein: 3g | carbs: 24g | fiber: 3g | sodium: 105mg

Mascarpone and Fig Crostini

Prep time: 10 minutes | Cook time: 10 minutes | Serves 6 to 8

1 long French baguette	1 (8-ounce / 227-g) tub mascarpone cheese
4 tablespoons (½ stick) salted butter, melted	1 (12-ounce / 340-g) jar fig jam

1. Preheat the oven to 350°F(180ºC). 2. Slice the bread into ¼-inch-thick slices. 3. Arrange the sliced bread on a baking sheet and brush each slice with the melted butter. 4. Put the baking sheet in the oven and toast the bread for 5 to 7 minutes, just until golden brown. 5. Let the bread cool slightly. Spread about a teaspoon or so of the mascarpone cheese on each piece of bread. 6. Top with a teaspoon or so of the jam. Serve immediately.

Per Serving:
calories: 445 | fat: 24g | protein: 3g | carbs: 48g | fiber: 5g | sodium: 314mg

Cretan Cheese Pancakes

Prep time: 15 minutes | Cook time: 25 minutes | Serves 4

2 cups all-purpose flour, plus extra for kneading	5 tablespoons crumbled feta cheese
½ cup water	2 tablespoons olive oil
2 tablespoons olive oil, plus extra for frying	½ cup chopped nuts of your choice
1 tablespoon freshly squeezed lemon juice	⅛ to ¼ teaspoon ground cinnamon, for topping
1 tablespoon brandy	1 tablespoon honey, for drizzling
1 teaspoon sea salt	

1. In a large bowl, stir together the flour, water, olive oil, lemon juice, brandy, and salt until a ball of dough forms. Turn the dough out onto a lightly floured surface and knead for 10 minutes. If the dough is too wet, add a little more flour. If it's too dry, add some water. 2. Divide the dough into 5 equal pieces and roll each piece into a ball. Place a dough ball on a lightly floured surface and roll it out into a 6-inch-wide circle about ¼ inch thick. Place 1 tablespoon of the feta in the center, fold the dough over, and knead the dough and cheese together. Once the cheese is well incorporated, roll the dough out flat to the same size. Repeat with the remaining balls of dough. 3. In a large skillet, heat the oil over medium-high heat. Place one round of dough in the skillet and cook for 5 to 6 minutes on each side, until golden brown. Transfer the cooked pancake to a paper towel–lined plate to drain. Repeat to cook the remaining dough pancakes. 4. Sprinkle the pancakes evenly with the nuts and cinnamon, drizzle with the honey, and serve.

Per Serving:
calories: 480 | fat: 24g | protein: 11g | carbs: 57g | fiber: 3g | sodium: 396mg

Olive Oil Ice Cream

Prep time: 5 minutes | Cook time: 25 minutes | Serves 8

4 large egg yolks	cup whole milk
⅓ cup powdered sugar-free sweetener (such as stevia or monk fruit extract)	1 teaspoon vanilla extract
	⅛ teaspoon salt
2 cups half-and-half or 1 cup heavy whipping cream and 1	¼ cup light fruity extra-virgin olive oil

1. Freeze the bowl of an ice cream maker for at least 12 hours or overnight. 2. In a large bowl, whisk together the egg yolks and sugar-free sweetener. 3. In a small saucepan, heat the half-and-half over medium heat until just below a boil. Remove from the heat and allow to cool slightly. 4. Slowly pour the warm half-and-half into the egg mixture, whisking constantly to avoid cooking the eggs. Return the eggs and cream to the saucepan over low heat. 5. Whisking constantly, cook over low heat until thickened, 15 to 20 minutes. Remove from the heat and stir in the vanilla extract and salt. Whisk in the olive oil and transfer to a glass bowl. Allow to cool, cover, and refrigerate for at least 6 hours. 6. Freeze custard in an ice cream maker according to manufacturer's directions.

Per Serving:
calories: 168 | fat: 15g | protein: 2g | carbs: 8g | fiber: 0g | sodium: 49mg

Peaches Poached in Rose Water

Prep time: 15 minutes | Cook time: 1 minute | Serves 6

1 cup water
1 cup rose water
¼ cup wildflower honey
8 green cardamom pods, lightly crushed
1 teaspoon vanilla bean paste
6 large yellow peaches, pitted and quartered
½ cup chopped unsalted roasted pistachio meats

1. Add water, rose water, honey, cardamom, and vanilla to the Instant Pot®. Whisk well, then add peaches. Close lid, set steam release to Sealing, press the Manual button, and set time to 1 minute. 2. When the timer beeps, quick-release the pressure until the float valve drops. Press the Cancel button and open lid. Allow peaches to stand for 10 minutes. Carefully remove peaches from poaching liquid with a slotted spoon. 3. Slip skins from peach slices. Arrange slices on a plate and garnish with pistachios. Serve warm or at room temperature.

Per Serving:
calories: 145 | fat: 3g | protein: 2g | carbs: 28g | fiber: 2g | sodium: 8mg

Roasted Honey-Cinnamon Apples

Prep time: 15 minutes | Cook time: 20 minutes | Serves 2

1 teaspoon extra-virgin olive oil
4 firm apples, peeled, cored, and sliced
½ teaspoon salt
1½ teaspoons ground cinnamon, divided
2 tablespoons low-fat milk
2 tablespoons honey

1. Preheat the oven to 375°F(190°C). Grease a small casserole dish with the olive oil. 2. In a medium bowl, toss the apple slices with the salt and ½ teaspoon of the cinnamon. Spread the apples in the baking dish and bake for 20 minutes. 3. Meanwhile, in a small saucepan, heat the milk, honey, and remaining 1 teaspoon cinnamon over medium heat, stirring frequently. When it reaches a simmer, remove the pan from the heat and cover to keep warm. 4. Divide the apple slices between 2 dessert plates and pour the sauce over the apples. Serve warm.

Per Serving:
calories: 285 | fat: 3g | protein: 2g | carbs: 70g | fiber: 10g | sodium: 593mg

Poached Pears with Greek Yogurt and Pistachio

Prep time: 10 minutes | Cook time: 3 minutes | Serves 8

2 cups water
1¾ cups apple cider
¼ cup lemon juice
1 cinnamon stick
1 teaspoon vanilla bean paste
4 large Bartlett pears, peeled
1 cup low-fat plain Greek yogurt
½ cup unsalted roasted pistachio meats

1. Add water, apple cider, lemon juice, cinnamon, vanilla, and pears to the Instant Pot®. Close lid, set steam release to Sealing, press the Manual button, and set time to 3 minutes. 2. When the timer beeps, quick-release the pressure until the float valve drops. Press the Cancel button and open lid. With a slotted spoon remove pears to a plate and allow to cool to room temperature. 3. To serve, carefully slice pears in half with a sharp paring knife and scoop out core with a melon baller. Lay pear halves on dessert plates or in shallow bowls. Top with yogurt and garnish with pistachios. Serve immediately.

Per Serving:
calories: 181 | fat: 7g | protein: 7g | carbs: 23g | fiber: 4g | sodium: 11mg

Greek Yogurt Chocolate "Mousse" with Berries

Prep time: 15 minutes | Cook time: 0 minutes | Serves 4

2 cups plain Greek yogurt
¼ cup heavy cream
¼ cup pure maple syrup
3 tablespoons unsweetened cocoa powder
2 teaspoons vanilla extract
¼ teaspoon kosher salt
1 cup fresh mixed berries
¼ cup chocolate chips

1. Place the yogurt, cream, maple syrup, cocoa powder, vanilla, and salt in the bowl of a stand mixer or use a large bowl with an electric hand mixer. Mix at medium-high speed until fluffy, about 5 minutes. 2. Spoon evenly among 4 bowls and put in the refrigerator to set for at least 15 minutes. 3. Serve each bowl with ¼ cup mixed berries and 1 tablespoon chocolate chips.

Per Serving:
calories: 300 | fat: 11g | protein: 16g | carbs: 35g | fiber: 3g | sodium: 60mg

Olive Oil Greek Yogurt Brownies

Prep time: 5 minutes | Cook time: 25 minutes | Serves 9

¼ cup extra virgin olive oil
¾ cup granulated sugar
1 teaspoon pure vanilla extract
2 eggs
¼ cup 2% Greek yogurt
½ cup all-purpose flour
⅓ cup unsweetened cocoa powder
¼ teaspoon salt
¼ teaspoon baking powder
⅓ cup chopped walnuts

1. Preheat the oven to 350°F (180°C) and line a 9-inch square baking pan with wax paper. 2. In a small bowl, combine the olive oil and sugar. Stir until well combined, then add the vanilla extract and mix well. 3. In another small bowl, beat the eggs and then add them to the olive oil mixture. Mix well. Add the yogurt and mix again. 4. In medium bowl, combine the flour, cocoa powder, salt, and baking powder, then mix well. Add the olive oil mixture to the dry ingredients and mix well, then add the walnuts and mix again. 5. Carefully pour the brownie mixture into the prepared pan and use a spatula to smooth the top. Transfer to the oven and bake for 25 minutes. 6. Set the brownies aside to cool completely. Lift the wax paper to remove the brownies from the pan. Remove the paper and cut the brownies into 9 squares. Store at room temperature in an airtight container for up to 2 days.

Per Serving:
calories: 198 | fat: 10g | protein: 4g | carbs: 25g | fiber: 2g | sodium: 85mg

Light and Lemony Olive Oil Cupcakes

Prep time: 10 minutes | Cook time: 24 minutes | Serves 18

2 cups all-purpose flour
4 teaspoons baking powder
1 cup granulated sugar
1 cup extra virgin olive oil
2 eggs
7 ounces (198 g) 2% Greek yogurt
1 teaspoon pure vanilla extract
4 tablespoons fresh lemon juice
Zest of 2 lemons
Glaze:
1 tablespoon lemon juice
5 tablespoons powdered sugar

1. Preheat the oven to 350°F (180°C). Line a 12-cup muffin pan with cupcake liners and then line a second pan with 6 liners. Set aside. 2. In a medium bowl, combine the flour and baking powder. Whisk and set aside. 3. In a large bowl, combine the sugar and olive oil, and mix until smooth. Add the eggs, one at a time, and mix well. Add the Greek yogurt, vanilla extract, lemon juice, and lemon zest. Mix until well combined. 4. Add the flour mixture to the batter, ½ cup at a time, while continuously mixing. 5. Spoon the batter into the liners, filling each liner two-thirds full. Bake for 22–25 minutes or until a toothpick inserted into the center of a cupcake comes out clean. 6. While the cupcakes are baking, make the glaze by combining the lemon juice and powdered sugar in a small bowl. Stir until smooth, then set aside. 7. Set the cupcakes aside to cool in the pans for about 5 minutes, then remove the cupcakes from the pans and transfer to a wire rack to cool completely. 8. Drizzle the glaze over the cooled cupcakes. Store in the refrigerator for up to 4 days.

Per Serving:
calories: 225 | fat: 13g | protein: 3g | carbs: 25g | fiber: 1g | sodium: 13mg

Tortilla Fried Pies

Prep time: 10 minutes | Cook time: 5 minutes per batch | Makes 12 pies

12 small flour tortillas (4-inch diameter)
½ cup fig preserves
¼ cup sliced almonds
2 tablespoons shredded, unsweetened coconut
Oil for misting or cooking spray

1. Wrap refrigerated tortillas in damp paper towels and heat in microwave 30 seconds to warm. 2. Working with one tortilla at a time, place 2 teaspoons fig preserves, 1 teaspoon sliced almonds, and ½ teaspoon coconut in the center of each. 3. Moisten outer edges of tortilla all around. 4. Fold one side of tortilla over filling to make a half-moon shape and press down lightly on center. Using the tines of a fork, press down firmly on edges of tortilla to seal in filling. 5. Mist both sides with oil or cooking spray. 6. Place hand pies in air fryer basket close but not overlapping. It's fine to lean some against the sides and corners of the basket. You may need to cook in 2 batches. 7. Air fry at 390°F (199°C) for 5 minutes or until lightly browned. Serve hot. 8. Refrigerate any leftover pies in a closed container. To serve later, toss them back in the air fryer basket and cook for 2 or 3 minutes to reheat.

Per Serving:
1 pie: calories: 137 | fat: 4g | protein: 4g | carbs: 22g | fiber: 2g | sodium: 279mg

Crispy Apple Phyllo Tart

Prep time: 15 minutes | Cook time: 30 minutes | Serves 4

5 teaspoons extra virgin olive oil
2 teaspoons fresh lemon juice
¼ teaspoon ground cinnamon
1½ teaspoons granulated sugar, divided
1 large apple (any variety), peeled and cut into ⅛-inch thick slices
5 phyllo sheets, defrosted
1 teaspoon all-purpose flour
1½ teaspoons apricot jam

1. Preheat the oven to 350°F (180°C). Line a baking sheet with parchment paper, and pour the olive oil into a small dish. Set aside. 2. In a separate small bowl, combine the lemon juice, cinnamon, 1 teaspoon of the sugar, and the apple slices. Mix well to ensure the apple slices are coated in the seasonings. Set aside. 3. On a clean working surface, stack the phyllo sheets one on top of the other. Place a large bowl with an approximate diameter of 15 inches on top of the sheets, then draw a sharp knife around the edge of the bowl to cut out a circle through all 5 sheets. Discard the remaining phyllo. 4. Working quickly, place the first sheet on the lined baking sheet and then brush with the olive oil. Repeat the process by placing a second sheet on top of the first sheet, then brushing the second sheet with olive oil. Repeat until all the phyllo sheets are in a single stack. 5. Sprinkle the flour and remaining sugar over the top of the sheets. Arrange the apples in overlapping circles 4 inches from the edge of the phyllo. 6. Fold the edges of the phyllo in and then twist them all around the apple filling to form a crust edge. Brush the edge with the remaining olive oil. Bake for 30 minutes or until the crust is golden and the apples are browned on the edges. 7. While the tart is baking, heat the apricot jam in a small sauce pan over low heat until it's melted. 8. When the tart is done baking, brush the apples with the jam sauce. Slice the tart into 4 equal servings and serve warm. Store at room temperature, covered in plastic wrap, for up to 2 days.

Per Serving:
calories: 165 | fat: 7g | protein: 2g | carbs: 24g | fiber: 2g | sodium: 116mg

Individual Apple Pockets

Prep time: 5 minutes | Cook time: 15 minutes | Serves 6

1 organic puff pastry, rolled out, at room temperature
1 Gala apple, peeled and sliced
¼ cup brown sugar
⅛ teaspoon ground cinnamon
⅛ teaspoon ground cardamom
Nonstick cooking spray
Honey, for topping

1. Preheat the oven to 350°F(180°C). 2. Cut the pastry dough into 4 even discs. Peel and slice the apple. In a small bowl, toss the slices with brown sugar, cinnamon, and cardamom. 3. Spray a muffin tin very well with nonstick cooking spray. Be sure to spray only the muffin holders you plan to use. 4. Once sprayed, line the bottom of the muffin tin with the dough and place 1 or 2 broken apple slices on top. Fold the remaining dough over the apple and drizzle with honey. 5. Bake for 15 minutes or until brown and bubbly.

Per Serving:
calories: 250 | fat: 15g | protein: 3g | carbs: 30g | fiber: 1g | sodium: 98mg

Chocolate Pudding

Prep time: 10 minutes | Cook time: 0 minutes | Serves 4

2 ripe avocados, halved and pitted ¼ cup unsweetened cocoa powder ¼ cup heavy whipping cream, plus more if needed 2 teaspoons vanilla extract	1 to 2 teaspoons liquid stevia or monk fruit extract (optional) ½ teaspoon ground cinnamon (optional) ¼ teaspoon salt Whipped cream, for serving (optional)

1. Using a spoon, scoop out the ripe avocado into a blender or large bowl, if using an immersion blender. Mash well with a fork. 2. Add the cocoa powder, heavy whipping cream, vanilla, sweetener (if using), cinnamon (if using), and salt. Blend well until smooth and creamy, adding additional cream, 1 tablespoon at a time, if the mixture is too thick. 3. Cover and refrigerate for at least 1 hour before serving. Serve chilled with additional whipped cream, if desired.

Per Serving:
calories: 205 | fat: 18g | protein: 3g | carbs: 12g | fiber: 9g | sodium: 156mg

Red Grapefruit Granita

Prep time: 5 minutes | Cook time: 0 minutes | Serves 4 to 6

3 cups red grapefruit sections 1 cup freshly squeezed red grapefruit juice ¼ cup honey	1 tablespoon freshly squeezed lime juice Fresh basil leaves for garnish

1. Remove as much pith (white part) and membrane as possible from the grapefruit segments. 2. Combine all ingredients except the basil in a blender or food processor and pulse just until smooth. 3. Pour the mixture into a shallow glass baking dish and place in the freezer for 1 hour. Stir with a fork and freeze for another 30 minutes, then repeat. To serve, scoop into small dessert glasses and garnish with fresh basil leaves.

Per Serving:
calories: 94 | fat: 0g | protein: 1g | carbs: 24g | fiber: 1g | sodium: 1mg

Minty Cantaloupe Granita

Prep time: 10 minutes | Cook time: 5 minutes | Serves 4

½ cup plus 2 tablespoons honey ¼ cup water 2 tablespoons fresh mint leaves, plus more for garnish	1 medium cantaloupe (about 4 pounds/ 1.8 kg) peeled, seeded, and cut into 1-inch chunks

1. In a small saucepan set over low heat, combine the honey and water and cook, stirring, until the honey has fully dissolved. Stir in the mint and remove from the heat. Set aside to cool. 2. In a food processor, process the cantaloupe until very smooth. Transfer to a medium bowl. Remove the mint leaves from the syrup and discard them. Pour the syrup into the cantaloupe purée and stir to mix. 3.

Transfer the mixture into a 7-by-12-inch glass baking dish and freeze, stirring with a fork every 30 minutes, for 3 to 4 hours, until it is frozen, but still grainy. Serve chilled, scooped into glasses and garnished with mint leaves.

Per Serving:
calories: 174 | fat: 0g | protein: 1g | carbs: 47g | fiber: 1g | sodium: 9mg

Blueberry Panna Cotta

Prep time: 5 minutes | Cook time: 0 minutes | Serves 6

1 tablespoon gelatin powder 2 tablespoons water 2 cups goat's cream, coconut cream, or heavy whipping cream 2 cups wild blueberries, fresh	or frozen, divided ½ teaspoon vanilla powder or 1½ teaspoons unsweetened vanilla extract Optional: low-carb sweetener, to taste

1. In a bowl, sprinkle the gelatin powder over the cold water. Set aside to let it bloom. 2. Place the goat's cream, half of the blueberries, and the vanilla in a blender and process until smooth and creamy. Alternatively, use an immersion blender. 3. Pour the blueberry cream into a saucepan. Gently heat; do not boil. Scrape the gelatin into the hot cream mixture together with the sweetener, if using. Mix well until all the gelatin has dissolved. 4. Divide among 6 (4-ounce / 113-g) jars or serving glasses and fill them about two-thirds full, leaving enough space for the remaining blueberries. Place in the fridge for 3 to 4 hours, or until set. 5. When the panna cotta has set, evenly distribute the remaining blueberries among the jars. Serve immediately or store in the fridge for up to 4 days.

Per Serving:
calories: 172 | fat: 15g | protein: 2g | carbs: 8g | fiber: 2g | sodium: 19mg

Fruit Compote

Prep time: 15 minutes | Cook time: 11 minutes | Serves 6

1 cup apple juice 1 cup dry white wine 2 tablespoons honey 1 cinnamon stick ¼ teaspoon ground nutmeg 1 tablespoon grated lemon zest 1½ tablespoons grated orange	zest 3 large apples, peeled, cored, and chopped 3 large pears, peeled, cored, and chopped ½ cup dried cherries

1. Place all ingredients in the Instant Pot® and stir well. Close lid, set steam release to Sealing, press the Manual button, and set time to 1 minute. When the timer beeps, quick-release the pressure until the float valve drops. Press the Cancel button and open lid. 2. Use a slotted spoon to transfer fruit to a serving bowl. Remove and discard cinnamon stick. Press the Sauté button and bring juice in the pot to a boil. Cook, stirring constantly, until reduced to a syrup that will coat the back of a spoon, about 10 minutes. 3. Stir syrup into fruit mixture. Allow to cool slightly, then cover with plastic wrap and refrigerate overnight.

Per Serving:
calories: 211 | fat: 1g | protein: 2g | carbs: 44g | fiber: 5g | sodium: 7mg

Individual Meringues with Strawberries, Mint, and Toasted Coconut

Prep time: 25 minutes | Cook time: 1 hour 30 minutes | Serves 6

4 large egg whites	diced
1 teaspoon vanilla extract	¼ cup fresh mint, chopped
½ teaspoon cream of tartar	¼ cup unsweetened shredded
¾ cup sugar	coconut, toasted
8 ounces (227 g) strawberries,	

1. Preheat the oven to 225ºF (107ºC). Line 2 baking sheets with parchment paper. 2. Place the egg whites, vanilla, and cream of tartar in the bowl of a stand mixer (or use a large bowl with an electric hand mixer); beat at medium speed until soft peaks form, about 2 to 3 minutes. Increase to high speed and gradually add the sugar, beating until stiff peaks form and the mixture looks shiny and smooth, about 2 to 3 minutes. 3. Using a spatula or spoon, drop ⅓ cup of meringue onto a prepared baking sheet; smooth out and make shapelier as desired. In total, make 12 dollops, 6 per sheet, leaving at least 1 inch between dollops. 4. Bake for 1½ hours, rotating baking sheets between top and bottom, front and back, halfway through. After 1½ hours, turn off the oven, but keep the door closed. Leave the meringues in the oven for an additional 30 minutes. You can leave the meringues in the oven even longer (or overnight), or you may let them finish cooling to room temperature. 5. Combine the strawberries, mint, and coconut in a medium bowl. Serve 2 meringues per person topped with the fruit mixture.

Per Serving:
calories: 150 | fat: 2g | protein: 3g | carbs: 29g | fiber: 1g | sodium: 40mg

Almond Pistachio Biscotti

Prep time: 5 minutes | Cook time: 1 hour 20 minutes | Serves 12

2 cups almond flour or hazelnut flour	2 large eggs
½ packed cup flax meal	2 tablespoons extra-virgin olive oil
½ teaspoon baking soda	1 tablespoon unsweetened almond extract
½ teaspoon ground nutmeg	
½ teaspoon vanilla powder or 1½ teaspoons unsweetened vanilla extract	1 teaspoon apple cider vinegar or fresh lemon juice
¼ teaspoon salt	Optional: low-carb sweetener, to taste
1 tablespoon fresh lemon zest	⅔ cup unsalted pistachio nuts

1. Preheat the oven to 285°F (140°C) fan assisted or 320°F (160°C) conventional. Line one or two baking trays with parchment paper. 2. In a bowl, mix the almond flour, flax meal, baking soda, nutmeg, vanilla, salt, and lemon zest. Add the eggs, olive oil, almond extract, vinegar, and optional sweetener. Mix well until a dough forms, then mix in the pistachio nuts. 3. Form the dough into a low, wide log shape, about 8 × 5 inches (20 × 13 cm). Place in the oven and bake for about 45 minutes. Remove from oven and let cool for 15 to 20 minutes. Using a sharp knife, cut into 12 slices. 4. Reduce the oven temperature to 250°F (120°C) fan assisted or 285°F (140°C) conventional. Lay the slices very carefully in a flat layer on the lined trays. Bake for 15 to 20 minutes, flip over, and bake for 15 to 20 minutes. 5. Remove from the oven and let the biscotti cool down completely to fully crisp up. Store in a sealed jar for up to 2 weeks.

Per Serving:
calories: 196 | fat: 17g | protein: 7g | carbs: 7g | fiber: 4g | sodium: 138mg

Lemon Berry Cream Pops

Prep time: 10 minutes | Cook time: 5 minutes | Makes 8 ice pops

Cream Pops:	Coating:
2 cups coconut cream	1⅓ cups coconut butter
1 tablespoon unsweetened vanilla extract	¼ cup virgin coconut oil
Optional: low-carb sweetener, to taste	Zest from 2 lemons, about 2 tablespoons
2 cups raspberries, fresh or frozen and defrosted	1 teaspoon unsweetened vanilla extract

1. To make the cream pops: In a bowl, whisk the coconut cream with the vanilla and optional sweetener until smooth and creamy. In another bowl, crush the raspberries using a fork, then add them to the bowl with the coconut cream and mix to combine. 2. Divide the mixture among eight ⅓-cup ice pop molds. Freeze until solid for 3 hours, or until set. 3. To easily remove the ice pops from the molds, fill a pot as tall as the ice pops with warm (not hot) water and dip the ice pop molds in for 15 to 20 seconds. Remove the ice pops from the molds and then freeze again. 4. Meanwhile, prepare the coating: Place the coconut butter and coconut oil in a small saucepan over low heat. Stir until smooth, remove from the heat, and add the lemon zest and vanilla. Let cool to room temperature. 5. Remove the ice pops from the freezer, two at a time, and, holding the ice pops over the saucepan, use a spoon to drizzle the coating all over. Return to the freezer until fully set, about 10 minutes. Store in the freezer in a resealable bag for up to 3 months.

Per Serving:
calories: 549 | fat: 8g | protein: 3g | carbs: 58g | fiber: 3g | sodium: 7mg

Avocado-Orange Fruit Salad

Prep time: 10 minutes | Cook time: 0 minutes | Serves 5 to 6

2 large Gala apples, chopped	1 tablespoon extra-virgin olive oil
2 oranges, segmented and chopped	½ teaspoon grated orange zest
⅓ cup sliced almonds	1 large avocado, semi-ripened, medium diced
½ cup honey	

1. In a large bowl, combine the apples, oranges, and almonds. Mix gently. 2. In a small bowl, whisk the honey, oil, and orange zest. Set aside. 3. Drizzle the orange zest mix over the fruit salad and toss. Add the avocado and toss gently one more time.

Per Serving:
calories: 296 | fat: 12g | protein: 3g | carbs: 51g | fiber: 7g | sodium: 4mg

Chocolate Lava Cakes

Prep time: 5 minutes | Cook time: 15 minutes | Serves 2

2 large eggs, whisked
¼ cup blanched finely ground almond flour

½ teaspoon vanilla extract
2 ounces (57 g) low-carb chocolate chips, melted

1. In a medium bowl, mix eggs with flour and vanilla. Fold in chocolate until fully combined. 2. Pour batter into two ramekins greased with cooking spray. Place ramekins into air fryer basket. Adjust the temperature to 320°F (160°C) and bake for 15 minutes. Cakes will be set at the edges and firm in the center when done. Let cool 5 minutes before serving.

Per Serving:
calories: 313 | fat: 23g | protein: 11g | carbs: 16g | fiber: 5g | sodium: 77mg

Flourless Chocolate Brownies with Raspberry Balsamic Sauce

Prep time: 10 minutes | Cook time: 20 minutes | Serves 2

For the raspberry sauce
¼ cup good-quality balsamic vinegar
1 cup frozen raspberries
For the brownie
½ cup black beans with no added salt, rinsed
1 large egg

1 tablespoon olive oil
½ teaspoon vanilla extract
4 tablespoons unsweetened cocoa powder
¼ cup sugar
¼ teaspoon baking powder
Pinch salt
¼ cup dark chocolate chips

Make the raspberry sauce Combine the balsamic vinegar and raspberries in a saucepan and bring the mixture to a boil. Reduce the heat to medium and let the sauce simmer for 15 minutes, or until reduced to ½ cup. If desired, strain the seeds and set the sauce aside until the brownie is ready. Make the brownie 1. Preheat the oven to 350°F (180°C) and set the rack to the middle position. Grease two 8-ounce ramekins and place them on a baking sheet. 2. In a food processor, combine the black beans, egg, olive oil, and vanilla. Purée the mixture for 1 to 2 minutes, or until it's smooth and the beans are completely broken down. Scrape down the sides of the bowl a few times to make sure everything is well-incorporated. 3. Add the cocoa powder, sugar, baking powder, and salt and purée again to combine the dry ingredients, scraping down the sides of the bowl as needed. 4. Stir the chocolate chips into the batter by hand. Reserve a few if you like, to sprinkle over the top of the brownies when they come out of the oven. 5. Pour the brownies into the prepared ramekins and bake for 15 minutes, or until firm. The center will look slightly undercooked. If you prefer a firmer brownie, leave it in the oven for another 5 minutes, or until a toothpick inserted in the middle comes out clean. 6. Remove the brownies from the oven. If desired, sprinkle any remaining chocolate chips over the top and let them melt into the warm brownies. 7. Let the brownies cool for a few minutes and top with warm raspberry sauce to serve.

Per Serving:
calories: 510 | fat: 16g | protein: 10g | carbs: 88g | fiber: 14g | sodium: 124mg

Pomegranate-Quinoa Dark Chocolate Bark

Prep time: 10 minutes |Cook time: 10 minutes| Serves: 6

Nonstick cooking spray
½ cup uncooked tricolor or regular quinoa
½ teaspoon kosher or sea salt

8 ounces (227 g) dark chocolate or 1 cup dark chocolate chips
½ cup fresh pomegranate seeds

1. In a medium saucepan coated with nonstick cooking spray over medium heat, toast the uncooked quinoa for 2 to 3 minutes, stirring frequently. Do not let the quinoa burn. Remove the pan from the stove, and mix in the salt. Set aside 2 tablespoons of the toasted quinoa to use for the topping. 2. Break the chocolate into large pieces, and put it in a gallon-size zip-top plastic bag. Using a metal ladle or a meat pounder, pound the chocolate until broken into smaller pieces. (If using chocolate chips, you can skip this step.) Dump the chocolate out of the bag into a medium, microwave-safe bowl and heat for 1 minute on high in the microwave. Stir until the chocolate is completely melted. Mix the toasted quinoa (except the topping you set aside) into the melted chocolate. 3. Line a large, rimmed baking sheet with parchment paper. Pour the chocolate mixture onto the sheet and spread it evenly until the entire pan is covered. Sprinkle the remaining 2 tablespoons of quinoa and the pomegranate seeds on top. Using a spatula or the back of a spoon, press the quinoa and the pomegranate seeds into the chocolate. 4. Freeze the mixture for 10 to 15 minutes, or until set. Remove the bark from the freezer, and break it into about 2-inch jagged pieces. Store in a sealed container or zip-top plastic bag in the refrigerator until ready to serve.

Per Serving:
calories: 290 | fat: 17g | protein: 5g | carbs: 29g | fiber: 6g | sodium: 202mg

Greek Island Almond Cocoa Bites

Prep time: 5 minutes | Cook time: 0 minutes | Serves 6

½ cup roasted, unsalted whole almonds (with skins)
3 tablespoons granulated sugar, divided
1½ teaspoons unsweetened

cocoa powder
1¼ tablespoons unseasoned breadcrumbs
¾ teaspoon pure vanilla extract
1½ teaspoons orange juice

1. Place the almonds in a food processor and process until you have a coarse ground texture. 2. In a medium bowl, combine the ground almonds, 2 tablespoons sugar, the cocoa powder, and the breadcrumbs. Mix well. 3. In a small bowl, combine the vanilla extract and orange juice. Stir and then add the mixture to the almond mixture. Mix well. 4. Measure out a teaspoon of the mixture. Squeeze the mixture with your hand to make the dough stick together, then mold the dough into a small ball. 5. Add the remaining tablespoon of the sugar to a shallow bowl. Roll the balls in the sugar until covered, then transfer the bites to an airtight container. Store covered at room temperature for up to 1 week.

Per Serving:
calories: 102 | fat: 6g | protein: 3g | carbs: 10g | fiber: 2g | sodium: 11mg

Banana Cream Pie Parfaits

Prep time: 10 minutes | Cook time: 0 minutes | Serves 2

1 cup nonfat vanilla pudding
2 low-sugar graham crackers, crushed

1 banana, peeled and sliced
¼ cup walnuts, chopped
Honey for drizzling

1. In small parfait dishes or glasses, layer the ingredients, starting with the pudding and ending with chopped walnuts. 2. You can repeat the layers, depending on the size of the glass and your preferences. 3. Drizzle with the honey. Serve chilled.

Per Serving:
calories: 312 | fat: 11g | protein: 7g | carbs: 50g | fiber: 3g | sodium: 273mg

Halva Protein Slices

Prep time: 5 minutes | Cook time: 0 minutes | Serves 16

¾ cup tahini
⅓ cup coconut butter
¼ cup virgin coconut oil
1 cup collagen powder
½ teaspoon vanilla powder or
1½ teaspoons unsweetened

vanilla extract
½ teaspoon cinnamon
⅛ teaspoon salt
Optional: low-carb sweetener, to taste

1. To soften the tahini and the coconut butter, place them in a small saucepan over low heat with the coconut oil. Remove from the heat and set aside to cool for a few minutes. 2. Add the remaining ingredients and optional sweetener. Stir to combine, then pour the mixture into an 8 × 8–inch (20 × 20 cm) parchment-lined pan or a silicone pan, or any pan or container lined with parchment paper. Place in the fridge for at least 1 hour or until fully set. 3. Cut into 16 pieces and serve. To store, keep refrigerated for up to 2 weeks or freeze to up to 3 months.

Per Serving:
calories: 131 | fat: 13g | protein: 2g | carbs: 3g | fiber: 1g | sodium: 33mg

Ricotta with Balsamic Cherries and Black Pepper

Prep time: 10 minutes | Cook time: 0 minutes | Serves 4

1 cup (8 ounces/ 227 g) ricotta
2 tablespoons honey
1 teaspoon vanilla extract
3 cups pitted sweet cherries (thawed if frozen), halved

1½ teaspoons aged balsamic vinegar
Pinch of freshly ground black pepper

1. In a food processor, combine the ricotta, honey, and vanilla and process until smooth. Transfer the mixture to a medium bowl cover, and refrigerate for 1 hour. 2. In a small bowl, combine the cherries, vinegar, and pepper and stir to mix well. Chill along with the ricotta mixture. 3. To serve, spoon the ricotta mixture into serving bowls or glasses. Top with the cherries, dividing them equally and spooning a bit of the accumulated juice over the top of each bowl. Serve chilled.

Per Serving:
calories: 236 | fat: 5g | protein: 7g | carbs: 42g | fiber: 1g | sodium: 93mg

Strawberry-Pomegranate Molasses Sauce

Prep time: 10 minutes | Cook time: 5 minutes | Serves 6

3 tablespoons olive oil
¼ cup honey
2 pints strawberries, hulled and halved
1 to 2 tablespoons pomegranate

molasses
2 tablespoons chopped fresh mint
Greek yogurt, for serving

1. In a medium saucepan, heat the olive oil over medium heat. Add the strawberries; cook until their juices are released. Stir in the honey and cook for 1 to 2 minutes. Stir in the molasses and mint. Serve warm over Greek yogurt.

Per Serving:
calories: 189 | fat: 7g | protein: 4g | carbs: 24g | fiber: 3g | sodium: 12mg

Chapter 14 Staples, Sauces, Dips, and Dressings

Berry and Honey Compote

Prep time: 5 minutes | Cook time: 15 minutes |
Serves 2 to 3

½ cup honey
¼ cup fresh berries

2 tablespoons grated orange zest

1. In a small saucepan, heat the honey, berries, and orange zest over medium-low heat for 2 to 5 minutes, until the sauce thickens, or heat for 15 seconds in the microwave. Serve the compote drizzled over pancakes, muffins, or French toast.
Per Serving:
calories: 272 | fat: 0g | protein: 1g | carbs: 74g | fiber: 1g | sodium: 4mg

Green Olive Tapenade with Harissa

Prep time: 5 minutes | Cook time: 0 minutes | Makes
about 1½ cups

1 cup pitted, cured green olives
1 clove garlic, minced
1 tablespoon harissa
1 tablespoon lemon juice

1 tablespoon chopped fresh parsley
¼ cup olive oil, or more to taste

1. Finely chop the olives (or pulse them in a food processor until they resemble a chunky paste). 2. Add the garlic, harissa, lemon juice, parsley, and olive oil and stir or pulse to combine well.
Per Serving:
¼ cup: calories: 215 | fat: 23g | protein: 1g | carbs: 5g | fiber: 2g | sodium: 453mg

Seedy Crackers

Prep time: 25 minutes | Cook time: 15 minutes |
Makes 24 crackers

1 cup almond flour
1 tablespoon sesame seeds
1 tablespoon flaxseed
1 tablespoon chia seeds

¼ teaspoon baking soda
¼ teaspoon salt
Freshly ground black pepper
1 large egg, at room temperature

1. Preheat the oven to 350ºF (180ºC). 2. In a large bowl, combine the almond flour, sesame seeds, flaxseed, chia seeds, baking soda, salt, and pepper and stir well. 3. In a small bowl, whisk the egg until well beaten. Add to the dry ingredients and stir well to combine and form the dough into a ball. 4. Place one layer of parchment paper on your counter-top and place the dough on top. Cover with a second layer of parchment and, using a rolling pin, roll the dough to ⅛-inch thickness, aiming for a rectangular shape. 5. Cut the dough into 1- to 2-inch crackers and bake on parchment until crispy and slightly golden, 10 to 15 minutes, depending on thickness. Alternatively, you can bake the large rolled dough prior to cutting and break into free-form crackers once baked and crispy. 6. Store in an airtight container in the fridge for up to 1 week.
Per Serving:
2 crackers: calories: 65 | fat: 5g | protein: 3g | carbs: 2g | fiber: 2g | sodium: 83mg

Spicy Cucumber Dressing

Prep time: 5 minutes | Cook time: 0 minutes | Serves 2

1½ cups plain, unsweetened, full-fat Greek yogurt
1 cucumber, seeded and peeled
½ lemon, juiced and zested
1 tablespoon dried, minced

garlic
½ tablespoon dried dill
2 teaspoons dried oregano
Salt

1. In a food processor, combine the yogurt, cucumber, lemon juice, garlic, dill, oregano, and a pinch of salt and process until smooth. Adjust the seasonings as needed and transfer to a serving bowl.
Per Serving:
calories: 209 | fat: 10g | protein: 18g | carbs: 14g | fiber: 2g | sodium: 69mg

Crunchy Yogurt Dip

Prep time: 5 minutes | Cook time: 0 minutes | Serves
2 to 3

1 cup plain, unsweetened, full-fat Greek yogurt
½ cup cucumber, peeled, seeded, and diced
1 tablespoon freshly squeezed lemon juice

1 tablespoon chopped fresh mint
1 small garlic clove, minced
Salt
Freshly ground black pepper

1. In a food processor, combine the yogurt, cucumber, lemon juice, mint, and garlic. Pulse several times to combine, leaving noticeable cucumber chunks. 2. Taste and season with salt and pepper.
Per Serving:
calories: 128 | fat: 6g | protein: 11g | carbs: 7g | fiber: 0g | sodium: 47mg

Skinny Cider Dressing

Prep time: 5 minutes | Cook time: 0 minutes | Serves 2

2 tablespoons apple cider
vinegar
⅓ lemon, juiced

⅓ lemon, zested
Salt
Freshly ground black pepper

1. In a jar, combine the vinegar, lemon juice, and zest. Season with salt and pepper, cover, and shake well.

Per Serving:
calories: 2 | fat: 0g | protein: 0g | carbs: 1g | fiber: 0g | sodium: 0mg

Red Pepper Hummus

Prep time: 5 minutes | Cook time: 30 minutes | Makes 2 cups

1 cup dried chickpeas
4 cups water
1 tablespoon plus ¼ cup extra-virgin olive oil, divided
½ cup chopped roasted red pepper, divided
⅓ cup tahini

1 teaspoon ground cumin
¾ teaspoon salt
½ teaspoon ground black pepper
¼ teaspoon smoked paprika
⅓ cup lemon juice
½ teaspoon minced garlic

1. Place chickpeas, water, and 1 tablespoon oil in the Instant Pot®. Close the lid, set steam release to Sealing, press the Manual button, and set time to 30 minutes. 2. When the timer beeps, quick-release the pressure until the float valve drops. Press the Cancel button and open lid. Drain, reserving the cooking liquid. 3. Place chickpeas, ⅓ cup roasted red pepper, remaining ¼ cup oil, tahini, cumin, salt, black pepper, paprika, lemon juice, and garlic in a food processor and process until creamy. If hummus is too thick, add reserved cooking liquid 1 tablespoon at a time until it reaches desired consistency. Serve at room temperature, garnished with reserved roasted red pepper on top.

Per Serving:
2 tablespoons: calories: 96 | fat: 8g | protein: 2g | carbs: 10g | fiber: 4g | sodium: 122mg

Cider Yogurt Dressing

Prep time: 5 minutes | Cook time: 0 minutes | Serves 2

1 cup plain, unsweetened, full-fat Greek yogurt
½ cup extra-virgin olive oil
1 tablespoon apple cider vinegar
½ lemon, juiced
1 tablespoon chopped fresh

oregano
½ teaspoon dried parsley
½ teaspoon kosher salt
¼ teaspoon garlic powder
¼ teaspoon freshly ground black pepper

1. In a large bowl, combine the yogurt, olive oil, vinegar, lemon juice, oregano, parsley, salt, garlic powder, and pepper and whisk well.

Per Serving:
calories: 402 | fat: 40g | protein: 8g | carbs: 4g | fiber: 1g | sodium: 417mg

Kidney Bean Dip with Cilantro, Cumin, and Lime

Prep time: 10 minutes | Cook time: 30 minutes | Serves 16

1 cup dried kidney beans, soaked overnight and drained
4 cups water
3 cloves garlic, peeled and crushed
¼ cup roughly chopped

cilantro, divided
¼ cup extra-virgin olive oil
1 tablespoon lime juice
2 teaspoons grated lime zest
1 teaspoon ground cumin
½ teaspoon salt

1. Place beans, water, garlic, and 2 tablespoons cilantro in the Instant Pot®. Close the lid, set steam release to Sealing, press the Bean button, and cook for the default time of 30 minutes. 2. When the timer beeps, let pressure release naturally, about 20 minutes. Press the Cancel button, open lid, and check that beans are tender. Drain off excess water and transfer beans to a medium bowl. Gently mash beans with potato masher or fork until beans are mashed but chunky. Add oil, lime juice, lime zest, cumin, salt, and remaining 2 tablespoons cilantro and stir to combine. Serve warm or at room temperature.

Per Serving:
calories: 65 | fat: 3g | protein: 2g | carbs: 7g | fiber: 2g | sodium: 75mg

Zucchini Noodles

Prep time: 5 minutes | Cook time: 0 minutes | Serves 4

2 medium to large zucchini

1. Cut off and discard the ends of each zucchini and, using a spiralizer set to the smallest setting, spiralize the zucchini to create zoodles. 2. To serve, simply place a ½ cup or so of spiralized zucchini into the bottom of each bowl and spoon a hot sauce over top to "cook" the zoodles to al dente consistency. Use with any of your favorite sauces, or just toss with warmed pesto for a simple and quick meal.

Per Serving:
calories: 27 | fat: 1g | protein: 2g | carbs: 5g | fiber: 2g | sodium: 13mg

Citrus Vinaigrette

Prep time: 2 minutes | Cook time: 0 minutes | Serves 4

Zest of 1 lemon
3 tablespoons fresh lemon juice
Pinch kosher salt

Pinch freshly ground black pepper
2 tablespoons olive oil

1. In a small bowl, whisk together the lemon zest, lemon juice, 3 tablespoons water, the salt, and the pepper. While whisking, gradually stream in the olive oil and whisk until emulsified. Store in an airtight container in the refrigerator for up to 3 days.

Per Serving:
calories: 65 | fat: 7g | protein: 0g | carbs: 2g | fiber: 0g | sodium: 146mg

Pepper Sauce

Prep time: 10 minutes | Cook time: 20 minutes | Makes 4 cups

2 red hot fresh chiles, seeded
2 dried chiles
½ small yellow onion, roughly chopped

2 garlic cloves, peeled
2 cups water
2 cups white vinegar

1. In a medium saucepan, combine the fresh and dried chiles, onion, garlic, and water. Bring to a simmer and cook for 20 minutes, or until tender. Transfer to a food processor or blender. 2. Add the vinegar and blend until smooth.

Per Serving:
1 cup: calories: 41 | fat: 0g | protein: 1g | carbs: 5g | fiber: 1g | sodium: 11mg

Harissa Spice Mix

Prep time: 5 minutes | Cook time: 0 minutes | Makes about 7 tablespoons

2 tablespoons ground cumin
4 teaspoons paprika
4 teaspoons ground turmeric
2 teaspoons ground coriander
2 teaspoons chili powder

1 teaspoon garlic powder
1 teaspoon ground caraway seeds
½ teaspoon cayenne powder

1. Place all of the ingredients in a jar. Seal and shake well to combine. Store in a sealed jar at room temperature for up to 6 months.

Per Serving:
1 tablespoon: calories: 21 | fat: 1g | protein: 1g | carbs: 4g | fiber: 2g sodium: 27mg

White Bean Hummus

Prep time: 10 minutes | Cook time: 30 minutes | Serves 12

⅔ cup dried white beans, rinsed and drained
3 cloves garlic, peeled and crushed

¼ cup olive oil
1 tablespoon lemon juice
½ teaspoon salt

1. Place beans and garlic in the Instant Pot® and stir well. Add enough cold water to cover ingredients. Close lid, set steam release to Sealing, press the Manual button, and set time to 30 minutes. 2. When the timer beeps, let pressure release naturally, about 20 minutes. Press the Cancel button and open lid. Use a fork to check that beans are tender. Drain off excess water and transfer beans to a food processor. 3. Add oil, lemon juice, and salt to the processor and pulse until mixture is smooth with some small chunks. Transfer to a storage container and refrigerate for at least 4 hours. Serve cold or at room temperature. Store in the refrigerator for up to one week.

Per Serving:
calories: 57 | fat: 5g | protein: 1g | carbs: 3g | fiber: 1g | sodium: 99mg

Red Pepper Chimichurri

Prep time: 10 minutes | Cook time: 0 minutes | Serves 4

1 garlic clove, minced
3 tablespoons olive oil
1 tablespoon red wine vinegar or sherry vinegar
¼ teaspoon freshly ground black pepper
1 shallot, finely chopped

1 large red bell pepper, roasted, peeled, seeded, and finely chopped (about 1 cup)
3 tablespoons capers, rinsed
3 tablespoons chopped fresh parsley
½ teaspoon red pepper flakes

1. In a small bowl, stir together all the ingredients until well combined.

Per Serving:
calories: 113 | fat: 10g | protein: 1g | carbs: 5g | fiber: 1g | sodium: 157mg

Olive Mint Vinaigrette

Prep time: 5 minutes | Cook time: 0 minutes | Makes ½ cup

¼ cup white wine vinegar
¼ teaspoon honey
¼ teaspoon kosher salt
¼ teaspoon freshly ground black pepper

¼ cup extra-virgin olive oil
¼ cup olives, pitted and minced
2 tablespoons fresh mint, minced

1. In a bowl, whisk together the vinegar, honey, salt, and black pepper. Add the olive oil and whisk well. Add the olives and mint, and mix well. Store any leftovers in the refrigerator in an airtight container for up to 5 days.

Per Serving:
2 tablespoons: calories: 135 | fat: 15g | protein: 0g | carbs: 1g | fiber: 0g | sodium: 135mg

Southern Italian-Style Tomato Sauce

Prep time: 5 minutes | Cook time: 15 minutes | Makes about 3 cups

3 cups canned whole tomatoes, drained
¼ cup plus 2 tablespoons olive oil
4 cloves garlic, lightly crushed

½ teaspoon salt
¼ teaspoon freshly ground black pepper
1 tablespoon finely chopped fresh basil or flat-leaf parsley

1. Remove and discard the tomato seeds. Place the tomatoes in a medium bowl and crush them with a fork or potato masher. 2. Heat the olive oil in a medium saucepan over medium heat. Add the garlic and cook, stirring frequently, until it softens and turns golden. Stir in the tomatoes, salt, and pepper. Simmer for 15 minutes. Discard the garlic cloves and stir in the basil just before serving. For a smoother sauce, use an immersion blender to purée the sauce or put it in a food processor, countertop blender, or food mill.

Per Serving:
calories: 66 | fat: 7g | protein: 1g | carbs: 1g | fiber: 1g | sodium: 99mg

Traditional Caesar Dressing

Prep time: 10 minutes | Cook time: 5 minutes | Makes 1½ cups

2 teaspoons minced garlic
4 large egg yolks
¼ cup wine vinegar
½ teaspoon dry mustard

Dash Worcestershire sauce
1 cup extra-virgin olive oil
¼ cup freshly squeezed lemon juice
Sea salt and freshly ground black pepper, to taste

1. To a small saucepan, add the garlic, egg yolks, vinegar, mustard, and Worcestershire sauce and place over low heat. 2. Whisking constantly, cook the mixture until it thickens and is a little bubbly, about 5 minutes. 3. Remove from saucepan from the heat and let it stand for about 10 minutes to cool. 4. Transfer the egg mixture to a large stainless steel bowl. Whisking constantly, add the olive oil in a thin stream. 5. Whisk in the lemon juice and season the dressing with salt and pepper. 6. Transfer the dressing to an airtight container and keep in the refrigerator for up to 3 days.

Per Serving:
calories: 202 | fat: 21g | protein: 2g | carbs: 2g | fiber: 0g | sodium: 14mg

Orange Dijon Dressing

Prep time: 5 minutes | Cook time: 0 minutes | Serves 2

¼ cup extra-virgin olive oil
2 tablespoons freshly squeezed orange juice
1 orange, zested
1 teaspoon garlic powder

¾ teaspoon za'atar seasoning
½ teaspoon salt
¼ teaspoon Dijon mustard
Freshly ground black pepper, to taste

1. In a jar, combine the olive oil, orange juice and zest, garlic powder, za'atar, salt, and mustard. Season with pepper and shake vigorously until completely mixed.

Per Serving:
calories: 284 | fat: 27g | protein: 1g | carbs: 11g | fiber: 2g | sodium: 590mg

Versatile Sandwich Round

Prep time: 5 minutes | Cook time: 2 minutes | Serves 1

3 tablespoons almond flour
1 tablespoon extra-virgin olive oil
1 large egg
½ teaspoon dried rosemary, oregano, basil, thyme, or garlic powder

(optional)
¼ teaspoon baking powder
⅛ teaspoon salt

1. In a microwave-safe ramekin, combine the almond flour, olive oil, egg, rosemary (if using), baking powder, and salt. Mix well with a fork. 2. Microwave for 90 seconds on high. 3. Slide a knife around the edges of ramekin and flip to remove the bread. 4. Slice in half with a serrated knife if you want to use it to make a sandwich.

Per Serving:
calories: 354 | fat: 33g | protein: 12g | carbs: 6g | fiber: 3g | sodium: 388mg

Appendix 1: Measurement Conversion Chart

MEASUREMENT CONVERSION CHART

VOLUME EQUIVALENTS(DRY)

US STANDARD	METRIC (APPROXIMATE)
1/8 teaspoon	0.5 mL
1/4 teaspoon	1 mL
1/2 teaspoon	2 mL
3/4 teaspoon	4 mL
1 teaspoon	5 mL
1 tablespoon	15 mL
1/4 cup	59 mL
1/2 cup	118 mL
3/4 cup	177 mL
1 cup	235 mL
2 cups	475 mL
3 cups	700 mL
4 cups	1 L

VOLUME EQUIVALENTS(LIQUID)

US STANDARD	US STANDARD (OUNCES)	METRIC (APPROXIMATE)
2 tablespoons	1 fl.oz.	30 mL
1/4 cup	2 fl.oz.	60 mL
1/2 cup	4 fl.oz.	120 mL
1 cup	8 fl.oz.	240 mL
1 1/2 cup	12 fl.oz.	355 mL
2 cups or 1 pint	16 fl.oz.	475 mL
4 cups or 1 quart	32 fl.oz.	1 L
1 gallon	128 fl.oz.	4 L

TEMPERATURES EQUIVALENTS

FAHRENHEIT(F)	CELSIUS(C) (APPROXIMATE)
225 °F	107 °C
250 °F	120 °C
275 °F	135 °C
300 °F	150 °C
325 °F	160 °C
350 °F	180 °C
375 °F	190 °C
400 °F	205 °C
425 °F	220 °C
450 °F	235 °C
475 °F	245 °C
500 °F	260 °C

WEIGHT EQUIVALENTS

US STANDARD	METRIC (APPROXIMATE)
1 ounce	28 g
2 ounces	57 g
5 ounces	142 g
10 ounces	284 g
15 ounces	425 g
16 ounces (1 pound)	455 g
1.5 pounds	680 g
2 pounds	907 g

Appendix 2: The Dirty Dozen and Clean Fifteen

The Dirty Dozen and Clean Fifteen

The Environmental Working Group (EWG) is a nonprofit, nonpartisan organization dedicated to protecting human health and the environment Its mission is to empower people to live healthier lives in a healthier environment. This organization publishes an annual list of the twelve kinds of produce, in sequence, that have the highest amount of pesticide residue-the Dirty Dozen-as well as a list of the fifteen kinds ofproduce that have the least amount of pesticide residue-the Clean Fifteen.

THE DIRTY DOZEN	THE CLEAN FIFTEEN
• The 2016 Dirty Dozen includes the following produce. These are considered among the year's most important produce to buy organic:	• The least critical to buy organically are the Clean Fifteen list. The following are on the 2016 list:

Strawberries	Spinach	Avocados	Papayas
Apples	Tomatoes	Corn	Kiw
Nectarines	Bell peppers	Pineapples	Eggplant
Peaches	Cherry tomatoes	Cabbage	Honeydew
Celery	Cucumbers	Sweet peas	Grapefruit
Grapes	Kale/collard greens	Onions	Cantaloupe
Cherries	Hot peppers	Asparagus	Cauliflower
		Mangos	

• *The Dirty Dozen list contains two additional itemskale/collard greens and hot peppers-because they tend to contain trace levels of highly hazardous pesticides.*

• *Some of the sweet corn sold in the United States are made from genetically engineered (GE) seedstock. Buy organic varieties of these crops to avoid GE produce.*

Appendix 3 Recipes Index

Made in the USA
Las Vegas, NV
04 October 2023

78565042R00083